Library of Davidson College

VOID

HORIZONS IN THEORY AND AMERICAN CULTURE
Bainard Cowan and Joseph G. Kronick, Editors

The ROMANTIC THEORY of the NOVEL

The ROMANTIC THEORY OF THE NOVEL

Genre and Reflection in Cervantes,
Melville, Flaubert, Joyce, and Kafka

PIOTR PARLEJ

LOUISIANA STATE UNIVERSITY PRESS *Baton Rouge and London*

Copyright © 1997 by Louisiana State University Press
All rights reserved
Manufactured in the United States of America
First printing
06 05 04 03 02 01 00 99 98 97   5 4 3 2 1

Designer: Michele Myatt
Typeface: Trump Mediaeval
Typesetter: Impressions Book and Journal Services, Inc.
Printer and binder: Thomson-Shore, Inc.

Library of Congress Cataloging-in-Publication Data

Parlej, Piotr, 1959–
    The romantic theory of the novel : genre and reflection in
Cervantes, Melville, Flaubert, Joyce, and Kafka / Piotr Parlej.
        p.   cm. — (Horizons in theory and American culture)
    Includes bibliographical references and index.
    ISBN 0-8071-2141-X (cloth : alk. paper)
    1. Romanticism.   2. Fiction—History and criticism—Theory, etc.
I. Title. II. Series.
PN56.R7P37   1997   97-9301
809.3'9145—dc21   CIP

The paper in this book meets the guidelines for permanence and durability of the Committee on Production Guidelines for Book Longevity of the Council on Library Resources. ∞

To my mother, father, sister, Michelle, and Jane

CONTENTS

Acknowledgments	xi
Abbreviations	xiii
Introduction	1
I The Genre of Involution in *Don Quixote*	66
II Genre as Mood in *Pierre*	114
III Genre and *la Syncope* in *Madame Bovary*	157
IV Genre as Example in *Ulysses*	202
V The Genre of the Neuter in *The Trial*	248
Bibliography	291
Index	301

ACKNOWLEDGMENTS

I am grateful to Henry Sussman, the reader who made the writing possible. I would like to thank Troy Thibodeaux for invaluable assistance in preparing the text for print. Finally, I would like to thank my friends—in Poland and in the United States—for their friendship.

ABBREVIATIONS

Primary Works

CS	Franz Kafka, *The Complete Stories*
DQ	*Don Quixote*
MB	*Madame Bovary*
P	*Pierre; or, The Ambiguities*
U	*Ulysses*
T	*The Trial*

Works of Friedrich Schlegel

DP	*"Dialogue on Poetry" and Literary Aphorisms*
F	*"Lucinde" and the Fragments*
LN	*Literary Notebooks, 1797–1801*
SL	*Schriften zur Literatur*

Criticism

CCP	Alan Udoff, ed., *Kafka and the Contemporary Critical Performance*
FS	Hans Eichner, *Friedrich Schlegel*
G	Maurice Blanchot, *"The Gaze of Orpheus" and Other Literary Essays*

IC	Maurice Blanchot, *The Infinite Conversation*
L	Jorge Luis Borges, *Labyrinths*
LA	Philippe Lacoue-Labarthe and Jean-Luc Nancy, *The Literary Absolute: The Theory of Literature in German Romanticism*
SA	Rodolphe Gasché, "The Sober Absolute: On Benjamin and the Early Romantics"
TM	Philippe Lacoue-Labarthe, *Typography: Mimesis, Philosophy, Politics*
TU	Peter Szondi, *"Textual Understanding" and Other Essays*

The ROMANTIC THEORY of the NOVEL

Introduction

Even a cursory glance at romanticism's pronouncements on the novel reveals that besides the statements that use fairly clear and direct terms there also appear statements whose expository status is not so clear and not so direct. For example, in Idea 11, Friedrich Schlegel places the novel in a rather puzzling context: "Only through religion does logic become philosophy; only from it comes everything that makes philosophy greater than science. And instead of an eternally rich, infinite poetry, the lack of religion gives us only novels or the triviality that now is called art" (F, 242).[1] The configuration of terms—religion, logic, philosophy, science, poetry, novel, art—not only typifies romanticism's predilection for thinking in terms of the system, but it also determines the specific context of romantic thought about the novel. Schlegel's "definition" implies that when speaking of the novel it is not enough to provide an Aristotelian definition that specifies the genus and the species and that defines the term in its difference from all other terms; neither is it enough, Schlegel says, to trace the historical circumstances, influences, and theories. Rather, when speaking of the novel, one must at the same time mention "religion, logic, philosophy, science, poetry, art" to suggest that the novel intimately

---

1. References to Schlegel's Fragments in English are to the translation as found in *Friedrich Schlegel's "Lucinde" and the Fragments*, trans. Peter Firchow (Minneapolis, 1971). The German texts of the *Critical Fragments, Athenaeum Fragments*, and *Ideas* are taken from *Charakteristiken und Kritiken I, 1796–1801*, ed. Hans Eichner (Munich, 1967), Vol. II of *Kritische Friedrich-Schlegel-Ausgabe*, ed. Ernst Behler in cooperation with Jean-Jacques Anstett and Hans Eichner. All the works cited as well as the translations cited have been consulted in the original language.

belongs to a system of concepts and closely interacts with this system's components.

Schlegel's account of the novel differs considerably from those accounts that are concerned with constructing a history of the genre in terms of historical mutations of an otherwise identifiable form. These two opposed types of theoretical reflection have dominated the modern (that is, postromantic) theory of the novel. To use a recent schematization by Anthony Cascardi, this is the difference that separates the tradition represented by Georg Lukács' *Theory of the Novel* from the tradition represented by Ian Watt's *The Rise of the Novel*, Michael McKeon's *Origins of the English Novel*, Fredric Jameson's *The Political Unconscious*, and J. M. Bernstein's *The Philosophy of the Novel*. While both reconstructions of the novel, the philosophical path represented by Lukács and the "empirical" or "formal" paths represented by Watt and others, claim to be "historical," they are based on radically different categories of beginning and of history. Cascardi writes that for Lukács "the novel is a form of literature which 'thinks' in terms of totality even in a disenchanted or detotalized world." Ian Watt's *Rise of the Novel*, on the other hand, "failed to link the various aspects of form within the context of any larger (social, historical, or conceptual) whole."[2]

This split in the twentieth-century theory of the novel can be traced to the double sense of the term *der Roman*. This ambiguity is at work in the distinction (which is also an implied value judgment) made by Friedrich Schlegel in "The Letter on the Novel": "It must be clear to you why, according to my views, I insist that all poetry should be romantic and why I detest the novel insofar as it wants to be a separate genre."[3] In his insistence, on the one hand, to condemn the novel

---

2. Anthony Cascardi, "Totality and the Novel," *New Literary History*, XXIII (1992), 610–11. Georg Lukács, *The Theory of the Novel*, trans. Anna Bostock (Cambridge, Mass. 1987); Ian Watt, *The Rise of the Novel* (Berkeley, 1957); Michael McKeon, *The Origins of the English Novel, 1600–1740* (Baltimore, 1987); Fredric Jameson, *The Political Unconscious* (Ithaca, 1981); J. M. Bernstein, *The Philosophy of the Novel: Lukács, Marxism, and the Dialectics of Form* (Minneapolis, 1984).

3. *Friedrich Schlegel: "Dialogue on Poetry" and Literary Aphorisms*, trans. Ernst Behler and Roman Struc (University Park, Pa., 1968), 101. "The Letter on the Novel" ("Brief über den Roman") is part of "Dialogue on Poetry" ("Gespräch über die Poesie"), which also contains "Epochs of Literature" ("Epochen der Dichtkunst"), "Talk on Mythology" ("Rede über die Mythologie"), and "Essay on Goethe" ("Versuch über den verschiedenen Stil in Goethes früheren und späteren Werken"). References to the German texts of these essays are to *Friedrich Schlegel: Schriften zur Literatur*, ed. Wolfdietrich Rasch (Munich, 1970).

as a specific genre but, on the other, to preserve its etymological derivative, "romantic," as a dominant characteristic of "all poetry," Schlegel is asserting a complex term whose ambiguous, even contradictory, reference has systematically confounded traditional terminology and all too often led institutionalized literary studies astray. The word *novel* (*der Roman*) is ambiguous because it denotes *both* the presence of the transcendental subject to itself, as postulated by Kant's philosophy, *and* a literary genre inherited from antiquity. Expressed in terms of the divergence in critical approaches to the novel distinguished by Cascardi, this ambiguity invites either a philosophically oriented study of the novel as an emblem of totality or a literary-critical study of the novel as a merely formal unity.

The romantics were quite well aware of the word's ambiguity but thought that the risks of misunderstanding were far outweighed by the felicitous unity of a literary genre and the philosophical operation that this genre was expected to perform.[4] If this imprecision is, as Lacoue-Labarthe and Nancy presume, a trap set by Schlegel that required "the lucidity of a Benjamin" to detect (*LA*, 15), and if, despite Benjamin's insight, we cannot now escape this trap, can we at least articulate the *trappings*?

To understand the romantic theory of the novel, we must first present the philosophical and historical contexts in which it acquired its shape. In the philosophical realm, the brief episode of the Jena romanticism (for it is this romanticism, particularly the two years of the *Athenaeum*, 1797–1800, that concerns us here) offers one among three solutions to what is called the "Kantian aftermath," the other two being speculative idealism (Fichte, Schelling, Hegel) and Hölderlin's "poetry of poetry." As responses to the crisis precipitated, or opened up, by Kant's system, these three options postulate and aspire to effectuate, each in its own way, the subject as a necessary "part" of the system defined by Kant.

The disquieting legacy of Kant's philosophy is that the agency (the subject) of judgments cannot be present in these judgments—not, that is, within the limits of reason defined by Kant as the conditions of possibility for these judgments. Let us first consider the realm of pure reason. Kant assumes that in the realm of pure reason every manifold of experience (any group of sense perceptions, or intuitions) must be

---

4. The complex history of the meaning of the word *romantic* is treated in *FS*, 51; in Eichner's "Germany: Romantisch—Romantik—Romantiker," in *"Romantic" and Its Cognates: The European History of a Word*, ed. Hans Eichner (Toronto, 1972), 98–156; and in *LA*, 31.

unified if it is to become available for the understanding. This unity, in turn, presupposes a unified subject that in each moment perceives the manifold and relates this manifold to itself as a unified subject.

Here an important distinction must be made. As it registers representations, the subject is sometimes aware of itself making these representations. For Kant this self is merely "empirical" because the moments of its self-awareness are a matter of contingent incidents occurring in time: the self sometimes becomes aware of itself and sometimes loses itself in perception. In contrast to the empirical self-perception (apperception as understood by Leibniz), Kant postulates "pure" or "original" apperception. As the subject of pure apperception, Kant's subject is the unity of perception and the thought that thinks this unity, a unity of thinking and perceiving that Kant expresses in the formula "I think." Within Kant's system, however, this unity cannot be thought as it is in itself but only as the condition of possibility under which the unity of the manifold can each time be understood by a unified subject and under which the subject itself can function as a unity. Kant phrased the transcendental condition in the well-known proposition: "It must be possible for the 'I think' to accompany all my representations; for otherwise something would be represented in me which could not be thought at all, and that is equivalent to saying that the representation would be impossible, or at least would be nothing to me."[5]

The difference between the empirical self and the self of pure apperception can be stated in the following terms. The empirical self can occasionally become aware of itself, but then it appears under the form of time; hence it is merely an object for the self. Empirical self-awareness offers a representation that is inadequate to the self as it is in itself. The self of pure apperception, on the other hand, does not have to appear to the self; all that is required for the unity of cognition is the *possibility* that pure apperception accompany our representations. Hence, while the empirical self can occasionally appear to the subject in objective representation, pure apperception is present at all times in the subject's acts as the condition of possibility for these acts.

In both cases, however, the self as it truly is cannot be made accessible to itself. The empirical self is aware of itself only as a representa-

---

5. Immanuel Kant, *Critique of Pure Reason*, trans. Norman Kemp Smith (New York, 1965), B131–32.

tion in time and space, while, in terms of Kant's system, the subject as such does not exist under these forms. In its turn, pure apperception thinks the subject as it exists outside of time and space, but precisely for this reason it can represent the subject neither for the understanding (as an object) nor for the senses (as an intuition) but only as the possibility *that* it exists: "In the synthetic original unity of apperception, I am conscious of myself, not as I appear to myself, nor as I am in myself, but only that I am. This *representation* is a *thought*, not an intuition.... Accordingly, I have no *knowledge* of myself as I am but merely as I appear to myself."[6]

The Kantian subject can know itself only as an object in time and space, or only as a condition of possibility that accompanies the subject's cognition of the manifold of intuitions. It cannot, however, know itself truly, as the thing-in-itself outside of time and space—it cannot *intuit* (*anschauen*) itself as itself:

> Just as for knowledge of an object distinct from me ... so for knowledge of myself I require, besides the consciousness, that is, besides the thought of myself, an intuition of the manifold in me, by which I determine this thought. I exist as an intelligence which is conscious solely of its power of combination; but in respect of the manifold which it has to combine I am subjected to a limiting condition (entitled inner sense), namely, that this combination can be made intuitable only according to relations of time, which lie entirely outside the concepts of understanding.[7]

As the subsequent discussion will show, the Kantian "intuition" became the central issue for the romantic theory of the novel.

Kant's *Critique of Judgment* sought to resolve the problem of the deficiency, or the lack, of the subject by invoking the reflective judgment and the transcendental imagination. However, here too the project failed to reach its ultimate goal. The reflective judgment, which operates in the judgment of taste as it sets in motion the free play of the imagination, "brings about the unity of the subject only insofar as the subject sees itself in the image (*Bild*) of something without either a concept or an end" (*LA*, 31). The subject remains inaccessible to itself, representable only in the contemplation of works of art and in the self-formation (*Bildung*) of humanity as a whole, an infinite self-perfecting that indicates, symbolically, the "form" (*Bild*) of the subject.

6. Ibid., B157–58. Kant's italics.
7. Ibid., B158–59.

It is here, in Kant's conclusion that the subject is absent from the most pertinent and proper presentation (its presentation to itself), that the philosophical articulation of the romantic project begins to intersect with the historical formulation. It is approximately at the time when the absence of the subject emerged as philosophy's most immediate and most challenging task that philosophy (beginning with Kant) also inaugurated a systematic study of aesthetics and that it began to study art through its history. The nature and the extent of the coincidence are sufficiently indicated by the fact that the authors who inquired into the history of ancient literature adopted Kant's philosophical terminology to describe the predominant types of sensibility and the literary genres that expressed this sensibility. The Kantian vocabulary of "subject" and "object" thus entered the discourse of aesthetics and came to describe the systematic relations among the genres of antiquity: the lyric (subjective), the tragic (objective), and the epic (objective/subjective or subjective/objective).

It may be perhaps most appropriate to analyze the specific ways in which romanticism erected the relation between philosophy, history, and aesthetics in the work and accomplishment of Friedrich Schlegel. Friedrich Schlegel not only exemplifies romanticism's passionate interest in history but also represents this interest in its vital relation to the theory of the novel. In his vigorous study of classical antiquity, especially of Greek and Roman literature, Schlegel, like many other intellectuals of his time, viewed Greek art as an "idealization" of the human form and Greek culture as a natural formation unspoiled by the artifice of civilization.

This view of natural perfection, and even of its superiority over the moderns, posed serious problems, however, when examined in terms of the contemporary philosophies of history advanced by Kant and Johann Gottfried von Herder. In distinction from the conceptions of history prevalent before Giambattista Vico, in which history was a series of *exempla* based on the finite set of biblical themes, Kant's and Herder's theories allowed time and change to play a considerable role in the historical process. For example, Kant's progressive philosophy of history is composed of three stages: subjugation to instinct in harmony with nature, fall into freedom and arbitrariness of choice, and recuperation of this arbitrariness in the autonomous (free) subject. In the third moment, humanity will, in asymptotic infinity, approach the goal of history posited by Reason. In an alternative model, Herder defined the historical process of the formation of civilizations as a natural cycle in which cultures are born, mature, and face inevitable decay.

As Hans Eichner observes, it was obvious to Schlegel that Kant's thesis about the progress of humanity "was not very easily compatible with the history of the ancient civilizations" (FS, 20). If the "Golden Age" lies in the past, it is difficult to argue that humanity is progressing towards a "Golden Age" located in the future. It was apparent that the theory of the original "Golden Age" was more easily compatible with Herder's theory of natural growth and decline. Schlegel was forced to devise a more complex solution in order to reconcile the conflicting imperatives of preserving the grandeur of antiquity and of assuring the relevance of modernity. He reasoned that Greece, considered in itself as a separate age, conforms to Herder's description. But considered in the Kantian model as the origin of the infinitely progressive process, Greece marks the first moment in the speculative philosophy of history. This double proposal led Schlegel to posit two kinds of civilizations, "each subject to its own law of development: the 'natural' civilization, which obeys the laws of Herder's philosophy of history, and the 'artificial' civilization, which embodies Kant's notion of infinite progress" (FS, 21). The adjustment helped Schlegel reconcile the classicist thesis about the superiority of the Golden Age with the progressivist thesis about history's infinite march forward.

Schlegel developed the solution in terms of a division into two types of civilizations in his essay "Über das Studium der griechischen Poesie." The solution resembles the model of "naïve" and "sentimental" poetry proposed by Schiller in his study "Über naïve und sentimentalische Dichtung." (Schlegel's *Studium* was sent to the publisher in December, 1795, at the time when Schiller's essay began to be published.[8]) In Schiller's model "naïve," or "natural," poetry proceeds, not as art in the sense of artifice (aesthetics), but in an immediate fashion, art as a natural impulse. Furthermore—in an aspect important to Schlegel—the development of art forms in a "naïve" culture follows a "natural" course through stages that "naturally" complete the cycle of this civilization. Each of these stages is defined by a dominant, characteristic genre. Thus, the *Studium* identifies the sequence of

---

8. On the details of the temporal coincidence, see Hans Eichner's article "The Supposed Influence of Schiller's *Über naïve und sentimentalische Dichtung* on F. Schlegel's *Über das Studium der griechischen Poesie*," Germanic Review, XXX (1955), 260–64.

epos, lyric, and tragedy (although, as will be shown in a moment, Schlegel hesitated whether this sequence was one of development or decline), all of which reached their perfection in themselves, and as a configuration and sequence, these genres describe the process of development and the identity of this culture. As such a complete process, "Greek poetry is in its totality a maximum and canon of natural poetry, and every single product of it is the most perfect of its kind" (*FS*, 22).

We have already observed that the image of Greece as an age of pristine innocence and natural unity can function only within Herder's view of history as a series of enclosed ages that have nothing in common and that cannot become part of continuous historical development. This realization challenged Schlegel to devise a mechanism that would make possible the transition from the self-enclosed natural civilization to the infinitely progressive artificial one; it challenged him to articulate the efficient harmony of Herder's and Kant's philosophies of history. At stake were three fundamental assumptions behind modernity's understanding of history: the assumption that antiquity and modernity could be compared and related to each other (even if only in the negative juxtaposition of the "Battle of the Ancients and the Moderns"), the prevalent assumption that modernity represents an indisputable improvement over antiquity, and the belief in the unity of history.

The task of bridging the gap between antiquity and modernity posed enormous difficulties, and Schlegel, far from denying them, was quick to recognize them and to exploit their significance: "In the ancients, we see the perfected letter of all poetry; in the moderns we see its growing spirit" (Critical Fragment 93—*F*, 154); "All the classical poetical genres have now become ridiculous in their rigid purity" (Critical Fragment 60—*F*, 150); "The ancients are masters of poetical abstraction; the moderns are better at poetical speculation" (Critical Fragment 107—*F*, 155); "Perhaps one has to be arch-modern in order to gain a transcendental perspective on antiquity" (Athenaeum Fragment 271—*F*, 200; *cf.* Athenaeum Fragment 149—*F*, 181).[9] These and other attempts to capture the relation between the ancients and the mod-

---

9. The fragment further elucidates the transcendental perspective with the following examples: "Winckelmann felt the Greeks like a Greek. Hemsterhuis, on the other hand, knew how to circumscribe modern amplitude beautifully with ancient simplicity, and from the height of his culture he cast, as if from a free frontier, equally meaningful glances into the old and the new world" (*F*, 200–201).

erns in ever new models and metaphors testify not only to Schlegel's sharp awareness of the chasm but also to the elusive complexity of the problem. Indeed, his expertise in the subject makes him a prime example of the necessary qualification (being "arch-modern") specified in the last fragment quoted above. I will try to argue that Schlegel has proved himself worthy to be called "arch-modern": in a historic step, his romantic treatment of antiquity has made possible the subsequent transformation of "arch-modernity" into "post-modernity."

In order to present Schlegel's solution to the dilemma of antiquity and modernity, it is first necessary to show how this dilemma was approached by Schiller. Having constructed a "naïve" and a "sentimental" civilization, Schiller also found himself under the obligation to elaborate the nature of the relation between the two. For his part, Schiller hoped to build a bridge between the ancients and the moderns in a dialectical give-and-take that promised a recuperation of both moments in a synthetic unity. What the "artificial" civilization has lost in the natural realm—regulation, predictability, rhythmic flowering—it gains in the realm of artifice—freedom, caprice, invention, unpredictability of development, and ultimately, as Schiller emphasized, the infinite possibility, in the freedom from the bonds of nature, of striving after perfection.[10]

Schlegel's *Studium* and Schiller's "Über naïve und sentimentalische Dichtung" represent two basic modern responses to classical antiquity

10. Schiller's inchoate dialectic of the historical-aesthetic process has additional significance in the present discussion insofar as it structures those theories of the novel that think in terms of totality. The indebtedness to the Schillerian dialectic can be seen in the gesture of placing the modern novel in the tripartite scheme that begins with the condition of natural unity, passes through a negative moment of aridity and disintegration, and seeks redemption in a future time of restored harmony. For example, in *The Theory of the Novel* Georg Lukács identifies the immediate unity and natural harmony of Greek antiquity with the Homeric epos. The contemporary novel labors in a world without totality, longing for the ancient epos and hoping for the "new epos," of which Dostoevsky is, for the early Lukács, the notable harbinger. This is also the structure of Bakhtin's theory of the novel. In its constant references to the ancient menippea, Bakhtin's *Problems of Dostoevsky's Poetics* (trans. Caryl Emerson [Minneapolis, 1984]) implicitly relies on Greece as an exemplar of authentic and complete sensibility. Finally, René Girard's *Deceit, Desire, and the Novel* (trans. Yvonne Freccero [Baltimore, 1985]) advances a theory of the novel organized by "triangulated mimetic desire," by a scheme in which proper mediation degenerates into an improper relation that can only be corrected by abandoning the false mediation and by restoring the immediate relation with the True Mediator (Christ).

(although one must remember the original position of Hölderlin).[11] While Schlegel chose in the *Studium* to side with antiquity and to criticize modernity from classicist positions, Schiller recognized the need to leave antiquity behind and look forward to a completion in a future time of fulfillment. But it did not take long for Schlegel to recognize the value and the potential of Schiller's insight. Schiller's praise for "sentimental" poetry, "the splendid justification of the moderns," affected Schlegel so profoundly that he "did nothing for several days but read it and make notes" (*FS*, 28). Under the impact of this reading, Schlegel moved to revise his views presented in the *Studium*. As scholars frequently observe, Schlegel reversed his view of modernity: the grounds for negative judgment of the moderns now became the reasons for their emulation.

Schlegel decided to rethink the condition of the moderns along the lines of the "dialectical" resolution indicated by Schiller. However, the revelation provoked by Schiller's essay vindicated the moderns in the eyes of Schlegel in a sense completely different from, and one may risk stating, far less "influential" than, the models of resolution that came to control contemporary historical, philosophical, and aesthetic thought. Schlegel's model differs from the "dialectical" resolution intimated by Schiller, from the asymptotic approximation offered by Kant, and from the procedures of speculative idealism developed by Hegel. Schlegel's "sublation" of this opposition persists on the fringes of the models sketched above, largely unperceived and, in Hegel, entirely misunderstood and ridiculed as "subjective."

Schlegel defined the mechanism of transition from the natural to the artificial civilization as the process of completion. It can be seen that, defined in general terms, the problem of completion belongs equally to the Schlegel of the *Studium* as it does to the Schlegel who read Schiller. In the first place, the demand for the completion of antiquity calls for an imitation of the greatness of Greece in a work of art—and

---

11. In his essay "Hölderlin and the Romantic Tradition" (*Romanticism and Contemporary Criticism*, ed. E. S. Burt, Kevin Newmark, and Andrzej Warminski [Baltimore, 1993], 123–36) Paul de Man makes this difference clear in a passage that was crossed out by the author and appended in a footnote by the editors: "While in Schiller Greece and the West are opposed as nature is opposed to consciousness, in Hölderlin there is a dialectical reversal: our experience of nature is like the Greek's experience of consciousness and vice versa. What is naive to them is self-conscious to us (art)" (206n13).

in artistic genius—comparable to the standards handed down from antiquity. This is the option of classicism. In another sense, however—and this moment complicates completion beyond the sense of reproduction or matching—the task involves the completion of what in the perfection and grandeur of Greece remained imperfect and incomplete. In a sense, this imperfection at the heart of Greece is modernity's only chance to compete with, or surpass, antiquity. This is the romantic option.

The historical context in which Schlegel was elaborating this option is aptly expressed by the title of E. M. Butler's study *The Tyranny of Greece over Germany*. The peculiar character of this "tyranny" emerges as a double bind in Johann Joachim Winckelmann's famous sentence: "The only way we can become great, and, if this is possible, inimitable, is by imitating the Ancients" (*TM*, 236). The relation between the ancients and the moderns is a function of this double call, a call at once to imitate and to surpass, a call whose logic exhibits at its very core a certain excess powerful enough to set in motion a mechanism of an essential *in*completion of completion.

To explain this double bind it may be helpful to recall a similar structure found at the very center of Greek sensibility, the complex dependence between nature (*phusis*) and art (*tekhne*). Indeed, it would appear that the duplicity of the romantic completion of antiquity is a modern answer to the original Greek condition expressed by this dependence. Philippe Lacoue-Labarthe summarizes: for Aristotle (*Physics* II, 8, 199a) "there are ... two forms of mimesis. First, a restricted form, which is the reproduction, the copy, the reduplication of what is given. Then there is a general mimesis, which reproduces nothing given ... but which *supplements* a certain deficiency in nature, its incapacity to do everything, organize everything, make everything its work—*produce* everything. It is a productive mimesis, an imitation of *phusis* as a productive force, or as *poiesis*. It accomplishes, carries out, *finishes* natural production as such" (*TM*, 255–56).

This brief analysis reveals that Greek mimesis is structured on art's supplementary relation to nature. The supplement "reverse[s] the traditional relation between art and nature and decree[s] the first, in its very function of supplementation, superior to the second" (*TM*, 256). And it is this reversal that characterizes Schlegel's conception of the completion of antiquity. In this distinctly romantic option—different from the dialectical and the asymptotic models—the relation between a natural and an artificial civilization is controlled by the structure of the supplementary reversal: according to Schlegel, the artificial civilization is more important, and perhaps superior, because it alone is capable of understanding the natural civilization in its natural character, because it itself looks at this civilization from the artificial position, which is external to it, that is, from the arch-modern (*erzmodern*) perspective defined in Athenaeum Fragment 271: "Perhaps one has to be arch-modern in order to gain a transcendental perspective on antiquity." Postponing to a later moment a discussion of the implications of Schlegel's "arch-modernity," we may for now interpret Schlegel as saying that the organic unity of the natural civilization would be nothing without the romantic/modern gesture of completion: *indeed, this romantic conception of modernity creates the possibility of the historical existence of antiquity.* Romanticism proposes that modernity constitutes antiquity in the sense of supplementing it.

But there is more. Supplementarity not only allows for the possibility that the second moment could be, in a certain sense, the first moment; it also makes evident an originary absence in the apparently perfect unity. The discovery of supplementarity has made possible a critique of the notion of Greek "natural" civilization, a rethinking that has paved the way for the thesis about an *other* aspect of Greece. Schlegel's Idea 133: "To begin with, I speak only to those who are already facing the Orient," leads to Nietzsche's "Dionysian" element (see *FS*, 43). The romantic completion, then, not only heals an imperfection in the Greek ideal, but it discovers that this imperfection is structural—because no completion can ever hope to correct it—and transcendental—because without this incompletion no attempt at completion would make sense. Romanticism presupposes the primacy of lack (of incompletion) over the positive act of completion: the romantic completion acquires meaning and rationale from the antecedent, transcendental lack. The romantic completion of antiquity is, therefore, a matter of supplementing an original absence. This is why the different romantic projects that follow upon this discovery are marked with the characteristic stamp of supplementarity, preeminently the notion of *criticism*, which completes the work, and of *irony*, which presupposes the work's incompletion as the condition of its aspiring to perfection.[12]

12. Writing in *What Is Neostructuralism?* (trans. Sabine Wilke and Richard Gray [Minneapolis, 1989]) about the lack of center in structure, Manfred Frank links this lack with the supplementary logic of the romantic notion of criticism: "In the field of art criticism the early German romanticists already recognized this, and they considered

How did Schlegel understand this profound implication in the context of his own project? The structure of supplementarity has driven a wedge into the image, developed by Schlegel himself in the *Studium*, of Greece as an organic whole, as "one poem" that developed (or declined) in the natural stages of the epic, the lyric, and the tragic. In view of the supplementarity in the Greek concept of nature, the "possibility of the classical in modernity" is not simply the question of the mere possibility of equalling it in reproduction or, perhaps, even surpassing it, but primarily—and this is the other, unsuspected consequence, glimpsed by Schlegel alone, of the "splendid justification of the moderns"—a question of defining the essence of the transcendental lack.

Laboring under the terms of the Kantian crisis, the crisis of the absent subject, the romantics discovered, in the very process in which they sought to construct and comprehend universal history, a constitutive lack at the origin of this history. From now on, the goal of romantic thought is, as Lacoue-Labarthe and Nancy put it, "to construct, to produce, to effectuate what even at the origin of history was already thought of as a lost and forever inaccessible 'Golden Age'" (*LA*, 11). It will not be too pedantic to emphasize that the Golden Age in question is not to be understood as a form of sensibility, as a mythical Cytherea that fertilizes aesthetic imagination. To put it in philosophical terms, romanticism understood the Golden Age as the original unity of the subject with itself. Romanticism's inquiry into the origin of history has found the Golden Age to be affected by the law of incompletion. As originally absent, the Golden Age is the index of disunity, of lack of synthesis in the transcendental sense in which the Kantian subject lacks the form of representation adequate to itself.

At this point we can begin to define with more precision the specific manner in which romanticism conceived the relation between the post-Kantian crisis of the absent subject and the study of history (antiquity). Both the philosophical and the historical inquiries have yielded a constitutive absence. As if this crisis were not enough, the

---

literary criticism a supplement to an irreducible blemish in the work of art itself" (64). Frank adds: "Each interpretation ... presents ... a suggestion as to how one can replace the missing central meaning of the text and how one can determine it (provisionally, with reservations). Since the central meaning, however, is missing, interpretation is not so much a matter of *finding* (*Finden*) (finding presupposes the presence of something that can be found) as *inventing* (*Erfinden*), i.e. a supplement, an addition to the text" (64).

romantics also reasoned that the division itself between philosophy and historical aesthetics was the supreme symptom of the disunity. Faced with a subjectless philosophy, with an originless history, and (transcendentally) with a divided human spirit, the romantics saw their only hope for completing philosophy in transcendental poetry (where poetry is to be understood in the Aristotelian sense as making, production, as *poiesis*). They hoped to unify, to connect again—*re-ligio*—the separate realms that had, already in classical Greece, been sundered (Schlegel's *Ideas* are written from the point of view of this unity). When Schlegel speaks in Idea 11 of the inferiority of novels where "religion" is lacking, he indicates the time in which such transcendental unity has not yet been achieved.

Before presenting the nature and the goals of the transcendental unity advocated by romanticism in its specific reference to the romantic theory of the novel, we must first discuss in more detail how romanticism understood and represented the disunity discovered at the heart of Greece. Schlegel's use of the Homeric epos to represent the problematic unity of Greece becomes pertinent from the point of view of the means available to romanticism for completing the incompletion of the epos.

Having discovered the unity of ancient Greece to be originally incomplete, Schlegel reasoned that the genre that represents this essential condition of Greek culture must itself bear the formal signs of this incompletion. Hence, in order to select the ancient genre suitable for romantic completion, Schlegel first faced the task of determining which Greek genre represents the disunity of Greek sensibility in the purest form. The issue demands precision. As Peter Szondi observes, Schlegel hesitated whether the sequence of the epic, the lyric, and the tragic describes an evolution or a devolution of Greek civilization.[13] If the epic captured the moment of gestation after which Greek sensibility evolved through the lyric and reached its peak in tragedy, then the

---

13. Peter Szondi, "Friedrich Schlegel's Theory of Poetical Genres: A Reconstruction from the Posthumous Fragments," in *TU*, 85–89. Schlegel's hesitation branched out into many options and variants, not only as an alternative between epic and tragedy, but also as one between epic and lyric. For example, in 1799 Schlegel writes: "Epic = objective poetry, lyric = subjective poetry, drama = objective-subjective poetry." A year later he asserts that "Epic = subjective-objective, drama = objective, lyric = subjective" (85). Szondi adds: "we again find the definitions: lyrical = 'merely *subjective*,' dramatic = merely '*objective*,' epic = subjective-objective" (89).

primacy would have to be assigned to the *tragic* genre; if, however, the epic represented the highest moment of Greek culture, after which the culture declined through the lyric into tragedy, then the defining condition of Greek sensibility would be expressed by the *epic*.

It is necessary to clarify Schlegel's reasoning behind his choice of the epic over the tragic and the lyric, for as I hope to show later, this choice has left an indelible stamp on postmodern romantic sensibility.[14] Unlike Hölderlin, Schlegel saw in tragedy and lyric little or no potential for speculative construction; most likely, he reasoned that to choose the tragic or the lyric as the defining genre of modernity would amount to forcing (literary) history to regress and atrophy back to Greece.

The regression in question refers to the relative simplicity and complexity of a particular genre. Hölderlin, for instance, guided by the assumption that Greece excelled by its immediacy and naturalness, pursued the idea of a modern, pure lyricism, one so pure that it would be free even of lyricism itself; Schlegel, on the other hand, judged a genre by its ability to combine literary forms, types of sensibility, and modalities of philosophical mood. The tradition that starts with Plato perceived the epic as a combination, or union, of different poetic modes. As Lacoue-Labarthe and Nancy phrase it, the epos is not a pure genre because "it occupies the middle . . . between *diegesis* and *mimesis*, between dithyramb and tragedy; as the romantics will say, it is neither purely subjective nor purely objective, but subjective-objective" (*LA*, 96). The complexity of the epos as a subjective and objective form reaffirmed for Schlegel his newly formulated awareness that the pristine unity of the antique world is no longer a valid assumption. The epos represents, already at the beginning of (literary) history, an internally divided and complex form of sensibility. As an expression of "the Mystery of the articulation of the subjective and the objective,

14. Schlegel himself experimented with this possibility: "*Three dominant genres.* (1) *Tragedy* among the Greeks. (2) *Satire* among the Romans. (3) The *novel* among the moderns" (*TU*, 87; Fragment 32 in *Literary Notebooks, 1797–1801*, ed. Hans Eichner [Toronto, 1957]). In analyzing the two options, Schlegel must have been experiencing the contradictions between the Herderian and the Kantian philosophies of history—the contradictions of historical thought par excellence—very acutely. Greek civilization was both immutable and separate as "one poem," and mutable, a mere moment (albeit a glorious one) in history's march towards the romantic age. The hesitation between the epic and the tragic as candidates for representing the essence of modernity calls for a decision as to "what part of ancient poetry is still alive enough to be simultaneously killed and conserved, as Hegel would say—or resuscitated" (*LA*, 95).

necessity and freedom, the instinctive and the intentional, etc." (*LA*, 96), the Homeric epos seemed a suitable vehicle of romantic synthesis, a model ("the matrix-like genre"—*LA*, 96) for the even more complex modern sensibility that romanticism sought to capture and articulate.

Having established the epic form as the genre representative of Greek sensibility, Schlegel proceeds to determine the modern form corresponding to this genre. From the objective/subjective complexity of the epos, Schlegel derives *the novel* as the genre capable of representing this complexity. Besides this similarity—a merely external, perhaps accidental, similarity of two literary forms belonging to two separate historical moments—the novel is selected because it is the modern genre proper for healing the original split in human sensibility, the genre capable of completing the original lack. Szondi writes: "If, among the forms of Greek poetry, it is only the ancient epic (and not the tragedy or the lyric) that can be 'romanticized,' this is because the epic corresponds to the novel" (*TU*, 89). And it is the epic, rather than the lyric and the tragedy, that "corresponds" to the novel because, as Schlegel writes, "the poetry of nature is either subjective or objective," while "the mixture of the subjective and the objective is not possible in a natural formation" (*TU*, 89). The synthetic, that is, subjective-objective, character of the epic approaches most closely the complex unity of the modern, "artificial" civilization in the reflection of objective and subjective moments.[15]

It is nearly impossible to gauge the consequences of positing the epos as already a synthesis. If the unity has already taken place, Lacoue-Labarthe and Nancy ask, "is there anything left to do?" (*LA*, 96). Perhaps the unity is accomplished as already lost. Or, in one more possibility, has the unity already taken place on the objective side of the pair (in the Homeric epos), and the subjective task still lies ahead? It is perhaps most proper to say that Schlegel's solution took account of all these possibilities. For him the completion of the original lack be-

---

15. Novalis captures this advancement in Logological Fragment 34: "The poetry of primitive people is a narrative without beginning, middle, or end. The pleasure that it gives them is merely pathological—simply pastime, mere dynamic activation of the power of imagination. Epic poetry is the ennobled form of primitive poetry. In essence, altogether the same. The novel already stands much higher. The former continues, the latter grows. In the former there is a rhythmic progression, in the novel, geometric" ("Logological Fragments, in *German Romantic Criticism*, ed. A. Leslie Willson [New York, 1982], 69).

comes thinkable in the novel: the novel (*der Roman*) is the modern version of the ancient epic with respect to the reflected unity of the subjective and the objective; it is an appropriate vehicle for healing the discord and chaos of modern sensibility that he so precisely characterized in the *Studium*. Schlegel writes in "The Letter on the Novel," "Just as our literature began with the novel, so the Greek began with the epic and dissolved in it" (*DP,* 101). A similar process took place, according to Schlegel (Athenaeum Fragment 146), in Roman literature with regard to satire: "Just as the novel colors all of modern poetry, so satire colors and, as it were, sets the tone for all of Roman poetry, yes, even the whole of Roman literature" (*F,* 180). The novel completes antiquity by *romanticizing* the dispersed and complex sensibility of Greece—by repeating this disunity in a form suited to the moderns.

Keeping in mind the important premise that the romantic theory of the novel is defined by the horizon of the transcendental subject, we may now proceed to discuss the main outlines of this theoretical enterprise. We have seen that the romantics proposed the *Roman* in the context of resolving the duality of the subjective/objective Greek epos. In other words, the novel represented for romanticism the genre suitable for accomplishing the modern synthesis of the objective and the subjective (on the side of the subjective, in view of the Kantian aftermath), for accomplishing the self–presentation of the subject. Friedrich Schlegel expresses the potential of the novel to present the subject to itself in the following formula: "Every theory of the novel must itself be a novel" [*Eine solche Theorie des Romans würde selbst ein Roman sein müssen*] (*DP,* 102/*SL,* 319).

The discussion of Schlegel's formula that is to follow must be prefaced with several disclaimers. All too frequently, Schlegel's formula is mistakenly applied to the purely technical aspects of literary compositions written during and after the romantic period, aspects such as narratorial self-consciousness, various types of formal self-reflexivity, and, as it is generally put, "the presence of the author in the work." The literary works (Cervantes' *Don Quixote,* Sterne's *Tristram Shandy,* Tieck's *Märchen,* his plays *Prince Zerbino* and *The World Topsy-Turvy,* Jean Paul's *The Invisible Lodge,* Novalis' *Heinrich von Ofterdingen,* Brentano's *Godwi,* Solger's *Erwin*) invoked or created by romantics as models of the new novel have contributed to the subsequent erroneous identification of romantic reflection with matters of mere technique, while the question of the transcendental subject, with which the romantics began and with which alone they were concerned, became eclipsed.

The formula is also mistakenly understood as "raising to the second power" ("potentiation"), an infinitely expansive, elusive, capricious undermining of all statements in the notoriously "subjective" romantic irony. In the wake of romanticism, institutional literary criticism has found this particular distortion of the meaning of romantic reflection most palatable and, perhaps, most readily adaptable to classroom circulation.

Unfortunately, the intended content and the implications of Schlegel's proposition do not become clearer in light of his own criticism of contemporary novels in "The Letter on the Novel." The works singled out by Schlegel for positive evaluation from the point of view of conformity to the romantic theory of the novel only remotely indicate the ideal that Schlegel had in mind. Schlegel speaks in "The Letter" of Sterne, Diderot, Jean Paul, and Goethe, who represent satire, grotesque epic, and *Bildungsroman*, respectively, and who variously mix self-irony, arabesque, and the fantastic. Beyond these—in his opinion, inadequate—indications, Schlegel bemoans the inferiority of contemporary novels, which lack "a possible effective presentation of the unifying principle—that is, of the subject" (*LA*, 99).

Schlegel invites even more misunderstanding when he illustrates his concept of "transcendental poetry" with such "romantic novelists" as Dante, Cervantes, and Shakespeare. Although intended as illustrative paradigms, these examples manage to throw the precise meaning of the term "novel" in romanticism into even deeper confusion. This is the despairing response of Arthur O. Lovejoy, who, dismayed to find in "The Letter" this triumvirate under the label of "novelists," concluded that the romantic theory of the novel resists definition and for this reason no longer concerns scholarship as a valid issue.[16] At any rate, Schlegel's statements in "The Letter" sufficiently indicate that his "novel" is far removed from the genre of the fictional, realistic, psychological third-person narrative that took hold in Europe after romanticism. At the same time, however, one can see how his illustrations may invite erroneous reconstructions.[17]

---

16. Arthur O. Lovejoy, "The Meaning of 'Romantic' in Early German Romanticism," in *Essays in the History of Ideas* (New York, 1955), 206.

17. The issue of finding empirical examples of the romantic novel has been, of course, complicated by Schlegel himself. On the one hand, Schlegel's transcendental theory of genres rejects empirical evidence in principle. In Fragment 115 in his *Literary*

In this situation we may do well to redirect the analysis back to Schlegel's formula that "every theory of the novel must itself be a novel." It may be useful to begin an examination of this thesis by having a closer look at the term *theory*. Schlegel explains *theory* immediately before giving his formula, and he explains it as it is used in this definition: "If such examples [of romantic works] became known, then I would have the courage for a *theory of the novel* which would be a theory in the original sense of the word; a spiritual viewing of the subject with calm and serene feeling, as it is proper to view in solemn joy the meaningful play of divine images" (*DP*, 102).

The transcendental thrust of Schlegel's novelistic enterprise is indicated by the terms *viewing* (*Anschauung*) and *meaningful play of divine images* (*das bedeutende Spiel göttlicher Bilder*). As will be indicated later, the romantics understood *theory* in the sense of reflection, and *reflection* as "(intellectual) intuition." For now it may be sufficient to state that Schlegel's formula about the theory of the novel institutes the reflective identity of each novel with its theory. This identity determines the *romantic* character of the *theory*. The circular formula is romantic because the demand that the theory of the novel be a novel romanticizes—potentiates—not the narrowly defined novelistic genre but, more fundamentally, a genre's *being a genre*—the novel's being itself, *a novel*. The romantic novel reflects (works) on itself to produce itself (the work) and, in this production, to accomplish itself as itself.

As in the thematics of the Kantian subject, at issue is the production of the subject in its proper form, the production of the subject as *this subject's* subject. Expressed in terms of Kantian philosophy (although it is not part of Kant's system), the novel describes the work of the subject to achieve the presentation adequate to itself—not as a representation in space and time, and not as a condition of possibility of its cognitions, but as the subject's intuition (*Anschauung*, "spiritual viewing") of itself as the manifold of its own intuitions. The romantic

---

Notebooks, he says that Goethe had a "wrong idea of the novel" [*schlechte Idee vom Roman*] because "in his search for the spirit of the poetical genres [he] proceeds *empirically*"; in the case of the novel, however, "the character of this particular genre cannot be discovered in a full and exact manner by the empirical method" (*TU*, 80/*SL*, 29). On the other hand, however, Schlegel was not at all reluctant to identify among existing works adequate examples of a truly romantic novel. Thus, his "Letter on the Novel" mentions Rousseau's *Confessions* as adequately representing the presence of the subject in its work.

novel enables the subject, who was incapable of self-presentation in the Kantian system, to achieve self-presentation as its own subject. This self-presentation is effectuated as the presence of the subject in the entirety of the work. The complete presence of the subject in the work yields the original, reflective, "intuitive" unity of the subjective and the objective moments: the subject is the work, and the work is the subject. Schlegel's ensemble of the romantic novel and its theory describes the production of the work that is its only subject, that is only the subject and nothing else. The only work-of-the-subject is the presence of the subject to itself in its proper form of self-knowledge. In the infinite work of this dissolution of the subject-work, the subject knows itself as the knower of this knowledge: this knowledge is "the meaningful play [das bedeutende Spiel] of divine images."

A parallel thought concerning the romantic meaning of *theory* is expressed in Novalis' *Monologue:* "If it were only possible to make people understand that it is the same with language as it is with mathematical formulae—they constitute a world in itself—their play is self-sufficient, they express nothing but their own marvellous nature, and this is the very reason why . . . they are the mirror to the strange play of relationships among things. Only their freedom makes them members of nature, only in their free movements does the world-soul express itself and make of them a delicate measure and a ground-plan of things."[18] Echoing Kant's model of the "free play" of the mind's faculties, Novalis sees language as a strictly theoretical process of activity and self-expression, not only unconditioned in its origin and autotelic in its goals, but also originally united with itself and expressing nothing more than this primordial unity. This unity of language is "reflective"; as a vehicle of the original unity, language carries, for the romantics, the minimal relation of reflection, the germ cells, or, as Novalis calls them, the "grains of pollen," of the whole system. It is also on this "intuitive" unity capable of extrapolation that Schlegel founded his theory of the romantic fragment.

Keeping in mind the way that the sense of romantic theory determines the meaning of Schlegel's formula, we can now proceed to examine the origin and the place of romantic theory in the context of contemporary philosophical debates. As Lacoue-Labarthe and Nancy

---

18. Friedrich von Hardenberg [Novalis], "Monologue," in *German Aesthetic and Literary Criticism: The Romantic Ironists and Goethe,* ed. Kathleen Wheeler (New York, 1984), 92–93.

demonstrate, the romantic theory of the novel is parallel, as *theory*, to Hegel's absolute knowledge. In Hegel, knowledge is absolute "less because it is limitless knowledge than because it is knowledge that knows itself even as it knows what it knows, and which thereby forms the actual infinity of knowledge" (*LA,* 53). It is clear that Schlegel's formula—"every theory of the novel must itself be a novel"—rigorously specifies the knowledge of the absolute: the act of knowledge ("the theory") knows the object ("the novel") and at the same time it knows itself in this act ("it itself is a novel"). Finally, the subject of absolute knowledge in Schlegel's model, as a subject that is the knower and the known, is *dissolved* in this self-knowledge—it becomes the subject-work. It is inarguably a telling choice, made by the modern age, when it decided against the romantics' original solution and in favor of Hegel's speculative idealism, which places the subject (the "Spirit") in relation to everything in the transparency of the concept.

This parity between the romantic (literary) and the dialectical (speculative) solutions has not asserted itself with sufficient tenacity in literary criticism. At best, criticism eagerly endorsed Hegel's shrill condemnation of the "subjective" character of the romantic solution, of the fact that romanticism dissolves the subject in the work-of-the-subject. At worst, criticism concluded that romanticism was simply an attempt to see literature, an art form inherited from classical antiquity, as an "aesthetic" version of philosophy. In the latter misprision, literary studies assumed that romanticism merely added to literature an exotic philosophical "flavor" of its own. This assumption itself rests on a more fundamental misunderstanding, that literature possesses a stable identity different from that of philosophy. In order to halt this trend of systematic misprision and, perhaps, to explain, partly at least, the reasons behind the facile accommodations, it may be helpful summarily to trace the rich historical-philosophical context, the polemical stakes, and the potential pitfalls of the romantic solution.

Perhaps the term that best captures the specificity of the romantic solution is "the literary absolute," introduced by Philippe Lacoue-Labarthe and Jean-Luc Nancy. Both words play an equally important role in the phrase, as they locate the romantic solution within, and delimit it from, the other dominant systems emerging in German philosophy in the wake of Kant's *Critiques*. By speaking of the literary *absolute,* the romantics emphasized their allegiance to the new generation of thinkers—Fichte, Schelling, and Hegel—who set out to heal the divisions bequeathed by Kant; by speaking of a *literary* absolute, the romantics demarcated their efforts from the speculative solution, as they privileged the positive over the negative moments in the construction of the absolute.

To address both dimensions it may be helpful to discuss some aspects of romantic speculative thought developed by one of the core members of the Jena group, Johann Gottlieb Fichte. It may be remembered that Fichte's search for the transcendental unity of the self was provoked by Kant's undeveloped thesis about transcendental apperception, about the self-knowledge of the subject expressed in the statement "I think." As Dieter Henrich shows, in the course of his philosophical career, Fichte adopted at least three different models of the absolute.[19] Determined to give a full account of this synthesis, Fichte assumed that the structure of the absolute possessed the elusive simplicity of the self; he expressed this structure in his famous formula "I = I." At the first stage, this formula is given a reflective sense. However, Fichte was also the first to discover the fallacy of this model. Henrich writes "The possibility of reflection must be understood on the basis of this primordial essence of the Self," while "the theory of reflection proceeds in the opposite direction and explains the Self as an instance of the reflective act. Consequently, it interprets the primordial, but obscure essence of the Self with the help of the manifest, but secondary phenomenon of reflection" (22).

Fichte abandoned the model of reflection and proceeded to account for the original relation "I = I" with an amended model of positing (*setzen*), expressed by the formula: "The Self posits itself absolutely and unconditionally" (24). Henrich comments that this model avoids the trap of the reflection theory (where the self was merely a "secondary phenomenon"), for here there is no "Subject-Self prior to self-consciousness; rather, the subject, too, first emerges at the same time as the whole consciousness expressed in the identity 'I = I.' " Henrich adds that "the whole of self-consciousness . . . will not emerge from any one of its factors [subject, object], but simultaneously with them all" (25). The model, it can be seen, relies on the notion of immediacy—"the fact that the entire Self emerges all at once" (25) and without dependence on anything external or alien to it. Defining the pre-

---

19. Dieter Henrich, "Fichte's Original Insight," in *Contemporary German Philosophy*, trans. David R. Lachterman (University Park, Pa., 1982), I, 19, hereinafter cited parenthetically by page number in the text.

cise nature of this immediacy became a task of paramount importance for Fichte, for the romantics, and for Hegel.

As he made the transition from the reflection model to the positing model, Fichte acknowledged that the latter introduced a new component, that of *production*. As Henrich writes, "the act of production is taken here to be a real activity, while the product is taken to be the knowledge of this act" (26). Thus, Fichte asserted that "to be a Self is to perform an act" and that the only product of this act was the knowledge of this production *and* the production of this knowledge (27). Fichte rounded off this thought with an improved version of the previous formula: "The Self posits itself absolutely *as* positing itself" (29). With this improvement, which, Henrich comments, determined self-consciousness as "intuition and concept at the same time" (29), Fichte has irreversibly broached the fundamental Kantian distinction between concept (*Begriff*) and intuition (*Anschauung*) by declaring the two to be "equiprimordial (*gleichursprünglich*)" (cf. 30, n. 17).

Perhaps the most important breakthrough in Fichte's thought—from the point of view of the present argument regarding the romantic theory of the novel—occurred in a mystical moment, in a dream that Fichte documented in three sonnets (cf. 39). This stage of the "inserted eye," as it testifies to Fichte's fascination with sight, also points out the affinity of "sight" with the original meaning of romantic theory as "spiritual viewing." For Fichte the eye "must have in its sight the activity-of-the-eye *as* such" (33 italics in original). At this stage, self-consciousness is a "look that sees itself and in each case is already this act of seeing" (33). Here the coherent totality of the "I = I" structure emerges for Fichte in a nexus of five moments (too technical to be discussed here at length), all of which must be explained not only as the content of the activity but as the necessary moments of the absolute self-relation.

Always cautious not to derive the phenomenon of self-consciousness from any one of its constitutive factors, Fichte now proposes "a state of knowledge in which there is no knowing subject" (36). Fichte's subject emerges simultaneously with the structure in which it functions. Henrich notes that "if every item of knowledge really had a subject, the subject itself could not be an item of knowledge. Otherwise we would have to assume a subject of this subject and thus surrender to the infinite regress that Fichte so much feared. The idea of the Self would sink into the abyss. The paradox of subject-less knowing is preferable to that" (36).

This rough outline of the stages of Fichte's thought on the self points out three characteristics of the romantic thought on the novel. First, it shows that in its attempts to construct the absolute, romanticism followed the rigor of speculative thought; more specifically, it illustrates the circular economy of this thought and its central requirement, that of accounting for every moment of the absolute relation in terms of this relation itself. In short, Schlegel's formula that "every theory of the novel must itself be a novel" is parallel in its rigor and in its objectives to Fichte's thought on the circular (speculative) relation "I = I." Second, Fichte's intellectual efforts prepare the proper context for presenting the romantic transformations of the theme of "subject-less knowing" into the theme of dissolution.

Third, and perhaps most important, Fichte's thought illustrates in what sense the romantic project of the novel is inextricably linked with the thematics of the subject-self. Like Fichte's project, romanticism drew its impulse from the Kantian "I think"; like Fichte, the romantics sought to determine the unity of pure apperception in the circular-speculative formula; and, like Fichte, they reached the stage of the subject-less activity. However, in a crucial divergence from Fichte, who set forth the "I" and the "non-I" as determinations mutually delimiting each other (*Wechselbestimmungen*), Schlegel did not allow any play of the negative in the progress towards the absolute relation (a choice, as I will soon show, severely criticized by Hegel). Instead, romanticism opted for what Walter Benjamin has called the "medium of reflection" (*das Reflexionsmedium*), a continuum of forms that constitutes the "literary absolute."[20]

Furthermore, as we have seen, Fichte moved beyond Kant and declared the primordial self to be a unity of intuition and concept—for this reason, among others, Schlegel, in Athenaeum Fragment 281, called Fichte "a Kant raised to the second power" [*ein Kant in der zweiten Potenz*] (*F,* 202). But, in contrast to Schlegel, who understood the primordial unity of the self solely as a function of concept, Fichte understood intuition as sensory. It is necessary to bear this capital difference in mind when reading Schlegel's declaration (Athenaeum Fragment 76) that "An intellectual point of view is the categorical imperative of any theory" [Die intellektuale Anschauung ist der kategorische

---

20. Walter Benjamin, "Der Begriff der Kunstkritik in der deutschen Romantik," in *Gesammelte Schriften,* ed. Rolf Tiedemann and Hermann Schweppenhäuser (Frankfurt am Main, 1972), Vol. I, Pt. 1, p. 36.

Imperativ der Theorie] (*F,* 170). (Firchow translates incorrectly, of course; Schlegel means "intellectual intuition.")[21] Intellectual intuition may be taken either as sensory or conceptual; in this case it is, of course, the latter, the romantic sense—and this sense is decisive for our subsequent discussion of Schlegel's "theory of the novel." As we shall see, the choice of the conceptual over the sensory has important implications for the role of romanticism in the history of modern aesthetics.

In order to develop the differences and specificities of romantic thought in more detail, it may be useful first to discuss the romantic absolute by adopting a helpful alternative term proposed by Benjamin, the "poetic Absolute."[22] The reason why the romantic absolute is poetic becomes clear when we recall that this concept originated from the romantics' concrete interests, namely, their preoccupation with the aesthetic history of classical antiquity. We have already examined certain aspects of this preoccupation in the case of Friedrich Schlegel, and we have noted that the study of an aesthetic epoch implied for him the elaboration of a conceptual system that presupposed a unity of the epoch and a unity of the concepts that organize this epoch.

The same imperatives of totality that guided his historical pursuits also came to shape his critical enterprise. Eager to break with the classicist notion of critical rules and norms as standards of evaluation of empirical works of art, Schlegel proposed the existence of immanent laws that are applicable and valid for each work taken separately. The classicist conception implied not only that aesthetic rules preexist every concrete work, but also that the collection of such rules makes

---

21. Firchow ill-advisedly resorts to another bad translation in the following fragment: "These are the intellectual insights of criticism: the feeling of the infinitely subtle analytic quality of Greek poetry, and that of the infinitely rich mixture of Roman satire and Roman prose" [Die intellektualen Anschauungen der Kritik sind das Gefühl von der unendlich feinen Analyse der griechischen Poesie und das von der unendlich vollen Mischung der römischen Satire und der römischen Prosa] (*F,* 239/*Charakteristiken,* 254). The passage illustrates two points relative to the romantic sense of "intellectual intuition." First, it shows that the romantics treated criticism as a cognitive activity that belongs to the movement to(ward) the literary absolute. Second, it shows the inapplicability of Fichte's meaning as "sensory intuition," for in that case criticism would designate the process of the "I" grasping itself, rather than the process of a minimal reflection's becoming potentiated and dissolving in the absolute.

22. In this exposition I am following the direction suggested by Rodolphe Gasché in "The Sober Absolute: On Benjamin and the Early Romantics," *Studies in Romanticism,* XXXI (1992), 433–53.

up the idea of art; this position in turn implied that the idea of art is an abstraction from empirical works and that art originates in a fund of rules held in store by this abstract idea (*cf.* SA, 446). On the other hand, romanticism also resisted another contemporary fallacy—represented by the aesthetics of *Sturm und Drang*—that the work is the product of the subjective powers of the author. In contrast to these solutions, romanticism maintained that the Idea of Art is immanently present in each empirical work, neither as an abstraction, nor as an infusion of the author's subjectivity, but as an infinitization of the finite work's kernel of self-consciousness and reflection. As endowed with this kernel of reflective capacity, each work is already "criticizable," that is, it belongs, through the agency of romantic criticism, to the continuity of forms that, taken together, make up the poetic absolute.

The romantic thesis about the continuity of individual centers of reflection in the realm of art, the thesis about the "medium of reflection," marks the point at which Fichte and the romantics part company in a decisive way. Perhaps nobody has addressed this central problem of the romantic enterprise with more insight than Walter Benjamin in his classic study of the period, "The Concept of Art Criticism in German Romanticism." The first point of divergence concerns the treatment of negativity, or, more specifically, of infinity. As Rodolphe Gasché notes, while Fichte restricted reflection "to a self-positing I," the romantics extended it to "mere thinking, or thinking in general" (SA, 438). For the romantics everything was, by virtue of the kernel of self-consciousness, capable of (being) thought. Hence, something was either a self, and therefore immediately and a priori knowable, or it was not a self, and therefore non-existent (as object of knowledge). Also, while Fichte's "I" knew itself in sensory intuition, the romantic self knew itself in conceptual intuition. Finally, as Gasché writes, "the early romantics redefined infinity, seeing it no longer, in contradiction to Fichte, as continuous advance, but rather as an infinitude of connectedness" (SA, 438). Romanticism's poetic absolute is this connectedness.

According to Benjamin, the most precipitous consequence of such an unleashing of infinity becomes evident when one examines its impact on Fichte's formula of self-positing, "I = I." Fichte expressed this primary relation in the canonical Ur-Form, as "the thinking of thinking." As "second level reflection directed upon first level reflection whose subject matter is mere thinking with its correlative thought," this thinking "achieves completion in the self-positing I" (SA, 440). By contrast, the romantics turned this relation into an endless chain: Fichte's "thinking of thinking" expands into "the thinking of thinking of thinking," and so on.

But the romantics expose thought to mortal danger, says Benjamin, when they set the canonical Ur-Form adrift at the third level, because, as Gasché writes, "the rigorous Ur-Form of second-level reflection, in the third-level reflection, occupies both the position of the object and the subject of thinking" (SA, 440). While in Fichte the infinite regress of positing and thinking was controlled by self-limitation (*Selbstbestimmung*), in the romantics the proper form of reflection escalates without restriction (for it knows no delimitation), unfolding "into an ever more complex plurality of meanings at each successive level" (SA, 440, Gasché quoting Benjamin). The canonical form of reflection thus becomes irrevocably lost: as "absolute reflection" it is dissolved in the absolute.[23]

And for Benjamin it is precisely here that the danger to thought arises. The absolute now becomes continuous with the canonical form of thought, which has proliferated into ambiguous levels of subjective and objective positions. Moreover, the fact that the romantics described the relation of the absolute to itself in essentially the same terms in which they accounted for *thought grasping the absolute*, makes of the absolute, for Benjamin at least, an entity of the same order that characterizes reflective thought (Benjamin's comment on

---

23. As Samuel Weber lucidly argues ("Criticism Underway: Walter Benjamin's *Romantic Concept of Criticism*," in *Romantic Revolutions: Criticism and Theory*, eds. Kenneth R. Johnston *et al.* [Bloomington, 1990], 311), the issue of subject-less knowing in Fichte and Schlegel is complicated by its connection with reflection. Reflection for Fichte becomes exposed to infinite regress when, as the romantics want it, the barriers of self-delimitation (*Selbstbeschränkung*) are lifted; without the "non-I," the "I" falls into the abyss. In turn, the romantics regarded Fichte's model of the "I" and the "non-I" as endless, empty self-mirroring without advance. Romantic reflection is not based on consciousness but on the self in the realm of art, where "form" and "criticism" delimit infinity. Schlegel intimates the romantic self that is not a Fichtean "I" in his essay "On Incomprehensibility" (F, 259–71), where he speaks of "a Single Subject," the "Subject of Subjects" (259), "the invisible power of World Spirit"; this Subject "emanates" as "the purest and most genuine incomprehension ... from science and the arts ... and from philosophy and philology." The language of this Spirit is Kant's table of categories; it will reveal "the power and source of all activity," and with this language "the human spirit can transform itself and thereby perhaps at last bind its transforming and ever transformed opponent in chains" (260–61). This "Subject of Subjects" is *not* a consciousness and, therefore, has little to do with the "subjectivism" so vigorously denounced by Hegel.

the double meaning of the "medium of reflection" underscores this double aspect of the romantic absolute).[24] Benjamin makes note of this logical arrogance when he says that Schlegel not only sought to grasp the absolute systematically but to grasp the system absolutely. As Gasché puts it, "By contending that there is a steady continuity between lower forms of reflection and absolute reflection, the Absolute loses its distinctness, its univocity, in short everything that separates it from the lower orders" (SA, 441).

The implications of this indictment may become more palpable when Benjamin's critique is applied directly to Schlegel's formula that "every theory of the novel must itself be a novel." While formally parallel to Fichte's thesis "I = I," and while, like this thesis, faithful to the protocol of the speculative construction of the absolute, at its very heart Schlegel's formula at the same time foregrounds a difference that makes it radically irreducible to Fichte's account. Understood in the context of the romantics' philosophical enterprise, the specificity of the romantic absolute can be formulated in the following thesis: because the poetic absolute belongs to the continuum of self-reflexive forms and, moreover, because it knows itself in the same mode of knowledge in which the lower forms know it, the absolute can differ from the lower forms of reflection only in *quantity* and not in *quality*. The difference between the lower forms—for example, the forms and works of art—and the romantic absolute (which is the continuum of these forms) is merely a difference of *degree*. Keeping in mind this aesthetic theory, we can translate Schlegel's formula as follows: "Every theory of the novel—every mode of being of the Idea of Art (the absolute, the theory) that grounds and links up specific empirical works of art (every novel) to itself—must itself be a novel (must itself be a work of this type, level, or *genus*)." Concerning Benjamin's reservations about this solution, Gasché writes "The romantic theory ... condemns the medium of reflection, or the Absolute, to being *only* the enhanced reflection of whatever is reflectively raised to that higher level. By holding that the totality of all works is a work—however invisible or purely intelligible it may be—is to determine the Absolute as a mere potentiation of the singular works that it embraces. Such an understanding of the Absolute ... entails a loss of the force of transcendence and the relativization of difference" (SA, 447).

The capital mistake of this theory, according to Benjamin, is that it confuses the concept of universality (called for in this context) with

---

24. Benjamin, "Der Begriff," in *Gesammelte Schriften*, 36, n. 60.

that of abstraction (disastrous here) (*cf.* SA, 446). For Benjamin concepts, even those of the purest abstractions, are "incommensurate with the realm of the idea, or the Absolute" (SA, 447). Hence when Schlegel determines the absolute in terms of a being from a lower order—for example, when he determines the Idea of all works to be itself a work—he gives the absolute the status of a mere abstraction, of the *individual:* "Made present as an individuality, or a work, the Absolute is stripped of what makes it absolute, *i.e.,* cut off, not only from all sensible but all intellectual presentation as well" (SA, 447). By confusing the levels of generality and by implicating the highest universal in the exchanges with the forms of a lower ontological order, Schlegel has contaminated the realm of the absolute and mixed it with that of the actual. "As individuality or work, the absolute has been surrendered to the profane" (SA, 447). This profanation is perhaps the most profound legacy and burden bequeathed by romanticism. It is indispensable to realize that it is this momentous content and meaning that the terms *literary absolute* and *poetic absolute* are intended to convey. Finally, it is equally indispensable to remember that this profanation is a result of the romantic understanding of "intuition" as purely conceptual.

From the above discussion we have seen that romanticism has arrived at "the poetic absolute" by slowly modifying, or by departing from, certain critical stages of Kantian, speculative, and logical paths. Unlike Fichte, romanticism chose conceptual over sensory intuition for its model of reflection. Also in contrast to Fichte, it redefined infinity to denote infinite connectedness; it also allowed for the infinite extension of reflection. Finally, by mixing the levels of generality, it let abstract concepts into the domain reserved for universality.

Perhaps the most severe contemporary criticism of the romantic profanation came from Hegel. Hegel's first objection to the romantic model of the absolute was that it did not include the negative and the limited; the romantics allowed the finite to be dissolved in the absolute, rather than allowing it to be accounted for as a legitimate and separate moment in the movement of the absolute. The totality of this absolute deprived of the negative moment Hegel called "abstract totality": in Hegel's famous dictum, such an absolute is like the night in which all cows are black. Hegel's second objection concerns the systematic status of the absolute, or its character as a system (of knowledge). According to Hegel, the romantic absolute is not internally coherent, because the romantics failed to achieve (or chose to ignore) the objective totality of knowledge. As Gasché writes, "[The] exposition of the content of the Absolute cannot remain dependent on a subjective and contingent act, as in the case of Romanticism, since it corresponds to an objective need of the Absolute itself."[25] Hegel claimed that the romantics indulged in "mystic rapture" and neglected to develop their project along truly philosophical lines.

In this second point of his critique, Hegel was probably targeting the romantic attitude expressed by Schlegel in the Athenaeum Fragment 53: "It's equally fatal for the mind to have a system and to have none. It will simply have to decide to combine the two" (F, 167). To preserve polemical balance in this debate, it is necessary to remark that Hegel's criticism has itself come under vigorous attack. A critique most pertinent in our context is Philippe Lacoue-Labarthe's essay "The Unpresentable," which examines the references made by Hegel in *The Philosophy of Fine Art* to Friedrich Schlegel's novel *Lucinde*.[26] Among other things, the essay compares the image of femininity in Schlegel's novel with Hegel's account of the nude human figure in Greek sculpture as the progression of the self-manifestation of the Spirit in symbolic, classical, and romantic art. Lacoue-Labarthe argues that Hegel perceived that *Lucinde*, like his own philosophical system, marked the end of philosophy. However, Lacoue-Labarthe proposes that, while both philosophers speak of dissolution (*Auflösung*), careful analysis of Hegel's references to *Lucinde* would seem to indicate that Hegel is unable to control and restrict, with the conceptual apparatus developed in his monumental aesthetics, the double meaning of *Auflösung*.

It is this vagueness that provokes Hegel to allege the immorality of *Lucinde*; Schlegel's conception of femininity disrupts Hegel's dialectical conception of the self-manifestation of the Absolute Spirit in the dialectic of nudity and the concealment of nudity. *Lucinde* is the epitome of romanticism's moral scandal in light of Idea 128: "Mysteries are female; they like to veil themselves but still want to be seen and discovered" (F, 253). *Lucinde* derails Hegel's system from the position of a certain lateral exteriority, one which resists the "work of the negative" that would eventually lead to its recuperation and subjugation

25. Rodolphe Gasché, *The Tain of the Mirror: Derrida and the Philosophy of Reflection* (Cambridge, Mass., 1986), 59. For a useful contextualization of the standoff between Hegel and Friedrich Schlegel, see Ernst Behler's article "Friedrich Schlegel und Hegel," *Hegel-Studien*, I (1963), 203–50.

26. Philippe Lacoue-Labarthe, "The Unpresentable," trans. Claudette Sartiliot in *The Subject of Philosophy*, ed. Thomas Trezise (Minneapolis, 1993), 116–57.

through sublation (*Aufhebung*). In other words, Schlegel's conception of *philosophical thought as feminine* puts into question Hegel's system and, by implication, philosophy as such: Schlegel's novel is "*dissolution* itself."²⁷ Lacoue-Labarthe defends Schlegel's hesitation, in Athenaeum Fragment 53, over the status and role of the system, by claiming that the undecidability, or the optionality, of the romantic "system," far from being a contingent choice of a capricious subjectivity, is a valid option external to and more powerful than Hegel's system. This is to say that Hegel cannot determine whether speculative dissolution, the crowning concept of his dialectical system, encompasses and includes the romantic dissolution, or whether, on the contrary, the opposite is the case, or *even whether romantic dissolution can at all constitute a dialectical opposite to his system.*²⁸

At any rate, it is quite clear that it would be a mistake to underestimate the cumulative result of the romantic intervention in the speculative enterprise. As Jean-Luc Nancy argues in "*Menstruum universale* (Literary Dissolution)," the theme of dissolution, in its version as the romantic *Witz* or as Novalis' *menstruum universale* (related to Fichte's term for reciprocal determination, *Wechselbestimmung*), attacks the Western model of thought in which identity, while mediated by non-identity, is always recuperated in sameness. In the dissolution proposed by its theory of the novel, romanticism introduces an alternative model for thinking identity: the novel is "thought itself," anterior to the law of identity, anterior to the separation into self and non-self

---

27. Ibid., 186, n. 15.
28. For Weber ("Criticism Underway") this ambiguity is the direct consequence and primary manifestation of romantic irony, or "subjectivity." Romantic irony "parodies and ultimately betrays the dialectical progression of aesthetics rather than enacting it" (303). Weber continues: "It is as though the romantics' lack of seriousness, a point on which Hegel places such emphasis, tended to contaminate his own treatment of them, preventing him from taking them as seriously as their position would seem to require. As a result, what is left open is precisely the question of this position: Is it that of a *precursor* or of a *usurper*? Or could it be both?" (304). When Schlegel says, in "On Incomprehensibility," that he "made [his] *Lucinde* reveal the nature of love in an eternal hieroglyph (*ewigen Hieroglyphe*)" (F, 261), he is not indulging in an obscure language game; as "eternal hieroglyph," *Lucinde* dissolves (Hegel's) aesthetics because it discloses the "nature of love" to be the unity of intention and instinct, of system and chaos, as explained by Schlegel in Athenaeum Fragment 50: "In its origins true love should be at once completely premeditated and completely fortuitous, and seem simultaneously a result of necessity and free will. But in its character it should be both lawful and virtuous, and seem both a mystery and a wonder" (F, 167). This original synthesis eludes Hegel.

(the model without which Fichte's system would be inconceivable). Schlegel's *Lucinde* exhibits the power of the romantic novel to dissolve philosophy and, as Nancy writes, to signify thought itself.[29]

The romantic novel, in other words, signifies the possibility of total dissolution and, what is more, the possibility that this *Auflösung*, rather than being simply an undeveloped moment in the movement of the Concept, as Hegel has it, encompasses and dissolves dialectical dissolution in itself. But how can one gain access to this possibility if, by definition, it encompasses the conceptual mode of understanding? How can one *understand* dissolution if, as Lacoue-Labarthe writes, the novel is a "nongenre (or a unique 'genre'), that is, *literature* itself . . . or even *transcendental poetry*?" How can one *grasp* the theory of the novel if it signifies precisely the mixing of everything conceptual (of genres of thought), a transcendental mélange, an absolute *sui generis* (or a *sui generis* absolute)? How can one *think* the theory of the novel if, as satire did for Rome, the novel has *satura*ted modernity, if it has thought all the possibilities of thinking—if, as Kant's "I think," it is *thought thinking itself*?[30]

It is this danger that Benjamin anticipated—in the romantic presentation of the poetic absolute as the individual—as the danger of dissolution and profanation. And as Gasché shows in his discussion of Benjamin's essay on romanticism, Benjamin detected the systematic nature of this profanation in the romantics' treatment of prose. The romantics adopted the term *prose* to designate the dissolution that was effected by the romantic theory of the novel: prose names the individuality of the poetic absolute. The romantic novel can manifest the continuity of forms of the poetic absolute—and it can give individuality to this absolute—because it has discovered the absolutely dissolving power of prose (*cf.* SA, 449) Prose signified, for the romantics, the potential for indefinite encompassment that defies all conceptual thought and all systematic construction of the absolute. The romantics found this signification in the following manner. In the first, ordinary sense, prose refers to speech without poetic meter, speech close to ordinary speech, *ungebundene Rede*. However, as Gasché comments, "in addition to its proper meaning, prose has a fig-

---

29. Jean-Luc Nancy, "*Menstruum Universale* (Literary Dissolution)," *SubStance,* XXI (1978), 30.

30. Lacoue-Labarthe, "The Unpresentable," in *The Subject of Philosophy,* 185, n. 15; 126.

ural, improper meaning, namely prosaic, plain, ordinary, sober. Furthermore, this improper meaning cannot properly be distinguished from the proper. But it is this very lack of differentiation, this ambiguity of meaning, that predestines prose to become the comprehensible manifestation of the Absolute" (SA, 449–50).

It is through this constitutive ambiguity of prose that romantic dissolution can both solicit and undo (dissolve) conceptuality. Instead of denoting an *ens altissimum*, the romantic absolute signifies, in prosaic dissolution, the obliteration of the distinction between the proper and the improper, subject and object, and so on. The poetic absolute receives individuality from *oratio soluta*. This is the significance of Schlegel's Athenaeum Fragment 395: "In true prose everything has to be underlined" (F, 227). It is through this ambiguity of prose, through the *sober* absolute, that romanticism has stamped the present age as the age of profanation (cf. SA, 450).[31]

The progression in Schlegel's aesthetic history through the ages of literary dissolution now emerges in full clarity, as does the power of dissolution that the romantic *theory* of the novel brings to bear on history as a whole. Greece dissolved in the epos (DP, 101); Rome dissolved in satire (F, 180); at the last stage, modernity dissolves in the romantic (theory of the) novel. It is in this sense of dissolution as *Auflösung* that "the novel colors all of modern poetry" and that "all poetry is or should be romantic" (Athenaeum Fragment 116—F, 176). The movement from the subjective/objective unity of the epos, through the Roman saturation, to romantic dissolution in prose warrants the following enhancement of Schlegel's thought in Athenaeum Fragment 116: "All poetry has always been implicitly romantic." Beginning with the Kantian "I think," through Fichte's self-positing "I," and ending with the poetic absolute, romanticism has transformed the thematics of the self, ultimately dissolving it in the interminable self-manifestation called *literature*. It is time now to examine other aspects of the romantic profanation.

Romanticism chose to call "literature" the infinite, dissolved unity of the subject with itself. Because romanticism associated the term *literature* with the central problem of the unity of the subject, the term

---

31. Weber ("Criticism Underway," 303–304) helpfully contextualizes Hegel's perplexity over the romantic concept of prose and his own idea of proper, "philosophical prose" developed in *The Philosophy of Fine Art*.

has a highly specific function in the overall project of the romantic completion of antiquity—both in the philosophical sense, as the completion of the Kantian system, and in the historical sense, as the aesthetic completion of antiquity. In both aspects, the completion took place with respect to the presentation of the subject. The inaugural gesture of romanticism, the founding of literature, must again be presented in its proper context.

First, in an obvious if not banal sense, literature had been written before romanticism. Second, one may be quick to grant this originality in the limited sense, to wit, that romanticism invented yet another—avant-gardiste—meaning of the term *literature* and that this new meaning entered the semantic field as a species of the familiar genus. Resisting such hasty conceptualizations is especially difficult when, with Maurice Blanchot's analysis of romanticism in "The Athenaeum," one acknowledges the ambiguities, contradictions, obfuscations, and deliberate provocations that the romantics either ignored or themselves propagated.[32] In sum, this new sense of *literature* cannot but appear superadded to the stock of existing definitions, if one ignores the fact—and this neglect is most frequent—that *literature* was romanticism's name for that which was presented in the course of the deduction of the subject-work. Romanticism's *terminus technicus, literature* designates writing as infinite scripting (of) scripting itself.

These typical misconstruals lead us back to the question of romanticism, the question of what is named, in the dissolution of the subject in the work, as literature? It may be most useful at this point to analyze the single cause that is responsible for the historical occlusion of the romantic concept of literature, a cause centrally important because it proceeds directly from the inquiry that produced it. Lacoue-Labarthe and Nancy call this condition "equivocity" (*LA*, 121–27).

To do away with division—to rectify the absence of the subject from the Kantian system and to effect the unity of antiquity and modernity—romanticism has offered Schlegel's formula of the romantic novel. However, the speculative formula of the subject's self-

---

32. Maurice Blanchot, "The Athenaeum," in *IC*, 351–59. An example of this strategy can be seen in Schlegel's "On Incomprehensibility." Published in the *Athenaeum* at the end of the Jena phase of romanticism, the essay was intended as both an explanation of the romantic rationale and a parting shot for Schlegel's uncomprehending public. The essay played with the journal's readership, satisfying both the demand for the wit of parlor conversation and the concerns about the transcendental requirements for the unity of consciousness.

presentation constitutes a mechanism of identity that produces a unity that now begins to escape its determination in the very system in which it was produced. The language of an excess, of "absence" (Blanchot), "exergue" (Lacoue-Labarthe), "intussusception" (Kant), "*menstruum universale*" (Novalis), suggests, not a quantitative or substantive deformity, deviation, failure, or ambiguity, but the result of a unity in which presentation is coextensive with itself, beyond the distinction into subject and object, content and form, etc. Schlegel's theory of the novel gives rise to excessive presentation, to what Lacoue-Labarthe has called "the unpresentable." This dissolution of the subject in the subject-work lies at the heart of romantic equivocity.

The originary identity of the "dissolved" subject, of the subject dissolved in itself, which is the result of the romantic project to achieve the presentation adequate to the subject as such, is characterized by a certain excess or surplus. The surplus that results from the subject's self-presentation arises from the nature of this self-presentation as originary *self-production*. This excessive moment can be illustrated in the context of romanticism's preoccupation with Kant. In the solution that romanticism called the "fragment," romanticism brought about the presentation of the Idea as a necessarily finite presentation, as this particular idea, in a subjectivity (identity) proper only to this idea. The fragmentary nature of this presentation accounts for the originary coincidence of the idea with itself in such a way that the presentation is nothing but the self (of this idea). Yet, paradoxically, instead of a transparent identity and perfect overlapping, the fragmentary solution yields a strange surplus. The surplus appears, writes Gasché, as "an incline, a declivity, of sorts, between two sorts of wholes, or totalities—the idea of totality and its self-presentation."[33] The difference between the idea of totality and the totality itself is not a "differential" difference but a function of identity completely unified with itself. As the figure of totality in which the totality accomplishes itself as this totality, the romantic fragment resists hermeneutic accounts of totality, for it is both insufficient and excessive in relation to any potential transparency.

This curious consequence of the romantic "mixing of genres"—in the "fragment," in "religion," in "criticism"—the question, in other words, of "what is the nature ... of fusion or union" (*LA*, 91), is the

---

33. Rodolphe Gasché, "Foreword: Ideality in Fragmentation," in *Friedrich Schlegel's "Philosophical Fragments,"* trans. Peter Firchow (Minneapolis, 1991), xxxi.

paramount question of the romantic theory of the novel.[34] It not only defined romanticism's own historical moment, but it also persisted into the future, not as a potential to be developed by posterity, but as the imperative of completion that romanticism defined for the first time with regard to antiquity. This heritage is the excess of what is self-identical, that which remains outside of the work of the subject: the *exergue* (*LA*, 48).

As we have seen, the profanity introduced by the romantic theory of the novel consisted in the claim that the novel is a *unique* genre, a nongenre, or a transcendental genre. In it, all genres, including the genre of thought itself, achieve dissolution. This is why it is frequently stated that romanticism "mixed" genres and that the romantic novel is not a specific genre known to classical poetics but a *process* of unifying genres. This statement, however, requires two qualifications. First, the mixing in question is performed, not on genres insofar as they denote literary genres (Mikhail Bakhtin's "hybrid" pursues this mixing), but on genres (lyric, tragic, epic) as they imply, in their separate individuality, the division, the split within human sensibility and, ultimately, within history. The synthesis of genres will produce the transcendental synthesis of the subject.[35]

But we need to add a second, related qualification. To bring out the difference between the mixing of empirical genres and the profanation that results from a transcendental conception of genre, it may be useful to discuss briefly romanticism's fascination with Socrates. The romantic turn to Socrates is based on a philosophical understanding of irony. As Søren Kierkegaard showed a few decades after the high point of romanticism at Jena, Socrates' *daimon*, philosophy's first figure of subjectivity, shifts the Greek sense of authority from an external source, the oracle at Delphi, to the interior of the individual, where it becomes an indeterminate, subjective agency that dictates moral action only by negative urgings.[36] As is well

---

34. Timothy Bahti ("Fate in the Past: Peter Szondi's Reading of German Romantic Genre Theory," *Boundary 2*, XI [1983], 111–25) persuasively argues that the romantic theorems—translation, irony, criticism—operate in romantic literature, the conception of which is indebted to speculative philosophy of history.

35. Schlegel sharply distinguishes his conception of transcendental genre from the empirical taxonomies most authoritatively represented at that time by Goethe's *Dichtarten*. In Fragment 115 of his *Literary Notebooks*, Schlegel completes his critique of Goethe's empiricism with the following additional comment: "Goethe has filed down (smoothed out, rendered tame [*abgeschliffen*]) the (sharp) edges of all genres" (29).

36. Søren Kierkegaard, *The Concept of Irony: With Constant Reference to Socrates*, trans. Lee M. Capel (Bloomington, 1965). The book was submitted as a thesis in 1841.

known from the *Apology*, Socrates' earnest admission that he cannot describe or otherwise demonstrate this mysterious agency made the court even more suspicious of his moral integrity. Kierkegaard explains Socrates' bewilderment by suggesting that the irony of Socratic subjectivity cannot be determined in positive terms because this irony is "absolute infinite negativity": "It is negativity because it negates; it is infinite because it negates not this or that phenomenon; and it is absolute because it negates by virtue of a higher which is not. Irony establishes nothing, for that which is to be established lies behind it."[37] Socrates is the figure of this subject, for in him, or through him, the subject speaks as itself, "beyond" the historical particularity of the Athenian philosopher, "beyond" the positive formulas of the law, and "beyond" the intentionality of language. The word "beyond" appears in quotation marks because, defined romantically, Socratic irony is not external to the speaker but rather remains hermetically internal to him. It remarks the presence of that which speaks in what is spoken: as Hölderlin would say, what is speaking is the subject of speech, or *speech itself*. What makes this agency "subjective" is not, as in Hegel's pejorative reference to romanticism, arbitrary and purposeless caprice but the presence of subjectivity *as such* in every (moral) act.

It is in this sense that we must understand Schlegel's Critical Fragment 26: "Novels are the Socratic dialogues of our time" (*F*, 145). For Schlegel (Critical Fragment 108), Socratic irony is "the only involuntary and yet completely deliberate dissimulation. It is equally impossible to feign it or to divulge it.... It originates in the union of *savoir vivre* and scientific spirit, in the conjunction of a perfectly instinctive and a perfectly conscious philosophy. It contains and arouses a feeling of indissoluble antagonism between the absolute and the relative, between the impossibility and the necessity of complete communication. It is the freest of all licenses, for by its means one transcends oneself; and yet it is also the most lawful, for it is absolutely necessary" (*F*, 155–56). In other words, Schlegel's formula about the genre of the novel—"every theory of the novel must itself be a novel"—ought to be read as an *ironic* formula, insofar as Socratic irony reveals the subject as such. (One thinks of Socrates' own version of this generative reflection: "I know that I do not know.") Socratic irony typifies the reflective nature of the romantic theory of the novel and, by extension, the ironic nature of the romantic genre; it presents the subject in the work

---

37. *Ibid.*, 278.

(the genre) in such a way that the subject (the genre) is the only work of the work. Schlegel's circular formula, which postulates the presence of the subject in the object produced by the subject (by stipulating that the agency that articulates the novel must itself be a novel) characterizes the romantic genre as marked by a "declivity of sorts." As such declivity, romantic irony specifies the concrete manner in which romantic genre comes to the fore. In the reflective self-presencing in which the subject speaks itself, Socratic dialogues afforded the romantics a vehicle for unifying poetry and philosophy. Socrates accomplishes the unity of thought and form, for when the subject itself speaks, the form and truth of this speech are one—their difference is dissolved. Romanticism saw the Socratic synthesis of mimesis and diegesis as paradigmatically transcendental, as the dissolution of the subject in its own speech: Plato's *Dialogues* are "the work and reflection of the work . . . 'a genre' beyond all genres and containing a theory of this 'beyond' within itself" (*LA*, 86).

Here one might inquire why the romantics hoped that Socratic dialogues would accomplish the presentation of the subject and achieve the transcendental unity of diegesis and mimesis if, as we have seen, they had already found that the epos could do just as well? Is not the romantic reference to Socratic dialogues superfluous? One might speculate that, while the epos bequeaths to the romantics the *problem* for completion as the complex unity of diegesis and mimesis, the subjective and the objective, the ironic reflection of Socratic dialogues furnishes the romantics with the *method* of this completion. In other words, the model of Socratic irony makes it possible for Schlegel to define the romantic theory of the novel explicitly as the work of the *subject*. Schlegel offers insight on this point in Athenaeum Fragment 51, where he discusses the relation of irony to the complex unity of intention and instinct:

> Naïve is what is or seems to be natural, individual, or classical to the point of irony, or else to the point of continuously fluctuating between self-creation and self-destruction. . . . The beautiful, poetical, ideal naïve must combine intention and instinct. The essence of intention in this sense is freedom, though intention isn't consciousness by a long shot. . . . Intention doesn't exactly require any deep calculation or plan. Even Homeric naïveté isn't simply instinctive; there is at least as much intention in it as there is in the grace of lovely children or innocent girls. And even if Homer himself had no intentions, his poetry and the real author of that poetry, Nature, certainly did. (*F*, 167)

Besides implicitly arguing for a structural affinity between the Homeric epos and Socratic irony, the fragment also states that the central concern of the romantic synthesis, *the unity of instinct and intention*, or the unity of the subject, is inseparable from the work of irony.

Moreover, the framing of the synthesis of the subject in terms of the unity of instinct and intention, as it sheds light on the central concerns of the romantic theory of the novel, gives the reader a glimpse of Schlegel's intellectual brilliance, later confirmed by Nietzsche's philologico-philosophical thesis. The romantic theory of the novel sought to capture the unity of instinct and intention expressed by Homer. Seen from this point of view, Schlegel's Athenaeum Fragment 51 anticipates with astonishing accuracy Nietzsche's solution to the "Homeric question." As a postromantic formulation of this problem, Nietzsche's essay "Homer and Classical Philology" discusses the history of the concept of the author as the history of the concept of personality. This "personality" (to be distinguished from the concrete, empirical person) is the unity of the ideal and the real conceptions of the author of the *Iliad* and the *Odyssey*. Rejecting the crude "romantic" view (originated by Vico) of Homeric poetry as the embodiment of "folk-spirit," Nietzsche expressed a belief "in the one great poet of the *Iliad* and the *Odyssey—yet not in Homer as this poet.*" As David R. Lachterman notes, this formulation "separates the question of the unity of authorship from the question of the author's identity." The name "Homer" stands for the poetic act which "mak[es] events."[38] As Lacoue-Labarthe and Nancy comment: "Here, well in advance of the formation of any concept of the work . . . and of any philosophical subjectivism, the work operates itself; and perhaps even *it* operates itself, for although the romantics did not invent the Nietzschean usage of *it*, 'what' else could be in question when the 'true author' of the greatest work, the Homeric epic, is 'nature' (*A* 51), but the 'nature' of a thought that . . . is preoccupied with undoing all its links with any 'naturality'?" (*LA*, 121—"*A* 51," in original, refers to Athenaeum Fragment 51).

Schlegel's Athenaeum Fragment 51 deserves one more comment in this context. The romantics brought the novelistic project to a culmination when they sought to name the mystery of the unity of the subjective and the objective (which was represented by the Homeric epos)

38. David R. Lachterman, "*Die Ewige Wiederkehr des Griechen:* Nietzsche and the Homeric Question," manuscript of a lecture delivered at the comparative literature department of SUNY-Buffalo, February, 1991, 22, 24. Nietzsche's text translated by Lachterman.

in terms of the "Book." Schlegel develops the romantic concept of the Book in Idea 95:

> The new, eternal gospel that Lessing prophesied will appear as a bible: but not as a single book in the usual sense. Even what we now call the Bible is actually a system of books. And that is, I might add, no mere arbitrary turn of phrase! Or is there some other word to differentiate the idea of an infinite book from an ordinary one, than Bible, the book per se, the absolute book? And surely there is an eternally essential and even practical difference if a book is merely a means to an end, or an independent book, an individual, a personified idea. It cannot be this without divine inspiration, and here the esoteric concept is itself in agreement with the exoteric one; and, moreover, no idea is isolated, but is what it is only in combination with all other ideas. An example will explain this. All the classical poems of the ancients are coherent, inseparable; they form an organic whole, they constitute, properly viewed, only a single poem, the only one in which poetry itself appears in perfection. In a similar way, in a perfect literature all books should be only a single book, and in such an eternally developing book, the gospel of humanity and culture will be revealed. (F, 249–50)

The relationship between the romantic novel and the project of the *biblos* as "an independent book, an individual, a personified idea," still remains to be explored.[39] Further remarks on this subject can be found in the last section of the introduction.

To summarize: the novel, as the synthesis of ancient and modern poetics, cannot be understood as a unification of the classical genres

---

39. As Michel Beaujour shows ("Genus Universum," *Glyph*, VII [1980], 15–31), the concept of "the Book" is not romanticism's original discovery. It still remains to be determined, however, whether the Renaissance genealogy of the romantic book described by Beaujour imposes the continuity of influence and of similar philosophical positions and goals, or whether the romantic book, like the romantic "literature," marks the birth of a genuinely new entity. Above all, scholarship should remain vigilant to avoid identifying the romantic "Book" with empirical texts and with text in a structuralist sense, as is done in Kevin Newmark's essay "*L'absolu littéraire:* Friedrich Schlegel and the Myth of Irony" (*MLN*, CVII [1992]; see especially 930, n. 22). In other words, it still remains to be determined whether the romantic book could coincide with any philosophically identifiable theme whatsoever—history, absolute, totality, etc. Because the novel (*der Roman*) is, according to Schlegel, a romantic book, it would appear that romantic potentiation and the historical interests of modernity are necessarily connected with totality (*die Ganze*). The romantic book would, then, appear to stand for the unity of history, philosophy, and literature, as a figure elevated far above the most sublime interests of even the most transcendental of inquiries.

in a preexisting generic category, in *another* genre better suited for modernity or for the future. The unity accomplished in the novel is, romantically, the original identity of genre (of subject) as *this* genre (as subject). Transcendental poetry heals the divided human spirit; it is "a spiritual viewing of the subject with calm and serene feeling, as it is proper to view in solemn joy the meaningful play of divine images." Yet the problem remains that romanticism's transcendental poetry produces excessive unity of genre with itself, and we must come to terms with the profanity of romanticism's transcendental poetics.

As we have said, the romantic poem, the *Mischgedicht*, is not identified by the variety of literary forms that appear in it but by the romantic, that is, novelistic, ability of its form to be equally present in all its "parts"—except, of course, that the hermeneutic discourse of parts and whole does not apply here. Indeed, the unity of genres mixed romantically cannot be determined in terms of a *form* encompassing this unity, any more than the *content* thus unified can be said to be in any sense different from that which does the unification. The subject-work conforms neither to the terms of unity adequate for the hermeneutic model of understanding (parts and whole) nor to those adequate for a formalist model (formal pattern). Indeed, the new "work" is a work exclusively in relation to the subject that seeks its own proper presentation. Completely saturated by the subject as its "content"—as Schlegel writes in Idea 95, "the esoteric concept is itself in agreement with the exoteric one" (*F,* 250)—the work's "form" is no longer organic but, as Hölderlin has it, "aorgic" (*TM,* 244). Instead of a resolution in the form of substantive synthesis, the romantic mixture of genres calls for a formal *dissolution* of the work, the identity of the subject with itself (see Athenaeum Fragment 111). Romanticism saw in the novel the origin of the modern age and expected this age to dissolve in it: "Just as our literature began with the novel, so the Greek began with the epic and dissolved in it" (*DP,* 101).

Examples of the profane romantic poetics can be multiplied. Echoing Schlegel's distinction, in Idea 95, between a book that is "a means to an end" and an "independent book," Maurice Blanchot speaks of the difference between transitive and intransitive speech: "To speak poetically is to make possible a non-transitive speech whose task is not to say things (not to disappear in what it signifies) but to say (itself) in letting (itself) say, yet without taking itself as the new object of this language without object" (*IC,* 357). This is the "night of speech," the condition in which language speaks itself as its subject alone, in which, as Blanchot writes, "true speech is the subject." In yet another phrase, Blanchot applies the intransitive mechanism to consciousness: "What exceeds consciousness is its inability to lose consciousness."[40] On the one hand, we live and act with the familiar sense of consciousness as clear light and openness to impressions and to knowledge. However, this clarity becomes clouded by the following realization: while consciousness interacts with the world of objects, it is unable to process as its content the fact that it, as consciousness, cannot lose consciousness. Thus, what seemed to be a ground of knowledge and of the subject's self-presence in its conscious being reveals a darkness at the very center of its clarity: what is both darker and brighter than consciousness is its being a consciousness. *As* consciousness, it itself is beyond the capacities of reflection and penetration that characterize its very nature of operation. In its original identity with itself, consciousness is, in strict adherence to romantic equivocity, more *and/or* less than itself.

When the subject is present in the work as work (when all that speaks is speech itself), the ground is laid for literature in the romantic sense of the word, that is, for the "independent Book," for nontransitive utterance, the self-productive manifesto as such. It is not an accident, and Blanchot articulates this collusion, that Schlegel's Athenaeum Fragment 216 identifies the French Revolution as one of the three "greatest tendencies" of the age, the other two being Goethe's *Wilhelm Meister* and Fichte's philosophy. As Henrich comments, the grand "pathos" of freedom uncovered by Fichte's formula that "the Self posits itself" lies not only in the unconditional and autonomous nature of the self and not only in the fact that freedom is a-causal and a-teleological. The pathos of this freedom lies primarily in the fact that the self manifests the "grounding One" in the circular fashion characteristic of the speculative absolute: "This One manifests itself finally in the Self in the form of what manifests itself."[41] In a similar fashion, what makes a romantic *literary* manifestation is the manifestation pure and simple, self-manifestation without object. In romanticism, writes Blanchot, "literature suddenly becomes conscious of itself, manifests itself, and, in this manifestation, has no other task or trait than to declare itself." Literature "is the site wherein poetry will no longer be content to produce beautiful,

---

40. Maurice Blanchot, "Literature and the Right to Death," in *G*, 45–46.
41. Henrich, "Fichte's Original Insight," 24, 42.

determinate works, but rather will produce itself in a movement without term and without determination" (*IC*, 354).⁴²

The dissolution of the division between the objective and the subjective (the real and the ideal) that can be heard in the "ab-solute" determines literature as the highest *poietic* act, as the making of making without an object. In Athenaeum Fragment 238 Schlegel calls this self-production without object "transcendental poetry": "There is a kind of poetry whose essence lies in the relation between ideal and real, and which therefore, by analogy to philosophical jargon, should be called transcendental poetry. . . . But just as we wouldn't think much of an uncritical transcendental philosophy that doesn't represent the producer along with the product and contain at the same time within the system of transcendental thoughts a description of transcendental thinking: so too . . . in all its descriptions, this poetry should describe itself, and always be simultaneously poetry and the poetry of poetry" (*F*, 195). Blanchot puts the same thought in the following terms: "Romanticism has the keenest knowledge of the narrow margin in which it can affirm itself: neither in the world nor outside the world; master of everything, but on condition that the whole contain nothing; pure consciousness without content, a pure speech that can say nothing" (*IC*, 356). And Schlegel again confirms that "Romantic poetry is a progressive, universal poetry. . . . It can . . . hover at the midpoint between the portrayed and the portrayer, free of all real and ideal self-interest, on the wings of poetic reflection, and can raise that reflection again and again to a higher power, can multiply it in an endless succession of mirrors. . . . The romantic kind of poetry is the only one that is more than a kind, that is, as it were, poetry itself: for in a certain sense all poetry is or should be romantic" (*F*, 175–76). Schlegel's statement that "every theory of the novel must itself be a novel" refers to this purity of transcendental self-production sustained

---

42. Novalis acknowledges this secret speech of language (of the subject) uttering itself in the following reflection from the "Monologue" (*German Aesthetic and Literary Criticism*, ed. Wheeler): "And though I believe that with these words I have delineated the nature and office of poetry as clearly as I can, all the same I know that no one can understand it, and what I have said is quite foolish because I wanted to say it, and that is no way for poetry to come about. But what if I were compelled to speak? what if this urge to speak were the mark of the inspiration of language, the working of language within me? and my will only wanted to do what I had to do? Could this in the end, without my knowing or believing, be poetry? Could it make a mystery comprehensible to language? If so, would I be a writer by vocation, for after all, a writer is only someone inspired by language?" (93).

between the subjective and the objective on "the wings of reflection," sustained in the infinity of self-grasping without term. As a production without an object—not the presentation of the ideal or of the real, but the self-presentation of the subject—"the romantic kind of poetry is the only one that is more than a kind, that is, as it were, poetry itself."

The excess, the profanation of transcendental poetics is contained in the phrase "more than a kind," which defines the unity of Genre with Itself as a hyperbolic relation of genre to itself (of totality to the idea of this totality). The hyperbolic relation is *not* metaphysical: while it points to a beyond, it does so not in the modality of transfer but in that of the dissolved subject. While romanticism's "infinite progressive poetry" has healed the division, it has also left an inescapable legacy: the "poetry of poetry"; this pure making of making has yielded a surplus, the excessive identity of the subject with itself. In effecting the self-sameness of the subject, the work of *poiesis* yields the work "outside-the-work (*hors d'oeuvre*)" (*LA,* 48)—the *exergue.*

Much of contemporary literary theory thinks in terms of "the other" because the romantic definition of "literature" as the transcendental process of the subject's self-production has disclosed the exergue in its blinding light as the infinite identity of the subject with itself. What characterizes this otherness is, to use romantic terms, allegorical, ironic, symbolic. Maurice Blanchot has articulated the nature of this referral to the other and defined the heritage of romanticism's "literature" as the pursuit of the other in the essay "Wittgenstein's Problem": "1) what is inexpressible is inexpressible in relation to a certain system of expression; 2) although there may be reason to regard the ensemble of things and of values as a whole ... the virtual ensemble of the different possibilities of speech cannot constitute a totality; 3) the Other of any speech is never anything but the Other of a given speech or the *infinite movement* through which a mode of expression ... contests itself, exalts itself, challenges or obliterates itself in some other mode" (*IC,* 337–38). It is no accident that Blanchot's "matrix of the other" is built with language as its central component. The reference to the founding role of language in the construction of the Other is sufficient proof that Blanchot is thinking from within the paradigm of the romantic absolute, from the saying that accomplishes itself in dissolution. To underscore the romantic roots of Blanchot's thought it is enough to quote again from Novalis' "Monologue": "It is amazing, the absurd error people make of imagining they are speaking for the sake of things; no one knows the essential thing about language, that it is concerned only with itself. That is why it is such a marvellous and fruitful mystery—for if someone merely speaks for the sake of speaking, he utters the most splendid, original truths. But if he wants to talk about something definite, the whims of language make him say the most ridiculous false stuff."[43] The historical significance of this thought and the influence it exerted on philosophy can be gauged from Martin Heidegger's comments on Novalis' notion of language. Referring to Novalis' "Monologue," Heidegger writes: "That title points to the mystery of language: language speaks solely with itself alone. One sentence in Novalis' text runs: 'The peculiar property of language, namely that language is concerned exclusively with itself—precisely that is known to no one.'"[44] Heidegger's reference to Novalis can be taken to indicate two moments. First, by referring to the romantic conception of the absolute as the self-uttering subject, Heidegger confirms our thesis about a strong structural affinity and parity between the romantic conception of the absolute and the conceptions that came to dominate the philosophical tradition, beginning with speculative idealism, such as Fichte's self-positing and self-producing "I," through Hegel's self-grasping Concept, and up to Heidegger's "(event of self-)appropriation" (*Ereignis*).

Second, in a significant circular return, Heidegger's postphenomenological method yields an absolute that is very close to the initial romantic conception. For in Novalis, language (the subject) itself speaks itself, exhausting itself and accomplishing itself in this speech without object (a similar circularity controls Schlegel's formula about the theory of the novel). For Heidegger the nature of language consists in the simple act that is proper (*eigen*) to language, the act of language itself speaking: the essence of language is that language speaks (*Die Sprache spricht*). While the romantic and Heideggerian conceptions of language as a vehicle of the absolute present an absolute that disappears, one that in itself is no-thing and does not "occur," they differ in their respective description of the drift of the absolute relation

---

43. Ibid., 92–93.
44. Martin Heidegger, "The Way to Language," in *On the Way to Language*, trans. Peter D. Hertz (San Francisco, 1971), 111. Novalis' thought is echoed by Schlegel himself in "On Incomprehensibility," when he says that "words often understand themselves better than do those who use them . . . that there must be a connection of some secret brotherhood among philosophical words."

produced in the self-uttering subject. Novalis' term, *menstruum universale*, absorbs every form into its interior and dissolves it beyond conceptual marking; Heidegger's *Ereignis* "carries" and "founds" the minimal relation of self-coincidence, which, while in itself empty and nonconceptual, accounts for every other form's being what it properly is. It may also be observed that taken together these two models of the absolute differ from the strong, total positivity of the conceptual absolute expressed by Hegel's *Begriff*, which accounts for all the relations of inclusion and exclusion that can occur in and among forms. For Hegel there is *no outside* to the founding relation, while for Novalis and Heidegger *it is precisely the outside (the Other)* that is the founding relation.

The romantic theory of the novel has provoked many critical commentaries; this criticism can only be alluded to in these pages, partly in acknowledgment and partly as indispensable synopsis. A paradigmatic example of the other that emerges when language is brought to speak itself can be encountered in Maurice Blanchot's theory of the *récit* ("The Song of the Sirens," in *G*, 105–13). In a gesture similar to Schlegel's lament in Idea 11, Blanchot regrets the degradation of the novel (represented by the French term *roman*) and seeks to preserve the properly romantic dimension of the theory of the novel in the *récit*.

Blanchot introduces this distinction when he divides Homer's *Odyssey* into two sections, a division critically determined by the episode of Odysseus' encounter with the sirens. While the journey prior to this encounter develops according to the dynamics of the infinite striving, the dynamics of the "tale" (*récit*), after the encounter the narrative takes on the characteristics of a novel (*roman*). According to the distinction, the novel denotes the familiar sense of a recounting of past and present events, while the tale enacts a movement towards the place of the sirens, which promises speech as long as the speaker disappears in this place (*G*, 110). Only as attracted by its impossibility—or, to put it romantically, only as solicited by the open-ended, vague promise of dissolution—can the story sustain itself, recounting (or simply *counting*) this movement: "The tale is a movement towards a point, a point which is not only unknown, obscure, foreign, but such that apart from this movement it does not seem to have any sort of real prior existence, and yet it is so imperious that the tale derives its power of attraction only from this point, so that it cannot even 'begin' before reaching it" (*G*, 109).⁴⁵ Blanchot's self-generating *récit* resembles Fichte's and Schlegel's subject-less absolute.

In its attention to the *récit*'s infinite completion of itself, Blanchot's account lays the ground for a postromantic reconstitution of the original *theory* of the *roman*. If the Homeric epos represented for the romantics the synthesis of the subjective and the objective, then Blanchot's turn to Homer not only adequately recognizes this romantic perspective but also remarks the point in the *Odyssey*, the sirens episode (Book XII), after which the romantic novel, which seeks to accomplish the transcendental unity of the subject, degenerates into prose fiction, which narrates the adventures of the empirical self.

The contours of the romantic theory of the novel can also be recognized in Philippe Sollers' essay "The Novel and the Experience of Limits." Like Schlegel, Sollers recognizes the need for the speculative imperative in the construction of the novelistic absolute: "Writing ... must tell what it does even as it does it." Like Schlegel in Idea 11 and Blanchot above, Sollers works within the model of the true and the degenerate novel: "The novel must therefore burn and consume every trace of the novel, or else resign itself to being only a novel." Referring to Proust, Joyce, and Kafka, Sollers emphasizes the intransitive nature of their writing, a description that echoes the romantic theorem of "the poetry of poetry," the *romanticization* of every discursive mode into itself. Finally, Sollers, in strict fidelity to romantic reflection and prompted by the romantic motif of dissolution, suggests that the potentiation of the sign equally *redoubles* form and *erases* it in a writing "that through its nuclear organization and *play* presents itself as continual excess [*dépassement ouvert*]." The excess of this dissolution "compels us to remain unconscious" of language's "radical operations."⁴⁶

---

45. Manfred Frank ("The Infinite Text," *Glyph*, VII [1980]) uses the same motif of the Homeric voyage to determine the infinite nature of the romantic conception of text: "The aimlessly drifting ship begins its passage upon the tide of speech itself, and poetic speech makes conscious this process as such" (72). In a similar gesture Michel Foucault ("Language to Infinity," in *Language, Counter-Memory, Practice: Selected Essays and Interviews*, ed. Donald F. Bouchard, trans. Donald F. Bouchard and Sherry Simon [Ithaca, 1977]) postulates that, beginning with the simple, material activity of alphabetical transcription, language duplicates itself beyond recovery, that, in being spoken, language "pursues itself unto infinity" (45).

46. Philippe Sollers, "The Novel and the Experience of Limits," in *Writing and the Experience of Limits*, ed. David Hayman, trans. Philip Barnard and David Hayman (New York, 1983), 200–201.

Sollers' essay also offers an opportunity to examine the redefinition of the concept of genre provoked by the romantic profanation. As Sollers significantly adds, the excessive immediacy of intransitive writing prevents an unproblematically taxonomic approach to the question of genre: "It will be clear that on this level distinctions between 'literary genres' inevitably collapse."[47] The relation between intransitive speech and the collapse of genre distinctions defines the path taken by contemporary genre theory as it struggles to come to grips with the romantic dissolution of genres. Because it accomplishes the unity of the subject with itself, the romantic theory of the novel breaks with the taxonomic treatment of genre and subjects genres to a transcendental treatment: it studies the conditions of possibility of genre, the genre's excessive self-identity without which genre as such cannot be *gener*ated.

The modern debate over genres—a debate that is one of the legacies of romanticism—concerns the taxonomic and the transcendental positions, the former embraced by Tzvetan Todorov and Gérard Genette, and the latter by Maurice Blanchot and Jacques Derrida. Todorov and Genette insist that the traditional taxonomic field can, with slight adjustments, absorb and control the romantic profanation of generic boundaries advocated by Blanchot. Referring to Blanchot's "fundamental modes, the narrative and the novel" (the *récit* and the *roman*), Todorov writes that, whenever the *récit* violates the generic law, it itself "requires a law"; indeed, "the norm becomes visible—comes into existence—owing only to its transgression."[48] Todorov believes that each transgression itself becomes the law; hence the destruction of one genre presupposes the creation of another genre, reaffirming the validity of taxonomy as a conceptual system.

Genette's objection to the transcendental treatment of genres resembles the direction suggested by Todorov. Genette finds it impossible to resolve the antinomy between the suprahistorical nature of the concept of genre and the historical mutability of genres encountered in literary practice. He addresses this problem by drawing on Goethe's distinction between content-oriented "genres" (*Dichtarten*), which find their application in literature, and form-oriented "modes" (*Dichtweisen*), which are used in general language practice.[49]

47. Ibid., 204.
48. Tzvetan Todorov, "The Origin of Genres," in *Genres in Discourse*, trans. Catherine Porter (New York, 1990), 14.
49. Gérard Genette, "Genres, 'Types,' Modes," *Poétique*, VIII (1977), 389–421.

It is intriguing that, in order to defend taxonomic genre theory, Todorov and Genette choose as an example of a generically stable category Blanchot's *récit*, precisely that form that Blanchot uses to repeat in postmodernity the romantic dissolution of genres. Derrida foregrounds precisely this coincidence when he brings the romantic potential of Blanchot's *récit* to bear on the debate. In the modern debate over taxonomic and transcendental genre theories, which can be termed "the debate over Blanchot's *récit*," Derrida seeks to make evident that Todorov's and Genette's approaches are insufficient precisely with respect to the genre that they single out as a generically stable category. Stated briefly, Derrida claims that the *récit* cannot be assimilated to Genette's distinction between genres and modes.[50] According to Derrida the *récit* dissolves, not in the simple sense of erasing taxonomic lines, but in the sense of remarking a momentary shutdown, or excess, of the classificatory field, a moment irreducible to the logic of the norm and the exception, a certain excessive economy of presencing and/or absencing, which determines the field of genericity as a field in the first place: the *récit* is "the nonthematizable thematic content of something of a textual form that *assumes* a point of view with respect to the genre."[51]

For Derrida, the *récit* is inhabited by a moment of repetition: "One might even say by citation or recitation (*ré-cit*) . . . the law that protects the usage, in *stricto sensu*, of the words *citation* and *récit*, is threatened intimately and in advance by a counter-law that constitutes this very law, renders it possible, conditions it and thereby renders it impossible. . . . The law and counter-law serve each other, citations summoning each other to appear, and each re-cites the other in this proceeding (*procés*)." It is this excessive moment that Derrida identifies in Blanchot's *récit The Madness of the Day:* "This supplementary and distinctive trait, a mark of belonging or inclusion, does not properly pertain to any genre or class. The re-mark of belonging does not belong. It belongs without belonging"[52]

The infinite relation between *citation* and *récit* in Derrida and Blanchot surpasses the taxonomic interests of Genette and Todorov, emphatically showing that the question of genre is inseparable from the transcendental dimension of discourse: the "poetry of poetry" prevents

---

50. Jacques Derrida, "The Law of Genre," *Glyph*, VII (1980), 202–32.
51. *Ibid.*, 210.
52. *Ibid.*, 204–205, 212.

any "speech act" from resting within a simple, delimiting formula of address, meaning, or type. If, as Manfred Frank indicates, "genres are rule-systems which make recognizable an aggregate of utterances ... as realizations of certain forms of intentionality," then the identity of the utterance "as the vehicle of some conventionally preassigned meaning" will stagger and disappear "when saying itself becomes absolute."[53] "Absolute saying" is romantic *poiesis:* in the making of making there is no genre, or else there is excess of genre.

What remains to be explored, aside from, but certainly in terms of, this rich critical, theoretical, and polemical context, is the question of what the romantic novel would or could be for us, both as a theory and as literary practice sensitive to this theory. This question addresses both the consequences that the romantic theory of the novel might have for genre theory and the implications it might have for the question of the subject.

At this preliminary stage it seems necessary to define initial boundaries in which such an inquiry into the modern legacy of the romantic novel could be conducted. To use a concrete illustration of the complexity of this task, we may quote Hans Eichner's statement on Gustave Flaubert: "While Schlegel correctly forecast the predominance which the novel acquired in nineteenth-century literature, he would have been bitterly disappointed by the way it developed; he would have regarded Flaubert as the very embodiment of what he liked to call the 'evil principle' in literature" (*FS*, 67). On the other hand, Eichner maintains, "Schlegel would have hailed such novels as Joyce's *Ulysses* or Thomas Mann's *Magic Mountain* as the beginnings—merely the beginnings—of a return to the great tradition" (*FS*, 67). The present study has been conceived as a work of such forecasting, less in the spirit of polemics than in that of preparatory interrogation.

Seen in the perspective of the question of what the romantic novel would look like in the time after romanticism, scholarship remains either reticent or vague. Among fruitful studies one must mention Manfred Frank's "The Infinite Text," which seeks to determine the essential parameters of romantic textuality (and that also means of the romantic novel) as potentiation, expression of the infinite, and the suspension of the referential aspect of language (Blanchot's nontransitive speech): "Every sign of a symbolic composition which carries

---

53. Frank, "The Infinite Text," 78.

within it an indication of the act of its making (its gener-ation) bears an index of its textuality."[54] In its most pertinent aspect, Frank's essay ignores the narrowly generic considerations, for the qualities of romantic textuality are exhibited, in his analysis, in a poem by Tieck, in Wagner's music, and in the poetry of Gerard Manley Hopkins. Unfortunately, important and influential studies on the projective powers of romanticism (such as Beda Allemann's *Ironie und Dichtung* or Karl Polheim's "Spätzeiten als Frühzeiten"[55]) have tended to focus on other aspects of romantic thought, leaving the questions of the theory of the romantic novel and of the production of the subject in novelistic practice largely unexplored. The goal of the present study is to begin to fill this lacuna.[56]

Perhaps the most important problem addressed by this inquiry is the question whether postromantic novelistic practice has reflected

---

54. *Ibid.*, 73.

55. Beda Allemann, *Ironie und Dichtung: F. Schlegel, Novalis, Solger, Kierkegaard, Nietzsche, Thomas Mann, Musil* (Pfullingen, 1956). Karl Polheim, "Spätzeiten als Frühzeiten," *Wirkendes Wort*, XI (1961), 74–82.

56. Paul de Man in "The Rhetoric of Temporality" (*Blindness and Insight: Essays in the Rhetoric of Contemporary Criticism*, [2nd ed., rev.; [Minneapolis, 1986], 187–228) suggests Stendhal's *Chartreuse de Parme* as "one of the few novels of novels, as the allegory of irony" because it faithfully realizes Schlegel's "permanent parabasis" (227–28). However, this choice becomes at least problematic considering that Stendhal's fiction belongs in the realist tradition of the nineteenth-century novel, precisely where Eichner has located the "evil principle" of literature, and where one would *not* expect to look for the romantic novel. De Man's choice must, of course, be seen in the context of the entire essay, which sets out to reconcile the allegorical and the ironic rhetorical modes and to revalorize them against the domination of symbolism. Still, although in trying to unify allegory and irony de Man seems to move beyond rhetoric towards philosophy, where romantic irony is properly located (I attempt a similar task in Chapter I, where I give Schlegel's "rhetorical" definition of irony as "permanent parabasis" a philosophical dimension in the unity of apostrophe and parabasis), his analysis of irony and the romantic novel does not recognize the centrality of the question of the absolute. And it is, perhaps, this omission of Schlegel that allows de Man to see romantic quality in Stendhal (for a further discussion of the differences between Stendhal and Flaubert see also note 20 in Chapter III). Samuel Weber ("Criticism Underway") confirms this analysis. While Weber credits de Man for attempting, in "The Intentional Structure of the Romantic Image" (*The Rhetoric of Romanticism* [New York, 1984], 1–17), "to (re)-introduce the perspective of German romanticism into English-language literary criticism," he is intrigued that de Man should "go to Hölderlin rather than to Novalis or Friedrich Schlegel to find his exemplary text" (304–305). Weber argues that "the dislocation of the romantic work, and perhaps of romanticism itself, depends on a process of allegorization for which the problematization of self and the process of reading are inseparably linked"

the romantic thought on the novel, and to what extent it is still correct, and even perhaps proper, to demand from this practice any form of adherence to this theory. This questioning imposes a relatively narrow but, it would seem, highly specific and relevant perspective on the readings of *Don Quixote, Pierre, Madame Bovary, Ulysses,* and *The Trial.* This is to say that, while the works selected for this study are canonically recognized "masterpieces" of the novel, my objective will be to examine these "novels" from the point of view of the romantic theory of the novel, to search for the transcendental and not the taxonomic genre markers—for the traces of the dissolved subject and not for the criteria of an empirical genre.

The readings will seek to examine the novels in the light of Schlegel's formula that "every theory of the novel must itself be a novel," to examine them as the sites, or modalities, of the presence of the subject to itself. Such methodology implies two directions of inquiry. First, the readings will attempt to bring to light the subject of the work as it pervades the work and saturates it. Second, such analysis must simultaneously address the problem of the romantic genre; it must ask the question: What makes these novels the hyperbolic genre, the Genre (of) Itself? *The inquiry into the generative reflection of the romantic theory of the novel cannot be separated from the question of the transcendental genre.*

I believe that the general thrust of the individual readings can be systematized with the following statement made by Schlegel: "A *Roman* is a romantic book [Ein Roman ist ein romantisches Buch]" (*DP,* 101/*SL,* 318). What is the romantic novel as a "book"? The formula,

---

(307). From here Weber argues that de Man's "allegory" derives from Benjamin's elaboration of the term in *The Origin of the German Tragic Drama,* which in turn develops the romantic conception of criticism as "setting forth" (*Darstellung*), an allegorical mourning of the work for the sake of its (critical) preservation. It would appear that Weber's observation might also imply a similar circuitous derivation of de Man's concept of theory from its romantic prototype; this conclusion is less likely, however, in view of the fact that the romantic "theory" is articulated in rigorous proximity to the romantic "novel." One might surmise that behind this reluctance to engage Schlegel's romantic speculation lies de Man's more general reluctance to work within (or with) the dialectical edifice. This reluctance would at least partly explain the numerous engagements with Hölderlin as the symbol of the overcoming of dialectics. At any rate, "The Rhetoric of Temporality," more than any other essay in contemporary criticism, makes palpable the difficulties of accommodating the philosophical core of the romantic novel, even in a most comprehensive and theoretically refined study of romanticism, when such a study is guided by the question of rhetoric.

again, raises the issue of romantic reflective circularity as the method of systematic description. Schlegel immediately addresses the charges of empty circularity: "You will pass that off as a meaningless tautology. But I want to draw your attention to the fact that when one thinks of a book, one thinks of a work, an existing whole" (*DP*, 101). While the definition may seem to be an empty tautology, says Schlegel, it describes the supreme task of the romantic theory of the novel; for to the extent that a theory of the novel is itself a novel, it produces the subject-work, it effects the presence of the operative subject in its work, which is nothing more than this subject as (at) work. As it indicates the work, the novel—as the subject producing itself—presents the whole (*die Ganze*), the completion of the subject in the intransitive totality of self-production. Schlegel calls the romantic novel "a book" to signify the totality of the subject's self-presentation: the romantic Book is the *non-objective, dissolved figure* of the excessive identity of the subject that has achieved its proper self-presentation.

In this infinitely self-enclosed totality of auto-production (*ein für sich bestehendes Ganze*), the novel executes—and this becomes the central concern of *Don Quixote*—the presentation of the subject by the subject itself in the totality called "the Book." What takes place in this reflective operation is the "unworking" (*désoeuvrement—LA*, 57) of the work, the excessive production whose result is what Maurice Blanchot calls "the absence of the Book" (*IC*, 422–34). The mechanism of "unworking" can be compared to the operations described by Blanchot with reference to consciousness. To modify Blanchot's phrase, we could say that "what exceeds the work is its inability to stop working." We have observed that the subject-work no longer satisfies the hermeneutic and the formalist conceptions of the whole, that it cannot be understood as a result of the interplay between parts and whole or between form and content. We have expressed this shift in the concept of the work as a transition from the "organic" to the "aorgic" theory of the work's unity. The "unworking" of the work corresponds to the aorgic (non-work) character of the entity. The identity of the subject with its work leads to the subject's complete disappearance in what works. As a result of the romantic production of the subject, the work considered as an organic entity separate from the productive subject ceases to exist, and the place of the work is taken by the subject-work, an un-worked, aorgic identity of the subject with itself in the form of presentation adequate to it. It is this dissolved, absolute absence/presence that Schlegel in Idea 95 named "the Book," that is, the unity of instinct and intention that would surpass the poetry of Homer and even that of Nature, that would achieve the effectiveness of Nietzsche's "it," that would sever all links to Nature, to *phusis* and *tekhne.* The readings in this study seek to uncover the mechanism of the romantic Book as the Whole that operates itself.

The romantic Book received a modern restatement in Roland Barthes' thesis about "the death of the author," a belated and potentially misleading (as misleading as Nietzsche's thesis about "the death of God") acknowledgment of romanticism's discovery that the Book is more originary than the historical subject, *agent,* or author.[57] The author makes room for the Book; the transcendental sphere, the subject speaking in what is spoken, is anterior to the empirical sphere of historical registers, styles, forms, and origins.

Significantly, romanticism's formula of the auto-productive subject assumes in modernity the form of repetition: the transcendental generative formula "poetry of poetry" captures the repetition of repetition repeating itself in the generative tautology later codified by Nietzsche's "eternal return of the Same." In the repetition of repetition, the subject of repetition recurs as the Same, and this recurrence cannot be articulated in the differential system of speech because it is speech speaking (itself). Similar to Hölderlin's hyperbolic formula "poetry of poetry" which produces no object, the tautological formula "repetition of repetition" does not produce an object but merely enacts the process of re-iteration. This pure declaration is modernity's way of actualizing romanticism's ab-solute subject.

It follows that this study posits a necessary link between the romantic theory of the novel and postmodernity in philosophy, specifically in the area of the subject. The connection arises with particular clarity in the case of the romantic sense of *theory.* Romanticism's thesis about transcendental poetry, transformed into its modern version as repetition, achieves the complete measure of the profanation that Benjamin detected in the romantic theory of the poetic absolute (of the novel). The subject of repetition, the modern absolute brings to completion the romantic absolute's potential for profanation and becomes postmodern. It is essential to note that modernity's repetition does not enjoy even a moment of independent existence (in a structural, not temporal sense), for under the pressure of the transcendental

---

57. Roland Barthes, "The Death of the Author," in *Image-Music-Text,* trans. Stephen Heath (Glasgow, 1977), 146.

mandate it inherited from romanticism, modern repetition *must immediately become* the postmodern exergue. This is perhaps the uncontrollable power of Schlegel's absolute degree for modernity, "arch-modern (*erzmodern*)" invoked by him as the condition of an adequate comprehension of antiquity from the transcendental point of view (Athenaeum Fragment 271). Schlegel's "arch-modernity" indicates that romanticism's transcendental theory harbors within itself the seeds of the postmodern surplus and that the seeds have now come to fruition. Romanticism reminds us that, in the battle between the Ancients and the Moderns, the Post-Moderns had always been standing by.

In selecting the novels for this study I have tried, first of all, to retain the basic model from "The Letter on the Novel," which defines the romantic novel in the work of the transcendental poets—Dante, Cervantes, and Shakespeare. I have chosen the Cervantine paradigm above all because *Don Quixote* deploys the central theme of the romantic theory of the novel, the question of the Book, in explicit and theoretically diversified terms.

I examine the five novels as instances of the presentation of the subject to itself. I will seek to discover in each novel a mode of the actualization of the dissolved subject, the vehicle of resurgence under whose guise the subject as such comes to the surface of conceptuality and, in so coming, disturbs this surface, rearranges it, and shows it to be an effect of romanticism's excessive presentation. My readings will also examine the impact that these modes of actualization may have on some of the dominant critical and philosophical strategies of interpretation.

The pressure of the Other originates in the excessive identity of each novel with itself, and in each case this identity is expressed by a specific transcendental genre that actualizes this identity. The genres of *involution* in *Don Quixote*, *mood* in *Pierre*, *la syncope* in *Madame Bovary*, *example* in *Ulysses*, and the *neuter* in *The Trial* describe the identity of the romantic subject; they are the forms of hyperbolic self-manifestation comparable to those described above by Lacoue-Labarthe, Benjamin, Novalis, Blanchot, Sollers, and Frank as *l'imprésentable*, the work, *menstruum universale*, the Other, *dépassement*, and absolute saying.

Treated here as a romantic search for transcendental origin, *Don Quixote* is read as the romantic reconstruction of Greece: Cervantes finds that the origin, rather than constituting a stable and self-identical unity, emerges as divided, elusive, and different. For him, the original difference is the transcendental relation par excellence, for it is a pure relay, an infinite texture. The divided origin is the transcendental original relation at work as Work. The work that emerges in the course of this production is without author, for the original relation, the *genre of involution*, is generative in the transcendental sense, as speech speaking itself in the difference from itself. The individual author Cervantes can establish his presence in the matrix of this speech only in an ironic curtailment of his own speech: he can join the totality that speaks as the Book only insofar as he allows the difference of origin to come forward in his speech.

The analysis of *Madame Bovary* begins with a study of the role and function of the technique of bricolage. In his use of bricolage, Flaubert remains close to the romantic understanding of arabesque. According to the standard definition, an arabesque is an ensemble of elements randomly put together; still, romantically considered, the chaos of the arabesque somehow pleases the eye because it invokes the totality without specifying the nature of its parameters (formal? hermeneutic?). The analysis proceeds to develop the implications of the technique of bricolage for the experience of reading *Madame Bovary* and for Flaubert's conception of the literary work. Bricolage presents Flaubert with the following dilemma: the parts of bricolage are already parts, yet they do not conform to the whole in which they are now assembled. Flaubert confronts a synthesis that has occurred without his participation. Hence the disconcerting realization: Flaubert uses language "parts" whose method of formation, whose original context, and whose "meaning" are alien to the author who is currently using them.

The realization—that there exist parts without their encompassing whole, that there exists a product without a producer—induces a specifically Flaubertian vertigo: the mind confronts neither order nor chaos but, romantically, order *and/or* chaos. The vertigo, the *genre of la syncope*, is pure vertigo—not only the loss of balance, or of consciousness, but the experience of this loss as loss, the Blanchotian discovery that what exceeds consciousness is its inability to lose consciousness. The analysis focuses on one concrete form of vertigo—Flaubert's realization that the book *Madame Bovary*, as a part without a final synthetic term, can, at best, only be assumed to be a book. Flaubert, in other words, is unable to determine the source and the content of his speech, for both merely point to an anterior moment, to an original synthesis from which the concepts of "form" and "content" can first be grasped. Aware of the distinction between form and content, Flaubert can first make this distinction from a higher, or anterior, plane for which there is no form or content. Organized by a synthesis not of his own making, Flaubert's prose instantiates the ironic (other) presencing of the subject of speech as such. Flaubert's vertigo is a reaction to the presence of an alien but indispensable agency, one that makes (human) speech possible but that itself exceeds this speech. As he foregrounds the clichéd aspect of language, Flaubert recognizes the anterior source of his speech as the presence of the subject of speech.

In the special case of Joyce (a case that, somehow, always manages to be special), the romantic novel is fulfilled in *Finnegans Wake*. The present choice of *Ulysses* is motivated by the need to describe, and to accentuate, the moment of transition from the prenovelistic *Bildungsroman* of *A Portrait of the Artist* to the transcendental, self-engendering subject of *Finnegans Wake*. The analysis of *Ulysses* concentrates on Joyce's conception of exemplarity, a conception far removed from the customary uses of the term. Joyce's use of exemplarity in *Ulysses* resembles Flaubert's use of bricolage in *Madame Bovary:* both techniques work with parts whose relation to the whole is problematic. Considered in light of this conception of exemplarity, *Ulysses* is a romantic arabesque, or, as Jean-François Lyotard suggests, its close cousin, the Kantian sublime; in either case, the example confronts the reader with an absent totality.[58]

As in the chapter on Flaubert, the analysis next examines the consequences of the arabesque character of the example for the experience of reading *Ulysses* and for Joyce's conception of the literary work. The discussion of the Joycean *genre of example* reveals that the romantic arabesque entertains its tenuous relation to the absent totality in the mode of echo, of repetition. The exemplary repetition is a transcendental relation both inadequate and excessive in relation to what it would repeat. What speaks in the example cannot be positively determined: the reader cannot know what the example is an example of, or

---

58. "Joyce allows the unpresentable to become perceptible in his writing itself, in the signifier. The whole range of available narrative and even stylistic operators is put into play without concern for the unity of the whole, and new operators are tried. The grammar and vocabulary of literary language are no longer accepted as given; rather, they appear as academic forms, as rituals originating in piety (as Nietzsche said) which prevent the unpresentable from being put forward" (Jean-François Lyotard, *The Postmodern Condition: A Report on Knowledge,* trans. Geoff Bennington and Brian Massumi [Minneapolis, 1984], 80–81).

what grounding form corresponds to the example in the first place (a book? history? the totality of language?). The example only shows that the relation between the detail and its grounding totality presupposes a minimal, merely formal relation of identity between the two. Joyce's example is an example of this original, exemplary identity; it is an example of the example as such coming to surface. *Ulysses* refines the concept of repetition to its last, *exemplary* stage before it indicates, in *Finnegans Wake*, repetition's pure subject.

Melville's *Pierre* and Kafka's *The Trial* stand as the paragons of the romantic novel insofar as they lead up to and carry out (*Pierre*), or simply carry out (*The Trial*), the presentation of the subject as subject in its proper form. The two novels seem to confirm the assumption that repetition is the central form in which modernity imitates and continues romanticism's transcendental project. *Pierre* exemplifies the romantic theme of the Book understood as the overcoming of the metaphysical (mimetic) economy of repetition. On the thematic level, the problem of repetition appears as the antinomy of moods and the self-identical subject. Melville attempts to preserve the unity of the subject, but he also wants to allow the subject to feel many contradictory moods. His problem is one of preserving identity in difference.

Melville resolves this antinomy by developing a nonmetaphysical conception of the subject. In the metaphysical conception of the subject, the antinomy of the subject and its moods is resolved by dispersing a self-identical term into a multiplicity of synonyms: difference is a finite field of play controlled by metaphysically guaranteed sameness. In his proposal, Melville offers sameness, not as a mathematical equation of identity or of correspondence, but as transcendental reflection.

However, the resort to the transcendental solution exposes Melville to the vagaries of romantic profanation. In the reflective understanding of identity as romantic tautology (a sense developed by Jean Paul), the two terms in the relation of identity ($A = A$) are affected by a speculative moment that is neither empty tautology nor a metaphysically controlled difference. Melville's romantic tautology defines the *genre of mood* as the vehicle of adequate presentation of the subject of repetition to itself. However, originally designed to ward off the drift and disintegration of the subject, this structure of repetition yields a romantic dissolved subject. Melville's subject is made up by moods, where mood (*Stimmung*) is the structure of the subject as such, the being-subject of the subject in terms adequate for this subject. What emerges in the medium of moods is not a unified subject but the subject *of* moods *as* moods.

The analysis of repetition in *The Trial* follows Maurice Blanchot's work on Kafka's, and literature's, *neuter*. On the thematic level, I address a certain specificity of Kafkan metaphor. The traditional metaphor is based on the exchange of properties that themselves are assured by the metaphysical conception of language as a system of properties (*Eigenschaften*). Kafka's metaphor and his conception of language depart from the metaphysical model in that they operate, not by exchanging properties or by asserting differences, but by utilizing the aspect of language indifferent to properties. Instead of asserting similarities among objects, Kafka seeks to disclose an indifference—the neuter—neither similar to nor dissimilar from anything. The *genre of the neuter* is a relation stronger than tropologically-exploited similarity: this romantic excess of identity renders figurative speech futile and exposes the literal use of language to uncontrollable tropological tremors. Because in Kafkan tropology language is constituted by transcendental repetition—Blanchot's *récit*—his language, romantically dissolved, becomes the prosaic absolute: *either* a metaphor of repetition *or else* a repetition of metaphor.

What makes Kafkan repetition transcendental is the absence of the object of repetition: the transcendental repetition repeats, as a minimal operation, repetition itself. Here repetition is the proper and the only subject. One may propose the following formula: the subject requires repetition to be a subject, and repetition becomes repetition only in the subject. The relation does not organize two preexistent entities; the relation is that of the romantic absolute, for the subject of repetition cannot be distinguished from the repetition in which it "becomes" a subject. The absolute as repetition implies that Kafkan origin is available only in repetition as this repetition. There is no preexistent point anterior to the operation, for origin occurs in repetition; conversely, the act of repetition itself can never present origin as origin—it can only bring origin forth as repeated. In Kafka the transcendental relation—that is, the original relation—is original in the hyperbolic sense, for it is the original relation of origin presenting itself as the infinite, original relating striving to originate itself.

As the novel of all novels, in many senses the original novel, *Don Quixote* serves in this study as the paradigm of the romantic theory of the novel. It has received its best critical *Vollendung*, as the book of all Books, in the work of Jorge Luis Borges (or of "Pierre Menard,

Author of the *Quixote*"). Cervantes is a romantic novelist because his *Don Quixote* parodies literature in the sense of belles lettres and because it proposes literature in the romantic sense of manifestation. Cervantes is an author, according to Schlegel's distinction (Critical Fragment 68): "How many authors are there among writers? Author means creator" (*F*, 151).

If there emerges a difference in the tenor of these readings, it concerns what might be called the level of intensity in the romantic response to the imperative of the Book, a hesitation, in this response, between an arabesque indication of the subject (Flaubert, Joyce) and a strict, that is, dissolved, ab-solute presentation of the subject (Melville, Kafka). I believe that this difference in the comportment towards the Book, between (Cervantes)-Flaubert-Joyce on the one hand, and (Cervantes)-Melville-Kafka on the other, can prove fruitful to a contemporary assessment of the romantic theory of the novel.

The question concerns the significance of this difference. Perhaps one way to assess this significance is to attempt to identify some passages in the romantic writings on the theory of the novel that would indicate an early awareness of this difference. We have seen that the romantic novel was intended to complete antiquity's epos and that the goal of this completion was the presentation of the subject to itself. However, we have also seen that the novel completes its historical labors by dissolving modernity in a supreme transcendental dissolution: "Just as our literature began with the novel, so the Greek began with the epic and dissolved in it" (*DP*, 101). Put briefly, in romanticism the subject becomes present by being dissolved in its excessive identity. Hence, if the romantic novel "colors all of modern poetry," it does so in the sense that the romantic project to unify antiquity and modernity immediately yields the postmodern exergue in excess of romanticism's enterprise.

The question can now be posed with more precision: What is the nature of the difference between the modern and the postmodern, considering that the difference is not temporal but denotes *merely the process of dissolution*, the instantaneous production of blinding prose, of the poetic absolute? Does this moment signify, as Lacoue-Labarthe intimates, the dissolution of difference as such? In that case it would be possible to argue that the romantic novel, as a figure of dissolution, defines the outline, the gestalt, of history itself and that the difference—represented by romantic dissolution—between modernity and postmodernity is the figure-less figure of history itself, the *topos* of the happening of history. We have returned to the paradox of attempting to *grasp conceptually* precisely that which eludes the grasp of the concept (*Begriff*).

The romantic novel, as the identity of the subject with itself accomplished in strict fidelity to Schlegel's formula that "every theory of the novel must itself be a novel," produces the dissolved, ab-solute subject. For this work-of-the-subject there is no proper figure, not even that of "work": romantic theory stands *outside* the novel as infinitely identical with itself. It is this transcendental externality, the "outside the work" that constitutes romantic profanation. The *exergue* is the figure of dissolution and the dissolution of figures (of all conceptuality, of all *gestalts*). This externality is the postmodern figure of romantic dissolution.

We can now see how the nontemporal difference/dissolution between/of modernity and postmodernity may be linked to the profanation of the romantic dissolution, to the figureless figure of the romantic "unworking." Stated simply, the product of the dissolution of modernity in postmodernity, the unworked subject, is nothing in two senses of the word: *the* nothing that was the goal of romantic dissolution, as indifference, the poetic absolute as the "medium of reflection" realized in the continuum of poetic forms; and *mere* nothing, a superfluous formation that has outlived its brief moment in history.

Put in different terms, this thesis would mean that romantic dissolution not only encompasses conceptual thought, as Lacoue-Labarthe argues in the case of Hegel, but that it recoils on itself and applies the ambiguity of its prosaic nature to its own operation. Not only does romantic dissolution undermine conceptual thought—it itself is unable to determine whether the dissolution proposed in the theory of the novel is a *contingent* or a *necessary* moment for the poetic absolute. In Hegel's terms, the romantic absolute is an abstract totality, a totality whose abstractness threatens its own existence: not only are all cows black in the dark—we do not even know *that* they are *cows*. In Schlegel's terms, "It's equally fatal for the mind to have a system and to have none. It will simply have to decide to combine the two" (Athenaeum Fragment 53—*F,* 167). It is obvious that at stake here is nothing less than the historical and intellectual validity of the romantic enterprise.

My thesis would seem to obtain circumstantial corroboration from several passages in Schlegel's writings. First, it is important to remember that, before Schlegel settled on the Homeric epos as the proper expression of the complex unity of ancient Greece, he had also considered as potential candidates the tragic and the lyric. We have mentioned that the tragic option did not seem viable to him (it did to Hölderlin). But Schlegel experienced serious hesitation over the lyric, specifically the Sapphic lyric. One can find strong evidence of this hesitation in Critical Fragment 119: "Sapphic poems must grow and be discovered. They can neither be produced at will, nor published without desecration. Whoever does so lacks pride and modesty.... And if lyrical poems are not completely unique, free, and true, then, as lyrical poems, they're worthless. Petrarch doesn't belong here: for the cool lover doesn't utter anything except elegant platitudes; and actually he is romantic [novelistic], not lyrical" (F, 157). Significantly, when contrasted with the lyric, the term "romantic" acquires here a pejorative connotation. The Schlegel of Critical Fragment 119 disagrees with the Schlegel of Athenaeum Fragment 51 (unity of intention and instinct in Homer) and of Critical Fragment 108 (unity of intention and instinct in Socrates). It would seem that Sappho had achieved the unity of the subjective and the objective moments infinitely better than did the Homeric epos and Socratic irony. Sappho knew the secret of poetry free from all bonds with Nature; Homer and Socrates belong to the second wave; they are the canonical masters of a naturality that already functions in modernity's conceptual/dialectical grid.

In that case Schlegel's choice of the novel as the modern genre that corresponds to the epos (and all the implications of this choice) will begin to hover over an abyss of arbitrariness and will most likely plunge and disappear in it. If it is indeed the case that Schlegel glimpsed the possibility that the novel might *not* be appropriate for the transcendental task of healing the division and of presenting the subject, then this "mistake" will begin to resonate with an urgency and drama that our age has experienced, not as the Hegelian possibility of the *end* of history, but as the Nietzschean possibility of the *lack* of history.

Let us reiterate that romantic equivocity allows for two undecidable options. The first moment of the romantic profanation is the arbitrary choice of the novel over the lyric. Here the romantic novel dissolves modernity because it was a wrong choice, a mere trifling with history, a nothing. On the other hand, the unworking may be a necessary consequence of romanticization. It is the sum of these options that makes for the prosaic ambiguity of romanticism and that makes up the figureless figure of postmodernity. The romantic novel, like Nietzsche's "eternal return of the Same," stands under the law of the exergue. Just as Nietzsche's "Same never reaches its sameness" (*LA*, 123), so the novel dissolves with infinite ambiguity into the poetic absolute. As a consequence of its equivocity, romanticism is unable—in terms of the dissolution that it has itself fashioned—to delimit the historical futility of its enterprise from its immanent necessity.

We touch in this critical moment on what could be, as Lacoue-Labarthe and Nancy say, Schlegel's "obsession" (*LA*, 100); we encounter perhaps the most ambiguous moment of romanticism, the most ambiguous because the ambiguity of its concept of dissolution is not directed at external thought systems but at itself. In this moment the possibility of triviality, contingency, irrelevance—of a *complete dead end*—coexists equivocally with the greatest triumphs, insights, and achievements of the romantic theory of the novel. Clearly, it would be devastating to acknowledge this equivocity, to rethink it and retroactively to implement it.

It will suffice to realize that already at the very dawn of its formulation by Friedrich Schlegel, the romantic theory of the novel recognized the theoretical validity of the lyrical option for the presentation of the subject in the form adequate to itself. It may be further assumed that Schlegel understood well that the unity of instinct and intention achieved in the Sapphic lyric is more "original" than that exhibited by the Homeric epos. One may further speculate that Schlegel recognized the lyric as the genre in which the unity of the subject has been adequately accomplished, not only for the ancient Greeks, but for the moderns as well. Schlegel must have also seen—and Hölderlin certainly did—that Sappho's lyrics had already accomplished the transcendental "speech of speech" in an originary sense, that is, without any extrinsic task whatsoever, even the supreme task, imposed by romanticism on the Homeric epos, of accomplishing unity. Above all, it should be realized that romanticism saw in Sappho's lyrics the origin of aesthetic history, the Golden Age of the synthesis of instinct and intention in relation to which the unity presented in the Homeric epos was already secondary, historical, and perhaps even derivative. We can be led to suppose that romanticism, faced with a unity already accomplished in the lyric, and threatened with "nothing left to do," had, perhaps, rejected the lyric's archaic unity and usurped for itself, for the *Roman*tic age, the privilege of fulfilling the Greeks' transcendental secret. We may say, in other words, that by rejecting Sappho romanticism gained the opportunity not only to complete antiquity but, above all, *to originate history.*

It is, I would propose, this need for history that emerges both as the primary objective of the romantic theory of the novel and as the justification for our criticism of this theory. I believe that the instantaneous transition from modernity to postmodernity, the nontemporal difference between Flaubert and Joyce on the one hand, and Melville and Kafka on the other, serves romanticism's purpose of inducing the illusion of progression. The difference expresses, for romanticism at least, the real distance of historical advance, a perceptible measure of the occurrence of history.

As such a measure of the historical, the difference articulates the romantic imperative, the imperative to engender history. It creates, and was intended to create, nothing but an *illusion*—a semblance—of history in the minuscule, instantaneous, inexorable movement in which modern completion dissolves into postmodern exergue. Romanticism has created its theory of the novel and the artifice of the distinction between antiquity and modernity (and postmodernity implied in it) solely for the purpose of creating a historical world in which it, romanticism, could play a significant, perhaps central role. In emphasizing the original lack in the Homeric epos and in intentionally overlooking the unity of the Sapphic lyric, romanticism saw a chance for itself in undertaking the project of completing antiquity in the highly specific and narrow parameters of speculative philosophy of history. By rejecting original unity accomplished *without speculation* and by inaugurating history as the speculative relation between antiquity and modernity, romanticism opened history up to artificial construals. That is, it opened up the history of "artificial" civilization, or even, perhaps, it opened *the artifice of history*, so that we, who come after the ancients, can—however briefly—participate in, and benefit from, a properly historical existence.

That Schlegel was not a stranger to such foundational thinking, and that he could conceive, however paradoxical it may sound, of a *foundational* role for romantic *dissolution*, can be seen from his declarations in Athenaeum Fragment 252. In his discussion of the possibility of a "philosophy of poetry," Schlegel contemplates extending the mandate of the theory of the novel to Plato's doctrine of Ideas and to his political theory, implying that the novel represents the true spirit of Platonism, or else that it deserves to redefine Platonism and its Ideas according to the doctrine of dissolution: "The keystone [of a philosophy of poetry] would be a philosophy of the novel, the rough outlines of which are contained in Plato's political theory" [*Eine Philosophie des Romans, deren ersten Grundlinien Platos politische Kunstlehre enthält, wäre der Schlußstein (einer Philosophie der Poesie)*] (*F,* 198).[59] Schlegel may be suggesting that by dissolving modernity romanticism is belatedly performing for history a task that Platonism was equipped to perform but failed to recognize as its highest historical mission.

Still, romanticism's flirting with the political (Schlegel's later political views, for example) is outweighed by the sheer power of dissolution as an independent and original treatment of the absolute. To extend Lacoue-Labarthe's thought, one could say that the dissolution that Schlegel's *Lucinde* exerted on speculative philosophy is equal in its impact to the influence that Heidegger claims Hölderlin's poetry exerted on modern thinking. This dissolution, the legacy of the romantic theory of the novel, has, as we have seen, a double meaning, a duplicity that accounts for the theory's profanity. Schlegel adds, in Athenaeum Fragment 252, that his philosophy of poetry is "something that—for those who are able to understand it at all—follows from the proposition I = I. It would waver between the union and the division of philosophy and poetry, between poetry and practice, poetry as such and the genres and kinds of poetry; and it would conclude with their complete union" (*F,* 198). Having created the artifice of history, romanticism now cannot distinguish, in the postmodern excess, the "union" from "the division," the work from the exergue. Having set conceptual thought adrift and "colored all poetry," the romantic novel itself is now caught up in the *menstruum* that exceeds both the Golden Age and history, nature and artifice. And yet, although the romantic theory of the novel spells the *désoeuvrement* of history, we should remember that without romanticism's transcendental poetry there would be no universal history, no work of art, and no present subject.

---

59. Again, Firchow's mistranslation obscures a subtle point: not "Plato's political theory," but "Plato's political doctrine of aesthetics"; the latter translation affects the modern sense of history by subjecting it to an aesthetic rigor (the *literary* absolute). Here, at last, we may imagine a way of including the romantic age in the scheme of Schlegel, side by side with the civilization of Greece, as a single aesthetic body, as one unified poem.

I
The Genre of Involution in *Don Quixote*

The *stage* of a good novel is the language in which it is written; but the *places* which are completely individual and are properly parabases are quite useless.

In Cervantes the presentation of folly is divine; however, the presentation of controversy, personality, and parabasis is quite ordinary.

For a genre cannot be conceived without an accompanying genre.

—Friedrich Schlegel, *Literary Notebooks*

The First Prologue to *Don Quixote* appears as one among several preambles to the novel.[1] Before reaching the prologue, the reader encounters the dedication (to the Duke of Béjar), the statement of price (the *tassa*, signed by Juan Gallo de Andrada), the approval of the censors (the *privilegio*, usually written by a cleric), and the copyright (issued by the prince of the realm).

The statements of financial, editorial, theological, and political orthodoxy alert the reader to the proximity of the literary event proper. Yet, while all these prefatory statements are primarily intended to confer formal approval on Cervantes' novel, it is possible to read in them an intention and, perhaps, an apprehension of a different nature. The prefatory matter seems to be as much concerned about the

---

1. Miguel de Cervantes Saavedra, *Don Quixote*, ed. Joseph R. Jones and Kenneth Douglas, Ormsby Translation, revised (New York, 1981). The parallel Spanish citations follow the text as found in Miguel de Cervantes Saavedra, *El ingenioso hidalgo Don Quijote de la Mancha*, ed. Joaquín Casalduero (Madrid, 1984).

strictly administrative matters of issuing formal approval of a literary work as it is concerned about its own grounds of authority in relation to this work. Put differently, although the official statements speak with authority about a text, although they officially *authorize* it, they themselves enter into a rivalry with this work precisely over the claim to the highest authority.

The statements from the Licentiate and from the King, and Cervantes' prologue, can be read as short treatises on the origin of authority—can, indeed, be seen as contestants vying for the privilege of pronouncing with authority on what is properly literary. When placed alongside one another, the three statements do not appear separated by the formal difference between administrative and literary writing. Instead, they all seem preoccupied with grounding their own authority as speaking positions. Clearly, the goal of self-authorization cannot be artificially isolated from the practical role each of the statements is expected to perform within the concrete political, social, and cultural context. Indeed, this goal can be detected and analyzed only in the forms used in these statements insofar as they serve precisely these historically conditioned practical purposes. As the prefatory pieces pursue one goal—to secure their own authority—each of them exemplifies a different approach to this apparently straightforward task.

And it is with reference to the problem of authority, and, secondarily, against the backdrop of the other prefatory statements, that Cervantes' prologue puts forth a theory of authority, of authorization, as a properly romantic act of self-constitution. To the extent that the act of establishing one's own authority is self-referential and reflexive, this act opens up the question of origin and originality. I want to argue that, in the course of the rivalry with *Don Quixote*'s other prefatory statements over the question of authority, Cervantes' prologue comes to define the self-reflexive act as the *literary act* in the romantic sense of "literature" as self-manifestation pure and simple. In the specific case of *Don Quixote*, this manifestation concerns the self-origination of origin.

Let us for a moment disregard the prologue and concentrate exclusively on the administrative statements. The administrative preambles represent two elocutionary positions. The first type is illustrated by the word from the Licentiate. Authority is external to the Licentiate. He speaks as a cog in a machine, one to whom the administrative hierarchy has temporarily delegated privilege and power. This situation has several implications. First, the Licentiate understands his audience impersonally; his form of address reads like a memo: "to whomever it may concern." Second, as he hides behind the hierarchy, which alone gives him his status, he believes that his message is *worth knowing*, but he believes so with the indifferent conviction of the dutiful employee. Third, he never questions the decrees that he passes on, for he is merely a docile functionary equipped with official power. But it is usually the case that authority assigned to a person elicits a zeal of enforcement equalling, if not surpassing, the whim of the absolute monarch himself. This is why it can be assumed that the Licentiate, who unquestioningly delivers his decision, expects, like a monarch, that his message will not be questioned. Finally, the speaking position of the Licentiate defines the nature of his authority. The Licentiate's authority has its origin in the structure of the organization to which he belongs. His power is derivative; it flows from the political hierarchy that he has freely entered. As a bureaucrat in a system of delegated power, the Licentiate does not authorize the message he delivers; and even if he does, it is only because he subscribes to the system of beliefs according to which a work of literature should receive such external authorization.

The second type of address is illustrated by the statement entitled "The King." The authority of the King differs from that of the Licentiate, and the difference is not merely a quantitative one of scope or a qualitative one of privilege. The two kinds of authority have different *origins*. The King does not delegate his authority; he merely conveys it to others from himself, for he himself is the source of this authority.

The King's self-authorization defines the form of "The King." In his address, any subject under discussion, including the book *Don Quixote*, is appended to the king's name. In its strongest version, the circularity of this movement appears at the end: "Yo El Rey." In the royal signature, the king has assumed both discursive positions (the royal "I" speaks to the "king"); he has spoken *to himself in himself*. The signature *Yo El Rey* becomes *El Rey El Rey*, and, finally, *Yo Yo*, a tautological echo that contains the minimal relation of authority.[2] As a minimal formulation, *Yo Yo* would imply the following conclusion:

---

2. The reduction to *Yo Yo* is only partly ironic. The simultaneous process by which, in feudalism, the collective *we* has evolved into the royal *we*, and the *you* has ceased to imply equality and assumed the relation of subordination and, ultimately, complete infantilization, has been traced by Immanuel Kant in "Note on the Formality of Egoistic Language," in *Anthropology from a Pragmatic Point of View*, trans. Victor Lyle Dowdell, ed. Hans H. Rudnick (Rev. ed., Carbondale, 1978), 13–14.

whether considered as administrative function or as royal privilege, the relation of authority demands a conferral, transmission, and delegation. While the Licentiate's authority is a function of bureaucratic position conferred on him by someone who occupies a higher position of power, the King's authority is a function of an absolute position conferred on the King by the King himself. The authority of kings is established within the person of each king, as this person's self-relation, as an intra-personal relay of authority. The King reminds his subjects that he possesses this relation of authority in his use of the royal *we*.

Let us return to the Licentiate. His speech is impersonal because his authority is impersonal; it is not created by himself for himself. For the same reason, the Licentiate always assumes that he speaks to an already constituted audience, for the communicative situation is not of his making. For his part, in uttering the royal *we*, the King utters the formula *Yo Yo*, which restates his person as the original relation of authority: "I am I." The restatement swallows up everything in the essential relation that the king entertains with himself: L'état c'est moi. The King's power to establish his authority also gives him the power to create his audience. To give an example from the courtly protocol, the court must stop whispering—at the risk of committing *lèse majesté*—whenever the king wants to speak. At the King's command, the noisy crowd becomes an attentive audience. Because he is the source of authority, the King must make sure that a proper communicative situation is first constituted; the King must first make sure that all the persons are in (their) place. The difference between the conceptions of authority that underlie the Licentiate's and the King's addresses can be summed up in the following generalization: the Licentiate is a person under authority, while the King defines the position in which he has the authority to be a person. Stated briefly, the origin of the King's authority is also the *origin of the order among persons.*

The phrase *Yo El Rey* adds a new meaning to the royal *we*. The formula *I am I*, which normally serves to identify and consolidate the speaker as a subject, here enacts a movement within the subject, which destabilizes the subject as a self-identical presence transparent and immediate in itself. In this self-reference, or self-reflection, who is the first "I" and who is the second "I"? What difference between the two instances of self is the King asserting when he says "Yo Yo"?

The leap from one's proper self, from one's own "I" to the other "I," splits the self-identical "I," creating two kings, or a king with two heads. (The French Revolution overlooked, in its regicidal appetite, the hydra-like potential of royalty, its power of restoration.) Or else the king hears voices inside his head—the king must be crazy. Or, finally, the king entertains, as Blaise Pascal suspects, "the thought in the back of his mind."[3] He knows that his being a king is a matter of convention and not of divine right; his royal decree shrewdly conceals this truth from his subjects. In all cases it is legitimate to suspect that the royal *we* has been invented to conceal a "third," threatening personality that emerges when the first and the second kings speak together. The voice of the "we" awakened by the discourse of the king is by no means the sum of its parts, nor is it identical with the collective speakers of the grammatical first person plural. The voice of authority speaks with the ironic logic of the Socratic subjectivity: it hosts two modalities, the voluntary (*ekon*) imperative and the involuntary (*akon*) imperative, the singular/plural *daimon*.

Although the inner voice arises when the first king speaks to the second king, it is not controlled by royal consciousness. It arises as a third option, lodged between the voice of the obedient functionary, the Licentiate, and that of the consummate narcissist, the King. It proceeds from nobody's mouth, and its message, likewise, falls on nobody's ears. It is this third voice of polycephalic madness that Cervantes hears in the word *ingenioso*.[4] It is this ingenious voice that *Don Quixote* resurrects from the old romances of chivalry as the voice of literature. It is this plural voice that orchestrates the prologue's convoluted exposition.

Establishing this plurality is the central concern of the first prologue to *Don Quixote*. The prologue, in other words, offers its own treatment of the problem of authority, as the problem of *literary* authority. The Licentiate merely engages in the exercise of power, but he himself has no control over it. The King, in his turn, has created his own au-

3. Blaise Pascal, "The First Discourse on the Condition of the Great," in *Works of Pascal*, trans. O. W. Wight (n.p., 1866), 474.

4. Otis H. Green, "El *ingenioso* hidalgo," *Hispanic Review*, XXV (1957), 175–93. Green explains "the course of Alonso Quijano's transition from a country gentleman of *choleric temper* to an *imaginative* and *visionary* monomaniac . . . in the light of . . . Greek-Arabic physiological and psychological theories regarding the balance and imbalance of the bodily humors" (176). Green argues that in his choice of the word *ingenioso* Cervantes was drawing on the popular impact of a book by Juan Huarte de San Juan entitled *Examen de Ingenios para las ciencias* (1575). The word also suggests the sterility invoked in the prologue—the *lack* (in-) of genius.

thority and insisted that his audience always recognize this royal origin. However, the case of the King has disclosed in the origin of authority a perplexing duality that is, perhaps, the duality of origin itself. Although he is the source of his own authority, the King (the first "Yo") must somehow give it to himself (to the second "Yo"). Hence origin is not immediate presence but, rather, a relation—a mediation—of privilege. The King has sought to conceal this truth of the original relation in the majesty of the royal *we*; Cervantes' prologue is designed to bring this relation to presence and to develop its *literary* implications.

In its bid to discover its own authority, the prologue focuses on the mediated nature of the original relation. What the King hoped to conceal in order to preserve authority for himself, Cervantes hopes to foreground as literary authority, as authority as such, which cannot be used for the exercise of power and which cannot be claimed either by a historical individual or by a concrete author. But it must first be recognized that literary authority remains very close to the authority of the King: it is that which is sustained in the original relation as the relating, relaying from the first "I" to the second "I." However, while the King, as we have seen, exploits this relation to confer on himself, in a decree given to himself, the authoritative, absolute privilege as such, the prologue establishes literary authority as this relation pure and simple. Properly speaking, the literary authority of the prologue is not established, for it abides in the split—it abides as the differing, as the constant arrival of relation into its own. Conversely, however, because this relation cannot be solidly established with any finality, it becomes impervious to all challenges: it can be neither usurped nor abolished. In his (political) *ingeniosidad*, the prologuist presents the original relation, the origin of originality, as pure relating.

The unique circularity of the question about the "origin of originality" adds another dimension to Elias Rivers' thesis that the prologue is an "anti-prologue."[5] The prologue is either circular or negative: it is a circular structure without beginning and end, or else it is an impossible project that can never begin. The prologuist writes: "Many times [*muchas veces*] I took up my pen to write it, and many I laid it down again, not knowing what to write" (*DQ*, 9). The phrase "many times"

---

5. Elias L. Rivers, "Cervantes' Art of the Prologue," in *Estudios literarios de hispanistas norteamericanos dedicados a Helmut Hatzfeld con motivo de su 80 aniversario*, ed. J. M. Solà-Solé, A. Crisafulli, and B. Damiani (Barcelona, 1974), 169.

stands in curious opposition to the formulaic beginnings of narratives, "once upon a time." The contrast between Cervantes' phrase and the stock formula may be described as the difference between what Roland Barthes has called "lisible" and "scriptible" narratives.[6] A lisible narrative uses stock narrative devices like "once upon a time" to present the work as transparent reading matter that "reads itself," inducing the reader to overlook the fact that the text is an artifice fashioned by an artisan. By contrast, a scriptible narrative foregrounds the quality of the work as an artifact, making it impossible for the reader to become absorbed in the naturalness of the text and reminding him of its indelible nature as a human product.

In keeping with this definition, the lisible phrase "once upon a time" conceals the arbitrariness of beginning, and even of writing itself (Why write stories?) and "naturally" launches the artifice into existence: as a *motif*, it motivates (gives rationale for) the work. By contrast, as a polemical counterpart to the lisible "once upon a time," Cervantes' "many times" disrupts the illusion of naturalness and of fictive temporality. The plurality of his *muchas veces* runs counter to the *lisible* "once upon a time," postulating not one ("once") but *many* instances of authorial toil. Cervantes upsets the lisible order by exposing the arbitrariness of the prologue's motivation. His prologue exists, not in order to launch a story, but exclusively in order to struggle for its own existence; the proper content of the prologue is the difficulty of being written. In the brackets of the *prologon* (taking up the pen) and the *epilogon* (laying it down), this single sentence describes whatever transpires when the pen is in the writer's hand—it expresses the perpetual writing of the prologue.[7]

---

6. Roland Barthes, *S/Z*, trans. Richard Miller (New York, 1974), 181–84.

7. This is why a mere reversal of Elias Rivers' model, proposed by Américo Castro, is still insufficient. Castro advances his model—the prologue is an epilogue—in the following passage: "En realidad, se trata de epílogos, redactados después de conclusa la obra; y no precisamente porque los prólogos suelan escribirse 'a posteriori,' sino porque en este caso su sentido no se revela sino a quien posea noticia muy cabal del libro" (*Hacia Cervantes* [Madrid, 1957], 205). Castro calls the prologue to *Don Quixote* an epilogue not simply because the documentary evidence of scholarship justifies this view (this evidence refers exclusively to the circumstances of composition—the fact that the prologue was actually composed after Part I of *Don Quixote* had been finished); Castro also argues from the hermeneutic premise: the reader will understand the prologue only after reading Part I. Still, although the hermeneutic argument helps to explain why the prologue was written a posteriori and why it is best read as an epilogue, this reliance on the temporality of the hermeneutic act fails to account for the unique temporality in

Cervantes, however, chooses to escape not only the narrow confines of naïve *readability* but also the more refined terms of the *scriptible* option. Let us look more closely at the time of the prologue's occasion. We read: "One of these times [*y estando una suspenso*], as I was pondering with the paper before me, a pen behind my ear, my elbow on the desk, and my cheek in my hand, thinking of what I should say, there came in unexpectedly a certain lively, clever friend of mine" (*DQ*, 9). In this passage, Cervantes transcends not only the lisible format but the scriptible format as well. The *muchas veces* are not only the *moments suspended (suspenso) between* the taking up of the pen and laying the pen down; the act of suspension itself can take place only within the *muchas veces*, within the prologically generated history of prological attempts. As we read the prologue, we are not alerted—as we are when we read scriptible narratives—to the process of the prologue's being written; because it is impossible to write the prologue, the reader sees the prologue as it hovers in suspension, "not-written." The prologue's content is neither actual (lisible) nor ideal (scriptible) but transcendental (inscriptible).[8]

---

which it first becomes possible to unite each prologue with its epilogue. When the (textual) prologue of the prologuist is combined with the (a posteriori) epilogue of the reader, when the reading act has been completed prospectively and retrospectively, there comes to the fore, in the purely theoretical, descriptive order, a temporality that suspends empirical time. This is the ecstatic time suggested by the prologuist in the phrase *y estando una suspenso:* he writes from within this ecstasis, the externality anterior to beginning and end.

8. As I will argue later, the prologuist's words, "Many times I took up my pen to write it, and many I laid it down again, not knowing what to write," typify the prologue to *Don Quixote* and the novel as a whole as a *literary* project. In this sentence Cervantes captures what Maurice Blanchot has called the "anomaly which is the essence of literary activity": The writer "has no talent until he has written, but he needs talent in order to write" ("Literature and the Right to Death," in *G*, 23). The complexity of this anomaly was first raised by Hegel, and Blanchot summarizes Hegel's description of work (and of literary creativity) as found in *Phenomenology of Spirit:*

> The writer only finds himself, only realizes himself, through his work; before his work exists, not only does he not know who he is, but he is nothing. He only exists as a function of the work; but then how can the work exist? ... If he does not see his work before him as a project already completely formed, how can he make it the conscious end of his conscious acts? But if the work is already present in its entirety in his mind, and if this presence is the essence of the work ... why would he realize it any further? Either: as an interior project it is everything it will ever be ... and so [the author] will leave it to lie there in its twilight ...

Cervantes' prologue implies a multiplicity of its prior instances, which, having all failed, furnish a ghost of a historical tradition, an *irreal* number of beginnings suspended in an ontological limbo. The condition in which any actual prologue comes into existence only against the backdrop of previous prologues suggests a *prological imperative:* the actual prologue exists in relation to a prological postulate; the real prologue exists in the shadow of an Idea of Prologue. Thus Cervantes postulates a unique condition of writing: his prologue mediates the relation between the real prologue, which we (currently) read, and the ideal Prologue, which the prologuist (perpetually) desires to compose.

This relation, which romanticism called "transcendental," inhabits neither the real nor the ideal realm but is lodged in the sphere between the two. Cervantes' prologue dwells in the transcendental sphere of "one of these times." Although set down on paper, every prologue is still identified as "one" of these "times"; while no longer ideal, it is not actual either, for it is not completely separated from "these times." The writing of the prologue, described in the passage above as the taking up of the pen and as the laying down of the pen, is the pure activity of writing—without a subject and without an object, without beginning or end. The transcendental prologue is the writing, the sustaining, of this suspended posture.

This is not to say that the prologue that we can read in Cervantes' book is the transcendental prologue *itself.* Rather, the physically available text describes the act of writing in which alone this infinite pos-

---

without writing it—but then he won't ever write, he won't be a writer. Or: realizing that the work cannot be planned, but only carried out ... he will begin to write, but starting from nothing and with nothing in mind—like a nothingness working in nothingness, to borrow an expression of Hegel's. ("Literature and the Right to Death," in *G,* 24)

Referring to Blanchot's account of Hegel, Andrzej Warminski extends this analysis of writing to the activity of *reading* and applies this new reading to Hegel's account of creativity ("Dreadful Reading: Blanchot on Hegel," *Yale French Studies,* LXIX [1985], 267–75). In the case of both writing and reading, Warminski proposes, Blanchot finds a way of bypassing the circular anomaly described by Hegel, by "rewriting Hegel in another place" and under "another negative" where something else is set to take place (*avoir lieu*) (269). This other place figures in Cervantes' prologue as the transcendental sphere in which the prologue and the prologuist become actual, not before, and not after, but only *in and during the act of their writing.* The dissolution of the author and the work, discussed later in the chapter, confirms the romantic, unconscious nature of the "other place" in which literary activity has its origin.

ture between the real and the ideal, which is a matter of writing itself, can be brought to presence. Cervantes' transcendental prologue is not a set of items, all of the same category, from which the writer draws one in order to actualize it; rather, to each attempt to write a prologue there corresponds this item's "being-a-prologue," which is not this prologue's ideal form but its identity, its prological self. The prologue's being a prologue, however, cannot be objectivized as reading matter, nor can it be controlled by the subject. The transcendental nature of the prologue is this prologue's being its own subject, *this prologue('s) writing itself.*

In this sense, Cervantes' prologue may be called "a prologue about/of a prologue" (*un prólogo del prólogo*), as Jean Canavaggio proposes.[9] Still, Canavaggio's term cannot be interpreted in the familiar models of the objective and subjective genitive, of exemplarity (this is the prologue of all prologues, the *shir hashirim*), or of meta-prologue. The relation in question cannot be produced objectively, as a concrete piece of writing, or subjectively, as the product of the writing subject, because the transcendental prologue both follows and precedes the subject's intentional acts. This is why the prologuist can neither write the prologue nor desist from writing it; he *cannot but* produce it, although, he assures us, he still *intends* to produce it. He is, then, simultaneously engaged in writing (intending to write) and free from it. He is, simply, an "idle prologuist" (the prologuist addresses his audience with the phrase "Idle reader!"). The writer offends the court, as Socrates did, both *ekon* and *akon,* voluntarily *and* involuntarily; he intends and dis-intends his work at the same time; he is a writer *manqué.*[10]

The prological condition defines the characteristic power of Cervantine irony. To apply the common notion of irony—which has been shaped by the Enlightenment—to the prologue's plural origin would impoverish the complexity of the phenomenon. The Enlightenment's antiphrastic theory of irony (saying the opposite of what one means) presupposes a single logical core and follows a simple logic of opposites. The intended meaning can be easily recovered and the extent of irony adequately measured. In the final analysis, the speaker always speaks *una voce,* clearly, rather than *suspenso.*

9. Jean Canavaggio, "Cervantes en primera persona," *Journal of Hispanic Philology,* II (1977), 35–44.

10. Friedrich Schlegel (Critical Fragment 23): "Every good poem must be wholly intentional and wholly instinctive. This is how it becomes ideal" (*F,* 145).

Cervantes' prologue belongs to romantic irony. The prologue's origin offers the possibility that, while irony is actually present, its original thought will remain inaccessible and unnameable, although quite concrete in its effects. In other words, we will forever remain unable to gauge the ironic distance from which the actual prologue is uttered: we will laugh *without knowing the reason* for the laughter. One can see how inadequate antiphrastic theory of irony is to the multiplicity opened up by Cervantes. For how does one decipher an irony that refers, not to a decidability between truth and lie, but, instead, to a *multiple, undecidable ground*?

Indeed, how can the ground remain at all if it oscillates with undecidability? Consequently, the plurality of the prologue's origin creates an odd communicative situation: many instances (*muchas veces*) determine, *in their multiplicity*, a multiple *meaning* of the single instance, and they determine it as suspended and incomplete (*y estando una suspenso*). The ironic suspension radically affects the meaning of the category of "meaning" by giving it two denotations. Here a felicitous English pun helps illustrate the point with more precision. In the first sense, *meaning* refers to "semantic content," as in the question "What do you mean?" In the second sense, *meaning* refers to "intention," as in the sentence "I did not mean to hurt you." In Cervantine irony both senses arise equiprimordially. The prologue means (intends) to convey a meaning (semantic content). Meaning as intention and meaning as semantic content emerge and "mean" in a relation of mutually originating difference. As long as Cervantes means (intends) to convey his meaning, he has not conveyed it *yet*, and as soon as the meaning (semantic content) has been conveyed, the intention behind this content has disappeared—semantic content can be delivered only in *the absence of the intention.*

The essence of this operation lies, not in temporal succession, but in what I would like to call *speculative involution* of the intentional and the semantic moments, in the undecidable co-presence of *y estando una suspenso*. This involution of meaning and intention resembles in its structure the ironic formula of Socrates, "I know that I do not know." As Louis Marin perceptively observes, Socrates' famous declaration is empty of positive content, for the knowledge it produces is the infinite, empty knowledge of one's ignorance.[11] In Cervantes'

---

11. Louis Marin, "On the Interpretation of Ordinary Language: A Parable of Pascal," in *Textual Strategies: Perspectives in Post-Structuralist Criticism*, ed. Josué V. Harari (Ithaca, 1979), 239.

involution, meaning is separated from intention so that the single instance of semantic meaning is now set adrift: it refers back to an intended meaning, but this specific intention can no longer be retrieved. This is the ironic condition of Cervantine "plural" meaning.

Cervantes' prologue has its origin in a nonspecific past of untraceable moments. If the prologue comes to us from *muchas veces*, from a plurality of beginnings, can one speak of origin*ality*? Can a *multiple* origin remain *original*? To understand the proximate involution of Cervantine origin, we must closely examine a passage from the prologue: "But I could not counteract Nature's law that everything shall beget its like; and what, then, could this sterile, uncultivated wit of mine beget but the story of a dry, shriveled, eccentric offspring?" (*DQ*, 9). The passage discusses the mechanism of similarity. On the face of it, the mechanism appears quite simple: according to "Nature's law [*orden de naturaleza*] . . . everything shall beget its like [*cada cosa engendra su semejante*]." Read *speculatively*, however, the phrase discloses an intriguing double bind: "Nature's law" legislates, not about one operation—resemblance—but about two operations—resemblance *and* production (begetting). In this double proposal, both operations occur simultaneously: similarity operates by begetting, and what is thus begotten is similar to the original.

We must be even more precise. The relation is circular: similarity begets similarity—it can only produce the same (*su semejante*); and infinite—only similarity identifies the product *as* product (of begetting). Proximate involution works to the fullest extent: the originating relation of begetting produces a replica; it duplicates itself, as a creative process, in similarity. Cervantes' mimetic concept of origin stands under the same law of proximate involution that controls intention and meaning.

It would be quite futile to resist this circularity. Similarity is an integral part of begetting, for the product of begetting is similar to that which has begotten it. Hence, if begetting is thought of as a process that does not involve similarity, then the product will disappear as a product similar to the original. The work will no longer resemble the original and will no longer be traceable to an originating instance. In a sense, this would be a desirable situation, to the extent that originality means "being unlike anything else that has come before." This is the avant-gardiste theory of artistic production. But the double bind cannot be overcome with the simple claim that the original does not belong to any recognizable tradition. For the word *originality* and the rhetoric of originality based on it hark back to origin as their rationale, even if this origin is explicitly repudiated. The sense of originality as a unique and unprecedented quality functions in constitutive proximity to the antecedent "origin" that it seeks to deny. Originality irrevocably links the product to its origin. Little is gained by negating originality altogether, for then one must be "unoriginal." Even when avant-gardiste art clarifies its position and says that it is original in the sense that it originates itself, it only repeats the sense of origin that Cervantes has discovered as the pure relation in origin itself, as the duality by which origin relates (to) itself.

This is why affirming the speculative circularity of mimesis is none too helpful, either. For, given free rein, transcendental mimesis, as the origin of origin, will not only cause the product to lose its *unmediated* relation to origin but will also take the work away from the begetting author, who will now cease to be recognized in his work (by his genetically encoded features, his unique style). And if the author is no longer recognizable in his work, then he will lose his character as authority, his *auctoritas* over the work. Here the crisis of originality escalates into a fundamental questioning. Can the work *remain a work* in the absence of its author? What name can denote, in the new situation, the "thing" that is not an object—for it lacks its (productive) subject—and not a relative similar to other products? Can the book, as orphan, at all *remain*?

This disconcerting question is taken up in the prologuist's conversation with the friend. We may remember that the friend offers his help at the very moment when the prologuist despairs of ever being able to write the prologue (*DQ*, 9). As the following analysis of the friend's exposition will hope to demonstrate, the logic of proximate involution, of infinite irony, lies at the heart of Cervantes' conception of originality.

The prologuist asks the friend to help him define the poetics suitable to writing an original novel. The friend offers essentially one remedy for the four difficulties that stand in the prologuist's way. The problems of writing the dedicatory sonnets that open a literary work, of writing the "references in the margin to the books and authors from whom . . . [he] take[s] the maxims and sayings" (*DQ*, 11), of writing the "annotations at the end of the book" (*DQ*, 12), and of writing the "references to authors" (*DQ*, 12) that the prologuist needs for his book are all solved with the help of quotations from classical authors chosen indiscriminately, and somewhat mechanically, to satisfy the literary protocol of the day.

The Genre of Involution in Don Quixote / 79

The friend's advice carries an important implication. Each of the prologuist's inventions has a classical predecessor, one by definition more impressive and sublime than anything the prologuist could ever hope to produce. In quotation, or in intentional imitation, literature is ruled by classical *topoi*. The friend makes it perfectly clear that a writer can attain originality only because there have been voices speaking in the literary past. At the same time, however, it becomes clear that an original source can be *nothing but* a source, an occasion for quotation. The solution lies in total quotation, in *quotas*. The prologuist faces the tragic condition of speech, the proximate involution, in the possibility that his own words *are not* his own.

It would be futile to resist this condition by avoiding all quotation. The prologuist valiantly declares: "Of all this there will be nothing in my book, for I have nothing to quote in the margin or to note at the end" (*DQ*, 10). Apparently the lack of adequate erudition would be the prologuist's natural ally—ignorant of authorities, he cannot quote any. But he finishes the sentence with the following words: "*and still less do I know what authors I follow in it*" (*DQ*, 10; italics mine). The inability to quote authorities is not a result of ignorance; rather, the prologuist realizes that whatever heights (or lows) of naïve originality or unpolished creativity he summons, he will still be unwittingly quoting other authors. The prologuist is doomed. Whatever he says will have already been said by the great authors from the past. Moreover, he will never know *whether his words repeat an old phrase or are his own*; his mouth speaks with many voices. A Cervantine author, unaware of his sources, still, in some sense, *quotes* these unknown sources. The quotation of unknown content is not, strictly speaking, a quotation; and if it is, then the author cannot put quotation marks around his content with adequate precision and ethical responsibility, for he does not know what is and what is not quoted. A Cervantine quotation escapes both the conscious and the unconscious moments. Indeed, the very ability to use language may be a function of quotation. Anticipating the poetics of repetition in Flaubert and Joyce, Cervantes claims that when we speak we are quoting language as a system that allows us to speak. Only within such an enabling structure can we come to say something in intentional language, but at the same time, every act of speech is marked by the totality of language; this totality escapes the intentionality of the speaking subject.

In other words, the enabling system itself cannot be uttered in the intentional modality. For Cervantes, the source (language as enabling system) is *both* inaccessible to conscious quotation *and* also already, excessively, nothing but a quotation. Even when he speaks his own words, the original author is only *quoting* (even himself). Cervantes' awareness of this condition is perhaps his most impressive creative accomplishment. He seeks to capture this original relation of language, to express language *as such* speaking. It is for his conception of writing as the unity of the intentional and the unintentional modalities that the romantics came to recognize Cervantes as a transcendental poet, a *novelist*.

The relation between the original source and its quotation is thus the work of speculative involution. If the pristine originality of a source text (of an *auctoritas*) is available only as a *quoted* source, how can one distinguish the original source of quotation *before* it is quoted from the source *as* quotation, in order to prevent the systematic conversion of source into quotation? *Don Quixote* explores the issue of originality in general, as well as the issue of its own originality, in the light of the possibility that the original source can be first apprehended, *qua* source (*fons, origo*), only in the speculative involution of source into quotation, in the daimonic synthesis of intention and instinct.

The same infinite involution characterizes the manner in which the prologuist directly turns to the reader. We read the first words of the prologue: "Idle reader [*Desocupado lector*]: you may believe me, without my having to swear [*sin juramento me podrás creer*]" (*DQ*, 9). The speaking situation resembles the address of the Licentiate; it leads one to assume that the speaker already exists and that the listener is ready for the message: "I am an author; you are a reader—let me introduce you to my book." But the prologuist's opening also contains a more rigorous perusal, one that follows the King's poetics: the speaker makes sure that the persons of the audience are set in place—his formula, "idle reader," assigns to the reader *his identity and role* as a reader.

But if the phrase is read with Cervantine irony as it has been developed in the prologue, the relation between the speaker and the listener will appear far removed from the speech of the Licentiate and of the King, far removed from the communicative situation described by the linguistic models of addressee, addressor, message, and code. These models are designed to assure the uninterrupted flow of information or to assert the position of power, and they describe the conditions under which these goals can be best realized. Cervantes pursues an entirely different goal. For him the communicative situation is not a functional input/output operation designed to accomplish a clearly defined goal but a configuration in which the total meaningfulness of speech as such comes to presence. Cervantes assumes that if two people are to speak to each other they must first understand that they indeed are going to participate in a communicative situation. In other words, they must acknowledge the existence of something in virtue of which their encounter, their "being together in this place and at this time," is a communicative encounter in the first place.

This prior understanding and initial agreement, what Jean-Jacques Rousseau has called "the original contract," are anterior to any contractual agreement into which the two parties enter during the course of negotiations. Indeed, any intentional contractual agreement can be signed and ratified only because the two parties have initially agreed to understand themselves as potential participants in a situation that could lead to communication. This first understanding, however, cannot be captured on paper, accepted, or revoked, for it denotes the minimal condition of common humanity under which agreement and disagreement can begin to make sense. This is also the reasoning of Immanuel Kant in his preliminary remarks in *Critique of Judgment;* if the judgment of taste, as subjective, produces disagreement among different individuals, this disagreement itself implies a prior condition of fundamental community (*sensus communis*) in whose light alone we can comprehend our adversary's disagreement in the first place. The prologuist's word *idle* (*desocupado*) may be an indication of this fundamental disposition of suspended intentionality as the *literary* condition of language that makes it possible for the reader and the prologuist to engage in communication.

It is to this prior condition that Cervantes refers in the appeal to the reader: "You may believe me, without my having to swear." The understanding that already obtains between Cervantes and his reader does not require a notarial, juridical approval by oath. The situation of anterior understanding is already established in the fundamental sense described above. No legal convention, no delegated authority, and no official ceremony can institute or solemnize this original contract. By refusing to swear, to perform a conventional ritual, the author points to a ground that antedates conventional uses of authority, language, and law.

It is in this original precommunicative condition that Cervantes' prologue positions the "idle reader." As "pro-logos," it enacts a *pre*-positioning, the original agreement in which the activity of communication itself becomes comprehensible. The *yo* of the prologuist and the *tú* of the reader establish a relation of persons outside of the dialogical positioning described by linguistic models; the original condition antedates the communicative protocol of the *polis*. In this original address, the speaking positions cannot be unproblematically objectivized as addressor and addressee (as linguistic pragmatics attempts to do in the formula "since I speak to you, you must be, by definition, a listener"). Besides its implicit coercive moment, such description becomes untenable because it quickly sinks in the infinite regress: it requires a next remove of objective distance that itself would not belong to the communicative situation, and so on. And while in principle such regressive meta-description is possible, it rests a priori on the original level proposed by Rousseau and Kant.[12]

Similarly, the periphrastic concept of ironic dissimulation cannot function in this model, for it would presuppose that the speakers are masters of the communicative contract and that they freely use lan-

---

12. As Jacques Derrida shows in his discussion of Montaigne's essay "On Friendship" ("The Politics of Friendship," *Journal of Philosophy, Law and Society*, LXXXV [1988], 632–44), this anterior, precontractual understanding itself is not free from the dangers of the infinite regress, of the *abyss*. The passage deserves additional comment. Derrida's exposition on friendship rests on themes that are of essential importance to the present discussion of Cervantine address. First, friendship requires that one's friends be addressed as "friends," in the name of an anterior bond; second, as I will make it clear in the following pages, the appeal to friendship is structurally bound to an infinite function of apostrophe; third, the anterior bond can only be expressed in the manner of quotation. To combine the three moments: it is remarkably suggestive that Cervantes' prologue does indeed resort to the elusive "friend" who appears in the suspended moment of transcendental inactivity. The reader may obtain a sense of these linkages and their relevance to the romantic "origin" from the following commentary by Derrida:

> But the apostrophe "O my friends" turns also toward the past. It recalls, it makes a sign toward that which must be supposed so as to let oneself be understood, if only in the nonapophantic form of prayer. You have *already* shown me this minimal friendship, this preliminary consent without which you would not understand me, would not listen to my appeal.... Without this absolute past, I could not, for my part, have addressed myself to you in this way. We would not be together in a sort of minimal community—but one which is also incommensurable with any other—speaking the same language or praying for translation within the horizon of the same language, even were it so as to manifest a disagreement, if a *sort* of friendship had not already been sealed before any other contract: a friendship prior to friendships, an ineffaceable, fundamental, and bottomless friendship, the one that draws its breath in the sharing of a language (past or to come) and in the being-together that any allocution supposes, including a declaration of war. (636—Derrida's italics)

guage to manipulate intentionality—in this case, to speak seriously. Since here it is language itself that speaks, irony appears, not as dissimulation by language users, but as the very condition of communication.

The prologuist's address to the reader lays the foundation for the voices that speak in the novel as a whole. To describe this foundation in more detail, it is necessary to expand the above interpretation of the prologuist's address to the reader. The explanation of Cervantes' notion of language with the help of preromantic theories of origin in Rousseau and Kant invites an inquiry into the fate and development of the concept of origin after Kantian philosophy underwent a romantic turn. For Kant and Rousseau, the "original contract," although undemonstrable, provided the unshakable foundation for critical philosophy. Romanticism, on the other hand, came to understand the common ground, not as a firm (albeit hidden) condition, but as reflection, as "romanticization." This operation differs from the Kantian solution in that it does not reach back to grounding "sufficient reasons" or to "conditions of possibility" but establishes origin in the infinity of reflection. This infinity follows a mode of operation that Friedrich Schlegel has called "transcendental poetry" (Athenaeum Fragment 238). The essence of this kind of poetry "lies in the relation between the real and the ideal" (F, 195); this poetry hovers "at the midpoint between the portrayed and the portrayer, free of all real and ideal self-interest, on the wings of poetic reflection, and can raise that reflection again and again to a higher power, can multiply it in an endless succession of mirrors.... The romantic kind of poetry is the only one that is more than a kind, that is, as it were, poetry itself" (Athenaeum Fragment 116—F, 175–76). The extension of the present argument concerning origin to the romantic notion of origin as reflection appears particularly justified if it is remembered that Cervantes earned the highest respect in early German romanticism as one of the three "novelists," as one of the great *romantic* authors.[13] The general question now is, How is reflective origin related to the actual form and structure of the romantic novel insofar as this novel, *Don Quixote*, for instance, is a *Roman*?

13. Friedrich Schlegel writes in "The Letter on the Novel": "This is where I look for and find the Romantic—in the older moderns, in Shakespeare, Cervantes, in Italian poetry" (*DP*, 101). For a summary of the relation between romanticism, the novel, and irony, see Lowry Nelson, Jr., "Romantic Irony and Cervantes," in *Romantic Irony*, ed. Frederick Garber (Budapest, 1988), 15–32.

The reflective relation within origin—or reflection as the original relation—is based on romantic irony understood as speculative involution. We can detect the involution in the prologuist's turn to the reader, in which the "original contract" is being established as the infinite transcendental relation that opens up the possibility of communication. In this transcendental infinity, language itself speaks, and this speech of speech ironically escapes the speaking subject.

The specificity of Cervantine origin comes to the fore in the prologuist's ironic turn to the reader. German romantics (above all Friedrich Schlegel) redefined irony in terms of *parabasis*, in opposition to neoclassical (French—Voltaire, and English—Swift) theories of irony as *antiphrasis*, or verbal dissimulation.[14] Of immediate interest is Schlegel's conception of *parabasis* as the vehicle of romantic irony: "Die Ironie ist eine permanente Parekbase."[15] In its "permanence," parabasis destroys classical theater's distinction between the body of the play and the occasional asides. In a sense, only the *-basis* remains, since the first turn can no longer be retrieved. Schlegel implies that, in the course (in the *coursing*) of these turns and re-turns, the position of the author is constructed as the point, or the *trace*, of coincidence that determines each new turn as an identifiable *re*-turn.[16] I would like to propose that Schlegel's "permanent parabasis" generates the endless succession of turns and returns that neither resolves into a simple address to the reader nor constitutes a stable condition like "text" because this parabasis enters into speculative involution with the traditional apostrophe.

The prologuist turns to the reader: "Idle reader" [*Desocupado lector*]. The phrase is an apostrophe, an invocation to a thing or person.[17]

14. Ernst Behler, "The Theory of Irony in German Romanticism" in *Romantic Irony*, ed. Garber, 53). See also Norman Knox, Introduction to *the Word "Irony" and Its Context, 1500–1755* (Durham, 1961).

15. Friedrich Schlegel, *Philosophische Lehrjahre, 1796–1806*, ed. Ernst Behler (Munich, 1963), Vol. XVIII of *Kritische Friedrich-Schlegel-Ausgabe*, ed. Ernst Behler in cooperation with Jean-Jacques Anstett and Hans Eichner. According to the *Oxford English Dictionary*: "Parabasis: [Gk *parabasis* lit. a going aside, digression, stepping forward, fr. *parabainein* to go aside, step forward. In ancient Greek comedy, a part sung by the chorus, addressed to the audience in the poet's name, and unconnected with the action of the drama]"

16. In Behler's words, Schlegel's permanent parabasis strategically determines the "emergence of the author from his work certainly in the broadest sense" ("The Theory of Irony in German Romanticism," in *Romantic Irony*, ed. Garber, 61).

17. "Apostrophe: [L, fr. Gk *apostrophe*, lit. act of turning away, fr. *apostrophein* to turn away, fr. *apo* + *strephein* to turn—more at STROPHE]: the addressing of a usu. absent person or a usu. personified thing rhetorically <Carlyle's 'O Liberty, what things are done in thy name!' is an example of———>" (*Webster's New Collegiate Dictionary*).

But the phrase may also function as a parabasis, in which case it would be interrupting some *other* utterance in order to produce this one. The speculative involution of the two operations generates an infinite turn to the reader. As a "turning away," apostrophe shares with parabasis the moment of interrupting one activity in order to engage in another. In addition, both operations share an exclusionary moment, the absent person in apostrophe and the exclusion of one activity in parabasis. Cervantes' rhetoric exploits this exclusionary moment to construct the infinite irony of the prological address.

Both devices turn to and against each other in the grip of speculative involution. In other words, Cervantes appends apostrophe to parabasis and coerces parabasis to engage apostrophe—an *agon* of rhetorical terms that neither (parabasically) disrupts the course of the "play" nor (apostrophically) addresses the "absent thing or person." The involution offers a minimal operation in which the "turning away" takes place *between* the two rhetorical terms themselves. In this internal strife, apostrophe asserts itself by amputating the preceding text essential in the operation of parabasis: with no text preceding it, apostrophe would have a *first* turn at speaking. In *its turn,* parabasis seeks to annul apostrophe's constitutive primary: it reinserts apostrophe into an anterior textual continuum so that a parabasic aside becomes possible. The position of the prologuist is generated according to the logic of this struggle in the original relating; his address is spoken, again, from within the rhetorically inarticulate, transcendental *y estando una suspenso.*

The prologue yields the infinity of speculative involution, in keeping with Canavaggio's formula *un prólogo del prólogo.* This involution is essential to the novel's romantic affinities, for the romantic original relation is a reflection. At this point I will examine the importance of the reflective relation of involution to *Don Quixote*'s narrative structure.

In order to see how Cervantine origin affects the novel in the very manner of its telling, it is necessary to discuss, however briefly, the novel's narrative technique. *Don Quixote* is narrated by several authors: criticism speaks of *el primer autor* (Cide Hamete Benengeli—the *historiador arábigo*), *el segundo autor* (the first-person editor—the avid reader who picks up every scrap of paper found on the street), and the translator—the Morisco boy.

We will begin the analysis of involution in Cervantes' narrative technique by examining the relation between the two main methods of narration used in the novel. On the evidence of the novel's fictitious *deposé*, the narrative is composed by editing (done by Benengeli, the "segundo autor") and translation (done by the Morisco boy). The two techniques are affected by speculative involution in a most intimate way.

Let us first look at translation. Translation is important for *Don Quixote* for several reasons. First, we must consider the role of the Morisco boy, who translates the entire text as a member of the novel's editorial board and who, in one of the parabases (*DQ*, 66-67), translates an Arabic manuscript for the distressed editor, allowing him to finish the story of Don Quixote's encounter with the Biscayan. In addition, we must also consider the strictly *literary* relation between Cervantes' novel and its subsequent translations. Finally, we must consider translation as the transcendental operation in which the novel hovers between truth and fiction, between origin and destination, between the real and the ideal.

Don Quixote is a translation from an Arabic original.[18] The relevant passage opens Chapter 44 in Book II:

> Dicen que en el proprio original desta historia se lee que llegando Cide Hamete a escribir este capítulo, no le tradujo su intérprete . . . como él le habia escrito, que fue un modo de queja que tuvo el moro de sí mismo, por haber tomado entre manos una historia tan seca y tan limitada como esta de don Quijote.

As John Weiger observes in his analysis of the passage, the reader learns here that "the interpreter failed to translate" something and that "the failure becomes apparent *when one reads the original.*"[19]

---

18. For mysterious reasons this point has not attracted much interest in Cervantes criticism. The *hermeneutic* fact that *Don Quixote* is a translation from Arabic must bring into play an added dimension to any treatment of Cervantes' novel as a parodic text. If the original text was written in Arabic, then its parodic intent acquires distinctly political, ideological, and, as Eugene Vance says, "commemorative" overtones ("Roland and the Poetics of Memory," in *Textual Strategies*, ed. Harari, 374–403). The invisible Arabic original may be viewed here as a vitriolic attack, an act of revenge by the Arab world—uttered by Cervantes—on the Spanish and European literary commemoration of the entire period of the Reconquista, beginning with the defeat of Charlemagne at Roncesvalles in 778 and ending with the destruction of the Caliphate of Cordoba and the taking of Granada in 1492. *Don Quixote* sings, for Arabs, what the *Chanson de Roland* sang for Europeans, the end of a grand Arab era in the Iberian Peninsula.

19. John G. Weiger, "The Prologuist: The Extratextual Authorial Voice in *Don Quixote*," *Bulletin of Hispanic Studies*, LXV (1988), 131 (Weiger's italics), hereinafter cited parenthetically by page number in the text. I am indebted for some of my points,

Yet one only has to glance at the different versions of this sentence, in Smollett, Ormsby, Ozell, and Putnam, to begin to suspect that the passage *ironically* involutes translation and interpretation.

> They say that in the true original of this history, as Cide Hamete wrote this chapter—which his interpreter did not translate as he wrote it—there was a kind of complaint the Moor made against himself for having taken in hand a story so dry and of so little variety as this one about Don Quixote. (Ormsby)

> We have it from the traditional Account of this History, that there is a manifest Difference between the translation and the *Arabick* in the beginning of this Chapter; *Cid Hamet* having in the Original taken an Occasion of criticizing on himself, for undertaking so dry and limited a Subject which must confine him to the bare History of Don *Quixote* and *Sancho*. (Ozell)

> They say that in the original version of the history it is stated that the interpreter did not translate the present chapter as Cide Hamete had written it ... owing to a kind of grudge that the Moor had against himself for having undertaken a story so dry and limited in scope as is this one of Don Quixote. (Putnam)

> The original of the history, it is said, relates that the interpreter did not translate this chapter as it had been written by Cid Hamet Benengeli, who bewails his fate in having undertaken such a dry and confined history as that of Don Quixote. (Smollett)

> Mówią, że w pierwotnym oryginale tej powieści stoi, iż rozdział ten, napisany przez Sidi Hameta, nie został wiernie przełożony przez tłumacza, a była to jakby skarga skierowana przez Maura przeciw samemu sobie, że podjął się napisania historii tak suchej i ograniczonej jedynie do Don Kichota. (a Polish translation)[20]

The semantic pliability of the very *passus* that speaks about translation and its inaccuracies discloses the ironic dimension of translation

---

both material and methodological, to this splendid article. Weiger's work on and continuing attention to the nature and (hypothetical) hierarchies of the voices in *Don Quixote*, in this essay and in other pronouncements as well, deserve the credit for initiating an entirely new and extremely promising approach to Cervantes.

20. *DQ*, 661–62. *Don Quixote,* trans. John Ozell (New York, 1967), 623. *The Ingenious Gentleman: Don Quixote de La Mancha,* trans. Samuel Putnam (2 vols.; New York, 1949), II, 788. *Don Quixote de la Mancha,* trans. Tobias George Smollett (London, 1986), 668. *Don Quixote,* trans. Anna Ludwika Czerny and Zygmunt Czerny (2 vols.; Warsaw, 1986), II, 269; no English translation of this translation is currently available.

as precisely interpretation.[21] In view of the ironic nature of translation, not only will different translations deliver a different meaning, but the meaning of a translation can be decided only by an additional ply of interpretation/translation.

This is to say that translation and interpretation occur *at the same time*, transcendentally, in a meta-relation (*una traducción de la traducción*). This meta-relation does not simply proliferate possible denotations but repeats the operation of translation itself in order to produce an interpretation. Consequently (or in other words), the only way in which the reader can decide whether he is reading the original work or its translation will be on the basis of an interpretation of translation and/or on the basis of a translation of an interpretation.

The ironic involution has important consequences for the hermeneutics of *Don Quixote*. Not only are all translations interpretations, but we will never know whether, on any given occasion, we are interpreting or *merely* translating. Hence the historical translations of *Don Quixote* continue the Morisco's work of translation, for the novel's original story can never be translated—it can only exist, *y estando una suspenso*, in translation. Cervantes' speculative involution realizes Friedrich Schlegel's permanent parabasis as translation without term.

It is in this sense that the historical translations of *Don Quixote* (preromantic—Smollett, and romantic—Tieck) may be defined as responses to the transcendental ancestor, to the original text, which is, infinitely, the origin of its translations. This interpretation of the passage leads to the conclusion that Cervantes' novel exists in endless translation: translation *shifts the novel to an origin* without ever translating it there. The incomplete nature of translation makes this shift *transcendental* in the rigorous sense given to the word by the romantics. According to this understanding, the transcendental task of the translator—what Walter Benjamin calls *die Aufgabe des Übersetzers*—does not consist in translating the text from the source language into the target language; rather, the translator must see to it that the work exists exclusively in and as translation, where translation is understood dynamically, as constant transfer, as a hovering

21. At II, 5, we find an intermediate variant of this relation. The translator, speaking directly to the reader, disagrees with the Arabic author as to the originality of a fragment: "The translator of this history, when he comes to write this fifth chapter, says that he considers it apocryphal, because in it Sancho Panza speaks in a style unlike that which might have been expected from his limited intelligence" (*DQ*, 447).

on the wings of translation (reflection) between the real and the ideal.[22]

The analysis must go even further. Translation is, in the case of *Don Quixote*, quite literally the only method of writing and reading the novel. In Cervantine translation the Spanish text not only occurs synchronically with the original Arabic production, it is, indeed, the *Doppelgänger* of the original text. As soon as the original Arabic text is written, it must be translated; translation is a necessary companion of writing made, by the mechanism of involution, proximate to this activity. Speculative involution shows original writing to be a matter of translation; in the loop of composition and translation the priority of either function cannot be established. This is why the technique of the novel's production is so prominent in the moment of parabasis at I, 8–9, when the novel ceases to exist, suspended between two chapters, only to reappear in the mouth of the Morisco *interpreter* (translator—English again felicitously captures the connection developed here); this is also why in the parabasis at II, 44 the passage that debates the precision of the novel's translation yields divergent translations by the historical translators. For the objective of Cervantine translation is not to render faithfully a semantic content but to make present the infinite occurrence of transcendental origination that, as transcendental, differs from both ideal conception and actual completion.

The nature of Cervantes' novel as a translation of an Arabic original, as it confirms our earlier analyses, would seem to preempt all dreams of originality expressed by the prologuist. However, the issue is not to be dismissed so hastily. The infinite involution of writing and translation resembles the infinite involution of source into re-source, which we have seen in the prologuist's conversation with the friend. Infinite involution gives *Don Quixote*'s parodic intent its distinctive meaning.

Don Quixote has come into existence for the sole purpose of destroying chivalric romances; the friend says that the book "is, from beginning to end, an attack upon the books of chivalry" (*DQ*, 13). However, as it remains focused on *Don Quixote*'s parodic enterprise,

---

22. Walter Benjamin, "The Task of the Translator," in *Illuminations: Essays and Reflections*, ed. Hannah Arendt, trans. Harry Zohn (New York, 1969), 69–82. Here another observation is in order. The passage says about translation that "no le tradujo su intérprete como él le habia escrito." The text's interpreter commits perjury with impunity because, in Cervantes' transcendental world, no authority remains, in the sense that no authoritative, final translation can ever be produced.

Cervantes criticism has overlooked other important implications of this declaration. The technique for the execution of the plan considerably departs from the declared intention.

This is to say that the friend's advice on how to parody chivalric romances also offers one of literature's first proposals for a distinct, personal *style*. The friend tells the prologuist "merely [to] take care that your sentences flow musically, pleasantly, and plainly, with clear, proper, and well-placed words, setting forth your purpose to the best of your power, and putting your ideas intelligibly, without confusion or obscurity" (*DQ*, 13). The friend defines literature as the art of "well-placed words," of *le mot juste*, the art of language for its own sake. Thus Cervantes' parodic work also fertilizes a larger project, the literature of the Enlightenment, of words "without confusion or obscurity," of ideas expressed "intelligibly." However, the friend quickly takes the book beyond rationalistic economy towards a romantic notion of literature. He leaves the book to purely formal devices, for the exhortation to "put . . . ideas intelligibly" provokes another question: Ideas *about what*? What is the new book?

The new book neither merely attacks other books in parody, nor classically imitates the first model, nor, as a stylistic exercise, promotes mere self-expression, nor yet naïvely spurns the tradition. The work "has only to avail itself of imitation in its writing, and the more perfect the imitation the better the work will be" (*DQ*, 13). *Imitation* is central. The term covers three meanings that constitute the three basic possibilities of mimesis. First, the classical sense: the novel should "avail itself of imitation in its writing"—it should imitate the classical predecessors. Second, the formal sense: the novel must follow linguistic propriety defined by the purists. Finally, the transcendental sense: mimesis lacks its model; it imitates *nothing*. By adopting transcendental mimesis, *Don Quixote* refines the friend's proposal (parody of chivalric romances) and overcomes the moment of production by an author (stylistic uniqueness); it applies proximate involution to representation (mimesis) itself. Cervantes' novel represents, or *originally presents*, representation as such, it presents *presence itself*, the "-self" of the "it-" in that which writes itself—*lo que se escribiere*.

The transcendental sense of mimesis as speculative involution differs significantly from the familiar sense of copying usually associated with the term. It is indeed remarkable that Cervantes successfully resisted this common understanding of the mimetic mechanism, which at the time of Spain's *Siglo de Oro* was enjoying revival in the friendly climate of neo-Aristotelian aesthetics. While the prevalent theory of mimesis promoted a simple static relation of imitation between the original and the copy, Cervantes saw in the mimetic mechanism a potential for infinite, transcendental mimesis in which the original imitates *only* itself.

Cervantes proposed, in what is perhaps his most important and lasting insight (one which it took the speculative powers of romanticism grappling with the Kantian aftermath to understand and formulate) that mimesis is an original relation par excellence. Instead of organizing the simple relation of resemblance between one object (model) and another (copy), Cervantine mimesis defines the field of interaction as a minimal relation of identity. What is resembled in this field is the self of resemblance, or, to use a different term, the identity of identity as such. The romantic novel, *Don Quixote*, for example, presents *self*-sameness, and Cervantes is concerned with the duality, the irony, of this essentially repetitive relation.

Romanticism seized on Cervantes' reformulation of mimesis as infinite reflection of sameness into itself because it understood that this mechanism was a particularly suitable tool for presenting its notion of transcendental reflection. In their discussion of Cervantes, romantics frequently observed his "divine irony," his spirit of "buffoonery," his skill in evoking the atmosphere of the fantastic, and his ability to sustain a sense of order in a work where chaos seemed to prevail. In these formulations romanticism was referring to the transcendental quality of Cervantes' work, to the hovering that entertains a tenuous relation to the real and, at the same time, never entirely escapes into the ideal, into romance, into fantasy. Cervantes' work is suspended in the middle, hovering "on the wings of reflection," in the realm of what Friedrich Schlegel calls "the poetic ideal" according to the following equation:

$$\text{The poetic ideal} = \frac{1}{0}\sqrt{\frac{FSM}{0}}\left(\frac{1}{0}\right) = \text{God}$$

which means, as Hans Eichner explains, "that the poetic ideal is the complete fusion and intermingling of the 'fantastic,' the 'sentimental,' and 'the mimic' " (*FS*, 65).[23]

---

23. Schlegel's consummate equation (Fragment 735 in his *Literary Notebooks*) is preceded by the following comment:

$$\frac{F}{0}, \frac{S}{0}, \frac{M}{0} \text{ are poetical Ideas [sind die poetischen Ideen]}.$$

We are here clearly in the presence of what the romantics understood as both the absolute origin and the origin of the (poetic) absolute.

Let us now apply this sense of the middle, of pure reflection concerned neither with the real nor with the ideal, to the mechanism of transcendental mimesis. We can see that this mimesis, rather than organizing the relations between two solid entities, enacts the pure movement of reflection, operates between the real and the ideal, engaging only the moment of resemblance, or of reflection, which minimally constitutes the mimetic interior. The infinite transaction does not imitate an object, a concrete substance; it imitates exclusively mimesis itself.

Don Quixote, a novel of/about all novels, redefines mimesis to bring this vibration to maximum pitch. To see the significance of this relation it should be assumed that it strategically controls the novel's narrative structure: it persists in the efforts of the narrators to ensure the text's fidelity to the original. Thus Cide Hamete Benengeli's Arabic text gives faithful account of Don Quixote's exploits, the Morisco boy carefully translates the Arabic original, and Cervantes' novel *Don Quixote* itself imitates Part I in Part II.[24] The internal tension occasioned by self-presentation describes the specific meaning of Cervantine mimesis: the novel's faithful imitation of "it" is controlled by the proximate involution of "it" into "it-self." "It" controls the relation of the Arabic original to the *verdadera historia,* "it" structures the translation of the Arabic original of the *verdadera historia,* and "it" supervises the process of editing the Spanish translation of the Arabic original of the *verdadera historia.* The "object" of imitation only comes into being by virtue of imitation; the movement of imitation is the only content of this mechanism. This "object" is not a solid point of origin anterior to the novel's narrative relay. "It" runs

---

24. In *The Order of Things* (New York, 1973), Michel Foucault notes the generative ability and power of the involution to produce literature:

> [Language] now possesses new powers, and powers peculiar to it alone. In the second part of the novel, Don Quixote meets characters who have read the first part of his story and recognize him, the real man, as the hero of the book. Cervantes's text turns back upon itself, thrusts itself back into its own density, and becomes the object of its own narrative.... Between the first and second parts of the novel, in the narrow gap between those two volumes, and by their power alone, Don Quixote has achieved his reality—a reality he owes to language alone, and which resides entirely inside the words. Don Quixote's truth is not in the relation of the words to the world but in that slender and constant relation woven between themselves by verbal signs.... Words have swallowed up their own nature as signs. (48)

through narrative communication as its in-articulate condition, a component of language itself beyond articulation. "It" is self-narration, self-relation.

The transcendental, ironic status of "it" is directly related to the question concerning the novel's speakers. In order to understand "it" in its complexity, we must turn to the narrators of Cervantes' novel and hear what "they say" about "it." At issue is *Don Quixote*'s famous, and much-debated, *es opinión* cluster, a narrative formula usually translated "so the story goes."[25] The formula appears in *Don Quixote* in interpolated tales and is used by the narrators of these tales to convey the story to the audience. The continuing debate over the cluster seeks to solve several questions raised by Cervantes scholarship. There is the specific question of Cervantes' reasons for adopting the formula; there is the question of the identity of the speakers who are implied in the cluster; and, finally, there is the general question whether Cervantes used the cluster with any measure of rigor, and if he did, to what end.

The present discussion addresses all three questions, but it does so from the point of view of the last problem, the question of Cervantes' consistent use of the cluster and of his reasons behind such use. This direction of inquiry coincides to a considerable degree with the analysis of the *es opinión* cluster offered by Weiger in "The Extratextual Authorial Voice." In his search for the origin of these utterances, Weiger concentrates on one special sub-group, those remarks which "originate at a level removed from the historian [Cide Hamete] himself" (130). One such mysterious instance of "them" appears at II, 44, a passage already analyzed. In the passage someone is hiding behind the phrase *dicen que*, "they say," and this "someone" informs the reader about an inaccuracy in the translation. Weiger seeks to identify the speaker of this and other similar phrases. He assumes that " 'they' are, in this instance, readers of the original Arabic work, and that they have communicated the discrepancy to our narrator" (131). Weiger postulates that an Arabic reading public was the first to read the original version of the novel and that this public first detected a discrepancy in the translation. That is, "they say" that there exists a discrepancy.

25. The cluster contains forms such as *es opinión, hay fama, dicen que, sólo le oyeron decir, digo que dicen, dicen que dijo, cuéntase (en la historia)*, and *a lo que se cree*.

Weiger speculates that in this passage (as well as in others)[26] "someone is responsible for the extraneous comments" (132), that is, for comments not uttered by any of the novel's three authorized speakers. This "someone" exists "wholly outside the boundaries that the reader has understood the text to have," outside, that is, the "work called *El ingenioso hidalgo* . . . by Cervantes, *within which* a narrator recounts the 'history' that, we soon learn, an Arabic historian has chronicled" (132; Weiger's italics). This "someone," Weiger proposes, stands above the level of the authors who produce the novel—the first author, the editor, and the Morisco boy.

For Weiger "There is only one individual," a textually represented speaker "*extraneous* to this configuration" who "stands apart from the text of the *verdadera historia* (as distinguished from the novel, complete with Prologue, Dedication, etc.) and who not only is in a position to insert an occasional marginal note to that *historia*, but who has been advised to do so: the prologuist" (132; Weiger's italics). The prologuist "is . . . a historian . . . [who] note[s] down, in the same manner as he has noted down the history of Don Quixote, the dialogue between himself and his friend, a task he is professionally equipped to perform" (136). Weiger believes that the prologuist parodies the scholarly urge to quote authorities by indiscriminately writing whatever "they" have said. He provides "a series of incidental annotations that give the semblance of contemporary authority and of the author's diligence in seeking sources: not only what the 'primer autor' has to say, but as well what 'they' have to say" (131).

The solution is as attractive as it is problematic. First, Weiger seems to imply, very boldly, that Cervantes adopted the *es opinión* cluster as a general device that performs in the novel the function of infinite parabasis, of an absolutely extrinsic position for what Weiger

26. The cluster of allusions to what "they" say comprises, in Weiger's argument, the marginalia at I, 9 (Dulcinea); at I, 16 (Cide Hamete and the muleteer); at II, 12 (reference to Cide Hamete's *other* works); and at II, 44 (reference to the true original of the story, in which Cide Hamete disagrees with the translator about the book). Weiger also adds, parenthetically: "This [phenomenon] is to be distinguished from comments *about* that manuscript, such as the translator's refusal to believe Sancho's wisdom in II, 5, his treatment of Cide Hamete's description of Don Diego de Miranda's house in II, 18, or the frequent scolding of the 'punctilious' historian for his failure to clarify certain details. The interjection of gratuitous remarks about the content is a characteristic of the romances of chivalry and to this extent such comments in the *Quixote* are a parodic device" (130).

calls the "extratextual authorial voice." In this proposal, what "they say" is always traceable to one speaking position that organizes the text "from above" and assembles this text into the unity of one book. Second, Weiger identifies the position of infinite parabasis created by the cluster with the prologuist, who supervises, "edits," the book. The prologuist occupies the extrinsic narrative position in the novel at the top of its vocal pyramid. By preserving "them" in the confines of the novel, although above the authorial personnel, Weiger manages to secure the stability of the novel's editorial *régime.*

Weiger's solution postulates a personal narrator identical with one of the fictional characters featuring in the narrative. This model differs little from the prevalent misprisions of romantic use of self-referentiality in fictional constructs as self-reflexive statements made by fictive narrators. In order to free the present analysis from such misconceptions and to recover the transcendental sense of reflection as it was understood by romanticism, it is necessary to look more closely at the Morisco boy, an excellent, novel-historical example of an Arab reader *in the act of reading/translating* the Arabic original of the *verdadera historia.* Let us look at one of the novel's well-known passages. In the parabasis that extends between the two chapters in question (*DQ*, 58–69, Book I, Chapter 8 and Chapter 9)—when the Biscayan's sword hangs, *y estando una suspenso,* over Don Quixote's head—the editor loses his working manuscript and, back in La Mancha, runs into an old Arabic text. The editor asks the Morisco boy to identify the text:

> When I told him what I wanted and put the book into his hands, he opened it in the middle and read a little. Then he began to laugh [*se comenzó a reir*]. I asked him what he was laughing at, and he replied that it was at something in a note written in the margin of the book. I asked him to tell me what it was.
>
> "In the margin, as I told you," he replied, still laughing, "is written: 'This Dulcinea del Toboso so often mentioned in this history, had, they say, the best hand of any woman in all La Mancha for salting pigs.' "
>
> When I heard Dulcinea del Toboso named, I was struck with surprise and amazement, for it occurred to me at once that these notebooks contained the history of Don Quixote. With this idea I urged him to read the beginning, and he did so, turning the Arabic into Castilian at sight. He told me it meant, "History of Don Quixote of La Mancha, written by Cide Hamete Benengeli, an Arab historian." (*DQ*, 66–67).

The passage presents the reader with daunting technical complexity. One aspect of this complexity is that the Morisco boy engages in self-narration, in *autodiegesis* ("as I told you" [*como he dicho*]). In addition, the passage displays one of the novel's secret places, the *topos* of the margins ("In the margin, as I told you" [*Está, como he dicho, aquí en el margen*]). It is also here that the reader comes in direct contact with the novel's mystifying, original authorial voice: "they say."

There is one more aspect of technical complexity here. Weiger sees in this passage an instance of what he considers to be the speaker of the *es opinión* cluster, an instance of the "author of the marginal note about Dulcinea [who] is *extraneous* to this [the novel's authorial] configuration" (132). In this reading, the prologuist, the ultimate (senior) editor, has arranged the available utterances and produced their textual version into which he has inserted the phrase "they say" to preserve the authenticity of narrative relay. But it is plausible that "they" can be traced to the person of the Morisco boy. In this reading, the boy provides a nonsubsumptive resolution of the hierarchy of speakers that Weiger has, as we have seen, closed off with the prologuist. We must take a closer look at the boy's mysterious, irritating laughter as he reads the marginal note about Dulcinea. The question, once again, is not only, as Weiger wants it, *Who* is the nebulous "someone"? but also, as the editor present at the bazaar anticipates, What are "they saying" if the Morisco's translation comes as *laughter*?

Again: " 'In the margin, as I told you,' he replied, still laughing, 'is written: *This Dulcinea del Toboso so often mentioned in this history, had, they say, the best hand of any woman in all La Mancha for salting pigs.*' " The passage deserves close attention because it assembles in one place and time the novel's *vocal apparatus*, its entire phonic pyramid: us, the historical readers; the editor (*segundo autor*); the translator *on hand*; the Arabic manuscript; a flesh-and-bone Arabic reader; and an instance of "them." (Cide Hamete is missing: he is now in the process of becoming one of *them*.)[27]

Undeniably, this *complete presence* could occur only "extratextually," as Weiger has it, only in the novel's margins. However, in contrast to Weiger's sense of extratextuality as a spatial or architectural externality, the Cervantine margin is both a place extrinsic to the text

---

27. R. M. Flores discusses the elusive presence and the multiple roles of the Arab historian in his essay "The Role of Cide Hamete in *Don Quixote*," *Bulletin of Hispanic Studies*, LIX (1982), 3–14.

and the transcendental movement constitutive of the text. And it is into this generative nexus that Cervantes inserts the anecdote about Dulcinea and pigs. The consequences of this insertion are multiple. The margin is the place of laughter; hence, because the translator is physically present with the editor, there remains *nothing more* for the latter to edit. Next, with the editor rendered idle (*desocupado*), the editing ceases as a practical task and becomes a transcendental undertaking: laughter resists editing. There is more: reading in the margin will cause laughter, which will persist even in the presence of articulated speech ("he replied, still laughing"); the interpretation of marginality will come as laughter. It follows that this (first) translation of the margin will come in the incomprehensible language of laughter.

Finally, the Morisco boy offers an alternative way of conceiving the hierarchy of speaking positions. Rather than consolidating "them" into a unified voice, the boy lets the speech of speech come to presence by reading the novel in *its true topos*, in the margin. In the Morisco boy's laughter we have the novel's first instance, not only of what "they" say, but of "them" actually saying it *in person*. Or, rather, not *in* the person of the Morisco, but *through* his person. The Morisco *romantically translates* "their" voice in his laughter, into the ungraspable, nonconceptual, infinite meaning of laughter. The margin gives audibility to the voice that speaks *originally*.

The laughter that articulates "their" voice is thus essentially related to origin. In Weiger's solution, the original speaker, the prologuist, sits atop the pyramid, as the chronicler, a role venerated in the Western, historically-minded world. Favored by this cultural privilege, the historiographer, the solitary observer, collects all the remarks said by "them." In this conception, origin denotes the point of departure.

To conceive an origin compatible with the laughter of the boy, it is necessary to separate origin from the static terminals of beginning and end. In order to conceive origin transcendentally, it is necessary to question Weiger's assumption that the original speaker is a "person" (and a *first person singular*). This model only reinforces the editorial model of history and of truth that dominates in the West. One should, instead, assume that the collective voice of "them," which takes over *Don Quixote*, does not necessarily point *back* to a *someone*, a single author. The Morisco boy is neither a member of a finite group of readers nor a person who speaks intentionally. His laughter is an empty, ironic marker, a trace that generates the narrative out of the infinity of the margin. In other words, a true break with the traditional paradigm is possible only in the novelistic plural author and, perhaps, at the outer margins of the margin, in a totality of voices that is neither "us" nor "them."[28] We must study the marginal note in more detail in order to determine the *genre of laughter* and to grasp the community of "their" voices, which "communicate" in this unusual semantics.[29] What is the Book of Total Laughter?

To formulate this answer we must first show that the passage in Book I, Chapter 9 is not a parabasis as it is defined by classical rhetoric but a parabasis in the romantic sense of an infinitely generative operation. It must be shown, in other words, that traditional parabasis does not sufficiently explain the laughter of the Morisco boy. The speculative involution developed in the prologue may be helpful here. We may recall that, in Cervantes' prological address to the reader, apostrophe and parabasis oscillate in an articulatory agon of infinite address. In light of this analysis, the Morisco boy's laughter is neither a strict parabasis nor a strict apostrophe. The boy is *both* anterior *and* posterior to his own words: a mere medium for transmitting messages, he stands, parabasically, in the margins, but, a skillful translator, he is, apostrophically, indispensable. Speaking and laughing—repeating and originating—at the same time, the boy achieves the simultaneous presence of two operations that are, by their classical definitions, mutually exclusive.

The *risible* energy, released when direct and reported speech collapse into *autodiegesis*—the ridiculous explosion of the presence of/about all presence, the laughable charge of *omnipresence* as such—is so potent that it gives birth to the novel. In the eye of the articulatory tornado, in the *topos* of the margin, *Don Quixote* appears for the first time, both in the realistic sequence of textual progression and in the irrecoverable "first" utterance of the collective, laughing authorship of "them." In the remark about Dulcinea and pigs we find out, for the first time, in a marginal note interpreted instantaneously ("at sight") in laughter, *what we are reading*: "With this idea I urged him

---

28. Arthur Efron, in *Don Quixote and the Dulcineated World* (Austin, 1971), speaks of a germ of unbounded identity symbolized in Don Quixote's dementia; the madness permeates the novel's fictional world, Efron claims, while every character denies its omnipresence and omnipotence. "Their" presence lacks topological determination.

29. The insufficiency of Weiger's model becomes evident in his limited, merely rhetorical or *comic* treatment of laughter in *Don Quixote*. See John G. Weiger, "*Don Quixote*: The Comedy in Spite of Itself," *Bulletin of Hispanic Studies*, LX (1983), 291.

to read the beginning, and he did so, turning the Arabic into Castilian at sight. He told me it meant, *'History of Don Quixote of La Mancha, written by Cide Hamete Benengeli, an Arab historian.'* " The only editing permitted by laughter, the only work left for the editor to perform, is officially to announce, solemnly to depose, that the novel *has now begun.*

The moment when translation and interpretation, involuted, burst out into laughter, instantiates, in what is perhaps the *locus classicus* of the novel, a *Cervantine* possibility of saturating the present moment with *presence itself*, of making the Novel coincide with, *appear in*, the novel. As the complete identity of the novel with itself, Cervantine laughter accomplishes Schlegel's formula that "every theory of the novel must itself be a novel." In view of the need for this coincidence, a modern novelistic poetics faithful to romantic intentions would explore the possible configurations that structure the simultaneous existence of original presence and its representation *in the same textual instance.* The poetics would foreground the mechanism responsible for the involution of any two orders and their *dissolution in each other.* Let us bring out the implications of this poetics in greater detail.

The play of involution has rich potential as a literary device. For example, Laurence Sterne's *Tristram Shandy* constantly reminds the readers that they are reading a fictitious representation of reality. In order to destroy *readerly* illusion, Sterne defamiliarizes "natural" perception of the real-world temporal sequence by stretching *ad absurdum* the textual representation of this sequence. The discrepancy of text and reality underscores the distance between *pure presence* and the means of its presentation. In *Gargantua and Pantagruel,* François Rabelais formulates this discrepancy as the distance between the human body and its textual representation. The resulting laughter is the measure of the incongruity between the inert material of the book and the supple vibrancy of sheer physicality. In *Moby Dick,* Herman Melville schematizes the distance in question as the discrepancy between the representative powers of a fictional plot and potential allegorical significance of this plot. Here, the incongruity between presence and the means of presentation emerges as the clash of presence inherent in static allegorical structures with the dynamic nature of narrative accounts. *Moby Dick's* narrative moves *infinitely* toward its proper allegory, in whose perspective alone the book as a whole will have attained sense. These diverse *topoi*—temporal sequence, morphology of the body, allegorical frame—are examples of the relation between presence and the means of *present*ation.

This basic model assumes a unique shape in Cervantes. Unlike Sterne, Rabelais, and Melville, who, in different degrees, emphasize the divergence between presence and various forms of representation extrinsic to the subject at hand (time, body, allegory), Cervantes relates the book to the form of the book—that is, to a *literary* form. Like Flaubert's *Bouvard and Pécuchet*, *Don Quixote* vibrates, *y estando una suspenso*, between presence and its means of presentation, between the totality of discourse and a concrete instance of this discourse, between scientific experiment and Science, between the book and the Book. Flaubert, however, as Eugenio Donato argues, projects the totality of scientific discourse on the spatial form of the *library*.[30] Cervantes, on the other hand, encloses his book in a form deprived of spatial parameters, in the form of *discursive* totality itself, in the book of/about the Book, in the presence of/about Presence.

The analysis can gain precision from another comparison. Cervantes is not concerned with a substantive or thematic type of presence (body, time, allegory, library) but with presence as such. Cervantes allows his book to be shaped by the inner demands of the subject matter, by the Book Itself.[31] Like Burton's *The Anatomy of Melancholy*, and like Walton's *The Compleat Angler*, *Don Quixote* advances anatomically: it discusses the chosen subject, chivalric love, by *exhausting* it. *Moby Dick* uses the same method: it anatomizes, exhausts, the subject of whaling, to point, through this saturation, to

---

30. Eugenio Donato, "The Museum's Furnace: Notes Toward a Contextual Reading of *Bouvard and Pécuchet*," in *Textual Strategies*, ed. Harari, 213–38.

31. Although, for Spitzer, *Don Quixote* speaks the genre of exhaustion, his analysis is limited by an antiphrastic theory of irony.

> [The novel is] written in the form of ... a sort of parasitic manner.... [*Don Quixote*] adopt[s] all the situations and devices of the type of novel ridiculed. Thus Cervantes ... imprisoned himself ... in a seeming subservience to a stale pattern of adventures, situations, themes—even words. The novel-of-chivalry-to-end-all-novels-of-chivalry must ... allow the story to unfold as if for the enjoyment of the credulous reader, at the same time suggesting slyly the reaction of the critic-author, which will often consist only of an ironical underscoring, whereby he achieves an original creation composed of ingredients borrowed from the works criticized: a re-creation of the old subject matter. (Leo Spitzer, "On the Significance of *Don Quixote*," in *Cervantes: A Collection of Critical Essays*, ed. Lowry Nelson, Jr. [Englewood Cliffs, N.J., 1969], 87–88)

some possible allegorical significance of the totality of this particular human discourse.

Still, the anatomy also fails sufficiently to accommodate, or explain, *Don Quixote*'s historic task. In the poetics of the anatomy, the work's form is dictated by the subject matter itself. Burton only has to follow the preestablished divisions of his subject, the anatomy of melancholy, and they will automatically determine the form of the work. But how is Cervantes to proceed if *Don Quixote*'s informing *gestalt* is the form of the Book? Where can he find the model if the model exists only to the extent that the thing itself is produced? Moreover, how can Cervantes anatomically exhaust the subject of the Book if the subject, which determines the form of the treatise, seeks identity with the treatise as the form of this determination? For we must remember that the goal of Cervantes' novel is to become *itself*. Precisely because of this complete identity with itself, the form of form will remain infinitely obscure.[32]

The anatomical option crumbles in the case of Cervantes, not only because his form is infinitely involuted with the subject matter (this was also the case with Burton), but because the involution occurs between the form and *its* Form, as the involution of form into Form. The anatomy sheds pertinent light on *Don Quixote* as a novel announcing a new notion of genre spoken by the Book itself. What is the book? In a romantic fashion, Cervantes' novel gives form to itself; that is, its essence is to seek its Form. Hence the romantic duality: to the extent that it seeks *its Form*, the work has already found it and begun to exist, but insofar as the work still *seeks* it, it does not exist yet. The novel hovers transcendentally between ideal conception and actual execution.

This is the sense in which *Don Quixote* is a romantic book, an infinite, originless *identity of identity with itself*. Because its sole concern

---

32. Leo Spitzer ("Linguistic Perspectivism in the *Don Quixote*," in *Cervantes: Modern Critical Views*, ed. Harold Bloom [New York, 1987], 9–35) seeks for a similar model of identity, and he finds it in the coincidence of *Don Quixote* with the *etymo*-logic of language. Spitzer and Don Quixote, like historical grammarians (Grimm, Verner, Bopp), believe that the (etymological) story of language will lead them to a proto-narrative, the original *verdadera historia* of all possible relations among words, to the mythical *biblos* of meanings. Don Quixote's stubborn exercises in quirky etymology and punning, as well as his general philological explanations, deserve a separate analysis in light of the romantic theory of the novel.

is to coincide with its form, *Don Quixote* cannot be a book *about* anything, except being a book about being a book. Because it exhausts itself in the aspiration to coincide with its proper form, the novel has reached a critical point, the point at which, to use a romantic theorem, it can be criticized, at which it becomes *criticizable*.[33]

Proximately involuted, *Don Quixote* is its own *pantomime*. The mechanism of involution nullifies all distance in the mimetic interior—let us remember that, as it imitates the Novel, *Don Quixote* seeks its proper form. Generated by Schlegel's formula that "every theory of the novel must itself be a novel," the proximity of the book to the Book reaches a maximum possible pitch: the only movement left in the gap is the purely formal *trace*, the turning from one order to the other. With nothing in between, *Don Quixote* is, transcendentally, the book of/about the Book, his language is of/about Language, and his literature is of/about Literature; it is Genre Itself. We must now study more closely the novel's transcendental genre.

In Weiger's proposal, the voices of the editorial hierarchy of *Don Quixote* and the anonymous voices of the *es opinión* cluster are all unified by the highest speaker, the single, identifiable voice of the prologuist. According to the present proposal, the novel's original voice can be heard in the marginal note in Book I, Chapter 9, in the lapse be-

---

33. The coincidence of the historical art work with its Idea and, ultimately, as romanticism expressed it, its "dissolution" (*Auflösung*) in the Idea of Art, is possible because the work is constructed on its own immanent principles valid only for itself. This relation lays the foundation for what Walter Benjamin calls "three basic theses of the romantic theory of the assessment of art works ... the principle of the mediacy of assessment, the principle of an impossibility of a positive value scale and the principle of the uncriticizability of the worthless or inferior work." The principles state that, first, "the assessment of a work must never be an explicit one, but in every case one implied in the *fact* of its romantic critique"; second, "if a work can be criticized, then it is an art work, otherwise, it is not—a mean between these two cases is unthinkable"; and, third, an inferior work simply cannot be placed in any relation to other works, to its own Ideal Form, and to the Idea of Art, it is inferior precisely because it cannot be criticized ("Der Begriff der Kunstkritik in der deutschen Romantik," in *Gesammelte Schriften*, unpublished translation by D. R. Lachterman). For romanticism, *Don Quixote* proved to be not only an example of a criticizable work but also a paradigm for the theory of criticism established, in the aftermath of Kant's critical philosophy, as the science of what is possible. In other words, *Don Quixote* is the condition of possibility for literature.

tween translation and interpretation.³⁴ The novel's editorial personnel—the *primero autor*, the *segundo autor*, and "they"—can begin to speak *at the same time in one utterance, through the Morisco boy's marginal language of laughter*. Finally, at the moment when, in the parabasis, "they" speak through the Morisco boy, the novel itself becomes originally present. The last task left for us is to attempt a description of the nature—the kind, the genre—of the original voice.

With this purpose in mind we will have a look at one of *Don Quixote*'s interpolated tales, the tale of the braying adventure (Part II, Chapter 25), in which *Don Quixote*'s plural voice resounds with unprecedented clarity.³⁵ According to the tale, an alderman has lost his donkey, and with another alderman he follows the animal into the forest. The men decide to bray from opposite ends of the forest to lure the animal out of the woods. Their braying, however, proves useless, as they take each other's braying for the donkey's. In the end, the men find the donkey dead, "devoured by wolves."

The relevance of the tale for the concept of genre in Cervantes lies in two remarks about story-telling made by the tale's narrator. As they involute the narrative with itself, the remarks indicate the mechanism of speculative involution that structures Cervantes' novel as a whole. The first meta-narrative reference reads as follows: "It is with all these details, and just as I am telling it now, that those who know all about it tell the story" (*DQ*, 563). With this remark the tale's narrator apparently wants to reassure his audience that his account is faithful

---

34. The disjunctive nature of the novel's unity is further elucidated by Raymond S. Willis, Jr.'s study *The Phantom Chapters of the "Quijote"* (New York, 1953), which examines *Don Quixote*'s chapter divisions. While the gaps lack verbal connectives, the chapters emanate "a transcendent unity . . . simultaneously textual and vital. . . . At the threshold of the gap the lines of force tend onward; at the posterior they tend backward" (17–18). We can add that Willis' perceptive study fails to account for Cervantes' dangerous proximity to the romances he parodies, although his model is readily adaptable to this purpose. Not only the individual chapters but also the novel as a whole "cannot be textually conjoined with [its] neighbors" (with romances of chivalry, with other books in general); it stands, *originally*, "poised upon the circumstances of the past while thrusting forward into the not yet."

35. The tale belongs to a nexus of interpolated tales—stretching from Chapter 20 to Chapter 27 of Part II—whose structure and content significantly amplify the points developed in the present analysis. The nexus, which encompasses the episodes of Camacho's wedding, the episode in the Cave of Montesinos, and Maese Pedro's puppet show, deserves a commentary in its own right.

to the original version. We read in the second reference: "These are the strange things I told you I had to tell, and if you don't think they are, I have got no others" (*DQ*, 565). The narrator declares that he has nothing more to tell. The two remarks set this narrative significantly apart from the novel's other tales in that they place in a new perspective the tale's (any tale's) relation to origin.

Let us consider the first statement. The words can, of course, be simply a conventional formula for ending an innocent *conte*, but they can also suggest that the story has become verbally identical with the original. The tale measures itself against both the original story as told by "them" and *against itself* as it has been just told. This proximity erases the distance between the original and the repeated accounts. The telling reaches an articulatory crisis and de*generates*—ceases to be a *genre*—into braying, into indifference. In the involution of the tale with itself, the reader will hear something speaking from both paradigms at once, the tale telling itself, something speaking *in the origin itself*.[36]

The second remark, I have "no other tales" (*no sé otras*), seems to corroborate the radical nature of this involution. The lack of more stories announces a last logical possibility in the mimetic model. There remains no *other* place, no *topos* other than that which has been told. "*No sé otras*" exhausts telling: *all* has been told. The tale is total, it has affinity with everything, not extensionally, as having addressed all subjects, but intensionally, as having projected *itself as its own proper topos* onto the grid of narration. The tale has found its Form, literally, in the end. In a transcendental fashion, it *can be* only when it is *no more*.

In the infinite relation, *mimesis has represented itself* in mimetic resemblance; the romantic Book denotes this infinity of self-presentation. Mimetically speaking, the tale has told everything it ("it") had to tell: "it" has told "itself." The novel's form consists in the constant tension, the perpetual arrival, the differing of this self-presentation. This infinity replaces the model of the relation of origin by personal speakers with the model of the relation of origin in which the voice of origin speaks (to) itself *y estando una suspenso*.

36. Foucault writes: "*Don Quixote* is the first modern work of literature, because in it we see the cruel reason of identities and differences make endless sport of signs and similitudes; because in it language breaks off its old kinship with things and enters into that lonely sovereignty, from which it will reappear, in its separated state, only as literature" (*The Order of Things*, 48–49).

The perpetually differing nature of origin raises the question whether a proper comportment to this original mystery is at all conceivable, whether, in other words, one can find the donkey alive rather than dead. It is in the context of this question that one should approach the short story by Jorge Luis Borges, "Pierre Menard, Author of the *Quixote*," in which Pierre Menard undertakes an unprecedented project to rewrite *Don Quixote*.[37] Menard claims to have written, in a paragraph "verbally identical" with a passage from *Don Quixote*, a new text of Cervantes' original title (*L*, 41–42). Significantly, the passage chosen by Menard comes from the parabasis in Book I, Chapter 9.

Borges observes: "It is a revelation to compare Menard's *Don Quixote* with Cervantes'. The latter, for example, wrote (part one, chapter nine): 'truth, whose mother is history, rival of time, depository of deeds, witness of the past, exemplar and adviser to the present, and the future's counselor.'" Borges comments: "Written in the seventeenth century, written by the 'lay genius' Cervantes, this enumeration is a mere rhetorical praise of history. Menard, on the other hand, writes: 'truth, whose mother is history, rival of time, depository of deeds, witness of the past, exemplar and adviser to the present, and the future's counselor'" (*L*, 43). And Borges explains: "History, the *mother* of truth: the idea is astounding. Menard, a contemporary of William James, does not define history as an inquiry into reality but as its origin. Historical truth, for him, is not what has happened; it is what we judge to have happened. The final phrases—*exemplar and adviser to the present, and the future's counselor*—are brazenly pragmatic. The contrast in style is also vivid. The archaic style of Menard—quite foreign, after all—suffers from a certain affectation. Not so that of his forerunner, who handles with ease the current Spanish of his time" (*L*, 43).

The difference between the two versions cannot be attributed—or reduced—to different historical conditions of reception. Neither can Menard's project be reduced to the familiar techniques of literary imitation: epigonism, plagiarism, pastiche, parody, satire, caricature, stylization. Like the romantics, and later the symbolists, Cervantes and Menard are concerned with the essence of the Book. The two historical voices speak from *one textual instance*, not from the fragment of Cervantes' novel, and not from Menard's "original" piece, but from the lapse, the abyss, the margin between Cervantes' book and the

37. Jorge Luis Borges, "Pierre Menard, Author of the *Quixote*," in *L*, 34–44.

Book, the gap that allows (and continues to allow) the two "interpretations" to come forth. Neither Cervantes nor Menard is anterior to the Book.

Menard shows quite concretely that the book is a function of editing and interpretation, a situation already encountered in Weiger's model. For Weiger, a "someone," the prologuist, unifies and controls the noisy crowd of speakers conjured up by the novel. Menard, however, understands Cervantes' point; like Cervantes, he works in a model of the text as *one abyss*, as *one voice-box* that speaks itself. The voice speaks itself pertinently—it is uttered by an infinity of speakers and is comprehensible in any historical time. Menard exploits a radical notion of text discovered by Cervantes: the origin inhabits the text, and the Book inhabits the book, but the Book cannot be assigned to any point in (literary) history because the Book appears each time only in epochal manifestations. This is the meaning of the philosophical notion of history: history is the need for truth to manifest itself differently in different metaphysical epochs. This is the complex relation expressed by Cervantes/Menard: "Truth, whose mother is history." The Book is both already here, with us, in *Don Quixote*, and in the absolute time of meaning, in perpetual transit, in romantic *translation*. The Cervantine margin in which the Morisco utters his translation reveals history *in its totality* to be a Book. As such a totality, the Book cannot be edited, if editing is understood as an originating operation of editorial mastery and control; on the other hand, the Book can only be edited, if editing is understood romantically as an encounter with preexistent material not originated by the author—an encounter with the Book.

The argument gains in strength in light of two additional circumstances. First, Menard chooses for his project *Don Quixote* over other literary works because he finds Cervantes' novel to be an "unnecessary," "contingent book" (*L*, 41). In contrast, he cannot imagine the world without Poe, without Rimbaud's "Bateau ivre" and Coleridge's "Ancient Mariner." As necessary, these works could only be written once; that is, their authors dominate the work, giving it the unique authorial stamp that diminishes the work and limits its power to speak originally. These works cannot, therefore, be reinserted into the Book. On the other hand, *Don Quixote*'s contingency, its essential incompletion, allows the writer—Cervantes or any other writer—to undertake the novel over and over again. Like its prologue, *Don Quixote* exists in the *muchas veces* of its origin, and these "many times" constantly reinsert, translate, the novel into the Origin—the Idea—of Art.

In the second place, Menard, as we have already noted, selects for his undertaking the passage in Book I, Chapter 9, the point of parabasis in which, we have seen, *Don Quixote* momentarily, and originally, comes into existence in the margin (*L*, 41). Menard's project coincides with what "they have said" in *Don Quixote*'s infinitely generative parabasis. In this parabasis one historical author, Cervantes, speaks to another historical author, Menard/Borges; the translator of the seventeenth-century text, the Morisco boy, speaks to the "translator" of the text's twentieth-century version, Menard. Finally, "Menard's" text brings out the structural possibilities of Cervantes' discovery; in the articulatory tornado of the parabasis, the author (Menard) is identical with the translator (Menard), in the same way in which the Morisco boy enacts the living unity of parabasis and apostrophe. At I, 9 we can hear at least two voices, *laughing*; we can hear the differing identity of the two texts as One Book, the romantic Book of which Menard writes: "My general recollection of the *Quixote*, simplified by forgetfulness and indifference, can well equal the imprecise and prior image of a book not yet written" (*L*, 41).

The margin, in other words, captures the generative power of origin as a pure relation without content and without term. As it sought to name this infinity, romanticism guarded against objective terms and substantive identifications and chose the term *Book* to refer to the perpetually self-differing nature of origin. The romantic book is the name for original, infinite reflection. How should this internally differing origin be described?

Let us once again look at the tale of the braying adventure. To provoke the donkey into a response, human imitation must adequately resemble genuine braying, but it also requires a *sufficient difference* to make the distinction between man and animal possible. Thus as a system of differences language *differs* from noise. But precisely as a systematic arrangement of differences, it is powerless to describe that which is external to difference, to describe inarticulate sound; it is helpless when confronted with *its own Other*. This difficulty does not apply to the donkey, whose "speech system" operates by indifference. While speech finds the indifferent system of the donkey incomprehensible and impenetrable, the indifferent donkey easily tells the essential, transcendental differing between *itself* and the *not-itself*.

The same logic applies to mimesis. Access to origin is possible in imitation; the derivative unit returns, reverts, to its primitive phase, by imitating origin. But, as the friend has made it clear to the prologuist, origin does not resemble its product—it is dissimilar from what it begets. The mimetic relation between origin and imitation is intransitive and irreversible. Upon finding the donkey, the aldermen blame the animal: it must have understood their braying, otherwise "it would have been no ass" (*no fuera asno*). Unwittingly, the aldermen articulate the uncanny status of the donkey's *indifference* to human braying as the possibility that there might exist meaning structures not organized differentially. Indifference resists meaning, yet it sufficiently defines the meaning of the donkey's existence. Expressed in transcendental terms, the aldermen's dilemma is that no amount of calling, of imitation, will ever make this indifference accessible to representation, will ever be able to *imitate* it. We must assume the only, the last, possibility, already indicated by the narrator's words, "*no sé otras*": the animal "would have been no animal." The phrase "*no fuera asno*" captures the self-differing, inimitable, untranslatable nature of the romantic origin. Origin "*no fuera origen*," it *differs* from itself.

The genre of origin, the *genus* "donkey," is, thus, a genus of self-differing, of involution, and it is this genre that determines Cervantine genology. As different from itself, this "genus" has no "species." The aldermen possess and express the knowledge of the difference only *unwittingly*. This unconscious expression is structurally necessary, for the difference "in-itself" defies the conventional order of articulation at our disposal. Indeed, the difference, because it "utters meaning in indifference," before or below the differential system of speech, is a "condition" of meaning. As such a "condition," it "itself" resists explicit articulation, for it "speaks" in what is spoken as the "other" of what is said, itself unsayable. One cannot *tell* this difference, for this difference precedes and orchestrates all telling, including its own. Speech can be spoken only unwittingly, and this unconsciousness defines infinite irony.

This language of origin, the *braying*, suggests a structure of the Book which always exceeds and, in exceeding, speaks through the individual author's voice. The "strangeness" mentioned by the tale's narrator indicates an *alien source*, unquotable yet omnipresent, a *topos deinon* of all texts, a "*no asno*." While the book *Don Quixote* can exist exclusively as a function of its source, the source itself does not resemble the book that it has produced. The source of the text *"no fuera texto"; it would have been no text.*

It is the power of infinite self-differing to bring forth the transcendental "text" that underlies the connection between the romantic conception of irony and the romantic theory of the novel. This connection itself, in turn, cannot be established without romanticism's equally ironic conception of genre. That which is uttered in Cervantes, the genre of his speech, can be uttered only with irony, and only in the novel, for at the heart of genre lies the same ironic hesitation, the same romanticization, which is responsible for the romantic theory of the novel, of *der Roman:* "every theory of the novel must itself be a novel."

As Peter Szondi shows in his essay on "Friedrich Schlegel's Theory of Poetical Genres," the romantic, speculative "deduction of genres" is a matter of the same irony that romanticism detected in speculative metaphysics.[38] More specifically, Szondi argues that Schlegel's genre theory is subject to the same antinomies of thought that, according to the romantics, make thought necessarily *speculative.* The antinomies place Schlegel in an unenviable *double* position: he either thinks his system out from the ingenuity of his intellect, or he *must* conduct his proof in the way he does. Szondi writes "It is impossible to determine if this [the complete elimination of the division of poetry into genres] is a logical consequence or the realization of an initial intention to transcend the poetics of genres" (*TU*, 93).

At issue is the question of *involution* as developed in the preceding analysis of Cervantes' novel. Is thinking infinite? Is it anterior to the concepts that it manipulates? Or, on the contrary, does it merely encounter concepts and merely recombine categories and genres as these are found in the objective world? The romantic answer to this dilemma can only be ironic. The irony that structures Schlegel's deduction of genres arises out of what romanticism took to be the basic condition of thought in general: every act of thought passes through a necessary and a free moment. The mind itself can never presume to decide which moment in a given act of thought is necessary and which moment is free, for such decision would require a higher position, and so on to infinity. The only judgment available to the understanding is the infinite, ironic awareness that in each act of thought there inhere two modalities: the conscious grasp of conceptuality

---

38. Peter Szondi, "Friedrich Schlegel's Theory of Poetical Genres," in *TU,* 75–94.

available for manipulation, and the indelible index of Thought Itself asserting itself in every moment of intellection. The romantic account of the origin of thought foregrounds a hyperbolic relation that exceeds dialectical models of identity: in every act of thinking, thought thinks itself; in every act of language, language speaks itself.

The irony of Schlegel's deduction of genres reverberates with the same *difference* that Cervantes hears inside origin. For Schlegel the two simultaneous conditions of thought can be reconciled by a romanticization of the contradiction. Thought as such, in its identity as thought, is constituted by an excessive moment. This excess escapes not only the manipulation by the thinking subject but also the determination *that* it is a thought. For the genre of Thought Itself to be thought in its unity, it must be thought both consciously, from an individual thinking subject and, at the same time, unconsciously, not from the subject, but from the system. For the thinking subject to think thought, it is necessary that Thought first think itself. Schlegel's famous Athenaeum Fragment 53 expresses precisely this generative suspension of thought: "It's equally fatal for the mind to have a system and to have none. It will simply have to decide to combine the two" (F, 167).

Schlegel's formula defines the transcendental positioning of the mind as it ironically "combines" order and chaos. The reconciliation of the two positions is not a Hegelian synthesis. Hegelian dialectic brings the play of opposites to rest in the absolute of the Concept (*der Begriff*), which grasps itself (*sich begreift*) *as* such grasping, as Concept. In contrast to this mode of operation, the romantic suspension of contradiction defines the very source, the beginning, of thought before the distinction into thought and non-thought. The ironic difference within thought, the self-differing, defines the genre of the source—of the origin—of Thought Itself. The origin (and the self-differing that vibrates in it) does not sustain a relation of productivity such as we know, for example, in the model of subject and object, or of artist and art object. Origin cannot, in other words, encompass the difference that constitutes it *as* origin. As hyperbolical, as the production of thought by thought itself, the origin of thought does not orchestrate the play of difference; it does not organize or reduce the differential play as a matrix of its identity. Rather, origin appears as one among several moments in the self-differing, the continuing recombination of free and necessary modalities. It is a possibility of romantic thought that it "could be no thought."

A romantic thinker (and a romantic writer) is romantic because in each of his acts both moments occur simultaneously, in a necessary irony that cannot be prevented but only arranged into form, into literary form. When Cervantes speaks, something speaks that is not his, and it is in virtue of this indeterminate otherness that Cervantes can speak *as* Cervantes in the first place. Cervantes can speak as self-identical subject only because something speaks in his speech that is different from him and that, in a fundamental sense, differs from, and within, itself. When the author acknowledges this voice of otherness as necessary and constitutive to the production of his work, then, and only then, does the work earn the right to be called a work *of* literature.

The novel, *der Roman,* is the medium of this romantic reconciliation, acknowledgment, and presencing. When it selected the existing genre of "the novel" to fulfill this role, romanticism gave the novel a sense far removed from the classicist meaning of the term. The romantic *Roman* describes the act by which the mind is infinitely aware of the double modality of Thought—instinct and intention—by which it brings the other of thought, the excessive identity of Thought with Itself, into the play of representation. In the *Roman* the mind *romanticizes* intentional thought in order to disclose this thought's other, the involuntary, ironic process of Thought Itself that accompanies finite intellection. The *Roman* is the infinite self-relation of thought as being-thought, just as Schlegel's formula that "every theory of the novel must itself be a novel" enacts the infinite identity of the subject with itself as being-subject. The simultaneous occurrence of Thought Itself in conscious thought constitutes the infinity of the romantic absolute knowledge, a process of dissolution in which what is being thought is the being-thought of thought—the subject of knowledge is the object of this knowledge: "every theory of the novel is itself a novel."

The simultaneous presence, in speculative infinity, of the intentional and unintentional modalities leads Schlegel to concede Cervantes' possibility. A stable, self-identical, intentional moment cannot appear except as accompanied by the other, necessary, alien moment: "For a genre cannot be conceived without an accompanying genre" (*LN,* 72). Because the other of thought cannot be subject to the intentionality of conceptual thinking, it can enter into the field of language and of thought only in the artist's, and the thinker's, voluntary surrender of the conscious power to create, in the ironic self-destruction of the conscious mind, in destroying the positive content. When the conceptual content is thus destroyed, or, as the romantics put it, *romanticized,* the other of thought can be indicated in the infinite, indeterminate insufficiency of positive content in relation to the inexhaustible abundance of the other. The mark of genius is the readiness to acknowledge the presence of the genre of the other, to allow the subject of knowledge as such to emerge, and to allow speech to speak itself.

The other, alien moment is not a genre, is not a thought, or perhaps it is more than mere genre, more than mere thought. Its otherness is such that it cannot be assimilated into an opposite, a contradiction, or antithesis. It is the "not" that underlies that which at each moment is asserted *intentionally in the self-identical thought* of the subject. The "not" is not the logical opposite of the conscious thought but rather the suppressed content, the self-differing that speech covers over in order to become the speech that speaks as a differential system. This self-differing is, in its pure "otherness," the ground of possibility for the "sameness" of speech, of the ability of speech to be self-identical. Indeed, what is each time recognized by humans as speech is not the specific historical language (Spanish, English) but speech as the structure of sameness and self-identity. We rely on this structure so fundamentally that we resort to it even when we recognize a foreign language *as foreign.*

The self-differing that is the other "side" of speech resides as something absent in the midst of language. To think identity, we must at the same time *think difference;* intentional thought occurs in the presence of the excessive self-identity of Thought Itself. This awareness, however, while accurate, cannot become an object for thought; it only solicits the mind with a nonconceptual, ironic drift. Perpetually differing from itself, the "other" genre is not—would have been no—genre.

The romantic case of Hölderlin's translations of Sophocles proves particularly pertinent in this context, for it employs the alterity that underlies all thought in the project of translation. Translation, for Hölderlin, mediates the classicist separation of the ancients from the moderns. The famous, and philologically notorious, interpretation/translation of *Oedipus Rex* and *Antigone,* speaks the third language, situated between Attic Greek and modern German. The "third" language of translation inhabits those regions of Language that, in each of the two national languages, always remain silent and that, as silent, possess the properties of the "absent" genre. What speaks in Hölderlin's translation, what unites both epochs, is the unrealized *other* of the two ages, the other of (Hesperian) modernity imitating that which in Greek antiquity had always remained unexplored. According to Hölderlin's solution, the task of the moderns is to say that which classical antiquity *had not said.* Hence Hölderlin defines the imitation of origin as the relation of increasing difference, as an imitation of that which in origin had not been there. For Hölderlin, to imitate origin is to imitate the original relation as infinite self-differing.

Ultimately, and this accounts for the scandal over his translations, Hölderlin argued that there had been no Greece (no neoclassically conceived Greece); what had been there was only an inimitable (and therefore inaccessible) *other* Greece, the *Orient.* The original Greek texts are unrecognizable in Hölderlin's translation precisely because, as transcendental, they foreground the alterity that constitutes thought, the self-differing by which origin infinitely relates (to) itself. As Philippe Lacoue-Labarthe writes, "The 'modern' was ... for Hölderlin something like the *après coup,* in the strict sense, of Greek art: that is to say, the repetition of what occurred there without ever taking place, and the echo of that unuttered word that nevertheless reverberated in its poetry" (TM, 221). Lacoue-Labarthe continues:

> This could explain ... the enterprise of *translation,* and the altering of the scheme of imitation (classicist or dialectical) that it presupposes. . . . For it was a matter of making Greek art say what it had not said—not in the manner of a kind of hermeneutics attempting to find the implicit in its discourse, but in quite a different manner, one for which I doubt very much that we as yet have a category. It was a matter of making it say by this means, quite simply, that which was said (but) *as that which was not said:* the same thing, then, in its difference [*en différence*]. En diapheron heauto. (TM, 221)

A genre cannot be thought in isolation but must be thought with *another* genre: articulate speech must be thought with inarticulate noise. And so, whether the Morisco boy laughs at the good quality of the original source or whether the source, *origo ridicula,* comes "as such" in the laughter itself must forever remain a properly romantic secret.

II
Genre as Mood in *Pierre*

Fathers are afraid that their children's natural love may be eradicated. What then is this nature which is liable to be eradicated?

Habit is a second nature that destroys the first. But what is nature? Why is habit not natural? I am very much afraid that nature itself is only a first habit, just as habit is a second nature.

—Blaise Pascal, *Pensées*

That which is creative must create itself.

—John Keats

In *Pierre*, Melville frequently comments on the moods that his characters experience in specific situations.[1] In their attention to moods, these comments—usually intended to explain and justify the character's action or reaction, or else to enhance the description of the character's state of mind—demonstrate the importance of moods in Melville's literary enterprise as useful sources of insight into human nature. To account for the power of moods, and to find a legitimate place for them in human life, Melville proceeds to formulate a concept of the subject that could accommodate moods in all their shades and intensities. His solution is fairly simple. For every action of the protagonist influenced or affected by mood, Melville creates a general

---

1. Herman Melville, *Pierre; or, The Ambiguities*, ed. Harrison Hayford, Hershel Parker, and G. Thomas Tanselle (Evanston, 1971).

condition of this mood under which the specific occasion is subsumed. In this solution Melville explains each particular mood by invoking a general formula (the formula reads, "Sometimes we are in this mood which makes us") and then subsuming the specific situation under this formula ("Pierre found himself in one of such situations"); thus a specific sensation falls under a general form of sensibility. This technique allows the subject to lose control and to experience momentary domination of a particular sentiment, but in principle it assumes that the *swings* of mood never threaten the subject in any fundamental way and that after each moody episode the subject regains full control.

Underlying the frequent, perhaps systematic references to the character's current mood is the assumption that this character is a constituted and stable subject who from time to time is seized by emotional fluctuations. After a brief reign, these fluctuations subside and vanish, leaving the subject free from the domination of the mood and restored to emotional balance. But this model exhibits serious limitations at its very center. Having allowed moods to play a role in the functioning of the subject, Melville cannot arbitrarily exclude from this process those moods that do not harmonize with the premise of the stable subject. For among the many moods that seize the subject, some moods are simply too strong and too unusual to tolerate subsumption under a general rule. We read, for example, "When a man is in a really profound mood, then all merely verbal or written profundities are unspeakably repulsive" (*P,* 207). The case of a "really profound mood" is a special case, a mood too powerful to be subsumed under a rule and too powerful for the subject to express it in language.

Melville's original model of moods comes under enormous pressure from such "really profound moods": "There is a dark, mad mystery in some human hearts, which, sometimes, during the tyranny of a usurper mood, leads them . . . to cast off the most intense beloved bond, as a hindrance to the attainment of whatever transcendental object that usurper mood so tyrannically suggests" (*P,* 180). The initial model was designed to subsume every emotional state under the general formula of sensibility. In this way Melville hoped to allow limited autonomy to the play of emotions in the field of the subject. It turns out, however, that the apparently harmless theory of the moody subject has opened the floodgates for runaway emotions, for "usurper moods" whose "tyrannical" command presents the subject with a "transcendental object" and leaves the subject fragmented and impossible to reconstitute.

This is to say that in his use of moods to contextualize a character's behavior Melville has taken a certain risk and that the risk now threatens to materialize. Melville's technique may create, across the totality of the narrative, a character whose moods can prove incompatible, both with one another and with the notion of the unified subject, and can for this reason give rise to a disturbed subject, or, even worse, Melville's technique may create a character whose moody profile will not coincide with the structure of the subject as a stable self-identical entity. Allowing moods to play a role in the existence of a subject (and explaining the subject's behavior as a function of these moods) provokes the following danger: while moods randomly fluctuate in the subject, the subject in which they fluctuate might never emerge. At its most tame and moderate, Melville's technique allows moods to occur in a presumably constituted and whole self; at its most extreme and daring, it allows moods to destabilize this self *only temporarily.* Yet it is possible that the sum total of the moods experienced by the subject may fail to disclose a stable constituted self; the inductive series of moods may resist synthesis. Indeed, the irreducible diversity and inconsistency of moods might indicate that the self had never been integrated and had never enjoyed initial stability, and as such an originally disintegrated subject, the subject could not have been destabilized in the first place.[2] A similar destabilization seems to affect Melville's metaphorics. Melville frequently announces his metaphors in formulas such as "seemingly," and "as if." Melville's critics are in general agreement, however, that the prolific metaphorical substitutions do not proceed from a consistent core of images, nor

---

2. Gerard W. Shepherd ("Pierre's Psyche and Melville's Art," *Emerson Society Quarterly,* XXX [1984]), attributes Pierre's "succession of moods" (84) to Melville's lack of "an integrated vision of the psyche" (85). For Richard H. Brodhead (*Hawthorne, Melville, and the Novel* [Chicago, 1973]), Melville's "fiction of the absurd" presents "character as a series of inconsistent appearances," without attempting "to uncover a hidden logic to bind them together" (184). Warner Berthoff speaks of "[Melville's] damaging uncertainty in ... *Pierre* as to what exactly it was that he wanted to present and explain" (*The Example of Melville* [Princeton, 1962], 209). For Robert Milder ("Melville's 'Intentions' in *Pierre,*" *Studies in the Novel,* VI [1974]), decentered moods make "*Pierre* ... a far more terrifying book than *Moby-Dick*" (191), "a 'negative *bildungsroman,*' a deliberate *reductio ad absurdum* of all metaphysics, all ethics, and all psychology, founded on the proposition that nothing can be known, least of all the knower himself" (190). See also Hershel Parker's essay "Why *Pierre* Went Wrong," (*Studies in the Novel,* VIII [1976], 7) and William Ellery Sedgwick (*Herman Melville: The Tragedy of Mind* [New York, 1962], 171).

can they be subsumed, a posteriori, in a meta-system of tropes. Having allowed the change of moods and the circulation of metaphor, Melville now finds himself unable to control their sliding.

In what follows I would like to argue that in *Pierre* Melville offers an original approach to this condition of the drifting subject. I want to argue that when Melville focuses on the "really profound mood" and on similar structures that exceed the field of play allowed within the subject, he seeks in these irregular formations the key to the subject's deepest constitutive structure. Melville treats moods and the other *topoi* as the privileged places of disclosure of what constitutes subjectivity, the being-subject of the subject. The subject of the play of changing moods comes into being in this play, and only in it. Instead of presenting the subject as an object, the play of moods enacts original presentation, the presence of the subject as such. Before discussing the question of the subject, however, we must first present the examples in question in order to introduce other relevant aspects of Melville's technique.

In all of these examples, dispersed throughout *Pierre*, Melville pauses briefly to digress on authorial presence in and control over the work. I want to argue that Melville selects for these digressions certain formulations which, as they comment on the author's progress, offer figures of unity or of synthesis of the totality of discourse in which they are placed. For it seems that all of these examples have one thing in common: as instances of discourse they all possess the power to make present, in however elusive a fashion, the unity of the subject in the midst of a seemingly chaotic diversity. For Melville, these selected terms are, in a mysterious way, the indemonstrable unity of discourse itself. Let us examine these terms more closely.

In the first explicit reference to the activity of writing, Melville debates two techniques of composing a narrative account. "By the one mode, all contemporaneous circumstances, facts, and events must be set down contemporaneously; by the other, they are only to be set down as the general stream of the narrative shall dictate; for matters which are kindred in time, may be very irrelative in themselves. I elect neither of these; I am careless of either; both are well enough in their way; I write precisely as I please" (*P*, 244). In this turn to the reader, Melville momentarily suspends the progress of the narrative in order to discuss his technique. In this aside he criticizes the two techniques most commonly adopted by writers. To escape the conflict between freedom and necessity, random association and causal linkage, chaos and order, Melville elects caprice; he rejects tested icons of sensibility and compulsive sensory immediacy and plunges into the unpredictable poetics of moods, of *pleasure*.

In a second reference to his technique of composition, which, like the previous passage, breaks narrative illusion, Melville speaks about his control of metaphoric substitutions: "But while nature thus very early and very abundantly feeds us, she is very late in tutoring us as to the proper methodization of our diet. Or,—to change the metaphor,—there are immense quarries of fine marble; but how to get it out; how to chisel it; how to construct any temple?" (*P*, 257). Significantly, this is Melville's only acknowledgment in the entire novel that something by way of conscious manipulation of metaphor is taking place. Moreover, the explicit change of the metaphor itself takes place in a discussion of the problem of transition from nature to artifice, from crude "marble" to sculpted "temple." "Nature" and "Culture" appear as two optional metaphors that themselves stand in for the unity (marble, temple) that the author's imaginative metaphors are supposed to capture. The ground of the unity of the two metaphors, Melville seems to suggest, is somehow present in the constant changing, the constant substitution, even circulation, of metaphors.

In the third instance Melville makes explicit the theme of moods. Melville departs here from the subsumptive theory of moods that predominates in the rest of the novel. In this scene (Book XIV), Pierre makes preparations to read Plinlimmon's pamphlet: "the ... strange clutching mood of his soul ... did also prevail in causing him now to retain the crumpled paper in his hand for an hour or more of that wonderful intense silence." (*P*, 205). Melville reverses the canonical form, in which the general formula subsumes the specific instance, for mood is presented here in its essential powers, as a seizing ("strange clutching") of the soul. Here it is the general formula itself that is seized by mood. The passage in question seems to imply that what is thus seized is the soul itself—a mood seizes the soul so that the soul becomes a soul. In another complication (to be developed later) Melville connects this formative power of mood with the act of reading.

In the fourth and final remark of this revelatory type, Melville suspends the irony with which he has been describing Pierre's juvenilia (Book XVIII). In yet another moment of authorial frankness, Melville confesses to his use of irony: "Inasmuch as by various indirect intimations much more than ordinary natural genius has been imputed to Pierre, it may have seemed an inconsistency, that only the merest magazine papers should have been thus far the sole productions of his mind. Nor need it be added, that, in the soberest earnest, those papers contained nothing uncommon; indeed—entirely now to drop all irony, if hitherto any thing like that has been indulged in—those fugitive things of Master Pierre's were the veriest common-place" (*P*, 257).

As in the case of Melvillean moods, empirical reality (for example, techniques of literary discourse) exhibits a diversity and prolixity allegedly controlled by a unifying order. But as the case of moods would seem to imply, the empirical diversity (moods) threatens to erase or overwhelm its unifying center (the subject of moods). Irony, an allegedly momentary disturbance in an otherwise serious utterance, actually dominates this utterance and allows a serious moment to flare up merely as an ephemeral ornament. In other words, in the four exceptional instances discussed above, Melville seems to suggest that some content—caprice, metaphor, mood (reading), irony—escapes the formula of generalization and subsumption, and that this content can escape this formula because it refers to its informing totality and it adequately indicates this totality's scope. I would like to argue that the four explicit remarks represent Melville's original poetics of the subject. As instances of discourse unassimilable in the stable subject, they present the unity of this very discourse; they present the subject as such, precisely in the form of instability, in an immediate, non-objective fashion.

Melville's choice of the four *topoi* provokes questions about the role that these *topoi* are supposed to perform. It would appear that Melville saw in some instances of discourse a privileged locus of disclosure of the totality of this discourse. This privileged locus, usually framed in *Pierre* as an explicit remark concerning the writer's craft, is able, according to Melville, to realize the presence of this discourse and, in this presentation, to unveil its unity. In the four explicit remarks, Melville's reader encounters the totality of discourse, for these remarks, themselves mere discursive moments, already enjoy a privileged comportment to this totality. Such explanation repeats Martin Heidegger's method of existential analysis, in which an ontic condition, the mood of anxiety, for example, reveals, through its power to negate the totality of beings, the ontological structure of (anxious) beings.[3]

   3. For a perceptive and synthetic account of this relation, in both its philosophical and literary aspects, see Stanley Corngold's *The Fate of the Self: German Writers and French Theory* (New York, 1986), 208–18. Anthony J. Cascardi ("The Logic of Moods:

Applied to the last of Melville's passages above, this analysis would imply that irony is a privileged form of comportment to totality, a comportment in which this totality is not revealed for inspection as an object but is, rather, experienced without conceptual presentation. This complex presentation can be expressed in the following dilemma: Is irony just an element in an open-ended field of drifting moods for which no descriptive and functional totality exists (for instance, the organizing frame of the "subject"), or does irony itself represent this subject as the totalizing formula of unity and function?[4] Expressed in terms of theories of irony, this question would read: Is irony an intentional modality available for the subject's manipulation, or is irony the very condition of intentionality? Does the subject reveal irony, or does irony reveal the subject? This essential ambiguity of ironic showing, the irony of presentation, characterizes the four discursive moments as the privileged vehicles of the disclosure of the center of unity. They "contain" the totality in themselves in such a way that they lose the ability to manifest this totality in direct, explicit showing. Here lies Melville's paradox: while the unifying subject is re-

---

An Essay on Emerson and Rousseau," *Studies in Romanticism*, XXIV (1985), 223-37) makes a similar argument about the "logic of moods" developed in European and American romanticism in the context of Kant's account of cognition as a succession of sensations held together by a postulate of the unified self (indeed, the difference between Kant and Emerson, Cascardi argues, lies in understanding this succession as either objective or subjective). The "logic of moods" manifests itself in Melville in an ironic modality.

4. This fundamental uncertainty as to the direction, intention, and scope of Melville's irony in *Pierre* continues to baffle Melville criticism. Alan Holder ("Style and Tone in Melville's *Pierre*," *Emerson Society Quarterly*, LX [1970]), while acknowledging a consistent parody fueled by ironic stance, confesses to a bafflement: "What we find, then ... is a kind of pressure exerted on a given passage by materials sharply different in tone and sometimes immediately adjacent to it. This pressure leaves us confused as to how the original passage should be taken" (82). Shepherd writes that the "unnamed, semi-omniscient narrator" is "superior in perspective to the subject ... capable of explaining Pierre's inner experience more fully and accurately than Pierre could in his own voice.... This reasonable strategy of the narrator's double perspective proves ... the main formal source of the work's failure. It is responsible from the beginning for a confusion of voices" ("Pierre's Psyche," 89; see also Holder, "Style and Tone," 76). The higher vantage point offered by the narrator creates, in Shepherd's view, the novel's many moods. Any discussion of Melville's manipulation of stylistic registers for parodic effect in *Pierre* is inextricably linked to the unprecedented use by Melville of the omniscient narrator, raising the question about this narrator's relation to the problem of the unity of consciousness.

vealed in irony (or in metaphor, mood, caprice, reading), the clarity of this showing exceeds, ironically, the clarity of explicitness itself.

In what follows I will argue that Melville's theory of the presentation of the self, described above with reference to irony and to other privileged *topoi*, conforms to the presentation of the subject as defined by the romantic theory of the novel. The subsequent discussion of mimesis, subject, metaphysics, and tautology as they are presented in *Pierre* is intended to establish and to describe a certain infinite moment within these familiar philosophical, literary, and aesthetic structures and forms. All these structures betray an elusive presence, a factor that can be detected *in* the concrete mechanism in which it appears, although it cannot be represented *by* it. Whether in the infinite chiasmus of mimesis, in the metaphysical structure of language, in portraiture, or in the reception of literary texts, the elusive element marks, I want to argue, the presence of the subject as such.

Finally, I want to argue that in *Pierre* the presentation of the subject reaches its complete form in the thematics of the self confronted with literature. It is here, when Pierre reads Dante and Shakespeare, that the separate *topoi* merge into one efficient system: the self, mood, otherness, chiasmus, and the metaphysical structure of language combine, each in its proper function, to present the subject in the form adequate to this subject.

Perhaps the supreme figure of this presentative unity in *Pierre* is the ironic, or romantic, concept of tautology. To the extent that tautology is based on repetition, it discloses the need for repetition in the constitution of the subject—the subject needs to be repeated in order to emerge in its sameness and self-identity as a subject. This role of tautology, in turn, reflects back on the constitutive function of moods in *Pierre*. As a guarantee of sameness, romantic tautology would appear to imply that moods are ultimately underwritten by a stable ground of sameness. However, Melvillean tautology no longer follows the metaphysical model of language; it reveals, as repetition, the subject of repetition as such. This subject occurs only in repetition, as the non-objective content of the act of repetition.

To the extent, then, that mood is the *genre of the subject* in *Pierre*, it accomplishes the presentation of the subject in the occurrence of moods. One could equally say that the subject of moods is the same and that it is different; these predicates are irrelevant to the excessive identity of mood with itself because this identity cannot be subsumed under the metaphysical terms of identity and difference. While the subject is presented, it is presented only in the infinite excessive presence of that which is present in each instance of mood as mood. Melville's conception of mood corresponds to the initial attunement expressed by the German word *Stimmung:* the term denotes both the harmony between two different entities and, implicitly, the unity of these entities in this harmony. In *Stimmung* the subject is attuned with itself and, so attuned, it becomes the subject of this attunement. The ground is laid for the romantic presentation of the subject in the form adequate to itself, according to Friedrich Schlegel's formula that "every theory of the novel must itself be a novel."

Let us resume the analysis. The same power that enables irony to present the subject as such can be observed in *Pierre*'s treatment of mimesis. Defined in technical vocabulary, mimetic representation is a process in which nature (*phusis*) produces a copy with the help of art (*tekhne*). The mimetic mechanism, as it has been described by Aristotle, allows for two conflicting determinations of nature, and Melville exploits this double potential to full extent. In its object-character (*natura naturata*), nature is the first moment in the movement from Nature to Culture. This scheme describes the progression of Pierre's personal relations, which proceed from biologically transmitted similarity (father, mother-son, brother-sister) towards culturally defined relations based on dissimilarity (citizen, wife). In the course of this movement, Nature becomes Culture, and "natural" similarity is erased. But in its productive capacity, as *natura naturans*, Nature *produces* Culture, and as such a source, it produces ambiguous results. Melville associates this ambiguity with the essence of textuality.[5] "So perfect to Pierre had long seemed the illuminated scroll of his life thus far, that only one hiatus was discoverable by him in that sweetly-writ manuscript. A sister had been omitted from the text" (*P,* 7).

The relationship between Nature and Culture follows Friedrich Schiller's model of the dialectic between a naïve and an artificial civilization developed in the essay "Naïve and Sentimental Poetry." According to this model, natural formation develops into cultural formation, losing the instinctive basis of its mechanism and gaining the freedom of artifice and unpredictability. Melville presents Nature as text, as Culture. Conversely, the network of relations, Culture, is

---

5. See Philippe Lacoue-Labarthe, "The Caesura of the Speculative," in *TM,* 222; "Diderot: Paradox and Mimesis," in *TM,* 256.

punctured by a hiatus, a gap that alone will indicate the represented entity (Nature). What Nature took away from Pierre in the natural realm, by depriving him of a sister, she gives back as a system of artificial relations whose central lacuna informs him precisely of this deprivation. Isabel, then, figures for Pierre as the missing component in his dream of complete Nature, but Pierre can determine that something is indeed *missing* from his dream only by representing nature as incomplete, as a text constituted by a hiatus.

The interplay of Nature and Culture, their *mimesis*, is determined by a tragic quality: "In the country then Nature planted our Pierre; because Nature intended a rare and original development in Pierre. Never mind if hereby she proved ambiguous to him in the end; nevertheless, in the beginning she did bravely" (*P,* 13). Pierre tries to reverse the dispersal into difference that constitutes nature's operation. The reversal, if it were possible, would suspend the disintegration into dissimilarity and produce a replica identical with Nature. For culture Pierre would substitute, literally, a "second" nature, the *nature* of Nature, and not, as did Pascal in *Pensée* 126, the *habit* of nature ("If habit is our second nature, then nature is our first habit"). In this attempt to *see Nature through*, Pierre understands similarity absolutely: in supplementing the missing relation—biological and structural—of a sister, he will see the work of nature completed *nontextually*. The tragedy of this undertaking lies here: a completion of nature will preempt all means of *representing this completion*. In the basic model, to use the terms from Schiller's essay, the "sentimental" artifice of culture represents—longs for—Nature's "naïve" unity. The hiatus, the absence of sister, the absence of nature in the cultural formation, is the only trace of nature's former unmediated existence; only the hiatus makes the text understandable in its artifice, *as* text, that is, by its *difference* from natural unity. Nature without Culture, nature in pristine condition, would be *unreadable*. The sentimental text is naïve nature's tragic fate. Pierre is a tragic hero.

Melville pursues the matter of mimesis further. He considers the possibility of reversal, as Pascal indicated in his *Pensée* 126. Melville speculates that nature must already be affected by a textual moment in order to be able, in *its* turn, to make a text appear natural. In this way Melville discloses in Pascal's chiasmus—nature leads to culture, culture mirrors nature—a mysterious entity that is neither natural nor cultural, neither life nor art. Mimesis shares in the power of irony to present the subject. Just as the fluctuation of moods makes present the self of these moods, so the relation between nature and culture discloses a perpetual absence of the first order (nature) in the second order (culture), which, in its turn, re-presents the lost unity. Nature has *always* been accessible *only* in a cultural (textual) formation.

The mimetic mechanism sheds useful light on Melville's notion of the subject. In Melville's mimesis neither nature nor culture exists separately before each enters the play of mutual presentation; they simultaneously in-form each other's identity. The mutual information of nature by culture in mimesis is responsible for the essential ambiguity of nature. Nature is ambiguous, not simply because it produces another meaning, because it represents another capacity of Nature, or because it produces an ambiguous *object*. Rather, and more fundamentally, nature as *natura naturans* produces pure ambiguity, not an ambiguous meaning, but a certain infinite ambiguity of the productive process itself. What nature produces could be either an object or it could just as well be no object at all. The ambiguity of the mimetic process is haunted by an infinite moment that exists only as re-presented. It exceeds nature and culture, for it is no longer nature and not yet culture but only something in between.

This infinite rupture operates constitutively in the figure of the titan Enceladus in Pierre's dream vision (*P*, 342–46). Enceladus represents—arguably—the creative human spirit emancipated from human and divine hierarchy. The description of his handless torso, a ruin of the human body, is ambiguous about the order of priority: Does the absence of hands reduce the art object to the condition of mere stone, or, on the contrary, does it confer on it a unique aesthetic value as an art object eroded by millenia? The ambiguity of the stone erases its aesthetic significations for human history. Enceladus is both pre-natural and post-cultural; a titan-no-more, he has accomplished his titanic task in full measure.

Ultimately, the infinitely chiasmic structure of mimesis forestalls all possibility of founding history on aesthetic models. Melville analyzes the relation between the modern, American Memnon, the Terror Stone in the vicinity of Saddle Meadows, and its ancient predecessor that hails from the Egyptian legend about Memnon. Melville writes: "Now as the Memnon Statue survives down to this present day, so does that nobly-striving but ever-shipwrecked character in some royal youths (for both Memnon and Hamlet were the sons of kings), of which that statue is the melancholy type. But Memnon's sculptured woes did once melodiously resound; now all is mute. Fit emblem that of old, poetry was a consecration and an obsequy to all hapless modes of human life; but in a bantering, barren, and prosaic, heartless age, Aurora's music-moan is lost among our drifting sands, which whelm alike the monument and the dirge" (*P*, 136). At issue is the possibility of comparing cultural epochs for the purposes of erecting a consistent philosophy of history. The ambition of any such philosophy (for example, Schiller's "Naïve and Sentimental Poetry") is to demonstrate humanity's progress measured in relation to an initial primitive condition. In his discussion of this comparability, Melville follows the romantic model of the speculative philosophy of history as the synthesis of the Ancients and the Moderns, in which modernity erects its evanescent and fragile identity over against the stately grandeur of antiquity. Melville, however, does not remain trapped in the chronological immediacy of this model. The greatness of Egypt was also established over against an archaic predecessor; the Statue of Memnon is also a product of cultural synthesis of a "modern" Egyptian culture and *its* archaic prototype. Applying the model to other historical moments, Melville sees into the essence of modernity as such.

This bold extrapolation allows Melville to expose the emptiness of the modernist *gestus* across the whole of history. Egypt's former grandeur and modernity's current momentary sheen are permeated by the power of the passing away of *both* antiquity *and* modernity. Indeed, the corrosive power inheres in the very attempt of speculative philosophy of history to relate cultural epochs in terms of *Bildung* (cultural formation), which was Schiller's ambition in *The Aesthetic Education of Man*. For the very same rivalry of aesthetic epochs that helps establish the modern vision of historical continuity as the progression of the human spirit also sets in motion the process of passing away, the "whelming," a mysterious formal lapse between epochs, which cannot be accommodated in dialectical aesthetic-historical models. Neither the sands of antiquity, a monument of historical magnificence, nor the sands of modernity, the illusion of the synthesis of history, can resist the power of erosion as such—the *ruin* of Enceladus, the postmodern, irreducible to the models of historical progression constructed on aesthetic homologies. The postmodern, as it "whelms alike the monument [antiquity] and the dirge [modernity]," disallows the construal of history as a rivalry of cultural epochs, exposing the inability of each such rivalry to shift to a new, higher, more hopeful time. The erosion represented by sands pulverizes any systematic notion of continuity into a dumb persistence of elemental particles resistant to beautiful accounts. Enceladus confounds history based on aesthetic comparisons: he is reducible neither to antiquity nor to modernity; he is "a demoniac freak of nature, or some stern thing of antediluvian art" (*P*, 345). The logic of Melville's image distorts the discourse of nature (in stone, nature is a freak) and extends history into prehistory (in stone, "art" preexists art). The American stone evades the rigorous dialectic between the Ancients and the Moderns:

> Not unworthy to be compared with that leaden Titan, wherewith the art of Marsy and the broad-flung pride of Bourbon enriched the enchanted gardens of Versailles;—and from whose still twisted mouth for sixty feet the waters yet upgush, in elemental rivalry with those Etna flames, of old asserted to be the malicious breath of the borne-down giant;—not unworthy to be compared with that leaden demi-god—piled with costly rocks, and with one bent wrenching knee protruding from the broken bronze;—not unworthy to be compared with that bold trophy of high art, this American Enceladus, wrought by the vigorous hand of Nature's self, it did go further than compare;—it did far surpass that fine figure molded by the inferior skill of man. Marsy gave arms to the eternally defenseless; but Nature, more truthful, performed an amputation, and left the impotent Titan without one serviceable ball-and-socket above the thigh. (*P*, 345–46)

"In its untouched natural state" (*P*, 345), Memnon is both preternatural and postcultural, produced neither by human hand, nor by elemental erosion, nor yet by an act of assimilation to an aesthetic sensibility. In its mimetic infinity, the postmodern moment, a distinctly—as Melville reminds us—*American* phenomenon, is external to history.

On the side of Nature, Melville represents the intractable moment of mimesis as the "face," on the side of Culture, as the "book." The mysterious "face" (of his half-sister Isabel) perplexes Pierre precisely with this economy of presence anterior to representable presence: "Most miraculous of all to Pierre was the vague impression, that somewhere he had seen traits of the likeness of that face before. But where, he could not say; nor could he, in the remotest degree, imagine" (*P*, 49). Confused, Pierre uses the "face" to connect the faces of real people with portraits, unaware of the face's transcendental powers, which are independent of resemblance.

The transcendental power of similarity fundamentally affects Pierre when he attempts mimetically to reconstruct his father by tracing the similarities in the two existing portraits, the chair-portrait, which shows the father when he "was becoming" Isabel's father, and the drawing-room painting, which reflects the father as seen by Pierre's mother. The chair-portrait claims superiority on the grounds that it represents pure possibility, youth unaffected by social identities: "Look again, I am thy father as he more truly was. In mature life, the world overlays and varnishes us, Pierre.... In youth we *are*, Pierre, but in age we *seem*" (*P*, 83). The passage demonstrates the impossibility of establishing historical continuity on the premise of similarity. Complete genealogical identification between father and son is possible, not in the pool of shared features, but only in the brief span of "youth," in the amorphous interval of pure possibility. In its turn, this fullness of being or of self-identical presence ("in youth we *are*") precludes mimetic representation and, hence, the experience of the father by the son. The son can identify with his father only to the extent that he, like the father in his youth, experiences the potentialities preparatory to fatherhood—he can experience his father *in the time before the father*. The son can represent the father only when he *cannot* represent the father (as father). Conversely, the father ceases to be representable to the son when *he* becomes *the son's father*. Rather than founding continuity, mimesis is disrupted by a transcendental moment anterior to the play of empirical similarity. The infinite moment that, we have seen, informed nature and culture, here operates as the condition of the father-son relation. Neither father nor son, it is an ever-persisting condition/deficit of all relations.

This deficit emerges in the unusual structure of Aunt Dorothea's story about the chair-portrait. The story describes Mr. Glendinning before he became Pierre's father and explains the resemblance between this non-father and the portrait. Aunt Dorothea says to Pierre: " 'now sit down again, and I will begin.—The picture was painted long ago, my child; you were not born then.' 'Not born?' cried little Pierre. 'Not born,' said his aunt. 'Well, go on, aunt; but don't tell me again that once upon a time I was not little Pierre at all, and yet my father was alive' " (*P*, 74).

The "once" that descends "upon a time" implicates resemblance and temporality in an intriguing nexus. The "once" preexists narrative temporality and is anterior to a topological fixation; it determines an intersection of the temporal and topological axes indefinable in terms of any relation, an archaic temporality before time, innocence before it is negatively defined in relation to experience. Each narrative account begins before "once upon a time," in a preexisting abundance of relations, which alone founds objective relations (between father and son). Applied rigorously, this anterior nexus affects, not only

Pierre, but also his father: if Pierre is "not born," then neither is his father his *father*.

As in the infinite chiasmus of mimesis, the moment that establishes the father-son relation subsists between the two objects as their condition but is itself reducible neither to the natural nor to the temporal dimension. This infinite moment, in which one is a father or a son "so much the more truly" (83), remains submerged, invisible, never born. All narratives begin with a positive determination, "once upon a time," but this determination itself is founded on the lack of origin (on being "not born"). The prehistoric time of not being born is the excess of indeterminacy; it precedes narration as essentially unrelatable.

The pregenetic reserve founds the unusual powers of portraiture. The chair-portrait mystically whispers: "Pierre, believe not the drawing-room painting; that is not thy father; or, at least, is not *all* of thy father. Consider in thy mind, Pierre, whether we two paintings may not make only one" (*P*, 83). Portraiture harbors a resemblance that preexists empirical correspondence and that is independent of it. The "only one" portrait that founds the similarity between the drawing-room portrait and the chair-portrait, that by which they appear as the sum of the adolescent and of the father, is a hypothetical resemblance that relates the two portraits to one another. Melville writes: "and the face in the picture still looked at them [the old aunt and the little child] frankly, and cheerfully, as if there was nothing kept concealed; and yet again, a little ambiguously and mockingly, as if slyly winking to *some other picture*," wondering what these two could possibly suspect in such an innocent face (*P*, 80; italics mine). The reference to "some other picture" indicates that the two portraits resemble one another because they themselves derive from a grounding portrait and that this third portrait is a pure structure of "otherness." The comparison of the two portraits reveals an "other" picture, portraiture itself, a transcendental similarity that itself remains unrepresentable. The "other picture" presents pure resemblance divorced from mimetic correspondence. And it is this pure otherness that confounds Pierre's comparative investigation of the origin of the "face": "Only the face, the face alone now visited him; and so accustomed had he been of late to confound it with the shapes of air, that he almost trembled when he thought that face to face, that face must shortly meet his own" (*P*, 111). Seeing the face "face to face" defines the tautology that grounds transcendental similarity. The "face" is not the source of the resemblances but the condition of their being resemblances. Pierre indeed *can* observe resemblance among empirically different pairs: real faces, portraits, etc., but resemblance itself belongs neither to the biological nor to the mimetic order. Resemblance "as such," the infinite moment, which, in the Memnon Stone, exceeds nature and culture, is the relation of the face to *itself*. This original presence cannot be re-presented, for it is a relation founded on an excess of presence: it is presentation itself.

As another passage, quoted by Melville from Dante's *Commedia*, will show, seeing the face "face to face" entails a direct access to, a "making explicit of," the resemblance of resemblance. What is thus made explicit, however, cannot, because it has been made explicit, be grasped as an object of knowledge, for it is both more luminescent and more obscure than any clear showing—it is anterior and posterior to lucid presence. In this presentation we see showing *showing itself.* Pierre, staring "at the transfixed face in the air... ejaculated that wonderful verse from Dante, descriptive of the two mutually absorbing shapes in the Inferno: 'Ah! How dost thou change,/Agnello! See! thou art not double now,/Nor only one!' " (*P*, 85) The "face," neither self-contained nor dispersed into resemblance, is determined by an excessive explicitness—noumenality—of presentation. What is, in the order of re-presentation, available as the echo—the echo, for example, of nature in cultural representation—is here available directly, as presentation, neither "double" nor "only one."

Melville associates the excessive presence, the pure image, with the art of portraiture, and the connection is as revealing as it is complex. Pierre speculates about a European portrait (of a man resembling his father) observed at an art exhibition: "The original of this second portrait was as much the father of Isabel as the original of the chair-portrait" (*P*, 353). Pierre still proceeds empirically, trying to identify the original person painted in the portrait as the father of Isabel and as his own father. But Pierre continues his musings on the European portrait: "But perhaps there was no original at all to this second portrait; it might have been a pure fancy-piece" (*P*, 353). Unexpectedly, the power to engender offspring is not simply shifted to a different source but is separated from any source whatsoever; the European portrait maintains resemblance to Isabel, although it may have been painted *without an original*. The powers of engendering that characterize portraiture violate biological relations; the European portrait's resemblance persists in the absence of any empirically demonstrable relation.

For Melville the transcendentally engendering power of portraiture lies here. Whether painted with or without an original, all portraits capture the "essence" of the subject; they make explicit the essential comparability of the subject *with itself*; they foreground the ground of similarity as such—self-representability. Precisely this power to represent itself, which exceeds mimetic clarity, gives transcendental similarity the power to originate—to engender. Indeed, as the passage about the chair-portrait indicates, the engendering is employed in self-generation exclusively for the sake of effecting presentation. Pierre perceives a resemblance of Isabel, not in the father "any way rememberable by him," but "vaguely... in the portrait; therefore, not Pierre's parent... but the portrait's painted *self* seemed the real father of Isabel; for, so far as all sense went, Isabel had inherited one peculiar trait nowhither traceable but to it" (P, 197; Melville's italics). And while the similarity emanating from portraiture—"strange relativeness, reciprocalness, and transmittedness"—can be referred to an empirical "this" or "that," it always returns to the portrait, to the generative space of art's "nowhither."[6]

The pure power of engendering, completely indifferent to the empirical realm, raises the question of *what* is engendered by it. Here we arrive at the theme of the Melvillean subject. Let us read the passage again: "Not Pierre's parent... but the portrait's painted *self* seemed the real father of Isabel." The phrase "the portrait's painted *self*" contains several semantic layers. It gives, first of all, a reference—this portrait, and no other among those mentioned in the novel. In addition, it implies that the portrait's self, the art object, must be painted in order to come into existence. We must rigorously demarcate here the difference between the portrait *of the father* (the resemblance between the figure on the canvas and Pierre's father) and the portrait *itself*.

6. The origin of Isabel, traceable "nowhither" but to the self-enclosed and perpetually withdrawing interiority of the portrait, invites parallels between the theory of art in Melville and the views on art expressed by Martin Heidegger in his essay "The Origin of the Work of Art" (*Basic Writings*, ed. David Farrell Krell [New York, 1977], 149–87). In a preliminary questioning, Heidegger speculates that the origin of the work of art can be found neither in the artist nor in the work itself, but in art alone (149). Melville's "nowhither" seems to confirm Heidegger's preliminary decision that art is the origin of the art work. In the subsequent elaboration of this answer, Heidegger defines the work of art as the place of the happening of truth in an infinite presentation of this truth in the work, as this work, as the "putting-to-work-of-truth" (165). While at the level of specific solutions parallels between Heidegger and Melville are yet to be explored, Melville's "nowhither" shows that his reflection on art corresponds to the direction formulated in Heidegger's essay.

The "portrait itself" is not intended here as the material on which the figure can be drawn (the canvas) but the portrait's being a portrait, its identity as portrait. "The portrait's painted *self*" presents presentation. The portrait is constantly being painted—it emerges as a structural relation between static presence and the activity of making present. One structural moment (the activity of painting) "engenders" another moment (the passivity of being painted). This relation becomes precisely a *relation,* a nascence of relations (of relatives), an infinite, self-enclosed engendering without external figure whose only purpose is the engendering of itself. The only goal of this infinity is to "gender," to maintain a relation with itself as a relation that constitutes it in this relation. This relation is prior to relating; the "gender" as such (before it becomes engaged in engendering external objects) is "one of a kind," the Genre (of) Itself, kinship as such always implying a next of kin yet primarily abiding in its self. The portrait's painted self exists very much in the manner of Enceladus: "Wrought by the vigorous hand of Nature's self, it did go further than compare."

Melville thus accomplishes an indissoluble, *mutually engendering and simultaneously originating* relation between identity and the means of presenting this identity. "The portrait's painted *self*" suggests that the incessant painting (gerund) of the self cannot be distinguished by any marker of ideality from the self in the painting (noun). Melville's italics finitize an infinite relation, or conversely, they infinitize a finite relation. The portrait's self makes present, as "self," that materiality of portraiture that cannot be foregrounded over against a semantically transparent aspect—the presence that the portrait cannot represent in any material, yet which founds all possibility of representation. Melville "romanticizes" the relation between the subject and the subject's self-presentation into an infinite, transcendental self-presentation; his hyperbolic genre of mood is a Genre of Itself that "cast[s] off the most intense beloved bond, as a hindrance to the attainment of whatever transcendental object that usurper mood so tyrannically suggests" (*P,* 180).

Melville's metaphorics and the subsumptive classification of "moods" are structured by the transcendental genre of "the portrait's painted *self.*" First, transcendental mimesis opens up dimensions both more figurative and less literal than those the substitutive mechanics of metaphor is capable of generating. It produces two economies of language related to each other in circular fashion: a metaphysical economy, with a ground of literality and a sphere of transposed meaning, and an economy indifferent to metaphysics, a "bantering, barren, and prosaic" (*P*, 136) medium without the figurative option, the economy of "prose."[7] Second, Melville's mimesis engenders a similarly circular relation between the materiality of the painting and the ideality of the self. His theory of presentation makes the self both more sensitive to all moods and yet originally indifferent to—unconscious of—all advances of the synthesis of the self. In both cases, presenting the self operates in the darkness that, as in the narrative about "Little Pierre," precedes ostensible content.

Perhaps Melville's insight into the "portrait's painted *self*" is most illuminating with reference to the theme of the self as such. Applied to the self, this insight would suggest that the self that dwells in darkness is not the empirical self suffering in the "hell of the soul." Rather, it is the activity of constant self-constitution of self by itself. While the commonly conceived self is a re-presentation, a retrospective acknowledgment of the loss of the self's unifying principle (the mimesis of Nature and Culture), Melville's infinite self is the remarking of the infinite moment between the being of the self and the self of being (the chiasmus between nature and culture). The difference between the two conceptions of the self, the humanist/subjective self and the transcendental self, is a difference between the identity of the self with itself and the infinite surplus produced by this identity.

It is here that Melville's irony exhibits a strong affinity with the romantic theory of the novel. We may recall that romanticism constructed this theory to present the subject to itself in the form of presentation adequate to this specific subject. In Schlegel's formula "every theory of the novel must itself be a novel," the relation of the theory to its object effects the identity of the self as the infinite reflection between the theory and this object: the knowledge of the object (in this case, of the novel) is itself a novel. In the properly romantic fashion, Melville sees this reflective constitution of the self as the ironic work of moods. The genre of mood, that is, represents for Melville the privileged locus of disclosure of the self, if the self is understood as the non-objective presence of the self as such. In the genre of mood the self (of the mood) becomes itself.

---

7. The prose creates infinite language in an economy exemplified by the figure of Enceladus. The titan's handless torso precludes symbolism based on physical counterparts; it presents a possibility of signification independent of the physical vehicle (without hands). In Enceladus, Melville's figurality loses its literal ground and erases the metaphysical nature of language.

Schlegel's infinitely generative formula of reflection is the relation of pure interiority, whose only goal is to constitute and maintain itself and to contain itself in and as this reflection. In Schlegel and Melville the self is the "figure" of the infinite relation, but this is so, not for reasons of an interest in the psychological subject, but for reasons inherent in the process itself—for only this relation is one of *self*-relation. Self-relation produces nothing (no object-nature) but itself, beyond the possibility of showing both the object of this production and the self as separate from this production. The self is both the stage and the content of this self-relation. As in Schlegel's ironic presentation, the Melvillean self presents itself in the dense, non-objective presence, in the "hellish essence of the soul."

It is imperative, in other words, to preserve Melville's preoccupation with the self in the field of the romantic theory of the novel because Melville is not concerned with the self as a constituted human subjectivity but with the self as the necessary and the only "object" of absolute presentation. This presentation is absolute because here the self presents itself as itself. Because of the narrow margin of difference, it is not difficult to confuse the "hellish essence of the soul," considered as the infinite relation without figure that truly founds the self as self(-relation), with the "hell of the soul," considered in the existentialist sense as temporary penal colony. The latter can easily degenerate into simplistic forms, such as unhappiness, depression, and versions of Hegel's "unhappy consciousness."

Unfortunately, the fraudulent sense all too frequently assumes prominence. Melville seems to suggest that the false, sentimental self would triumph and that the true self might never become uncovered were it not for the instrumental role of literature. Pierre discovers it in his reading of the classics:

> "Well, well;—'twill be a pretty time we'll have this evening; there's the book of Flemish prints . . . then, second, is Flaxman's Homer. . . . Then Flaxman's Dante;—Dante! Night's and Hell's poet he. No, we will not open Dante. Methinks now the face—the face—minds me a little of pensive, sweet Francesca's face—or, rather, as it had been Francesca's daughter's face—wafted on the sad dark wind, toward observant Virgil and the blistered Florentine. No, we will not open Flaxman's Dante. Francesca's mournful face is now ideal to me. Flaxman might evoke it wholly,—make it present in lines of misery—bewitching power. No! I will not open Flaxman's Dante! Damned be the hour I read in Dante! more damned than that wherein Paolo and Francesca read in fatal Launcelot!" (*P*, 42)

At this point the affinity between Melville's and romanticism's conceptions of the self can be further strengthened and developed in the context of Schlegel's views on romantic poetry. As has been already noted, Schlegel found the paradigmatic illustration of romantic imagination in the work of the "romantic novelists," Dante, Cervantes, and Shakespeare. Schlegel writes: "This is where I look for and find the Romantic—in the older moderns, in Shakespeare, Cervantes, in Italian poetry" (*DP*, 101).[8] The following analysis will seek to place Melville's notion of the self in the context of Dantesque and Shakespearean poetics, with an eye to bringing out the romantic dimension of their preoccupation with the self.

To begin the discussion of Melville's affinity with the romantic authors, it may be appropriate to recall René Girard's theory of mimetic desire.[9] According to Girard, desire and the self proceed "mimetically" from images of desire and of self defined by literature. In its revelatory function, literature, according to Girard, exposes the "romantic" delusion (*mensonge*), for example, chivalric love in *Launcelot*, by making explicit, through an act of reading, the derivative, imitative nature of all supposedly original experience. Paolo and Francesca, reading *Launcelot*, fall prey to the delusion; Dante criticizes the literary infatuation by "quoting" it in his epic.

But Melville asks the dark question, While we can win a measure of distance from literary illusion only by reading the "book about the book" (Dante's mention of Paolo and Francesca reading *Launcelot*), what force can prevent us from falling prey, in turn, to the "secondary" reading itself? Pierre cannot distinguish between the naïve and the critical levels, the primary and the secondary: "Damned be the hour I read in Dante! more damned than that wherein Paolo and Francesca read in fatal Launcelot!" There is a secret power in the act of reading *as such* that makes reading at the same time seductive (primary) and critical (secondary), one that converts seduction into a disillusioned critique and renders critique infinitely intoxicating. Indeed, to Pierre critical literature appears "more damned"; Paolo and Francesca's intoxication with represented experience pales in comparison to Pierre's

---

8. See also *SL*, 319.

9. Girard, *Deceit, Desire, and the Novel*, 11–17. Edgar A. Dryden (*The Form of American Romance* [Baltimore, 1988]) sensitively raises, in the context of *Pierre*, the complex of Girardian questions—the origination of all experience (also of creative experience) in the "already written" (77)—and he pays special attention to Dante's treatment of the episode of Paolo and Francesca.

intoxication with *the critical representation of this intoxication*. Can reading control its own "bewitching power"?

This is to say that Melville rejects the hierarchy, implied in Girard's model, of the erring "romantic" writers, who merely repeat the intoxication, and the enlightened "novelistic" writers, who demystify the illusion. For Melville, literature, at least the work of Dante and, to an even larger extent, that of Shakespeare, is at the same time "immediate" and "critical" beyond the parameters allowed by Girard's scheme. For him, Girard's inferior literature does not mediate experience for self-indulgent, sentimental consumption. Rather, it sets in motion a reading experience that makes explicit the representation of the self—makes explicit the self that can come into existence exclusively in *thus* being made explicit, in ironic presentation.

Guided by Dante the romantic author, Pierre discovers the essence of the self to be located in the night and in hell, and he interprets it as a condition of dejection, a sorry fate of a self consigned to misery—this is still Girardian. But Melville reads more in the "sublime Italian" (*P*, 54); he suggests that Pierre, by reading what Girard considers "critical literature," glimpses the *other* possibility, not an alternative solution, but the possibility of otherness as such—that is, the possibility that a critical disciplining of sentimental fiction exposes the otherness of hell as precisely the source of the self and not as its temporary penal colony. Dante's hell has the capacity to *constitute* the self.

According to Melville, the Dantesque self is not a function of a more or less successful critical uncovering of the Girardian *mensonge*. Although able, in its clarity of insight, to expose the dark powers of hell, the Dantesque self constantly abides in the presence of the *Inferno*, able neither to conquer it nor to leave it behind. For Melville there can be no inferior, "romantic" literature, as opposed to a "novelistic," critical one. Literature is, according to Melville, the making explicit of self-sameness under the inexorable mandate of infernal otherness. Literature is immediate and critical—primary and secondary—at the same time, in excess of sentimental immediacy and of critical distance. Melville's literature solicits the sphere of "not being born," the hell that precedes the tale. In rejecting the distinction between high and low, Melville offers a literature free from all hierarchy, one founded on "some other" book, on the premise and promise of hell. Literature stands, in Melville, for a reflexive confrontation of the self with itself, for a disclosure necessarily affected—as his reading of Dante shows—by the distortion inherent in this reflexivity. When critically read, the overpowering immediacy of naïve experience produces its converse, intoxication with critical insight.

The infinite identity of naïve immediacy and insightful critique comes to the fore when Pierre compares the truth of the human experience as defined by Dante with the truth of this experience as described by Shakespeare. Pierre reinterprets the two romantic authors, Dante and Shakespeare, in tandem: reading *Hamlet* he applies the logic of hell to the problem of decision. Pierre reads in *Hamlet:* "The time is out of joint;—Oh cursed spite,/That ever I was born to set it right!" (*P*, 168). At this point in the novel, Pierre reads the words as if he were one of Dante's damned characters; like Paolo and Francesca, he identifies with a fictional character and a fictive situation pertinent to his dilemma. Pierre is in hell—in the benign, systematic-technical sense that Dante gives to his well-ordered justice of *oeconomia divina*, the hell of unreflected reception of literary models.

But the Dantesque hell changes quickly into a Hamletesque one. Unlike Dante, Shakespeare gives his reader no guidelines about a second-degree decoding of his condition. *Hamlet* (itself a thing of "hell and night") stands in the following relation to the *Commedia:* "It is the not impartially bestowed privilege of the more final insights, that at the same moment they reveal the depths, they do, sometimes, also reveal—though by no means so distinctly—some answering heights. But when only midway down the gulf, its crags wholly conceal the upper vaults, and the wanderer thinks it all one gulf of downward dark" (*P*, 169–70). The passage from Dante and the passage from Shakespeare offer Pierre two responses to experience mediated by literature. The former critiques such experience by implying that naïve reading is a thing of hell, while the latter steps aside to open up onto its own indecision. Defined by Dante's cosmology, Hamlet stands "only midway down the gulf, its crags wholly conceal the upper vaults, and the wanderer thinks it all one gulf of downward dark."

Applied to *both* Dante *and* Shakespeare, the passage addresses their character as romantic novelists insofar as they are preoccupied with the structure of the self. To be more precise, the two authors exemplify romanticism's explanation of the origin of the self as pure self-presentation. Both in Dante and in Shakespeare the self is constituted by hell, by the "gulf of downward dark." The "gulf" is otherness "as such," an impenetrable darkness, which, as it halts the power of light, defines within this horizon a finite field of visibility. In relation to this darkness, Dante's *Inferno* denotes the bottom of all meaning, and *Hamlet*'s hell denotes the mid-air zone in the free fall of the interpreter—of Shakespeare's and Melville's despairing youth. A Dantesque self seeks to delimit and demarcate its relation to this darkness; it assumes that, while otherness cannot be brought to light, it can at least be shown to be darkness. A Shakespearean self also recognizes the constitutive role of darkness, but in contrast to the Dantesque self, it believes itself to be infinitely constituted by a process of delimiting and demarcating. The same process that, in Dante, serves to construct the self *in its integrated wholeness* over against darkness, serves in Shakespeare to constitute the self *as the infinite relation* to darkness. Hence Dante's sense of the abyss is hermeneutic, encompassed by a top and a bottom, and essentially comprehensible, while for Shakespeare the abyss is an unconceptualizable and immeasurable space, a field of nonmetaphysical meaning, a perpetual infinite middle.

For Melville's Dante, literature is essentially critical: it discovers the self on the verge of hell, it asserts that the self itself has created this hell, and it rescues the self from the precipice of otherness. Dante considers the naïve reading *sentimental* because it operates under the illusory assumption that the self can become constituted by merging with infernal otherness. The critique of Paolo and Francesca's simple reading competence is intended to correct the sinful fall of the self into otherness by retrieving the self from it. The *Commedia* accomplishes this critique as secondary reading; it supersedes the intoxication with the reading matter by subjecting naïve reading to a reading of the second degree, in order to expurgate all intoxication. By leaving nothing uninterpreted, Dante attains pure reading, the reading that, hermeneutically, keeps darkness at bay.

While Melville's reading of *Hamlet*, like that of the *Commedia*, acknowledges the essential role of hell in the discovery of the self, it brings forth a different infernal economy. The concealed meaning is concealed in principle, a mystery, *das Geheimnis*, the hell of meaning, while the interpretable versions represent the obvious clarity, the luminescence that unproblematically dwells in hermeneutic light. Melville presents Pierre's hesitation between these two senses of hell in the figure of chiasmic alternation, as in the title of Book IX, "More Light, and the Gloom of That Light. More Gloom, and the Light of That Gloom" (*P*, 165). In the situation where both light and darkness inhabit the domain of their opposites, all reading of despair will become infinite, a penumbral, desperate reading in which reference to understanding as vision makes little sense. Not accidentally, the chiasmic structure is announced, in Section II of this book, by the hymnic invocation to the impartial reader, which associates the chiasmic condition with a system of moods: "Judge ye, then, ye Judicious, the mood of Pierre, so far as the passage in Dante touched him" (*P*, 169).

It is the chiasmic relation between the two works that renders them both indispensable and useless in Pierre's predicament:[10] "Torn into a hundred shreds the printed pages of Hell and Hamlet lay at his feet, which trampled them, while their vacant covers mocked him with their idle titles. Dante had made him fierce, and Hamlet had insinuated that there was none to strike. Dante had taught him that he had bitter cause of quarrel; Hamlet taunted him with faltering in the fight" (*P*, 170). Both works reveal to Pierre the nature of meaning as determined by hell: one, a Dantesque hyper-reading, a *sur-lecture*, seeks to delimit and neutralize hell, while the other abides in hell, as absence, or excess, of reading. Action, Pierre discovers, produces either a *comoedia*, the assumption of total readability, or a *tragoedia*, the lack of all assumption, an infinitely dense reading.

Which hermeneutic method—the lucidity afforded by the critical reading or the dense darkness of complete immediacy—is "more" true? The infinity of the chiasmus condemns the subject to a futile exercise in fine discrimination, to infinite de-ciding: How is any comparison of the two works possible? What do they have in common, if the one claims to represent the essence of reading and, thereby, to offer the only correct insight (allegory) into the meaning of the sentimental Hamlet (*Hamlet*), while the other, driven by sentimental rage, ironi-

---

10. The parallels between *Hamlet* and the *Inferno* in *Pierre* are so "intensive," writes Nathalia Wright ("*Pierre:* Herman Melville's *Inferno*," *American Literature*, XXXII [1960]), "that Melville's work may be called—as is that of the author Pierre—another *Inferno*" (167). Perhaps the most stimulating treatment of the problem can be found in G. Giovannini's article "Melville's *Pierre* and Dante's *Inferno*" (*PMLA*, LXIV [March, 1949], 70–78). Giovannini understands the relationship between the two authors and works to be chiasmic: "The symbolical meanings of the two books support one another; the awareness of evil ideally represented by the *Inferno* issues in the frustration ideally represented by *Hamlet*. . . . The ironic side of the paradox, that truth intensifies despondency instead of impelling the will, is suggested in the chiasmic pattern of the title of Book IX, the first and second element of which refer respectively to Pierre's reading in the *Inferno* and *Hamlet:* 'More Light, and the Gloom of that Light; More Gloom, and the Light of that Gloom' " (74). Edward H. Rosenberry (*Melville and the Comic Spirit* [Cambridge, Mass., 1955]) adds: "Pierre's favorite books were *Hamlet* and the *Inferno*. The combination is significant, for the whole ambiguous problem of bright and dark . . . usually led him, quite unprotesting, straight to Hell" (151).

cally reflects on the critical theory of reading and exposes hermeneutics as essentially a matter of a lack of interpretive resolve, as exegetical indecision? If the *Inferno* keeps hell at bay in critical reading, how can it *enter into contradiction* with Hamlet's notion of reading as constituted by and inseparable from hell? While a Dantesque comedy keeps hell at arm's length in the distance of critical reading, a Shakespearean tragedy abides in hell immediately, reads hell explicitly. There is no room in Dante's *Inferno* for *Hamlet*'s hell on earth.[11]

The chiasmus between the two romantic authors makes it impossible to decide about the priority of a sophisticated and a naïve reading. One begins in the dark and arrives into a clear region of understanding, and one originates in clarity only to uncover the all-pervasive darkness: "More Light, and the Gloom of That Light. More Gloom, and the Light of That Gloom." Dante and Shakespeare cannot, each in terms of his respective poetics, appropriate the other into the hermeneutics of darkness that they independently disclose. "Judge ye, then, ye Judicious, the mood of Pierre, so far as the passage in Hamlet touched him" (*P*, 170).

The infinity of this chiasmatically produced indecision is a matter of Melville's genuinely *titanic* irony—the irony, that is, of the titan Enceladus. It alone can make the self explicit—as underwritten by the play of irony—as the infernal irony of presence. In Book XVIII, entitled "Pierre, as a Juvenile Author, Reconsidered," we read the opening paragraph: "Inasmuch as by various indirect intimations much more than ordinary natural genius has been imputed to Pierre, it may have seemed an inconsistency, that only the merest magazine papers should have been thus far the sole productions of his mind. Nor need it be added, that, in the soberest earnest, those papers contained nothing uncommon; indeed—entirely now to drop all irony, if hitherto any thing like that has been indulged in—those fugitive things of Master Pierre's were the veriest common-place" (*P*, 257). Melville admits,

---

11. Rita Gollin ("*Pierre*'s Metamorphosis of Dante's *Inferno*," *American Literature*, XXXIX [1968], 542–45) rightly suggests that Melville identifies hell with complete immediacy and loss of observer's (interpreter's) distance. This condition prevents one from saying, in common language, that "one is in hell." Hell denies us even the luxury of being "in" it, the comfort of spatial metaphorization; it denies any form of literal and figurative grasp of experience. Gollin also notes that "the most important difference [between Dante and Melville] is that in this final scene [the dungeon in the prison] the last vestiges of Pierre's earlier role as Dantean observer of a sinful world have completely vanished" (544). All hope for a narrator's distance towards events collapses: infernal irony is sheer immediacy.

explicitly, that irony has been at work in the description of Pierre's juvenilia, and that this irony is now "entirely" dropped. This delimitation of ironic stance tests both the reader's and the writer's competence. First, as explicit, irony can now, even for the writer, be only retrospective—irony, dropped now, comes to presence exclusively as a "having-been." Secondly, an explicit admission of ironic stance arms the reader against the author's future ironic traps.

Above all, however, the author's admission that he has been ironic and that he will not engage in irony in the future brings to surface the constitutive mechanism of textuality. The artifice of textuality alone can re-present the natural, pretextual condition. As we have seen in the analysis of Nature and Culture, Pierre can detect the natural order only as an absence (of Isabel), as a hiatus in the text of his life. Nature can be represented, in the strict sense of "re-presentation," as a "having-been," and the text is the proper vehicle of this re-presentation. Conversely, the text is represented as a second nature, as a natural product, in keeping with the first law of art, that the art work appear as if it were made by Nature herself.

Melville's ironic device (by no means his original invention) arrests these reversals: it stops representing nature textually, and it stops reproducing the text naturally. In its essence, this project is antimetaphysical. It will suffice for now to state that by giving irony the sense of a "having-been" and of a "not-coming-again" Melville attempts to present the text without resorting to the natural pretence. Textuality, if thought in the infinite chiasmus with nature as its opposite, is constituted by the infinite moment that structures the opposition between Nature and Culture. Textuality, presented rather than re-presented, is the "text's written self," its being itself. To present textuality as such is to weave together the texture of the text, to present the constant passing away of what had always been here and what is always ahead, the postmodern, titanically ironic being of the self as the not yet and the no longer. Irony is the constant transition of the act of presenting into the matter being presented. In irony—supposedly one textual moment among other moments—text manifests itself in its transcendental nature: as not yet and no longer a being, not yet and no longer a book.[12]

---

12. Melville's remark, "entirely now to drop all irony, if hitherto anything like that has been indulged in," follows in structure Friedrich Schlegel's phrase, in "On Incomprehensibility": "I wrote this fragment with the most honorable intentions and almost

The issue goes beyond the mere notoriousness and intractability of ironic, meta-textual remarks. Most fundamentally, Melville's irony opens up the identity of writing to a constant sliding into itself ("the writing's written *self*") or away from itself (to "some other" writing). Indeed, as the privileged locus of disclosure of the text and of the self, *the ironic mood* is the site of the occurrence of this excessive presence. This ironic showing exceeds the stability of objective presentation. Melville's ironic subject always modifies its mood according to the situation, yet these locally pertinent adjustments never reveal the subject who supposedly stands behind them.[13] Irony discloses the subject as the impersonal, *un*subjective, unconscious happening of moods, where the moods constitute the scene of attunement of the subject with itself. In this attunement, nothing objective or, for that matter, *subjective* is being shown, but only the tuning of the subject, the subject's settling into harmony with itself. In its infinity, Pierre's "combining consciousness" (*P,* 171) fails to "combine" into an objective figure of its unity, a failure of transcendental excellence that is the mark of a "much more than ordinary natural genius" (*P,* 257).

---

without any irony at all [*fast ohne alle Ironie*]" (*F,* 263). In both cases, the remark captures the infinity of the statement, not only in content, but, above all, in structure—one's own comment on one's exposition not only belongs to the exposition itself, and not only fails thus to comment on it, but it, first of all, remarks the moment in textual economy in which the exposition is for the first time constituted *as* an exposition. However, the very moment that constitutes a text cannot itself be comprehended in terms of, and as a function of, textual hermeneutics. Hence the title of Schlegel's piece. All texts are necessarily ironic—here, for example, comprehension is founded on incomprehensibility.

13. The deadlocked reality, the only one offered by hermeneutic procedure, leads to what Shepherd calls "suicidal urge" ("Pierre's Psyche," 88). As Richard Gray rightly observes (" 'All's o'er, and ye know him not': A Reading of *Pierre,*" in *Herman Melville: Reassessments,* ed. A. Robert Lee [New York, 1984]), suicide belongs to a certain conceptual chain; a retreat into incest leads to "self-absorption and self-enclosure leading inevitably, it seems, to self-destruction" (129). Still, suicide, in Melville's sense, only perpetuates the condition of undecidability, for it itself stands under the incision of scission. In Melville, sui-cide refers more to an arbitrary construal of self (the scission that separates, cuts off, the self from what is not the self)—arbitrary because, in light of the moody constitution of the self, suicide always concretely fails, for one is unable successfully to establish the distinction between the self and the nonself on which the act of suicide would have to be based. Because it is controlled by a cutting off, decision in suicide always separates the subject (sui-) from its own decision. Self-destruction is, in Melville, as impossible as self-determination (standing under one's own law, autonomy).

We have said earlier that the presentation of the self in Melville entails a stepping outside of the metaphysical structure of language. It may be perhaps helpful to preface our further discussion of Melville's original insight with an analysis of Plinlimmon's "Pamphlet," for the pamphlet sets forth the metaphysical nature of language in unequivocal, if disingenuous, terms. Plinlimmon's text, whose "conclusion was gone" (*P*, 206), discusses the dependence of the hermeneutic act on moods, a dependence that shatters the metaphysical foundations of knowledge and language.

The pamphlet, a parable on the nature of moods, represents, arguably, Melville's tour de force in his attempt to define cosmic irony and to accomplish the romantic, transcendental explicitness of showing. To read the pamphlet, the reader must be in a proper mood: "The ... strange clutching mood of his soul ... did also prevail in causing him now to retain the crumpled paper in his hand for an hour or more of that wonderful intense silence" (*P*, 205). For Melville, entrance into reading is a question of such originary, moody attunement. In the concrete instance of the pamphlet, the attunement takes place between the reader, Pierre, and the text. The properly transcendental dimension of this reading situation lies in the circumstance that the pamphlet discusses the nature of the originary attunement of reader and reading matter as a necessary precondition of its own reading. As a consequence of this grounding, the pamphlet's only subject matter is the meaning of this specific reading. However, this account of the conditions of reading is still "merely" hermeneutic, based as it is on the theory of interpretive *Einfühlung*, which presupposes the stable entities of reader, author, and text. Melville's model, however, radically departs from this description.

To see the extent of Melville's originality on this point we have to analyze Plinlimmon's pamphlet in more detail. Plinlimmon's objective is to reinterpret the old apology that sought to reconcile the goodness of the eternal God with the corruption and imperfection of the sublunar world. The pamphlet, a "printed document ... so metaphysically and insufferably entitled as this:—'Chronometricals & Horologicals'" (*P*, 207), organizes its argument in a metaphysical fashion: it has a tenor (the other world) and a vehicle (the earth). In the opening sentences Plinlimmon recasts the metaphysical division between God and the world in navigational terminology: "For peculiarly coming from God, the sole source of that heavenly truth, and the great Greenwich hill and tower from which the universal meridians are far out into infinity reckoned; such souls seem as London sea-chronometers (*Greek*, time-namers) which as the London ship floats past Greenwich down the Thames, are accurately adjusted by Greenwich time, and if heedfully kept, will still give that same time, even though carried to the Azores" (*P*, 211).

However, in the course of the argument, this analogy, designed to facilitate exposition ("Christ was a chronometer; and the most exquisitely adjusted and exact one, and the least affected by all terrestrial jarrings, of any that have ever come to us," [*P*, 211]) begins to assume an increasingly central role and comes to dominate the exposition. In this development, the empirical analogue (the earth) assumes the properties of a transcendent entity in such a way that it is now in relation to the *earthly* point of reference, Greenwich, and in terms of a *human* activity, navigation, that the metaphysical question is posed, examined, and resolved. In this way the pamphlet's transcendent *explanandum* becomes completely submerged in the empirical *explanans*, in the images specific to the practical art of navigation: "True, in nearly all cases of long, remote voyages—to China, say—chronometers of the best make, and the most carefully treated, will gradually more or less vary from Greenwich time, without the possibility of the error being corrected by direct comparison with their great standard" (*P*, 211). And Plinlimmon plods on, hopelessly entangled in his own conceit. The navigational miscalculation can be moderated by "skillful and devout observations of the stars by the sextant" (*P*, 211), by considering, in each calculation, the margin of error, so "that ascertained loss or gain can be readily added or deducted, as the case may be" (*P*, 211), and by comparing one's measurements "with the chronometer of some other ship at sea, more recently from home" (*P*, 211). The dissolution of the pamphlet's metaphysical subject in the *minutiae* of the craft of navigation represents a process by which the pamphlet's subject matter becomes infinitely identical with the method of its exposition.

Moreover, the text seems to support the hypothesis that this inversion of method into content is a matter of a certain necessity inherent in the nature of language. Plinlimmon uses navigation in his presentation of the metaphysical principle for a highly specific purpose: he wants to demonstrate nothing less than the condition under which heavenly perfection can lend itself to any analogy with the empirical, *finite* world. He inquires about the relation between the earthly and the heavenly realms by analyzing the suitability of the worldly system for founding the "stability" of the highest immutable point. It so happens that language is a suitable vehicle for this synthesis.

According to Melville, it would appear that humanity cannot, *in principle*, conceive of the ideal as such. However, the ideal (heaven) can be brought into view, but then *only* in the form or guise of an earthly equivalent or analogue (Greenwich). Moreover, the affinity (analogy) between heaven and its humble earthly equivalent must be already somehow imagined, constructed, and secured in an original synthesis. The origin of a supposedly immutable concept of ethics lies in "this world," to the extent that the immutable point of reference can be imagined only on the fragile *fundamentum* identified in the sublunar world in this immediate synthesis.[14]

It would seem, then, that the need to represent the infinite by the finite, to argue about the "other" world from "this" world, merely reaffirms the initial metaphysical intentions of the pamphlet and, by extension, Melville's loyalty to a metaphysical conception of language. However, in an insightful reversal, Melville uses precisely the metaphysical premise to subvert metaphysics. He applies the metaphysical premise to language with its fullest force, claiming that the schematization into the finite and the infinite is itself a product of the metaphysical structure of language. From here it is an easy step to claim that the identity of the exposition with the tools of the exposition is responsible for a transcendental illusion: the language in which the relation between "this" and the "other" world is discussed is itself already structured metaphysically into the literal and the figurative levels. The metaphysical distinction applied *ex post* to extralinguistic relations first constitutes language as such.

Expressed in terms of Plinlimmon's text, this thesis implies that language cannot but activate the transcendental illusion. In speaking metaphysically, we use speech transitively to talk *about* metaphysics

14. This point is, perhaps, crucial for determining the pamphlet's role in the novel. Melville criticism has been largely satisfied to examine Plinlimmon in the context of the "history of cultural ideas," focusing on Melville's place in the debate between institutional religion and secular trends. As Milton R. Stern observes (*The Fine Hammered Steel of Herman Melville* [Urbana, 1957]), the ineluctable materiality and circularity of the pamphlet invites a structuralist reading of its rhetoric: "In the very instrument with which he must search, the quester is foredoomed: he can only search with the being that is natural man, and natural man cannot reach ideality with nonideality. The ultimate irony is that existence cannot be anything but natural" (176). (See also Dryden, *The Form of American Romance*, 119.)

(the declared subject of the pamphlet—Christ), but speaking metaphysically also means that *we use speech intransitively, we simply speak.* Plinlimmon's parable makes these two points simultaneously and beyond distinction, for it speaks transitively about its intransitive possibility. Plinlimmon himself cannot control the duplicity of horologicals and chronometricals; he, too, must use the metaphysical nature of language to make a metaphysical point. It is this inevitability that makes the pamphlet a parable, and makes it necessarily so. Language is nothing more than a parable of its operation.

The pamphlet is a parable of language, in other words, by virtue of this constitutive condition of language: every exposition makes two points (*pointes*) simultaneously, and every utterance produces, necessarily, two meanings. It is, finally, this mechanism that defines the scope of Melville's irony in his treatment of the pamphlet. A metaphysical argument *can* be made in principle only because the language in which this argument is formulated is itself a metaphysical structure. No other argument can be made in language considered metaphysically. We use language to speak of metaphysics because *language is the speech of metaphysics.*

In this sense the pamphlet's choice of the analogy with earth exposes rhetorical completion and closure as nothing more and nothing less than *rhetorical gestures made necessary by the metaphysical operation of language.* Language is essentially, and first of all, figurative. Leaving Greenwich, we travel around the body of the earth only to come full circle at the point of departure. Although we have covered real distance, we have only managed to return to the point of departure, which, of course, after completing the journey, we proceed to call "destination." Our use of language, and our travels around the globe, are feeble attempts to generate the illusion of movement in an otherwise immovable and stationary (conceptual) universe. The creation of this illusion is made possible by using two names to denote the same object, for example "point of departure" (0 degrees) and "destination" (360 degrees) for Greenwich. In this way we can imagine that we cross seas and continents, and that we conduct fruitful metaphysical speculation; we vehemently insist that we have made real progress, when in fact we continue to stand in the same place.

In this metaphysical illusion we use language on two interdependent planes. The literal plane (horologicals) simultaneously activates the figurative plane (chronometricals). "And thus, though the earthly wisdom of man be heavenly folly to God; so also, conversely, is the heavenly wisdom of God an earthly folly to man." And Plinlimmon adds, with vertiginous irony: "Literally speaking, this is so" (*P*, 212).[15] Plinlimmon's brilliance lies in asserting the intrinsically metaphysical condition of language as circular dependence; the literal level automatically activates the figurative level, in whose light alone the literal level *first becomes* literal. We can speak literally because whenever we thus speak we must, "literally speaking," *also* speak figuratively. When we schematize the universe into "this" world and the "other" world, we do not display our intelligence as rational creatures but, less glamorously, merely submit to the inexorable mechanism of language.

The simultaneously literal and figurative structure of language condemns it to constitutive circularity, represented by Plinlimmon's navigational schematization. The metaphysically driven inquiry returns, having gone "around" the globe of what is conceptually possible, "chronometrically" to confirm the "horological" hypothesis.[16] By the same token, Pierre cannot say "sister" without saying "wife"; if he begins with a sister, he will reach the term of a wife, and if he begins with a wife, he will attain a sister. The two terms constitute the defining poles of Pierre's language, the formative parameters of his conceptual world in which his drama is acted out. *Wife* and *sister* represent, for Pierre, the metaphysical schematization in the field of social relations, insofar as they are two names for the same object.

To charge that Plinlimmon's conceit and Pierre's drama are merely circular (and they *are*) would be to ignore the extremely important fact that the analogues used by Pierre and Plinlimmon are themselves, in

15. The discursive entanglement of the phrase "literally speaking" is the key here. Literality normally denotes a solid ground of reference; this view, however, remains oblivious to the infinite relation, according to which literality exists solely in an implied reference to figurality. The literal is generated by its difference from the figurative. Jacques Derrida emphasizes this mutual dependence as the tending, the *tropism*, of tropes, toward the unattainable condition of meaning ("White Mythology," in *Margins of Philosophy*, trans. Alan Bass [Chicago, 1982], 207–73). Hence Plinlimmon's insistence that "literally speaking, this is so" specifies which meaning (literal or figurative) is intended *at the same time as* it stresses this statement's indebtedness to a rhetorical framework in which figurative language necessarily completes, "on the other side," the literal level. This is the metaphysical structure of language: the literal remains incomprehensible without the figurative that Plinlimmon—not without a measure of sophistry—so vigorously ostracizes.

16. Stern perceives this motion behind Melville's rhetoric in the novel: "The book constantly goes back to ultimate beginnings in the history of mortality's plight, and finds none; constantly hints forward to the end of mortality's plight, and finds none" (*The Fine Hammered Steel*, 185).

Genre as Mood in *Pierre* / 147

their intrinsic circularity, metaphysical entities. Pierre's journey takes place in the metaphysical world organized by a literal term, *nature,* and a figurative term, *culture.* The pamphlet uses the physical "vehicle" of the earthly globe to explain heavenly economy (tenor). The earthly sphere's circularity necessarily forces arguments about completability to follow the analogue of completion as *inherently circular.* In both cases, the grounding analogy itself refers to a circular (spherical) object, to *a physical symbol of hermeneutic completability;* hence, the circularity of the point of the exposition can no longer be disentangled from the materiality of the image. One cannot determine the metaphysical analogy independently as suitable to the point under investigation because analogy is yet another rhetorical possibility within the metaphysical schematization under which language, as inherently rhetorical, necessarily operates.

The consequences of this condition of language extend beyond language itself. The metaphysical schematization of language strategically controls the act of understanding in the hermeneutic model. For Melville, we may recall, the act of hermeneutic comprehension is essentially identical with the material point to be "understood" in such an act. Plinlimmon's pamphlet shows language itself to be *inherently hermeneutic:* one begins with a preconception of the subject matter and arrives at it from within this preconception. Melville formulates the conditions for comprehension as Meno's paradox: "If a man be told a thing wholly new, then ... it is entirely impossible for him to comprehend it" (*P,* 209). This deadlock implies the mechanism of the hermeneutic circle: "For—absurd as it may seem—men are only made to comprehend things which they comprehended before (though but in the embryo, as it were). Things new it is impossible to make them comprehend, by merely talking to them about it" (*P,* 209).

As a result of this correlation between the metaphysical structure of language and the hermeneutic nature of understanding, the pamphlet (and Pierre) fails to escape the confusion against which Melville warns his reader: "Such mere illustrations are almost universally taken for solutions (and perhaps they are the only possible human solutions)" (*P,* 210). The metaphysical structure of language underwrites the fundamental distinction made by the Western world between words and action as well as the distinction, within language, between constative and performative acts. In Melville's conception of language, actions can no longer speak louder than words: "Such mere illustrations ... perhaps ... are the only possible human solutions." The mere presentation, the "illustration," of a problem can be taken for a solution because we speak of metaphysics in a language that is itself metaphysical. The interdependence of the subject matter and the means of its presentation, of literality and figurality, and, finally, of action and words prevents a conceptualization of that which is thus presented. We are unable to delimit the noxious difference between the solution and its presentation; the descriptive formulation of the problem is its only possible solution. To solve a problem means to admit that there is a problem. The metaphysical circularity, the "one pervading ambiguity," is "the only possible explanation for all the ambiguous details" (P, 224).

The metaphysical nature of language evident in Plinlimmon's pamphlet helps explain the writing of the mysterious book in the pages of *Pierre*. Pierre cannot escape the metaphysical structure of language described in Plinlimmon's exposition. In metaphysical economy, the essence of a text, of creativity, and of art emerges as a function of either nature or artifice. The pamphlet teaches Pierre that these distinctions inhere in the metaphysical nature of language. In this preestablished operative mechanism of language, the literal presupposes the figurative, the book implies the Book.

The ballast of this connection is enormous. As we have seen, understanding is hermeneutic in the sense that we can understand only that which we *already* understand. This preconceptual attunement accounts for the fact that we can have no conscious awareness of having understood: "Could he [Pierre] . . . have carried about with him in his mind the thorough understanding of the book, and yet not be aware that he so understood it?" (P, 294) This latent, preconceptual understanding resembles the suppressed knowledge of death, which humans carry in the midst of life: "And here it may be randomly suggested, by way of bagatelle, whether some things that men think they do not know, are not for all that thoroughly comprehended by them; and yet, so to speak, though contained in themselves, are kept a secret from themselves? The idea of Death seems such a thing" (P, 294). At the root of understanding lies the denial of the inexorability of death, the repression of the knowledge that it is necessary for thought to conclude the reasoning process in order to achieve comprehension. Death is the terminus towards which understanding moves in order to achieve comprehension; it is the closure required for understanding to take place. Understanding creates temporal duration, which presupposes a terminus, presupposes its conclusion. This end, this death, is the condition of understanding's coming to a conclusion. The interdependence of temporality and hermeneutics comes to the fore at the very end of the novel, where the conclusion of Pierre's book is expressed as a convergence of chronometrical and horological time sequences: "Here, then, is the untimely, timely end;—Life's last chapter well stitched into the middle! Nor book, nor author of the book, hath any sequel, though each has its last lettering!—It is ambiguous still" (360). The end, the "last chapter," is "stitched into the middle."

The passage suggests that Pierre is not satisfied with the limited opportunities furnished by the hermeneutic formula. He cannot, in other words, be satisfied with writing a book whose existence, and whose meaning, would be generated automatically by the metaphysical structure of language. Pierre cannot write a simple *parable* on the model of Plinlimmon's shrewd pamphlet. The passage above indicates that Pierre seeks to subvert the metaphysical and the hermeneutic nature of the whole. If the end is "stitched into the middle," there can be no beginning, middle, or end. As in the ironic economy of textuality, the book comes to presence here in the stitching *as this stitching*, texture as infinite presentation without objective form. The middle perpetually constitutes the book at the point where the Book, language, begins and ends, "ambiguous still." Since there is no end, there is no death; at the same time, where there is no end, there is no comprehension. Melville's overcoming of metaphysics launches the intellect into infinite, inconclusive, insane hovering.

This is to say that, as he sets out to write the book outside of metaphysics, in the margins of what is conventionally taken to constitute literature, Pierre disrupts the metaphysical structure of language and, with it, the hermeneutic nature of understanding. Pierre discovers a dimension in language, neither literal nor figurative, which is not accountable to the metaphysical calculus. He discovers something extrinsic to the orthodox process in which Nature becomes Culture and stranger becomes wife, a ground of creativity determined neither by the human nor by the divine prerogative. Melville indicates such overcoming of the metaphysical opposition in a chiasmic process by which husband becomes brother and brother becomes husband, at whose center the postmodern relation emerges. The overcoming creates a neutral term, a lack of relation or an overdetermination of all relations: "I am Pierre, and thou Isabel, wide brother and sister in the common humanity,—no more. For the rest, let the gods look after their own combustibles" (*P*, 273). "Isabel," as half-sister and fictitious wife, transcends the metaphysical field of identities in which Pierre's mother is "mother" and Lucy is to be his "wife." Melville determines this neutral point as the condition of demigods: "The demigods trample on trash, and Virtue and Vice are trash! Isabel, I will write such things—I will gospelize the world anew, and show them deeper secrets than the Apocalypse!—I will write it, I will write it!" (*P*, 273).

Melville can disrupt the circular, hermeneutic structure of language by preventing the closure of the circle, by subjecting it to an endless, inconclusive spin. Like Plinlimmon, Melville is bound to the metaphysical structure of language. In this structure, the literal and the figurative, the physical and the meta-physical levels are the boundaries that delimit the field of meaning. To be more precise, what makes language metaphysical is not the claim itself that the sensible empirical realm is sustained by a suprasensible ontological sphere but, rather, the concealment of this hypothesis, the dissimulation of its arbitrary nature in the different names invented to designate one level as if it were two. For example, the pamphlet uses two terms for "time," *horologicals* and *chronometricals*. Indeed, the primary objective of metaphysical thinking is, according to Plinlimmon, dissimulation, *naming* ("sea-chronometers [*Greek*, time-namers]") of the one entity, in the double schematization, as two different things, as the figurative and the literal levels.

In order to disrupt the metaphysical network, Melville does not alter the schematization itself but only reduces it to the essential mechanism. Refusing to participate in the metaphysical game of artificial naming, he calls both levels of the metaphysical grid, the physical and the metaphysical, by one, the same, name. Melville exposes the circularity of the hermeneutic circle as pure repetition, as tautology.

But his critique of metaphysics does not stop here. Melville realizes that the division between the two elements of a structure is a necessary one and that this division can be articulated in several models. The terms can be diversified in the metaphysical game of synonyms (horologicals, chronometricals), or their identity can be reduced to absurdity in unreflective repetition that erases language. Or, finally, they can be repeated in an *ironized* recurrence of nonconceptual content, of the trace. Following Dante's insight, we can describe the meaning of the tautologically repeated term as "not double now, / Nor only one!"

In this reading of tautological structures, Melville is close to Jean Paul.[17] Jean Paul exploits interesting nuances of self-reflexivity in-

---

17. Friedrich Richter [Jean Paul], *School for Aesthetics*, in *German Aesthetic and Literary Criticism*, ed. Wheeler, 191.

volved in the repetition of the subject in the predicate. Melvillean tautology corresponds specifically to Jean Paul's "circular wit," in which "an idea first opposes itself then makes a peace of similarity, but not of equality, with its non-self.... It is so easy that it needs only be willed: 'to file the critical file,' 'to recover from a recovery,' 'to imprison the Bastille.'... Aside from its brevity this form pleases, because the mind, which must always move on, sees the same idea, such as 'recover,' appear before it the second time as its own contrary and is forced by the equality to discover some similarity between them" (191). Thus Pierre says "that his woe is woe" (P, 70) and speculates that "not his mother had made his mother" (P, 90). The two instances of "woe" and of "mother" both predicate and do not predicate, carving out a crevice where the formula is neither circular nor predicative. It is speculative, *romantic*.

The romantic conception of tautological infinity shapes Melville's poetics in its very core, in his view that critical commentary stands at the origin of the literary text. The fact that "conscientious Virgil" was "all eager at death to burn his Aeniad for a monstrous heap of inefficient superfluity" (P, 227) suggests that the literary work (the *Aeneid*) is always already tautological in relation to the world that it engages. Richter's formula, that the text appears before the reader "the second time as its own contrary," as commentary, carries implications beyond the sphere of letters. The romantic tautology refers—as Melville is aware—to the strictly philosophical question of epistemology and to the metaphysical structure of the world. For Melville, the mimetic relation between the world and the text entails a structure of commentaries with textual moments occasionally arising as secondary presences. Indeed, the text of the world shows the absolute lack of the primary moment that would, as in metaphysical models, hold the structure together; *the structure is constituted and held together exclusively by commentaries flexible enough to become texts for one another*. The relation between text and world, as mimetic, activates the same ever-persisting infinite moment that controls the relations between nature and culture. The infinite surplus, representable neither as world nor as text, abides between the two: as Melville's oxymoron "inefficient superfluity" indicates, this surplus is both more ("superfluity") and less ("inefficient") than the world and the text—it exceeds the metaphysical means of presentation. Between the literal and the figurative poles of language, infinite tautology finds the moment that can be uttered neither literally nor figuratively. Melville's romantic tautology makes possible a nonmetaphysical understanding of text, language, and world: it is the nonmetaphysical "bantering, barren, and prosaic" speech speaking itself (*P,* 136).

Applied to Plinlimmon's pamphlet, this analysis would propose that the pamphlet's circularity shows a point "anterior" to beginning and end, a movement not determined by departure or arrival. The pamphlet executes tautology (or hermeneutic circularity) outside of both metaphorics and metaphysics, in a saturation (*satura* = satire = saturation, filling in) of language in which language itself speaks. For to conceive the analogy between heaven and earth (sacred and secular, eternal and temporal, perfect and imperfect), one must first carry out the original synthesis of a minimal relation between the two spheres, *a synthesis for which neither sphere serves as a type or model.* In other words, to conceive this analogy one must first reside in *an "other" world.* This world, however, is the other of *both* worlds postulated in the metaphysical model of language; this outside is neither perfection nor imperfection.

It is the tautological infinity deprived of a center that founds the poetics of the book written by Pierre in the pages of *Pierre.* Melville indicates Pierre's newly discovered poetics of tautology when he recounts the fate of Plinlimmon's pamphlet. The text is discovered, "years after," by an "old Jew Clothesman" who "rummaged over a surtout of Pierre's." The man finds the pamphlet "between the cloth and the heavy quilted bombazine lining": it "had worked its way clean down into the skirt, and there helped pad the padding. So that all the time he was hunting for this pamphlet, he himself was wearing the pamphlet" (*P,* 294).

The pamphlet, securely lodged in the lining of the surtout, underscores the tautological nature of literary meaning. Following Jean Paul's paradigmatic structure—"recovering from a recovery"—Melville offers "padding the padding" and invites further neologisms of this type—"timing the time," "placing the place," "spacing the space," etc. Tautological reflexivity makes it possible for Pierre to "write the writing," to "texture the text," to "book the book"; it makes it possible for Pierre to write his cryptic book and hide it in the "lining" of *Pierre.*

At stake in the infinite difference/identity between the book and the Book is Melville's theory of originality. Composed in recognition of Jean Paul's tautological mechanism, Pierre's cryptic text testifies to Melville's belief that the sole product, the only work of creativity, is the Book as a commentary on itself, the relation between the Book and the book. On the one hand, books "are built round a circle, as atolls . . . digestively including the whole range of all that can be known or dreamed" (*P*, 283). On the other, Melville believes that "there is no such thing as a standard for the creative spirit; that no one great book must ever be separately regarded, and permitted to domineer with its own uniqueness upon the creative mind; but that all existing great works must be federated in the fancy" (*P*, 284). Defined in such a wide scope ("digestively") and narrow scope ("our own things"—*F*, 284), originality imposes on the writer two mutually exclusive tasks: the writer must simultaneously acknowledge all the great works and establish his originality over against these works. Defined in this two-fold fashion, extensionally and intensionally, originality precipitates the tautological solution: "The world is forever babbling of originality; but there never yet was an original man, in the sense intended by the world; the first man himself—who according to the Rabbins was also the first author—not being an original; the only original author being God. . . . For though the naked soul of man doth assuredly contain one latent element of intellectual productiveness; yet never was there a child born solely from one parent; the visible world of experience being that procreative thing which impregnates the muses; self-reciprocally efficient hermaphrodites being but a fable" (*P*, 259).

Defined by the tautological theory of literary originality, Pierre's efforts to compose his book appear as an undertaking of pure futility, a creative endeavor for which futility guarantees the preservation of "work" as an aesthetically meaningful term.[18] "From eight o'clock in the morning till half-past four in the evening, Pierre sits there in his room;—eight hours and a half!" (*P*, 303). The emancipation made possible by devotion to writing lies in the liberation of the writer—the liberation afforded by the tautological economy—into the awareness

---

18. The futility in question refers to the condition of oblivion, of "inspiration," in which great works are created, as it were, accidentally. Melville specifies this mood: "There is a singular infatuation in most men, which leads them in odd moments, intermitting between their regular occupations, and when they find themselves all alone in some quiet corner or nook, to fasten with unaccountable fondness upon the merest rag of old printed paper—some shred of a long-exploded advertisement perhaps—and read it, and study it, and reread it, and pore over it, and fairly agonize themselves over this miserable, sleazy paper-rag" (*P*, 206–207). Dryden (*The Form of American Romance*, 98–99) associates this involuntary activity with the unconscious: Pierre reading the pamphlet while traveling "resembles the person alone at breakfast intensely studying the back of an empty cereal box or the one absorbed in a year-old magazine in a doctor's office, for that which fascinates him is a discarded fragment of the past that now exists independently of both its original intent and content."

that authorship consists essentially in "writing the writing," the awareness that the book always only remains the book "of" the Book, the postmodern, nonmetaphysical trace born neither of nature nor of artifice, neither of leisure nor of labor:

> That which now absorbs the time and the life of Pierre, is not the book, but the primitive elementalizing of the strange stuff, which in the act of attempting that book, has upheaved and upgushed in his soul. Two books are being writ; of which the world shall only see one, and that the bungled one. The larger book, and the infinitely better, is for Pierre's own private shelf. That it is, whose unfathomable cravings drink his blood; the other only demands his ink. But circumstances have so decreed, that the one can not be composed on the paper, but only as the other is writ down in his soul.... Thus Pierre is fastened on by two leeches.... He is learning how to live, by rehearsing the part of death. (*P*, 304–305)

Authentic originality of the self-producing subject exhausts itself in the sufficient production of the self by the self, in the originality of the "self-reciprocally efficient hermaphrodite." As *originally tautological*, Melville's creativity overcomes both death and life. It will not produce any product, a book, but only the *ironic difference* between the book and the Book.[19] It is this difference that underlies Melville's belief that

---

19. In this sense, *Pierre*'s use of the omniscient narrator technique breaks several barriers in the Melville opus. The association of irony (as the distance between the omniscient narrator and the protagonist) with the menippean scripting of the invisible book deserves brief commentary. We have seen Shepherd refer to the "reasonable strategy of the narrator's double perspective" in his relation to Pierre ("Pierre's Psyche," 89). Accounts of the novel as "a book in which everything comments on its own origins, making, and development" (Gray, " 'All's o'er,' " in *Reassessments*, ed. Lee, 118) imply a dependence between a parodic intent and self-reflexive structure. Gray adds: "[Pierre] writes a book eventually, but the book he writes is not the one we read: on the contrary, it is the book we read *about—within* the book that an anonymous, third-person narrator writes" (124). Rosenberry uses the same image: "In Melville it [the ironic mask] is worn by hero and author alike and must be seen from the inside. *Pierre* is a Chinese puzzle in which we have, literally, a man writing a bitter book about a man writing a bitter book about a man writing a bitter book. In the resultant mirror image the mood of Hamlet becomes the mood of *Pierre* the book as well as of Pierre the man" (*Melville and the Comic Spirit*, 149). Dryden sees only failure in the "self-conscious form" of narration (*Melville's Thematics of Form: The Great Art of Telling the Truth* [Baltimore, 1968], 117–18). Dryden adds elsewhere about *Pierre:* "The life of its hero is the story of a reader who attempts to become a writer," but unfortunately, "the meaning of the story is difficult to decipher, and Pierre's attempt to read will generate a second and even more

"the age of authors [is] passing" (*P*, 264). It is also this difference that makes Pierre's subterranean book a menippea *sensu stricto*, "a blasphemous rhapsody, filched from the vile Atheists, Lucian and Voltaire" (*P*, 356). It is also Melville's conception of the infernal immediacy of his infinite "new book" that should inform contemporary assessments of Melville's dispute with the sentimental immediacy of the fiction of his day.[20] Finally, it is this postmodern scripting in the pages of *Pierre* that must guide our evaluation of the novel's stature in Melville's opus.

According to Melville, the infinite, transcendental caesura between the two books, between the literal (the real) and the figurative (the ideal) levels, is the proper domain of semi-divine creativity, of the mythological, titanic imagination. The dream-vision of Enceladus the Titan shifts Melville's theory of the tautological conception of origin to the terminology of myth. The discourse of myth solicits the reader to identify Pierre with Enceladus, but in a more cautious perusal, it should foreground the tautological, irretrievable nature of such identification. For authorship, a supposedly nonderivative condition (self-authorship), restates the original creation as a tautology, as "mere" *self*-creation of the self by the self. Challenging the gods uncovers the

---

entangled and problematic narrative, that of the novel itself" (*The Form of American Romance*, 96, 76). As I argued earlier, the introduction of the omniscient narrator has failed to clarify Pierre's character and to secure the novel's center. The collapse of the center, and of the omniscient point of view, again derives from the Melvillean, infernal understanding of irony as total immediacy devoid of ordering hierarchy. The problem inheres, partly, in the confusion at the heart of the notion of distance that defines a narrator as omniscient. Distance is necessary to narration, but it is also required in all ironic gestures; hence, all narratives are potentially ironic, and all irony passes through a narrative moment. In Melville, irony is the necessary ingredient of narration.

20. Holder discusses the notorious case of "the humming-bird passage" and its critical history ("Style and Tone," 76). The now-classic essay by E. L. Grant Watson, "Melville's *Pierre*," in *Critical Essays on Herman Melville's "Pierre; or, The Ambiguities,"* ed. Brian Higgins and Hershel Parker (Boston, 1983) speaks of "those inserted chapters of satirical commentary on American literature" (162). The evidence suggests Melville's menippean affinities. Milder writes about *Pierre*'s styles: "It is as if [Melville] were determined to take the trappings of the popular romance—the light and dark heroines, the melodrama, the 'elevated' style—and bend them to his purpose, producing a book which ... would be a diabolical parody of the romance, 'a vicious perversion of a formula so universally worshipped as to be sacrosanct' " ("Melville's 'Intentions' in *Pierre*," 193; Milder quotes Perry Miller's *Nature's Nation*, 243).

original incest between the mythological heaven and earth, an anterior identity that shows the highest work to be the work *of* work alone:

> Thus smitten, the Mount of Titans seems to yield this following stream:—
>
> Old Titan's self was the son of incestuous Cœlus and Terra, the son of incestuous Heaven and Earth. And Titan married his mother Terra, another and accumulatively incestuous match. And thereof Enceladus was one issue. So Enceladus was both the son and grandson of an incest; and even thus, there had been born from the organic blended heavenliness and earthliness of Pierre, another mixed, uncertain, heaven-aspiring, but still not wholly earth-emancipated mood; which again, by its terrestrial taint held down to its terrestrial mother, generated there the present doubly incestuous Enceladus within him; so that the present mood of Pierre—that reckless sky-assaulting mood of his, was nevertheless on one side the grandson of the sky. For it is according to eternal fitness, that the precipitated Titan should still seek to regain his paternal birthright even by fierce escalade. Wherefore whoso storms the sky gives best proof he came from thither! (*P*, 346–47)

Melville may have concealed in *Pierre* his greatest work. This work, however, can emerge only as concealed, as a cryptic reference to "some other work," and neither can it be called entirely *Melville's*, for it also is "the work's written *self*."

III

Genre and *la Syncope* in *Madame Bovary*

D'ailleurs c'est toujours les autres qui meurent.

—inscription on Marcel Duchamp's tomb

The opening scene of *Madame Bovary* describes the entrance of the young Charles Bovary into the classroom of his new school.[1] His incredible headgear attracts the attention of the pupils:

> It was one of those head-gears of composite order, in which we can find traces of the bear- and the coonskin, the shako, the bowler, and the cotton nightcap; one of those poor things, in fine, whose dumb ugliness has depths of expression, like an imbecile's face. Ovoid and stiffened with whalebone, it began with three circular strips; then came in succession lozenges of velvet and rabbit fur separated by a red band; after that a sort of bag that ended in a cardboard polygon covered with complicated braiding, from which hung, at the end of a long thin cord, small twisted gold threads in the manner of a tassel. The cap was new; its peak shone. (*MB*, 2)

The cap, a visual impossibility, is perhaps the most notorious and most celebrated among the many unusual objects featured in *Madame Bovary*, and it can rightly represent the technique of bricolage at its

---

1. Gustave Flaubert, *Madame Bovary*, Norton Critical Edition, ed. with a substantially new translation by Paul de Man (New York, 1965). The parallel references in French can be found in *Madame Bovary*, ed. Victor Brombert (Paris, 1986).

best.[2] The cap highlights two basic problems that confront any theory of this technique: first, the problem of our ability to identify the individual elements that compose it and, second, the problem of naming the order of composition (*l'ordre composite*) of bricolage.

It may be helpful to contextualize Flaubert's conception of bricolage and to address the questions it provokes with Gérard Genette's discussion of bricolage in his essay "Structuralism and Literary Criticism."[3] Bricolage has come to prominence in structuralist criticism, says Genette, following Claude Lévi-Strauss's discovery of its methodological importance to structural anthropology. Considered as a technique of artistic composition, bricolage jumbles together diverse materials regardless of their original function. According to Genette, literary criticism resembles bricolage in the preliminary stages of the technique, when the pieces are first selected and assembled. Like the primitive *bricoleur*, the critic freely selects the elements for his bricolage, taking them without too many scruples out of their original contexts and placing them together in new configurations.

But Genette hastens to distinguish the critic from the *bricoleur*, and the distinction is a telling one. The difference between a *critic* who practices bricolage and a mere *bricoleur* is one of awareness. A *bricoleur* is satisfied with the act of constructing a bricolage; he assembles odds and ends without reflecting on what potential whole might be produced in this process. The critic, on the other hand, speculates about the possible form of this unity by raising the bricolage to a higher level of complexity. Literary criticism believes that it can master bricolage by postulating a higher unity as its meaning.[4] Genette implies that the critic can claim superiority over the *bricoleur* because he searches for the *meaning* of bricolage.

Genette may be quite right in granting this superiority to the critic, for in his search for a concept of unity adequate to the elusive structure of bricolage, the critic encounters a most challenging task: he submits to a very rigorous test the very assumption of unity under which, as Kant has first demonstrated, the human mind must operate to achieve intellection. However, by giving the critic the special task

---

2. It is regrettable that Flaubert's friends, Maxime Du Camp and Alfred de Poittevin, advised him to eliminate the elaborate toy Flaubert intended for one of Homais' sons; a description of the toy took up, according to various reports, from four to ten pages.

3. Gérard Genette, *Figures of Literary Discourse*, trans. Alan Sheridan (New York, 1982), 3–4.

4. Ibid., 6.

and the accompanying privilege, Genette's critic has also exposed the mind to a fundamental crisis.

When the mind constructs a whole, it works with elements that become, in the process of the hermeneutic feedback between parts and whole, *parts* of this whole. It can be immediately observed that the unity of bricolage is not accountable to the hermeneutic mechanism. Every component of bricolage has previously functioned as a part in its original whole; placed in the new context, the pieces form an aggregate that fails to constitute a whole. This is perhaps why in Flaubert's description of the cap the only positive indication of the elements' unity points retrospectively to their former wholes ("one can find traces" [*où l'on retrouve les éléments*]) while the present unifying whole is a "composite order" [*l'ordre composite*]. The difficulty lies not merely in the formal incompatibility of the pieces. From the point of view of the actual process of understanding a whole by enacting the hermeneutic movement, the parts selected for a bricolage are already parts; hence, the mind can no longer synthesize them or be otherwise engaged in the process of understanding. Because in bricolage the parts are already parts, there is no work left for the mind to perform.

Bricolage thus confronts theoretical understanding with a hybrid object. The mind encounters parts, but these parts have been identified as parts without reference to a relevant hermeneutic totality and without engaging the mind in effecting the synthesis. Faced with an object of perception that has no contextualizing whole, the mind is quick to call it "monstrous," "incomplete," or "pure chaos." Even such labels, however, refer the curious object to totality, as lacking this totality. However, this conspicuous absence of totality in the midst of disconnected parts ought to be grasped in its purity, without the implicit reference to hermeneutic totality. The term *in-finity* may serve this purpose by indicating that bricolage represents a nonhermeneutic conception of unity. Bricolage is an infinite product because, hermeneutically speaking, it can be grasped only as an *un*finished product. Still, it is necessary to eliminate the implicit reference to hermeneutic totality that survives in infinity's negative prefix.

What is the infinity of bricolage? The question has two aspects. First, as parts without their encompassing whole, the elements of bricolage postulate an infinite act of understanding that stands in radical contrast to hermeneutic cognition. Hermeneutic cognition always presupposes a conclusion, a rounding up that accounts for all relations. Second, it presupposes an object (real or imaginary) in which the act of understanding comes to rest. Hermeneutically speaking, "object" denotes a wholeness required for cognition to take place. Cognition compares a physical object to the idea of (this) object; if successful, this comparative identification leads to re-cognition.

In some aspects, the act of apprehending bricolage resembles the hermeneutic process of cognition. Bricolage presents the mind with parts, challenging it to find an object proper for the assemblage of these parts. But these parts are already parts. The mind confronts an already integrated totality; it experiences a posthermeneutic condition in which the relation of the detail to totality is not mediate but immediate—it is not a relation but an infinite presence of totality in every "part" of the bricolage. In addition, the indifference of bricolage to hermeneutic completion suggests a unity not produced in the process of synthesis. The infinity of bricolage renders conceptual cognition of objects useless, not only because we do not know what unity the bricolage conforms to, but also because the spectacle of bricolage requires no hermeneutic effort, or any effort at all.

The infinite structure of bricolage, then, presents the mind with the absence of a recognizable totality; this absence, in turn, leaves our cognitive faculties with nothing to do. The present analysis will attempt to trace and develop these aspects of bricolage as they appear in *Madame Bovary* under different formal guises. In a close analysis of Flaubert's use of clichés, parenthetical remarks, punning, and jokes, I will concentrate on the capacity of these devices to activate the same infinite perspective that has been shown to characterize bricolage. Most importantly, the infinity in question will be viewed as a characteristically romantic component of Flaubert's poetics, perhaps a most significant influence on his literary credo.

In his use of bricolage and of other bricolage-like devices, Flaubert pays tribute to the romantic "arabesque." Romanticism follows the sense of the word *arabesque* as defined by Goethe during his trip to Pompeii and the Vatican. As Hans Eichner puts it, *grotesque* and *arabesque* refer to a work of art that makes "a synthesis of apparent chaos and apparent order" (*FS*, 64). In arabesques, "the caprice of the artist seemed subject to no limitation while yet producing a pleasing and coherent whole" (*FS*, 64). The distinctive feature of the arabesque is its ability to evoke a sense of totality without satisfying the mind with any identifiable indication of order, harmony, pattern, or whole. Although the arabesque lures the mind with intimations of order, it preserves the order in the shadow of an impending chaos.

Beyond these parallels with bricolage, the arabesque also shares with bricolage the radical function of undermining its own status as an object of cognition. The arabesque undermines its status as an object because, while it appears before the mind and solicits active cognition, it makes it impossible for the mind to identify it in the familiar pattern of objective recognition and prevents the cognitive process from coming to rest. The mind finds this cognitive encounter disturbing because it apprehends something that is not, properly speaking, recognizable. The radicality of this situation lies in the implication that the object created by bricolage affects with its disintegrative infinity the perceiving subject itself. In this way, the arabesque, like bricolage, undermines the very ground of objective cognition, the fundamental epistemological relation between subject and object. In the following pages I would like to propose that in its arabesque character *Madame Bovary* continues the romantic project of the novel precisely by destabilizing the subject-object relation. By denying the subject a stable object of cognition, the arabesque reveals a more original condition in which the subject is a subject, not in its relation to an object, but in the constitutive self-relating, in being-a-subject. *Madame Bovary* presents the conditions under which the subject can become conceivable outside of the relation to the object and can emerge exclusively as non-objective self-relation.

While the genre of involution in *Don Quixote* and of mood in *Pierre* enact the emergence of the subject as such, the genre of bricolage in *Madame Bovary* enacts the emergence of the subject as the subject *of* cognition. The difference lies here: when the infinity of Flaubertian bricolage plunges the mind into cognitive vertigo, into *la syncope*, the subject is disclosed not "as such," not in the infinite and excessive presencing of the self, but in the intimation of the self on the threshold of self-presence. While in *Pierre* the moody self comes into its own as self precisely by being seized by moods, in *Madame Bovary* the self experiences *la syncope*, a vertiginous condition preliminary to, but in itself not constitutive of, the true essence of the subject.

The difference can be made clearer with the help of Friedrich Schlegel's formula "every theory of the novel must itself be a novel." Melville's definition of the self in terms of moods is strictly reflexive, for the moods that objectively characterize the self also constitute the self as such. The self is produced in the very terms in which it is described (known). By contrast, when Flaubert describes the self in the genre of *la syncope*, the vertigo does not simultaneously constitute the self in its being. In other words, in *Madame Bovary*, Flaubert stops short of closing Schlegel's formula into a continuous loop of constitutive reflexivity; although described in terms of vertigo, the Flaubertian self is not at the same time constituted by it. As romantic arabesque, Flaubert's bricolage only intimates the preliminary horizon of the self's true constitution.

Before describing the characteristics of Flaubertian destabilization of the self, we should explore the specific manner in which the bricolage of Charles's cap challenges the mind. We have seen that the separate elements of bricolage import their original contexts into the new environment and that the clashing identities prevent the construction of a new totality. Applied to Charles's cap, this theory would explain the confusion the cap causes among the students. The cap seems so ridiculous that even the teacher, "who liked to joke," cannot resist an ironic remark and orders Charles to get rid of the "helmet" (*MB*, 2). The cap's identity is infinitely absorptive; it can be called a helmet or a cap. While traceable to several sources, the cap itself never emerges as a cap, its chaotic aggregate of incompatible parts fails to add up to a unifying principle. As is the case in many other passages in the novel, the teacher's irony falls flat since the cap may indeed be construed as a helmet. The cap both gives rise to, and nullifies, irony; it is so ridiculous that it is beyond a joke.

The lesson of Charles's cap is that bricolage, an anomaly of reference, defines the truth of linguistic naming and reveals the condition of all reference. The cap, in other words, reveals the basic assumption behind linguistic naming. It is not enough to state that a cap is, indeed, a cap. In uttering a name we do not simply (or only) recognize an object; we also *decide* to call this object by this name—otherwise the parts of any object would float aimlessly without the functional masterplan. Bricolage makes it apparent that every act of naming presupposes our initial familiarity with some principle responsible for calling a cap a *cap*. This principle, however, is not available for objective cognition.

This conclusion alters the previous analysis of the students' reaction to the cap. The situation would be, strictly speaking, ridiculous, if something determinate (say, an empty flower pot) had been put where a cap would normally be placed, creating an incongruity between two determinate contexts (head, flower pot). Here, however, the cap exceeds ridicule because it is not clear what thing has been put on Charles's head, not clear whether the object on Charles's head is indeed a cap. Because bricolage does not reveal a determinate totality, it is impossible to measure the extent of the cap's incongruity. Consequently, it is not clear whether this incident is funny or not. Bricolage threatens conceptual language in this fundamental way.

The disintegrative effect of bricolage on language is confirmed in the subsequent events of the novel's opening scene. Charles's first attempt to introduce himself results in "an unintelligible name . . . articulated in a stammering voice." Asked to repeat it, Charles produces "the same sputtering of syllables . . . drowned by the tittering of the class." The teacher pressures Charles even further, asking him to pronounce his name "louder": "The new boy then took a supreme resolution, opened an inordinately large mouth, and shouted at the top of his voice as if calling someone, the word 'Charbovari' " (*MB*, 2–3).

Frightened and confused, Charles utters a portmanteau word, which, from the point of view of linguistic structure, can be regarded as bricolage. The word *Charbovari*, neither one nor two, is an assemblage of parts that do not constitute a self-contained linguistic unit. The disruptive effect of bricolage on linguistic articulation invites close scrutiny. Language articulates meaning in successive production of separate components (Latin: *articulus*). The portmanteau word *Charbovari* violates both the principle of keeping linguistic components separate and the principle of articulating these components in succession. In all evidence, bricolage is to hermeneutic totality what simultaneous articulation is to language; totality cannot function if its components are not subordinated to it as its parts, and language ceases when its parts are not clearly demarcated by linguistic structure.

Given the cap's infinite identity as bricolage, Flaubert's description of the headgear is more than "a parody of symbolic reading," as Jonathan Culler puts it. For Culler, "The discrepancy between the prose and its object grows, displaying the ludicrousness of language spinning itself out in clauses piled one on the other, all in an attempt to comprehend an unworthy hat."[5] Flaubert understands the distance between the name and the thing not simply as a function of an optional stylistic device, in a theory of language that presupposes the separateness of the objective world and of the linguistic means of describing it. If Flaubert, like the students in the classroom, reacts with laughter to the discrepancy between the thing and the name, his

---

5. Jonathan Culler, *Flaubert: The Uses of Uncertainty* (Rev. ed.; Ithaca, 1985), 92.

laughter is not intended to ridicule an incongruity in the objective world. Instead, his laughter is the reaction of terror at the discovery that, rather than being a simple operation of recognition based on habitual familiarity with the world, every act of naming is an arbitrary decision, each time made in the presence of an unknown and unknowable entity. A stylistic analysis of the passage—and this principle applies to Flaubert's novel as a whole—that relies on positive notions of syntactic, ironic, and comic effects, cannot sufficiently account for the essential thrust of the passage, the absence of name in the midst of verbal cornucopia. This absence is not a simple effect of parodic anticlimax but an infinite absence; language is not a stable system of motivated signs but a continuous substitution of arbitrary names.

The cap is a disintegrative force. In the opening scene the teacher loses control of the class, and Charles cannot pronounce his name. To restore the order of language and to fend off the impending chaos, the teacher rereads and redictates Charles's name. Such repetition, as a means of restoring linguistic order, may itself invite disintegration. This danger becomes evident in the teacher's response to Charles's confused utterance of his own name. The teacher, apparently threatened by the portmanteau word, orders Charles to conjugate *ridiculus sum* twenty times. The repetition of the *syntagmatic* chain in all possible *paradigmatic* configurations effectively exhausts discursive possibilities, not only of self-expression, but also of appearing ridiculous *in discourse*. Just as naming the cap "a cap" was a risky enterprise, so calling someone "ridiculous" may not be quite appropriate, because in both cases that which provokes laughter may have no name. Exhaustive conjugation of language in strict conformity to grammar—the *satura*tion of language—makes bricolage of articulated speech.

The discrepancy between name and thing disclosed by bricolage raises challenging questions. The paramount question is the problem of what is presented in the infinity that does not resolve itself hermeneutically into an object of knowledge. There is also the question of what the infinity of bricolage says if its elements are programmatically disarticulated. Finally, and this problem includes the former two, the elements of bricolage, as prefabricated parts, confound the basic structure and order of cognition, confronting the mind with the following dilemma: Is the portmanteau word *Charbovari* a poststructural formation, composed out of two words created earlier by the structure of language, or does this entity preexist language as an amorphous mass to be later parsed and harnessed into articulation? Does the "unity" of *Charbovari*, or of the cap, antedate the structure or succeed it? Or, perhaps, we find bricolage so disturbing because it is not yet structural *and* because it is no longer structural *at the same time*?

At bottom, these questions probe the possibility that the unity of bricolage escapes all accounts of intentional production, whether of creative bringing forth, speculative synthesis, or material construction. Put differently, the unity of bricolage is infinite primarily because it can be explained in terms of neither artificial nor natural models of production. This hypothesis may be concretized in a comparison of two kinds of bricolage, Charles's cap and Hippolyte's clubfoot. In one of the novel's most famous episodes, Charles Bovary, under the instigation of his wife, who expects her husband to achieve fame and celebrity as a surgeon, undertakes the risky operation on the clubfoot of the house hand, Hippolyte. The descriptions of the foot merit brief analysis.

> But on the equine foot, wide indeed as a horse's hoof, with its horny skin, and large toes, whose black nails resembled the nails of a horse shoe, the cripple ran about like a deer from morn till night. He was constantly to be seen on the Square, jumping round the carts, thrusting his limping foot forwards. He seemed even stronger on that leg than the other. By dint of hard service it had acquired, as it were, moral qualities of patience and energy; and when he was given some heavy work to do, he would support himself on it in preference to the sound one. (*MB*, 126)

According to this description, which relies on a simple simile ("wide indeed as a horse's hoof") and an aristocratic touch ("the equine foot"), there is nothing wrong with the clubfoot. For all intents and purposes, it works. For his part, Charles Bovary sees a completely different foot: "Yet, to know which of Hippolyte's tendons had to be cut, it was necessary first of all to find out what kind of club-foot he had. His foot almost formed a straight line with the leg, which, however, did not prevent it from being turned in, so that it was an equinus combined with something of a varus, or else a slight varus with a strong tendency to equinus" (*MB*, 126). Charles's hesitant diagnosis of the foot (to diagnose: to "see through") indicates an encounter with a composite entity of bricolage type. As a bricolage produced by nature, the clubfoot (*pied-bot*) reveals the powers of bricolage that Charles's cap could not make quite explicit. In the case of Charles's cap, the infinite unity of bricolage can be reduced to a simple discrepancy: whatever is on the head must be a cap; the identification of the outrageous headgear as a cap is a way of resolving the threat of infinity. The clubfoot, however, does not afford the mind the luxury of reducing the mystery of bricolage to hypothetical, albeit incongruous and funny, contexts and identities. For what is named in the clubfoot does not provoke mere laughter and ridicule; on the contrary, because the foot resists analysis and provokes a circular hesitation that paralyzes diagnosis and medical intervention, it arouses the feeling of terror and indignation. While Charles's cap momentarily reveals the arbitrariness of every act of naming, Hippolyte's malformed foot reveals the ineluctable terror of the unnameable human condition as a whole. And while the former bricolage can be brushed aside as a temporary artifice, the latter refuses to go away, for it is a permanent reminder of a component of the human condition not forged by humanity. What does the bricolage term *clubfoot* articulate in its anatomical disarticulation?

To decide what specific kind of clubfoot he is dealing with, Charles studies the relevant medical literature: "while he struggled with the equinus, varus and valgus—that is to say, *katastrephopody, endostrephopody,* and *exostrephopody,* or in other words, the various deviations of the foot, to the inside, outside, or downwards, as well as with *hypostrephopody* and *anastrephopody,* or torsion below and contraction above" (*MB,* 125). The term *clubfoot* denotes a whole class of different deformities without being definitively associated with any one of them. The technical terms only give many names to the clubfoot depending on the particular *type* of deviation. There exists in language no *pure,* aspectually undetermined clubfoot. Every concrete clubfoot is *already* subject to certain spatial and linguistic constraints (inside, outside, upwards, downwards).[6]

Of course, the term *clubfoot* sufficiently serves the purposes of practical reference. However, the point is not whether or not we can know a clubfoot when we see one but how we can *recognize* a clubfoot if, etymologically speaking, *re*-cognition implies a prior knowl-

---

6. Dennis Porter ("*Madame Bovary* and the Question of Pleasure," in *Flaubert and Postmodernism,* ed. Naomi Schor and Henry F. Majewski [Lincoln, Nebr., 1984]) calls the repetition of anatomical terms "a word-merchant's delight in words as material objects independent of any referent" (123). The "comic cacophony" provokes "a crisis in the reader's relation to language insofar as it objectifies speech in its material strangeness" (123). Porter also detects in the passage an "interlinguistic irony in the fact that Flaubert takes the opportunity to turn the tables and make Greek for once seem 'barbarous'" (123).

edge of the ideal object outside of time and space. For whenever we encounter a particular clubfoot, it is always already an object in time and space, a *katastrephopody,* or any other form indicated by the appropriate prefix. There exists, then, no clubfoot that would not *already* appear in the actualization of an *ana-*, a *hypo-*, a *kata-*, an *endo-*, or an *exo-*. In other words, we encounter each clubfoot only in a historically specific turning; indeed, we encounter the clubfoot each time *only in other words.*

The laughter of the boys in the classroom is a reaction to the disruptive question, when is a cap a cap? The catastroph(od)ic question now is, What do we see when we see a bricolage? As an aggregate of parts without their proper home, bricolage, a linguistic and structural disarticulation, resists the reflective powers of the human mind. As an object of cognition, bricolage demands a cognitive act that is independent of reflective structuring; it postulates an original knowledge without reflection or re-cognition. At this primary level we cannot even say that the mind encounters pure odds and ends, for the very judgment that the odds and ends that compose a bricolage are *precisely* odds and ends already implies a prior moment of analytical separation and cognitive ordering. This seemingly rudimentary distinction is actually made at an advanced level of cognitive activity. The unity of bricolage is, however, anterior to this level. In the knowledge required for the proper cognition of bricolage, not even the luxury of this rudimentary appraisal is available to us; the mind knows no odds or ends—it knows only some original order, *or else* some original chaos.

This conclusion makes possible a preliminary definition of Flaubert's literary enterprise. Flaubert operates with the awareness that all discursive means at our disposal reflect only a local structure; they are infinitely—ironically—removed from pure meaning. Meaning appears to the mind in finite and limited moments and structures, while the fundamental unity that would ground the local experiences of harmony and unity remains a postulate and a hypothesis, a conjectural concept without an ideal or material equivalent or basis. As undemonstrable, the fundamental unity of discourse makes all language ironic in a constitutive way. All local meaning flirts with the possibility that it is grounded in the highest Meaning, but it could *also* be only a local meaning not referrable to any anchoring ground or framing totality. Flaubert's concept of irony, then, is not only positivistic—a deliberate and voluntary indication of the opposite of what is explicitly said—but speculative, or transcendental—an indication of the fundamental, inescapable ambiguity about the meaningfulness of what is each time said. Thus, not only does transcendental ambiguity confound our sense of the serious and the ridiculous, but it also, and above all, shatters the basis of language; for whenever we speak we do not know whether we speak in earnest or in jest.

As we have seen, bricolage is challenging, not simply because it is hard to see what kind of unity the new composite constitutes, but also because its original unity is inaccessible in retrospective analysis. The unity of bricolage, as infinite, preanalytical and postsynthetic, remains inaccessible to the operations that are normally performed in order to produce unity. To use the vocabulary of Charles's medical endeavor, bricolage is *inoperable.* Indeed, Charles's and Genette's efforts to comprehend bricolage should be placed in the context of the unanalyzable character of this unity. We may recall that Genette does not address the infinite nature of the unity of bricolage. Instead, he elects to construct, in critical reflection, a hypothetical meaning of bricolage and in this way to present the mind with an object accessible to hermeneutic cognition.

Charles Bovary's medical diagnosis represents a second possibility of responding to the original unity of bricolage. An accomplished analyst, Charles assumes that each unity can be freely disassembled and reassembled and that the deformity of Hippolyte's foot can be clearly defined as a type separate from other types: "Now, as it was an equinus, it was necessary to cut the Achilles tendon first; if need be, the anterior tibial muscle could be seen to afterwards to take care of the varus. For the doctor did not dare to risk both operations at once; he was already sufficiently worried for fear of injuring some important region that he did not know" (*MB,* 127). Although the clubfoot is a bricolage (for as an equinus *and* a varus it defies the successive order of articulation), it must be dealt with only as one thing at a time—it must be articulated. Charles articulates the foot again after the operation in a belated diagnosis: " 'But it was perhaps a valgus after all!' exclaimed Bovary suddenly, interrupting his meditations" (*MB,* 133).

The two types of intervention, reflective and analytical, fail to do justice to the original unity of Hippolyte's foot.[7] The two responses to the infinity of bricolage seek to determine the foot as a finite object

---

7. There is a third option. The pharmacist Homais tries to seduce Hippolyte into the operation. Here the contradiction of the equinus and the varus is resolved, not with a logical argument, but with an appeal to sexual attraction: "[Homais] even hinted that [Hippolyte] would be more likely to please women" (*MB,* 126).

available for cognition, and in this approach they follow the natural cognitive instinct to achieve completion. Still, in the seemingly innocent and well-intended aspiration to produce objective knowledge, the reflective and analytical reductions of infinity commit an impropriety. As they pursue taxonomic purity, and as they attempt to restore the world to orderly articulation, positive sciences remain blind to the demands of infinity.

In the infinite perspective, the deformity of the clubfoot lacks a name; it frustrates objective cognition and renders all corrective action ill-conceived. The foot represents a prespeculative synthesis achieved prior to mentation, a unity that the mind cannot objectify. In its infinity the foot confounds the corrective zeal; it does not require surgery, for Hippolyte "would support himself on it in preference to the sound one." Bricolage produces synthesis *and* supersedes it; it dissolves the object of cognition in an excessive efficacy that comes into full play in Hippolyte's limping *itself*. In this romantic poetics, the foot represents the prereflective lyricism of pure animality, "a deer" running "from morn till night." Turned both inwards *and* outwards, the grotesque (or arabesque) foot resists naming. It is a "being-turned," a flight from being named, a stepping away that is also the foot that does the stepping. Flaubert will neither reflect nor analyze, neither amputate nor correct.

It is, of course, quite difficult to demonstrate positively that this type of deformity, and of unity, does not require correction and that, perhaps, rather than representing an undesirable deviation, it describes a condition of perfection and unity to which the mind ultimately aspires and which human nature craves as its highest goal. A large part of this difficulty should be attributed to the elusive ambiguity of bricolage. In a certain sense, the ambiguous unity of bricolage— the presence of parts without their whole—represents one extreme end result of the rigorous application of reflection and analysis. The original unity of bricolage appears both ridiculous and threatening to the mind primarily because it is inaccessible to syllogistic thought. A mathematical analogy may help here. The infinity of bricolage can be recognized in the well-known paradox of the Cretan Liar. The essence of the paradox lies in the confusion of two levels of language: the level of the object-language, in which statements are made about states of affairs, and the level of meta-language, in which statements are made about the object-language. Bertrand Russell hoped to prevent the Cretan Liar paradox in set theory (there exist sets that are members of themselves) by formulating the rule that the statements made in the first-level language should not be confused with those made in the meta-language. Russell's rule belongs with the efforts of Genette and Bovary to master the original unity of bricolage and to make it conform to the prescribed ways of the mind's operation. But the "unity" of bricolage cannot be schematized mathematically into levels or divided anatomically into parts. As Christopher Prendergast shows, its inaccessible interior mocks the mind with an infinite paradox: "Within the infernal logic and infinite self-referentiality of the Cretan Liar paradox, the questions are theoretically almost endless.... Indeed, the perverse logic of the paradox is such that, in a kind of frenzied paroxysm, it must in the end turn against its own terms: in a happily mindless phonetic coincidence our Cretan turns out to be a cretin."[8] The infinite conversion of analysis and reflection into vicious circularity and unreflective repetition offers a disturbing measure of the ambiguous unity of bricolage. This ambiguity may have a sobering effect on the procedures of the critical, medical, and mathematical sciences; the difference between the solidity of the hermeneutic whole and sheer fantasy of wishful thinking, between anatomical perfection and malformation, and, finally, between conceptual precision and vicious circularity, is very thin indeed. The infinitely narrow difference defines Flaubert's conception of stupidity (*bêtise*) as the paralysis of the mind faced with its inability firmly to delimit one from the other.

This is the disconcerting message that bricolage offers to the mind as an "object" of knowledge: bricolage reveals to the mind that its valid insights dwell in dangerous proximity to its capacity to commit fatal errors. Put differently, the mind's only true knowledge is the awareness of its capacity for error. Wise to the extent that it knows its weakness but defeated by the knowledge that it is essentially fallible, the mind, simultaneously proud and humiliated, begins to resemble bricolage in the very method of its operation. Most alarmingly, the mind betrays the structure of bricolage in the most critical act of all, in transcendental self-diagnosis to determine its suitability to serve as a vehicle for cognition and to establish its authority as the subject of knowledge. The mind as a reliable instrument of critical knowledge can no longer distinguish itself from the impostor, the mind as the

---

8. Christopher Prendergast, *The Order of Mimesis: Balzac, Stendhal, Nerval, Flaubert* (New York, 1986), 192.

source of delusion and self-deception. Confronted with the lack of object in bricolage, the mind experiences itself non-objectively.

If Flaubert's prose is structured on the infinite unity of bricolage, it becomes urgent to examine in more detail how the infinity of bricolage is realized with regard to the conception of linguistic articulation and, most pertinently, with regard to the conception of the literary work. We have seen that bricolage resists naming in the essential sense that its incongruity is not one of inappropriate placement but one of infinite absence of identity. Since the parts of bricolage lack their proper home, the absent totality in which they are placed is a lack of home—it is "unhomely." We can say, using German etymology, that bricolage is uncanny (*unheimlich*).

The uncanny defines the sense of totality in bricolage as infinite in the most rigorous fashion. What the parts of bricolage make present is the unity that originally made them parts but that now remains absent. The uncanny element echoes the absent unity in a strictly infinite fashion, for the absence of the original home is not merely a matter of something that once existed in the past and is now lost but of something that never was originally present and that had always been lost. The original totality returns only in the scattered separated parts.[9]

We can see the uncanny sense of the absent totality in the bricolage of Hippolyte's foot. When Flaubert skips from the Latin *equinus* to the Greek *katastrephopody* and on to the vernacular "turning of the foot to the inside," he repeats a term that has had no historically or logically *original instance.* A *re-*cognition of the clubfoot is, strictly speaking, impossible. One can only point to the *different forms of deviation* over and over again; one can only repeat empirical instances as moments of the inaccessible Meaning. *Madame Bovary* is composed in accordance with this romantic philosophy of language. To create his novel (*der Roman*) Flaubert "uses," repeats, words in an uncanny evocation of totality. In this concept of language, Flaubert's method

---

9. The logic of the uncanny encapsulates in Flaubert, as Eugenio Donato has shown ("The Crypt of Flaubert," in *Flaubert and Postmodernism,* ed. Schor and Majewski, 30–45), the relation between the absent grounding unity and the surface play of the means of presenting this unity. Indeed, the unrepresentable content of the totality is presented only indirectly, in the inability of language to disclose this content. The mechanism of the "crypt" is propelled by the essential unrepresentability of totality; the uncanny totality is the en-crypted content accessible only in the drifting parts.

resembles James Joyce's use of repetition in *Ulysses*. *Ulysses* develops exemplarity as a romantic arabesque, for the examples in Joyce's novel stand separate from their framing totality. In the exemplary reference to totality, Joyce places the mind between chaos and order; he exposes the mind to the drift of repetition between the detail and the encompassing whole, without allowing it to complete the hermeneutic movement and come to rest in a determinate object of cognition. The suspended condition is, for Joyce, truly exemplary, for it alone prepares the mind for an encounter with itself as its proper object.

Flaubert's bricolage never shows its encompassing and completing whole, if the whole is understood as a notion developed in the process of hermeneutic comprehension. The unity of bricolage consists in an invisible and, at best, hypothetical relation of its individual parts to their original whole(s). The individual elements (*articuli*) of language all point to their totalities, but they do so not as indices produced by articulated language, for they are themselves, as parts, already indices of what speaks in them as the totality (totalities) of language. The "parts" of language, like the parts of bricolage, are related to totality infinitely. As the parts of bricolage are already constituted in their character as parts, so the parts of speech are, for Flaubert, a synthesis accomplished without work.

The conception of language as the work of the uncanny has far-reaching consequences for the notion of totality. In their morphemic variety, the anatomical terms exhibit the disturbing prolixity associated with classical rhetoric. The classical rhetorical repertoire—for example, hyperbole, parable, symbol, prolepsis, and metalepsis—comes to resemble, if not the anomalous *turn* of Hippolyte's twisted foot, then certainly the various modes of spatialization characterizing clubfeet: "inside, outside, downwards, torsion below or contraction above." Just as the clubfoot only specifies a concrete meaning identifiable in space and time without indicating the entity as such, so a rhetorical figure can only describe a particular construction of the world without giving any indication of what the world *as such* might be.

In a *sym*bol, for instance, the world appears as "thrown together," while in a *hyper*bole it is "overthrown." In classical rhetoric such tropological distortions are based on the well-known "deviation theory" of figurative language: the rhetorical distortion implies that there must exist an original, normal, *prerhetorical* measure in relation to which the distorting departure of the figure acquires rhetorical effect. To this Flaubert would reply that the logical and temporal priority of the "normal world" is falsely deduced from the rhetorical deviation. He would ask: In relation to what prior "worldly parameters" is a hyperbole an exaggeration? a symbol a unification? a parable a comparison? The commonsensical reply that the world is "there" for all to touch is easy to refute. Just as, in the case of the clubfoot, we can have no experience of the pure clubfoot *before* it undergoes the spatial turn, so, here, too, we can never experience the world *as such* before it becomes rhetorically altered. And this is so, not because of the immensity of the world's size (we know the numbers well enough), but because the world is a hypothetical *horizon,* an ungraspable, *inconceivable* sum total of all inversions of the linguistically (empirically) available suffixes. We encounter in each specific suffix, however, only the temporalized and spatialized particular moment, such as Hippolyte's clubfoot. Bricolage seems to show that reflection and analysis are intrinsically unable to "deduce" the concept of the "world" from the empirically available assemblage of parts. We encounter the world only as a bricolage of parts; as the encompassing whole, the world is uncannily absent.

Bricolage offers the possibility of meaning not based on hermeneutic relations between parts and whole. The significance of recognizing the cognitive challenges posed by the infinity of the clubfoot can be measured by the case of Madame Bovary herself. Critical responses to Flaubert's heroine have usually described her character as a complex combination of features that challenges the sensitive critic to find the proper name for this combination. Such method of inquiry overlooks the possibility of a reversal: bricolage is not a special case of a deformed object but an infinite entity that institutes the subject of cognition.

As intrinsically incompletable, bricolage challenges one of language's most essential functions, the function of naming. In view of the structural infinity of Charles's cap, of *Charbovari,* and of Hippolyte's clubfoot, one has strong reasons to despair about the legitimacy of any attempt to call these objects "cap," "language," and "clubfoot." At best, one would engage in such onomastics with the awareness that all naming is implicated in the repetitive nature of language. At worst, one may choose to perpetuate the illusion that objective naming will determine the hybrid formation. For example, medicine's rigorous art of naming, anatomy, would argue that the clubfoot represents a special case, an "infelicitous" exception as opposed to a "felicitous" majority (as in the linguistic theories of Austin and Searle). Confronted with a hybrid, the conceptual theory of language will seek to denote it, to finitize it, to *amputate* it.

The critical literature on Flaubert's novel has responded to the absence of the name with a flurry of taxonomic attempts, failing to see the inadequacy of such schemes to the infinite object under investigation. *Madame Bovary* and Emma Bovary have been usually subsumed under the rubric of exceptionality—a disfigured imagination (Gautier's *bovarysme*) or a perverse aesthetic sensibility (Girard's *mimetic desire*). Among the early critical responses, Baudelaire's review of the novel dwells most explicitly, although with a slight gender bias prevalent in his day, on the possibility that Emma Bovary represents a sensibility not lodged securely in any known pattern. Baudelaire expressed this idea in terms of the acquisition by Emma of strongly *masculine* features: of Emma the woman with "a strong tendency to" the masculine, or of the weakly masculine Emma with "a strong tendency to" the feminine.[10] More recently, Tony Tanner has labeled Emma's case as "adultery," a collapse of the boundaries that organize conceptual meaning.[11]

Taxonomic explications of the *case of Emma Bovary* are bound to ignore the infinity of the phenomenon and to overlook the crisis of naming that this infinity provokes. For, as everything in Flaubert's novel, Emma's experience and her character obey the regimen of bricolage with all its infinite implications. Before discussing several examples, we must first introduce a pertinent distinction in order to prevent the misunderstanding of the logic of infinity. The transgression of conceptuality in bricolage tends to be understood, and this is confirmed by the reaction of the pupils in the novel's opening scene, as mere incompatibility of two otherwise determinate objects (contexts). Compared with the infinite sense of bricolage, this simple failure of

10. Charles Baudelaire, "*Madame Bovary*, by Gustave Flaubert," *L'Artiste*, October 18, 1857. Naomi Schor ("For a Restricted Thematics: Writing, Speech, and Difference in *Madame Bovary*," in *Modern Critical Interpretations: Gustave Flaubert's "Madame Bovary*," ed. Harold Bloom [New York, 1988], 61–81) expands this thought with the model of androgyny, of Emma's "failure" to be a girl, a wife, a mother. Schor extends this motif to the formal dimension of the novel as a whole: "In the last analysis the 'bizarre androgyn' is neither Flaubert (Sartre) nor Emma (Baudelaire), but the book, locus of the confrontation, as well as the interpretation of *animus* and *anima*, of the masculine and the feminine" (81).

11. Tony Tanner, *Adultery in the Novel: Contract and Transgression* (Baltimore, 1979), 11–18.

contextualization appears quite innocuous. However, what is at stake in the infinity is the lack of all measure of compatibility or of incompatibility, for while one context of placement (Charles's head) is known, the other context solicits pure indeterminacy. As such an *infinite thing*, bricolage prevents articulation, determination, and closure, all of which are needed if a violation of taxonomic boundaries is to take place and make any sense at all.

The difference in question is captured by Dominick LaCapra's analysis of the scandal over the publication of *Madame Bovary*. LaCapra argues that the scandal erupted, not over specific points of private and public morality, but because Flaubert's novel disrupted the very foundation on which ethical distinctions are based. What went on trial, then, was the very idea of trial as such: "*Madame Bovary* was experienced as somehow unsettling or disorienting by its readers, but the reasons explicitly given for discomfort do not adequately account for the unsettling, even uncanny, effect of the text ... the trial attempts to process exclusively as ordinary crime—crime involving standard forms of deviation from established norms or values—what may in some sense be 'ideological' or political crime—'crime' that places in question the very grounds of the trial itself."[12] Paradoxically, Flaubert's reading public *defended* transgression, to the extent that it demanded the preservation of clear distinctions by which transgression would be detected. The public could not tolerate, however, the condition before clear lines are demarcated, for this original condition would not only prevent one from identifying concrete transgressions but would also make it impossible to know *what a transgression is*. *Madame Bovary* tells us that the act of judgment must first institute the boundaries of its own competence. Emma's bricolage-like experience, then, does not simply transgress the (ethical) boundary, for in that case the boundary would, in its solidity, assure a stable world of meaning and provide criteria for judging immorality. Emma experiences the boundary as such, in all its purity and indeterminateness, as the difference between two entities, itself empty and infinite.

The boundary that assures the self-identity and coherence of experience (for example, the boundary between fact and fantasy) does not appear in Emma's actions as a stable dividing-line but only as a transgressed moment. As the following examples will seek to demonstrate, Emma experiences neither this nor the other side of the boundary, but

12. Dominick LaCapra, *Madame Bovary on Trial* (Ithaca, 1982), 17–18.

the line, the border itself. Early in the novel Emma traces the imaginary state of bliss to the other side of the boundary, which she identifies with temporal segments of her life: the schooling in the Ursuline convent, her brief stay on her father's farm, the even briefer happiness immediately after marrying Charles, the courting of Léon, and so on. Later, however, Emma feels increasingly excluded from the other side of the boundary, no matter where she is: "She longed to travel or to go back to her convent. She wanted to die, but she also wanted to live in Paris" (*MB*, 43).

Flaubert presents Emma's yearning for the other side in various forms of auto-affection, such as self-perception, imagination, and mirrors. The auto-affective acts immediately start a domino effect of accumulation, remembering, and synthesis, not only of one's prior identities or personas, but of a collective identity spread among total strangers, types, or models. After being seduced by Rodolphe during the horse ride in the woods—after crossing over to fantasy—Emma examines herself in the mirror:

> But when she saw herself in the mirror she wondered at her face. Never had her eyes been so large, so black, nor so deep. Something subtle about her being transfigured her. . . . Then she recalled the heroines of the books that she had read, and the lyric legion of these adulterous women began to sing in her memory with the voice of sisters that charmed her. She became herself, as it were, an actual part of these lyrical imaginings; at long last, as she saw herself among those lovers she had so envied, she fulfilled the love-dream of her youth. (*MB*, 117)

As the novel progresses, Emma becomes less attracted by the other, inaccessible, or forbidden side of the boundary and becomes increasingly sensitive to the pure boundary itself. During her second liaison with Léon, Emma, now extravagant, impatient, and provocative, touches up the reality of the affair with the power of the image: "She wanted him [Léon] to dress all in black, and grow a pointed beard, to look like the portraits of Louis XIII" (*MB*, 201). Emma wants her lover to look, not like Louis XIII, but like *the portrait* of Louis XIII. She obviously knows that Louis XIII now lives only in his portraits; however, she understands that the image is, somehow, more original than the original face.

In asking León to look like the portrait, Emma offers a revealing glimpse into her sensibility. The original Louis XIII is the portrait's mimetic origin; he *en*genders the portrait as a structure resembling something—himself. Léon, in his turn, re-resembling the portrait's mimetic relation to *its* original, is transcendentally *en-gendered* by this relation: he assembles the similarity between Louis XIII and his portrait in a relation that embodies similarity, or portraiture, itself. Asked to look like the portrait, Léon is, in fact, asked to *become* a portrait, to become *resemblance itself*. Emma Bovary possesses an aesthetic skill of the first order: the ability to detect transcendental likeness, to see that which makes two objects similar. She not only is in touch with "the other side," with "the dreams beyond" (*MB*, 223) but also perceives the ground of identity, the sembling excess of being. The sembling is the center of the transcendental ambiguity; as it constitutes both re-semblance and dis-semblance, truth and falsehood, it itself remains *indifferent* to them. Emma's imagination is attuned to this indifferent boundary itself. When she hears the story about La Guérine, a woman allegedly suffering from hysteria, who recovered after she got married, Emma says, "But with me . . . it was after marriage that it began" (*MB*, 78). The contents of the real and of the imaginary are no longer relevant. The boundary alone, the pure boundary, remains. There, Emma is threatened by direct access to experience *before* it becomes expressed in language. The task of art (of Emma's life) is to enter into the presence of experience in its sum total, to enter the forgotten—*Lethe*—totality of experience, the lethal experience.

Emma's experience resembles bricolage, then, not because it is fragmented, but because it remains attentive to the infinite boundary, if the boundary is understood, not as a geometrical line, but as the imperceptible division implied by the uncanny reference of the parts to the essentially absent whole. The experience of the boundary, as the uncanny presence of parts without the whole, defines the Flaubertian sense of vertigo. The infinite vertigo, as a poetic response to the infinity of bricolage, denotes the condition of cognitive faculties confronted with an infinite object. This object invites comprehension, for it is apparently composed of parts, but it frustrates cognition insofar as it denies the closure of the hermeneutic process. It becomes imperative to apply the concept of bricolage to Flaubert's concept of the literary work and to see how the infinite vertigo can constitute the essence of a properly literary project.

To pursue this point we will closely examine a passage from *Madame Bovary* (Part II, Chapter 7, pp. 91–92) in which Monsieur Rodolphe Boulanger de la Huchette comes to Charles Bovary's house to bleed one of his peasants. What promises to be a simple medical procedure of blood-letting unexpectedly gets out of hand. First the peasant faints, and Justin, who was holding the basin, follows suit. Bovary himself turns pale at Justin's *syncope*. The present analysis of the passage proceeds on the general assumption that Flaubert's poetics is based on the infinity of bricolage. Seen in these terms, Flaubert's novel is an unanalyzable composite that cannot be objectified in a theoretical model of totality. Confronted with the bricolage of this scene, literary "analysis" may be tempted to follow Genette's "reflective" method and speculate about the hypothetical meaning of the scene, or it may, following Charles, analyze it into its components. The unmediated unity of the passage can be preserved only in a poetic reading. This reading, however, exposes the mind to infinite vertigo.

The scene is organized by vertigo in several dimensions. First, the reader may be upset by the potentially unpleasant aspect of blood-letting. Second, Flaubert narrates the scene as if it had been already narrated by someone else before him, giving the text the sound of a now untraceable repetition, the flavor of a cliché. Third, the parenthetical remarks used in the passage complicate the reading with additional layers of meaning. And finally, at the end of the scene Emma takes upon herself the burden of vertigo in its pure infinity.

By setting in motion the domino effect of fainting (the peasant, then Justin) Flaubert turns the scene of blood-letting into an allegory of fainting. The reader may experience vertigo not only because the scene is quite explicit in physical detail but also because it is permeated by an indeterminate *syncope*, which takes hold of the mind exactly when the mind seeks to grasp it and control its disruptive effects. The elusive vertigo can be sensed, for example, in the character of the scene as a medical and linguistic cliché, a quality repeatedly signaled by set phrases presented in quotations. On arriving at the house, Rodolphe asks Justin to announce him to Charles: " 'Tell him that M. Rodolphe Boulanger *de la* Huchette is here.' " Flaubert comments: "It was not out of affectation that the new arrival added '*de la* Huchette' to his name, but to make himself the better known." Informing the reader about Rodolphe's finances, Flaubert repeats the hearsay and places the amount in inverted commas: Rodolphe "was supposed to have an income of 'at least fifteen thousand francs a year.' "

Similarly, the action of the scene is treated as a ritualistic procedure that proves effective solely by being performed. The conviction that bleeding is "what one is supposed to do" is shared by the peasant, Rodolphe, and the doctor himself. First, we learn about the peasant's condition in a speech reported by Rodolphe. Second, Flaubert puts the peasant's description of symptoms in inverted commas: "[He wanted to] be bled because he felt 'as if ants were crawling all over him.' " The peasant also rejects all dissuasion with formulaic denials: " 'It will clear me out,' was his answer to all reasonable objections" to blood-letting.

The general sense of *dejá-vù* and *dejá-fait* deprives the scene of freshness and originality in other aspects as well. For example, the blood of the peasant loses its natural look at the very moment it appears "splashing against the looking-glass." The fresh blood never exists in itself; it is only seen as an image, diffused and refracted, as in the stained-glass windows in which *Madame Bovary* abounds. Psychological reactions also lack spontaneity. At the very moment when, in a display of courage, he is conquering his fear, Bovary cannot resist *playing the role* of the competent surgeon. " 'Sometimes,' answered the officier de santé, 'one feels nothing at first, and them [sic] they start fainting, especially when they're strong like this one.' " The answer is not an answer to the peasant's question (about the redness of his blood) but a discourse of the experienced surgeon intended for the audience; it is the voice of impersonal authority. The patient is terrified by the diagnosis furnished to him in place of the anticipated response. From this nonresponse of Bovary, the peasant *learns what happens* to strong men during a blood-letting procedure, and what he, a strong man himself, ought to do in this situation. Even the fainting of the ploughman, which could qualify as a genuinely spontaneous event, occurs according to Bovary's prescription; it is motivated by a scientific *image* of sampled faintings. "At these words the peasant dropped the lancet-case he was holding back of his chair. A shudder of his shoulders made the chairback creak. His hat fell off." Bovary plays the composed doctor and says: "I thought as much," and presses his finger on the veins—as if he could bleed his patients only *after* he has made them faint.

It is at the point when the peasant faints in reaction to Charles's fatuous formula that the connection between bleeding, fainting, and cliché emerges with full force. We have seen that in his description of the scene of bleeding Flaubert emphasizes the character of the procedure as the *cliché of the popular medical imagination.* We have also seen that, instead of providing a simple description, Flaubert narrates the scene as if it were *still being reported.* One may venture the following explanation. A cliché confronts the mind with a form of linguistic infinity, and fainting seems to be a proper reaction to this experience. A cliché neither reaches a final stage of having been conclusively uttered by the actual speaker (in which case its existence as a cliché would come to term; the cliché would disappear from language), nor does it allow itself to be uttered *for the first time* (in which case it would not have been a cliché *yet*). Because, as an incomplete utterance, it hovers suspended between origin and destination, the cliché *eternally synthesizes* the beginning and the end without ever accomplishing this synthesis. The blood-letting scene does not merely induce fainting; it is not merely an allegory of fainting but also the fainting of allegory: the vertiginous scene discloses vertigo to be *the very essence of reading.*

Obviously, nobody in the room exercises any control over the anonymous causality of syncopation (*la syncope*). The scene is thus thrown out of rhythm and is on its way to achieve full syncopation, to unravel in total vertigo. The vertigo overcomes Bovary when Justin faints. His first response to the crisis is to call his Emma: " 'My wife! get my wife!' " (This cry will be repeated later, when Emma contemplates hurling herself from the attic window after reading Rodolphe's farewell letter.) Emma "With one bound . . . rushed down the staircase," interrupting her window reverie. Seeing Justin still unconscious, Charles orders Emma to conceal the basin: " 'We must hide this from him,' said Charles. Madame Bovary took the basin to put it under the table. With the movement she made in bending down, her dress (it was a summer dress with four flounces, yellow, long in the waist and wide in the skirt) spread out around on the tiles; and as Emma, stooping, staggered a little in stretching out her arms, the pull of her dress made it hug more closely the line of her bosom" (*MB*, 92). In an aesthetics sensitive to dramatic tension this moment would deserve to be called climactic; however, the infinite dynamics of the action prevents such resolution. What is, perhaps, most mysterious about Emma's staggering is the possibility that the very pull of her dress helps her maintain her balance as much as it prevents her from placing the basin under the table. Emma staggers, pulled by the opposite vectors of the weight of the basin and the resistance of her dress. Bent down, she generates a field of energy, which, contained wholly in the compass of her physical being, sustains her by virtue of balance *and* imbalance. Emma does not know which is to be restored and which is to be avoided.

It is important to insist on the infinite logic of Emma's situation. Emma is not experiencing a momentary loss of balance in the process of handling the basin but stands at the borderline of two conditions.

The weight of the basin pulls her down, while the pull of her dress straightens her up. Standing in between, precariously balanced, Emma experiences a true *ekstasis*,[13] standing neither simply on the outside nor on the inside of herself, standing outside of this option, standing atopically, nowhere. The critical moment of this scene occurs, therefore, not simply in Emma's bending and staggering, but in the bending-and-staggering-that-is-Emma.[14] Emma's staggering, a result of two contradictory impulses (pulsions) resembles *catalepsy*, and it remains unclear what undergoes the seizure and what performs the seizing. Greek etymology does not help, since the addition of *kata* (down; in accordance with; by) to *lambanein* (to seize), while it signals some form of seizing, at the same time leaves the exact manner of such grasping in obscurity. Catalepsy seizes no specific object; rather, catalepsy is the being-seized, the seizure of the body in which the body seizes (upon) itself and becomes the object of its own seizing. One could say that the experience is not one *of* vertigo but that it *is* vertigo, to the extent that the originary construction of the idea of experience encompasses the totality of conditions under which a specific experience can take place. The vertigo in question is the form of experience that has this conditioning totality as its only content.[15]

13. Ecstasy: [ME *extasie*, fr. MF, fr. LL *ecstasis*, fr. Gk *ekstasis*, fr. *existanai* to derange, fr. *ex* out + *histanai* to cause to stand—more at EX-, STAND] 1 a: a state of being beyond reason and self-control; b *archaic*: SWOON" (*Webster's New Collegiate Dictionary*).

14. Tanner describes Emma's vertigo in similar terms; this vertigo is a matter of a hesitation in which the subject grasps itself in its identity as a subject (*Adultery in the Novel*, 233–35).

15. Philippe Lacoue-Labarthe gives a precise phenomenological description of this experience in his meditation "Poetry as Experience" (*SubStance*, LX [1989], 22–29). The article discusses Paul Celan's poem "Tübingen, January" to determine the relation between Celan's and Hölderlin's concepts of experience. Lacoue-Labarthe argues that poetic experience is not a "tourist's" *Erlebnis* but an *Erfahrung* (etymologically related to *Gefahr*, danger). The essence of the danger lies in vertigo: "A vertigo can arise (*survenir*); it does not 'happen' (*advenir*). Or rather, in it, nothing happens. It is the pure suspension of happening: caesura or syncope. . . . What is suspended, put on hold, balancing suddenly in strangeness, is the presence of the present (the present existence of the present). And what happens then, without happening (for it is such that by definition cannot 'happen'), is non-being, nothingness, the 'nothing-being' ('rien d'étant') (ne ens). Vertigo is the *experience* of nothingness, of the (non)occurrence 'its very self' (as Heidegger says) of nothingness" (25). Vertigo brings a "strange *gift of nothing* or this *present of nothing*—as we say of an insignificant gift, 'It's nothing.' And in fact it's never anything, it's *nothing*. . . . It's reported that Hölderlin, gone insane, repeated incessantly, 'Nothing happens to me, nothing happens to me' " (27).

Emma's vertiginous relation to herself brings the discussion back to the question of bricolage and of the effect of its infinity on cognition. Rather than momentarily disturbing the mind's cognitive operations, the infinity of bricolage discloses the condition under which finite objects can be known. Moreover, as the case of Emma suggests, the vertigo of bricolage constitutes the knowing subject *as subject* as well. The only mode of self-knowledge available to the subject is the reflux, the uncanny return of the totality of the self in the moment of vertigo. The self's infinite movement in vertigo towards itself exceeds the objective figures graspable by the mind's cognitive powers.

We have said that Emma experiences in her vertigo, not a momentary loss of balance in an otherwise stable world of empirical reality, but the totality of conditions under which a specific experience can take place. We have also said that the vertigo in question is the form of experience that has this conditioning totality as its only content. It is not clear exactly *what*, in objective terms, Emma is experiencing in this moment. In the vocabulary of phenomenology, Emma's vertigo is the result of the disclosure of the horizonal structure of human experience.

As John Sallis shows in his article "Art within the Limits of Finitude," phenomenological analysis of aesthetic experience considers the work of art as the privileged locus of disclosure of the totality of horizons in which the human subject enacts its existence. The concept of the phenomenological horizon refers to the necessary structure of preconditions that makes each specific intentional act possible. Sallis illustrates the horizonal structure with the following example of "inner horizon" disclosed in perspectival perception of empirical objects: "In perceiving such an object I directly view only one perspective of the object. However, the object as it appears under this one perspective cannot be identified with the object of my perception.... The direct seeing from this one perspective becomes a perception of the object only within a horizon constituted by all other possible perspectives from which the object might be viewed. The perception of objects in space thus always involves not only a direct viewing from a single perspective but also a general non-thematic givenness of this inner horizon of possibilities."[16]

---

16. John C. Sallis, "Art within the Limits of Finitude," *International Philosophical Quarterly*, VII (1967), 295.

While this example specifies the horizonal structure in the particular case of spatial perception, it may also be sufficient to indicate the concept of horizon that always accompanies the subject's intentional acts. Under normal conditions, the subject moves in the horizonal structure without reflection, encountering objects disclosed in each specific and pertinent context. A work of art radically changes this situation. Phenomenological analysis assigns a special function to the work of art to the extent that it considers art objects the privileged places of disclosure of the horizonal structure as such. While in the perception of objects we allow the horizonal structure to disappear *in* the act of perception, the perception of the work of art is directed by the art object away from the object-character of the work and towards the totality of the horizonal conditions. Here, the subject perceives, not a specific object within a horizon of "non-thematic givenness," but the horizon (or the totality of horizons) in which the object can be understood in its character as an object.

Phenomenological description of the perception of the art object applies to Flaubertian bricolage in the following manner. The art object makes the subject aware of the horizonal structure as such because the gaze is fixed, not on the object, but on the totality of conditions of perception. The art object solicits the mind to overcome perspectival limitations of objective perception and to focus on the totality of horizons that underlies this perception. Sallis gives two engaging examples of such an overcoming of perspectival limitations: Picasso's "Girl Before a Mirror" and Duchamp's "Nude Descending a Staircase." The former enhances spatial perspective in a cubist fashion, by superimposing dimensions, while the latter enhances temporal perspective, by freezing several frames of movement of the human figure. Both paintings, says Sallis, "may be understood as presenting a movement towards a surpassment of the perspectival horizonality of human perception, a movement in which through the presentation of a multiplicity of perspectives the object or event in effect disintegrates, ceases almost to be an object, and we are brought back to a more profound awareness of the perspectival-horizonal nature of the human encounter."[17]

It appears that the subject can encounter the horizonal structure as such only because the work of art "ceases almost to be an object." For

---

17. *Ibid.*, 296.

what the work of art discloses is not a concrete empirical shape but the totality of horizons in which objects can reveal themselves to the subject in the first place. The disintegration of the object thus indicates that the cognitive relation between subject and object is less central, or, as phenomenological thought puts it, less "primordial," than the totality in which this relation arises. To gain access to this structure, the subject needs to come into contact with a work of art, that is, with an "object" whose object-character disintegrates and, in this disintegration, reveals the horizon as such.

The structure of bricolage conforms in many ways to the phenomenological analysis of the work of art as a privileged locus of disclosure of the horizonal structure of human experience. For now it may be pertinent only to suggest that the genealogy that extends from the romantic arabesque to modern bricolage opens the possibility of an affinity between romantic and phenomenological epistemology in the realm of aesthetic reflection and in that of the cognition of objects in general. The connection appears particularly strong in the correlation between Flaubert's romantic vertigo and the dissolution of the object: the disintegration of the aesthetic object finds its counterpart in the disintegration of the subject. The "surpassment" of the subject-object cognitive model paves the way for a more "primordial" experience—the aesthetic experience of Flaubert and of Emma Bovary.

We have seen in what way Flaubert uses cliché and bricolage to present the infinity of experience. Before characterizing Flaubert's literary enterprise in general, we must first examine one more technique prominent in *Madame Bovary*. I want to focus on Flaubert's use of parenthetical remarks. The episode of bleeding the peasant is *framed* by Emma. First, Emma opens and closes the scene with her puzzling presence. Second, Emma can be said to frame the episode in the sense that, both in the initial scene with Emma at the window and in the description of her bending under the table, Flaubert inserts what I take to be very important parenthetical remarks.

In the opening of this scene, Emma's initial position is that of a dreamy spectator at the window in her room. With the narrator, we observe Emma observe the indistinct landscape, and we receive from the narrator *explicit instructions*, in parentheses, telling us how to interpret the scene: "Emma was standing in the open window (she often did so: in the provinces, the window takes the place of the theatre and the promenade) and she amused herself with watching the rustic crowd, when she saw a gentleman [Rodolphe] in a green velvet coat"

(*MB*, 91). The parenthetical comment refers to "the theater and the promenade," venues offering ample perspective and totalizing perception.[18] The parenthesis performs two functions. Its first function is to define the realistic parameters of the scene (this is *why* Emma is standing in the window). In addition, the parenthesis invites the readers into the narrator's professional intimacy to be spectators *perceiving* Emma *perceiving* her milieu.

In the second example (the description of Emma as she bends under the table), the parenthesis refers to Emma's dress: "(it was a summer dress with four flounces, yellow, long in the waist and wide in the skirt)." It appears that the second parenthesis lacks both rationales: first, because we read a "pure" description not intended to justify any subsequent action, and second, because the parenthesis, interpreted as instructions, does not add a next remove of spectatorship. Yet the parenthesis is there. To take another example, in the immediate vicinity of the comment about Emma's "yellow" dress, there is a reference to Rodolphe's "yellow gloves." Still, Rodolphe's gloves appear *outside* parentheses, while Emma's yellow dress appears within them. The two instances of "yellow," in a hypothetical logic of subsumption (loosely analogous to bracketing in mathematical formulas) confront the reader with a motivated and an unmotivated use of parentheses. How can the two be reconciled? One may speculate that Flaubert uses parentheses without a strict sense of what is essential and what is marginal to his subject matter, that he has eliminated the clear sense of inside and outside. Capable of appearing *anywhere*, Flaubert's shifting parentheses expose the reader to *la syncope*.[19]

18. Windows are vertiginous for most of us. Jean Rousset considers such elevated locale (*plongeur*) central to *Madame Bovary*. By identifying vertigo with the specific physical circumstance (fear of heights), Rousset places Flaubert's dizziness in empirical, and not in infinite, aesthetics ("*Madame Bovary:* Flaubert's Anti-Novel," in *Forme et signification: Essais sur les structures littéraires de Corneille à Claudel* [Paris, 1962], 109–33. An excerpt of this essay appears as "Windows and Panoramic Vision," in *MB*, 449–57).

19. This analysis of the optionality of parentheses coincides with Christopher Prendergast's understanding of quotation in Flaubert (*The Order of Mimesis*):

> On the one hand, quotation signifies a borrowing; it is a way of acknowledging a 'debt,' of recognising an 'authority' that supports and guarantees the truth or plausibility of what is being affirmed. . . . On the other hand, quotation can have the opposite function: it represents the insertion of a certain distance between the speaker and what is being said, and thus opens up the possibility of ironic negation. Flaubert's text plays systematically on and across these two contradictory functions, but at the same time immeasurably complicates and refines that

Flaubert's use of parenthetical remarks to set off marginal content from central content resembles Emma's staggering condition. Emma, we may recall, experiences the pure condition anterior (or indifferent) to balance and imbalance. In a similarly infinite interpretation Flaubert's parentheses denote the pure boundary that separates form from content. The boundary constitutes form and content and provides the meeting ground for their coincidence and divergence. In itself, however, the parenthetical space of this encounter is empty (of content) and without shape (formless).[20]

The meaning of the parenthetical function in general is quite intriguing. In mathematical formulas bracketing has many functions, all of which pass through the parenthetical moment. Brackets indicate a precedence of an operation (what is bracketed must be executed first), an option (disregard and/or include), or a tentative commitment (the operation might be performed or not). The logic of parentheses claims to delimit the pertinent content from what is marginal, but its operative possibilities betray a potential for excess and contradiction. If it

---

play by the device of *dropping the quotation marks*. . . . In this way, the text operates a simultaneous dialectic of simulation and subversion, in which paradoxically the force of the latter depends crucially on the efficacy of the former. (202–203)

Prendergast usefully defines the theme extended here to other aspects of Flaubert's prose: Flaubert's exploration of the possibility that parentheses and other graphological devices used to set off one content from another (bracketing, italics, quotation) might be invisible—transcendental.

20. This analysis is confirmed by Robert Morrissey in his essay "Breaking In (Flaubert in Parentheses)" (*SubStance*, LVI [1988], 49–62). Morrissey distinguishes Flaubert's use of parentheses from that of other nineteenth-century novelists, Balzac, Stendhal, and Zola. The realism of these writers "involves both telling the tale and explaining or justifying the tale, but it does not involve, as it does in Flaubert, reflexively showing the telling of the tale" (52). The "reflexive showing" gives rise to a "faceless narrator behind Flaubert's tales" who "could . . . be described in almost formal or institutional terms as a function" (53). If, still in quite a traditional manner, Flaubert's parentheses mark "the boundaries of referential illusion" (57), they differ from this convention because parenthetical "insertion becomes a manner of narrative assertion and, in so becoming, works against the realist illusion" (56). Flaubert "places realism at the service of meaninglessness" (54) to present a "pure, unattached, 'objectified' perception. . . . Between parentheses, Flaubert has posited what might well constitute the most radical narrative act: disconcatenation, the abolition of the tale, its fragmentation into an unnarrated state" (59). Morrissey adds: "That parenthetical insertions constitute a 'natural' gesture in Flaubert's writing is attested to by their frequency in his correspondence where they introduce a kind of 'dédoublement de soi,' or rather another voice that is nevertheless the same" (61, n. 18).

were possible to assemble all the operations allowed by the logic of bracketing and to execute them simultaneously, the resulting sum of operations would confound the mind by the contradictory nature of the instructions. Parentheses seem to perform an operation on themselves, for they exhaust the logic of exclusion and inclusion, of relevance and irrelevance, in a structure of infinity completely enclosed in its reflexive interiority. The content of parenthetical bricolage is the constant and insistent separation, according to the strict logic of its functions, of the function of inclusion from exclusion, of priority from suspension, and so on. The parenthetical infinity creates the insoluble equation as a sequence of arithmetical commands. Lacking a totality, the bricolage of components maintains itself in the pure, empty operation of parenthetical delimitation of itself from itself.

Let us apply these possibilities to Emma's presence in the scene of bleeding. She may be disregarded (shoved under the table), included (she is also there among other participants), temporarily suspended (let us wait and see), or given precedence (the equation will come out incorrect unless one first attends to Emma). Placed under the table, Emma, enclosed in the inconclusive sequence of mathematical parentheses, presents herself as the infinite object encountered by the mind in bricolage. An object beyond objectivity, an equation endlessly pursuing its solution, Emma, along with Flaubert's prose, becomes aesthetically—infinitely—*beautiful.*

Flaubert's poetics differs from that of the realism of his time. Realism bases its sense of "reality" on the correspondence of word and thing. But realism fails to observe that it can claim to achieve this correspondence only because its deeper premise is the distinction between word and thing; only with this initial chasm does realism's project of bridging the chasm become possible and meaningful. For Flaubert, on the other hand, the initial separation between word and thing does not constitute a gap that must be bridged but a space that makes the coincidence between word and thing possible and meaningful. Flaubert is not interested in presenting realistic content with the most appropriate combination of words (although this ideal is, of course, part of his project). Flaubert is interested in bringing to presence the very condition under which word and thing can meet in the first place. Flaubert seeks to bring to presence the boundary itself.

Flaubert's prose privileges infinite formations—bricolage, cliché, parentheses—in order to deemphasize the simple referential relation between word and thought predominant in the aesthetics of realism and, instead, in accordance with the aesthetics of romanticism, to bring to language something that is neither a concept nor a thing. The encounter of word and thing that, in the normal use of language, would produce communication or reference, produces, in the case of Flaubert, a slippage of meaning. The failure of word and thought to coincide foregrounds the pure margin anterior to both articulation (form) and meaning (content). In the language of vertigo, Flaubert's words lose their denotative balance, and at this precarious moment, they derail the thought that they were supposed to bring forth. Flaubert fails to reflect the world *adequately*, not in an attempt to ridicule the world, but because his language interrogates its own ability to coincide with the world.

The question is, again, as in the case of bricolage: What "object" is being presented to the mind in parenthetical economy? The shifting parentheses of unbounded, romantic imagination cordon the reader off both from empirical reality and from an ideal world. Flaubert's project is neither realism nor idealism nor satire; reading Flaubert's descriptions in *Madame Bovary*, the reader can neither reconstitute the world as it is nor postulate the world as it should be, and rather than distorting the real world for satirical effect, Flaubert aims to present the *distorting (in) which the world is*.

Without beginning and without end, the novel maintains itself on the wings of parentheses, able neither to demonstrate the ground of its operation nor to indicate the distance from some stable economy of signification. If the novel exercises any measure of irony, this measure is irretrievably buried in the unanalyzable unity of Flaubert's prosaic bricolage. The parts of the bricolage could theoretically function in a totality; they might signify in some conceivable structure of reference. Yet, because the mind has not been actively involved in the production of the parts, it merely uses the prefabricated parts as untraceable quotations that, by some infinite irony, have been denied the comfort of totality.

Flaubert's reader, his faculties frustrated by the bricolage of the novel, is sensitized to the empty boundary that, in the communicative use of language, disappears in the referential function. What speaks in the boundary is not reason, not history, not the historical author, Flaubert, not literary tradition, and not a fictional story about Madame Bovary, but, as Maurice Blanchot says, Literature, the essence of speech that always speaks in what is conceptually spoken.[21] Literature is not written to accomplish reference but to bring to speech the point of coincidence between concept and world. We have seen how Flaubert produces vertigo by exploiting parenthetical remarks to suggest that any phrase in the novel may appear in parentheses. This *staggering* realization characterizes Flaubert's prose in general. Quotation, cliché, and parentheses reveal the *condition humaine* as the vertiginous condition, as the *condition littéraire*.

In the final analysis, the vertigo is not exhausted by the graphological devices, for these devices are primarily used to indicate the work of *positivistic* irony, the sarcasm that is the lot of the novel's designated fool, Homais. While Flaubert's prose always appears to be a quotation, the highest source of this economy of inescapable repetition cannot be remarked with punctuation signs because what the prose as a whole repeats is, as in the case of bricolage, nothing objective or determinate, but the uncanny totality, the formless and contentless totality of horizons that makes language—the coincidence of word and thing—possible.

This romantic conception of irony as infinite constitution of denotation would seem to explain Flaubert's *Dictionary of Received Ideas* more adequately than the positivistic notion of irony as satirical unmasking of well-established meanings. The *Dictionary*, a representative compilation of petit bourgeois refinement, is widely understood as a debunking of popular opinion. Yet this view overlooks the possibility that Flaubert's ironic headings in the book attack, not only commonplace views, but the very possibility of having views, the very possibility of originality. To present common opinion as the property of dictionaries implies that the *Dictionary* occupies a position elevated above all discourse and radically different from discourse. Hence, if Flaubert has seen through the commonplace, he must have also seen through the unique and the extraordinary. Speaking from the origin of language, Flaubert's repetition of common opinion is no longer simply satirical, for it would then exhaust itself in attacking specific objects and issues for their mediocrity and banality. Such limitation would concede that there exist other objects and other issues that possess excellence and deserve our admiration and that they have remained outside of the *Dictionary*'s scope. These objects would guarantee an extrinsic position inaccessible to the limited uses of positivistic satire.

---

21. "Literature and the Right to Death," in *G*, 21.

Flaubert's discursive position *a fortiori* encompasses in its critique the entirety of speech. Flaubert speaks from the totality, but then he loses a firm hold on his intentionality. He speaks in the manner of repetition. For it would be devastating to answer the central question opened up by Flaubert's *Dictionary:* Who supplies the *Dictionary*'s ideas? Of course, empirically speaking, the ideas originate in society and are anonymously circulated by it.[22] However, in view of the comprehensive, uncompromising, and unforgiving satire that speaks in the *Dictionary*, it is not sufficient to identify the society and the speaker (writer) as concrete historical sources. The writer of the *Dictionary* criticizes, not only the commonplace opinions of his historical moment, but the very idea and the very possibility of common opinion as it (re)occurs across history. The voice of the *Dictionary*, then, is not the voice of cultural critique, however topical and pertinent, but of transcendental critique. As transcendental, the critique is concerned less with exposing the mediocrity of contemporary opinion than with presenting the condition under which any opinion can be expressed at all. The writer (and the common public) *receives the ideas* from the totality of speech.

Because it critiques the conditions of possibility for language, Flaubert's *Dictionary*, rather than repeating the clichés of public life, foregrounds the operation of repetition that normally remains unnoticed when speakers, basking in the glory of originality, utter these ideas for the first time or when they regurgitate them in blissful ignorance. Stated simply, Flaubert's *Dictionary* reminds us that if something can be said for the first time, it must be essentially iterable; that is, its first utterance must have already been a repetition. Even the highest, transcendental critique is a cliché.

The transcendental sense of repetition sets Flaubert's parodic project apart from the satirical and parodic uses of repetition. A comparison with Mikhail Bakhtin's theory of novelistic discourse may bring the difference in question into sharper focus. For Flaubert, as for Bakhtin, the genre of the novel denotes the locus of language use that

---

22. The pharmacist Homais suggests an interesting direction of inquiry. As Robert Niess argues ("On Listening to Homais," *French Review*, LI [1977], 22–28), the importance of Homais lies beyond the total saturation of his discourse with the *idées reçues* of the age. For Niess "Homais' discourse is largely composed of declarative sentences of very positive cast" (25), a strong sign of Flaubert's settling accounts with the Enlightenment. For *his part,* Flaubert reports, in free indirect discourse, *stupidly,* the clichés of that time, his recourse to stupidity no longer retaining the luxury of brackets to signal (Flaubert's) critical distance.

offers the writer the opportunity to intensify the *usability* of language to the point of wearing it off in an endless spiral of parodies that, as Bakhtin puts it, "distance the author still further from language." However, in contrast to Bakhtin, Flaubert questions the very "object" character of this object. For Bakhtin, speech is constituted by *empirical* repetition, by what he calls the "apperceptive background,"[23] the sum total of historically actualized uses internalized and assimilated by a historical reader. For Flaubert, on the other hand, speech is the result of *transcendental* repetition, of the fundamental iterability that makes it possible to recognize (and use) speech *as* speech. This fundamental repetition, however, cannot be represented *objectively in speech*. Flaubert saturates his language with clichés, not in a parodic project, directed, as in Bakhtin, against other literary works, but in a literary project par excellence, in the infinite pursuit of the possibility of language.

Here we arrive at the central problem of Flaubert's irony: its representability in writing. The writer (this writer, Flaubert) lacks the empirical proof that the first time is always already a second time. The vertiginous belatedness of all speech in relation to the first occasion that always remains unspoken, the inherently repetitive nature of language, cannot be demonstrated empirically. Indeed, Flaubert realizes that graphological markers can only distract the reader from the transcendental repetition with which he is concerned. Seeing the quotation marks in the blood-letting episode, for example, the reader may be led to assume that the unmarked portions of the text are somehow less marked and less ironic. An infinite reading of Flaubert's graphological conventions should remain sensitive to the possibility that whenever the irony is thus marked it refers less to the sarcasm recognized in the immediate context than to Flaubert's awareness of the infinite, vertiginous condition of speech as always and already repetition. To overstate the point for the sake of emphasis, the reader may be well advised to consider the graphological marks in Flaubert's text as inferior forms of an all-pervasive, infinite parenthetical irony in which language itself speaks (itself).[24]

---

23. Mikhail Bakhtin, "Discourse in the Novel," in *Dialogic Imagination: Four Essays*, ed. Michael Holquist, trans. Caryl Emerson and Michael Holquist (Austin, 1981), 309, 281.

24. As Christopher Prendergast suggests ("Flaubert: Quotation, Stupidity and the Cretan Liar Paradox," *French Studies*, XXXV [1981], 261–77), central to Flaubert's irony is not the positive remarking of ironic stance (specifically, quotation marks) but, on the contrary, the ironic function of the absence of such remarking. Prendergast writes that

Perhaps Flaubert's most important contribution to the theory of literary language, one indebted to a romantic concept of infinity, is the awareness that language comes to every speaker as a cliché, that it comes in invisible quotation marks. From the point of view of Flaubert's infinite model of language, referential language represents a finite, aesthetically less attractive option, something like a mercantile transaction between word and thing. As we have seen in this account of language the infinite moment of coincidence between word and thing is concealed by, and reduced to, the adequate "exchange rate" of the two items. But Cratylic transparency is deceptive to the extent that it renders the user of language oblivious to the infinite speech of speech that hovers as the boundary between word and thing.

While Flaubert understands well that this boundary cannot be objectivized, while he is aware that no objective analogy can express the source of speech, he privileges some analogues from the objective world insofar as their structure resists the construction of objects by the human mind. It may be helpful to examine briefly one of these structures, especially with an eye to demonstrating Flaubert's conception of language as invisible quotation. In a famous letter to George Sand, Flaubert writes: "I remember how my heart beat and what pleasure I felt on looking at the wall of the Acropolis, a naked wall (the one on the left when one ascends to the Propylaea). I wonder whether a book, regardless of what it has to say, could not produce a similar

---

> the absence of quotation marks is not wholly interpretable as the sign of a tongue-in-cheek game played by the narrator with the reader. Rather it could be seen as the sign of a certain modesty, an implicit concession of the equality of writer and reader before the ubiquitous text of *bêtise*. The dropping of the commas would thus be an oblique acknowledgement of the impossibility of transcendence, a refusal of the disingenuous ironic distance that might be implied by the retention of the marks, a way of signalling what one could call, although in a non-proprietorial sense, the necessary "plagiarism" of any activity of writing. (271)

Flaubert's invisible quotation marks carry a complex message. First, visible markers imply, in their iterability, the anterior markers of transcendental repetition. Second, the invisible markers can only be "marked" by the visible markers, a concession that compromises Flaubert's project and makes it indistinguishable from the familiar ironic stance. Third, the invisible marks make all speech plagiaristic, yet the owner of the "copyrights" is an impersonal source without intention or subjectivity; it is only after this original anterior tribunal is instituted that the violation of the rights can be legally alleged.

impression? Is there not an intrinsic quality, a kind of divine power, in the precision of the construction, the economy of the means, *the polish of the surface,* the harmony of the whole? (I am speaking as a Platonist)" (Flaubert's italics).25

The passage makes two claims. First, Flaubert asserts that the "naked wall" possesses "precision," "economy," and "polish" that all add up to "the harmony of the whole." Second, Flaubert would like to write a book resembling the "naked wall" in these aspects (of "precision," "economy," and "polish"). In what sense could the wall be a bricolage according to the meaning of the term developed earlier as an assemblage of parts without the whole? For apparently this is what Flaubert sees in the wall: an indeterminate object that, nevertheless, contains in itself the idea of its whole ("the harmony of the whole") or, in the second image, an art object (a book) whose unifying "meaning" would be incidental to its structural and formal integrity ("a book, regardless of what it has to say"). Undeniably, the flat wall of the Acropolis puts to a serious test the theory of bricolage as a nonobjective infinite entity. In what sense would a wall (and, by extension, a book) constitute a bricolage?

We can begin by speculating that the surface of the "naked wall" presents a logically untenable form of exposure. The nakedness of the wall can, of course, be understood in the "mercantile" logic of language as a flat surface without anything on it. But the infinite sense of the phrase lies close by: the point is not so much that the wall is exposed and flat, but rather that nakedness represents a certain scandal in the economy of naming (and a scandal for public morality). For as naked, the wall lacks the proper form of self-presentation. Its nudity cannot appear *as such* but must be couched in *a form,* in language.

French etymology may be helpful here. *Surface* means both "over" and "under face"; just as in "surrealism" the surreal entity is both more and less than real, so here the "wall" is both more and less than naked, more and less than expressed. The nudity of surface is its means of self-presentation, yet the content, the nakedness thus presented, cannot *pass over* into representation. A wall always appears *originally naked;* it is naked both before and after undressing. To name this entity "naked," then, as Flaubert has done in his letter, is to engage in linguistic monstrosity and aberration, it is both to cover a

---

25. Gustave Flaubert, *Correspondance,* ed. Louis Conard (9 vols.; Paris, 1926–33), VII, 294.

clothed entity and to expose nudity *even more*. Like Charles's cap, the wall is the crisis of language. In its infinite nudity the wall defies conceptualization.

Quite possibly, while looking at the wall Flaubert saw the essentially prelinguistic, inarticulate essence of bricolage, the mysterious original unity accomplished without hermeneutic synthesis. Here an important distinction is in order. Referential theories of language consider the lack of meaning as a failure of the object to conform with the categories of thought, a sufficient indication that the system of concepts should not bother with an "object" that cannot be named. For Flaubert, however, the absence of the name denotes a dynamic condition that first renders the mind sensitive to infinity. The lack is not a mere absence but a matter of a certain necessity, a *summons*. As Maurice Blanchot says, Flaubert encounters, perhaps provokes, this absence in its proper character by making his language sensitive to what Blanchot calls the "*Other* of speech."[26]

Flaubert believes that the referential relation between word and thing that controls ordinary language use tends to overshadow the more fundamental relation, the infinite sphere in which word and thing first come into contact. This boundary is neither word nor thing, but a constitutive infinity, "otherness," which underwrites language. Blanchot schematizes this aspect of Flaubert's prose as a dependence between "form" and "content":

> When Flaubert says, with naïveté and malice, "too many things," "not enough forms," he is not contrasting a richness (the richness of the unsayable real) to a poverty (the poverty of words that are too few and too awkward to say it). Although he does not know it, all he is doing is contrasting one language with another: one fixed at the level of its content and semantically full, the other reduced to its formal values and fixed in its pure signifying decision. This is an opposition he cannot affirm in either of these two languages, but using a third, and thus speaking from higher up, he pronounces his judgment: "Too many things," "not enough forms." (*IC*, 460)

Anterior to the dichotomy of form and content, which, in its simple opposition, defines the philosophy of realistic fiction, is an indeterminate reserve, neither content nor form, that cannot be named linguistically. The finite, linguistic relation between sign and referent relies

---

26. Maurice Blanchot, "Wittgenstein's Problem," In *IC*, 337.

on this infinite economy that is not language *yet* but that, as a certain excess, is not language *any more* either. Flaubert's recognition of this anteriority and of its constitutive role in the origin of articulate language provides a firm ground for reconstructing his "romantic" aesthetics.

Blanchot's notion of the anterior reserve that constitutes referential language becomes particularly useful in offering a fresh perspective on what criticism has called the central compositional device in *Madame Bovary*. Following Stirling Haig, we may define the structure as the alternation of two scenes that "antiphonally" invoke one another. The classical locus of this technique is the *comices agricoles*, the theatrical stage of Emma's seduction by Rodolphe. This aspect of Flaubert's compositional skills in *Madame Bovary* has received by far the most critical attention, mainly, as in Haig's study, for its virtuoso manipulation of rhetorical and stylistic devices responsible for each ironic effect.[27] The general point, however, applies with equal validity to the novel's other episodes constructed according to this principle.

Let us take as an illustration the famous scene of Emma's conversation with the parish priest, Monsieur Bournisien. Emma seeks religious guidance from the curé. The two converse inside the church, while the priest occasionally rebukes the boys waiting for religious instruction. We catch him during one such aside:

> "You look out, Riboudet," the priest cried angrily, "I'll box your ears, you scoundrel!" Then turning to Emma. "He's Boudet the carpenter's son; his parents are well off, and let him do just as he pleases. Yet he could learn quickly if he would, for he is very sharp. And so sometimes for a joke I call him *Ri*boudet (like the road one takes to go to Maromme), and I even say '*Mon* Riboudet.' Ha! ha! '*Mont* Riboudet.' The other day I repeated this little joke to the bishop, and he laughed. Can you imagine? He deigned to laugh. And how is Monsieur Bovary?" (*MB*, 80)

Emma's conversation with the priest is punctuated by extrinsic utterances directed at the pupils. The interference of extrinsic matter prevents the conversation from ever reaching its point and, in terms of the plot, dooms Emma, for whom the meeting with the priest was the

---

27. Stirling Haig, *Flaubert and the Gift of Speech: Dialogue and Discourse in Four Modern Novels* (New York, 1986), 73, 69–75.

last hope of resolving her confused situation. But the relationship between two parallel utterances exceeds the economy of anticlimax described by Haig, in the context of the *comices agricoles*, in terms of an "asymmetry" between "the 'superior' pursuits of the discourse of love and the 'inferior' ones of the barnyard."[28] Flaubert uses the antiphonal technique to achieve ironic effect in accordance with Blanchot's theory of Flaubert's prose as oriented towards its other. In this model, *Madame Bovary*'s antiphonal technique juxtaposes two utterances to produce the third position of "higher up," the transcendental position of the vertigo of speech.

One can detect a similar overcoming of anticlimactic effect in Flaubert's use of puns and jokes.[29] It is usually assumed that Flaubert uses puns as verbal irregularities to disturb the meticulously crafted Cratylic transparency of his prose, and in this way to achieve the effect of positivistic irony by ridiculing the accepted standards of clarity, rationality, and morality.[30] It is also argued that when Flaubert deliberately fails "properly" to tell a joke he seeks to achieve the extrinsic position of satirical superiority over his characters.[31] The bumbling jokes emphasize the profound idiocy of the life in the provinces that *Madame Bovary*, subtitled "A Story of Provincial Life" (*Moeurs de province*), at once portrays and ridicules.

Examined in the perspective of transcendental vertigo, the presence of puns in Flaubert's prose suggests more than a departure from an

---

28. *Ibid.*, 69.

29. Among the puns there are proper names: Madame Lefrançois, Dr. Larivière (la rivière = river), Charles Bovary (le bouvier = boor), Monsieur Lheureux (l'heureux = the happy one), Mère Rollet (le rôlet = small acting-part in a performance), Madame Tuvache (tu + la vache = you + cow). The structural variety of Flaubert's jokes in *Madame Bovary* can be appreciated in Tanner's exhaustive and penetrating analysis in *Adultery in the Novel*.

30. Tanner, *Adultery in the Novel*, 320–27.

31. Samuel Weber, "It," *Glyph*, IV (1978), 26–27. The article, a sort of arbitration piece on the controversy between Jacques Derrida and John Searle (and, by association, J. L. Austin) over the status of performatives and constatives, seeks to establish the validity of a "speech act" that remains irreducible to pragmatic models of communication. Weber offers a paradigmatic example of such a renegade "speech act" by critically examining Freud's theory of jokes. Weber shows that the spontaneous nature of the listener's reaction (laughter) to the joke makes it impossible to place this communicative situation, and this reaction, in the models of language practice (like those of Austin and Searle) that assume intentionality and, in general, a finite set of contexts in which speech functions. In sum, what makes, for Freud, a properly told joke, brings forth exactly that aspect of involuntary and uncontrolled reaction that defies pragmatic linguistic models.

ideal of prose. The crisis occasioned by Flaubert's polysemy resembles the crisis of Flaubertian rhetoric. The possibility of misunderstanding a joke or missing a pun indicates that these speech acts violate a logical norm (pun) or a psychological one (joke) in an *unspecified, undetermined degree*. The punning interludes signal textual gaps in a fabric thrown over (or under) some undetermined original economy of designation. The indeterminate economy points to a transcendental ground of meaning, itself neither serious nor jocose.[32] In this economy the roles are reversed: slips of the tongue are the norm, while the artifice of conceptual clarity called *le mot juste* becomes the exception. Flaubert's economy of language is ruled by an excess, an infinity of meaning that *automatically* produces a joke or a pun. The novel produces "improperly told" jokes; it tells jokes necessarily and involuntarily: the joke is a quite serious matter—a romantic *Witz*. Flaubert's jokes are not so amusing any more; on the other hand, *everything else* in the novel becomes *quite* funny.[33]

The difference, in Flaubert, between positivistic and romantic irony is measured as the contrast between stylistic registers, on the one hand, and the infinite, immeasurable joke of language, on the other. In the latter case, the irony abides in the infinite boundary at which word and thing meet; the boundary constitutes the original ground of meaningfulness on which the secondary function of linguistic reference is erected. In Flaubert's irony the reader first experiences the boundary as such, while linguistic reference remains secondary and optional.

In order to indicate the original utterance, the totality of discourse that always underlies each specific utterance, Flaubert punctuates his novel with moments of infinity: bricolage, cliché, parentheses. These moments, the infinite enunciations, underscore the necessary presence of an event, of an utterance, that is absolutely anterior to the events and utterances of the novel. They remark the presence of the infinite in the finite. This is to say that Flaubert uses repetition neither for its acerbic power nor out of a temperamental predilection for a

32. Porter speaks of "a sonorous subliminal buzz" (*"Madame Bovary* and the Question of Pleasure," in *Flaubert and Postmodernism*, ed. Schor and Majewski, 135).

33. Prendergast ("Quotation, Stupidity") correctly attributes this adverbial property of "quite" to the function of literality discovered by Flaubert in the self-conscious use of adverbs: "The implications of this potential for non-ironic, literal readings are very far-reaching indeed, and touch ultimately on the foundations of the theory and practice of mimesis itself. For if it is possible to take the literal sense seriously . . . if a literal interpretation of Flaubert's most banal phrases and sentences can be proposed *in good faith*, then this in turn implies at least the viability of a strictly mimetic reading of the text, in which the sceptical and ironic positions are decisively usurped" (273).

parodic view of the world. More fundamentally, Flaubert is attentive to the transcendental potential of repetition. In accordance with the logic of bricolage, Flaubert utters every phrase as a part *previously constituted by someone (or something) else.* When he encounters language, Flaubert detects in it, above all, that anterior condition that makes it possible for him to articulate language. In other words, Flaubert presupposes for every speech act an anterior, transcendental phrase without which this act could not take place. Aware of transcendental repetition, Flaubert remembers that the very ability to say something for the first time implies transcendental iterability: the fact that the word is now available for empirical utterance implies that it must have already been spoken in a transcendentally anterior instance.

An indication of the transcendental origin posited by Flaubert, and of the infinite irony based on this philosophy of language, can be gleaned from the mechanism described by Maurice Blanchot. When he says that there are "too many things," "not enough forms," Flaubert is "thus speaking from higher up," speaking, that is, in a discourse reducible neither to the discourse of content nor to that of form. In conformity to the rigor of otherness, whenever Flaubert uses the language of form and content, he is automatically invoking the transcendental position from which form and content can first be grasped in their separate essences.

While the transcendental position can never become an object for Flaubert's language of form and content because it is uncannily absent from what it makes possible, it nevertheless remains constitutively connected to it. Herein lies the fundamental difference between the transcendental attitude to infinity, represented by Flaubert, and the analytical approach, championed by Genette, Bovary, and Russell. Analytical approaches can only delimit the infinite paroxysm of the Cretan Liar paradox by arbitrarily imposing the rule that statements made in the object-language will not be used for meta-linguistic purposes. What these approaches overlook is the possibility that every act of language automatically invokes the level of meta-language in whose eyes alone the object-language can become a language in the first place. In other words, the philosophy of analysis ignores the possibility that the relation between the two levels may not be merely that of subsumption and logical structuring. For, as Flaubert intimates, the relation between object-language and meta-language can be understood as a generative relation: *the language of form and content can only occur in the productive presence of the higher position.*

Moreover, the relation between the two languages is intransitive. Whatever Flaubert says, he simultaneously remarks, in saying it, the necessarily anterior position, the first/second language in virtue of which he is each time using the language of form and content. As it remarks its enabling other, Flaubert's prose comes into being concurrently with the relation that alone gives it any real existence. This infinite, temporally incalculable simultaneity of origination produces the vertigo of Flaubert's prose, for language (writing) can begin to exist only in comportment to the higher language that alone gives it meaning. In order to be, Flaubert's prose must constantly strive to attain the higher position; this position, however, is intrinsically unattainable. Or, more precisely, the higher position cannot be *attained*, if attaining means grasping an object or performing an act; the higher position is necessarily implied, invoked, whenever language takes place. The higher position is the founding rationale that exists in infinite simultaneity with the language that it brings to existence, and it exists as soon, and as long, as the speaker utters language. Whenever he uses language, Flaubert posits, intransitively, an *other* language in whose presence alone he was able to use the first language. The higher position is unattainable, but without it the writing could not exist at all. Flaubert's prose is the infinite hovering between, as Friedrich Schlegel would say, "the real and the ideal." Its only objective and its only content is to sustain itself in the vertigo of the generative, originating simultaneity.

It is on this infinite referral to the constitutive otherness of speech that romanticism seized in its search for a proper definition of irony. This irony—and Flaubert understands it in this fashion—is infinite because it transcends the logic of form and content, not simply as another kind of speech placed above this logic, but because form and content begin to make sense only in the (absent) presence of this third locus. Perhaps the central aspect of this understanding of irony is that it escapes the conscious manipulation by the author; it "grounds" the intentionality of speech without itself being accountable to the intentional imperative. Blanchot writes that Flaubert can formulate his dilemma of "too many things," "not enough forms" from the higher position, but that this position remains constitutively concealed: "Although *he does not know it*, all he is doing is contrasting one language with another." The writer can write only insofar as he remains oblivious to the ground of this possibility. Likewise, the sole "content" of his literature is this original unconsciousness.

The condition of unconsciousness defines perhaps most adequately the proper response of the mind confronted with the original unity of bricolage. Facing form and content, the mind encounters components whose ground of unity, the "third position," is inaccessible but remains constitutive for the meaning of these components. In other words, the use of the aesthetics of form and content opens the subject up, in *la syncope* of the unconscious, to the uncanny ground of the unity of form and content. The subject's relation to literary language is possible only in this vertigo.

Alert to the original unity of form and content, Flaubert utters his speech in the presence of the ground of meaningfulness without which he could not say anything. The infinite irony of this situation is that, although Flaubert uses speech with greatest care, it is precisely this rigor that exposes him to transcendental vertigo: even as *he* speaks, Flaubert merely succeeds in allowing *speech to speak itself*. A Flaubertian novel places language in a systematic comportment to the transcendental ground or origin. Understood in its etymological sense of the novel as *der Roman*, *Madame Bovary* enacts the operation of allowing the original repetition to enter and shape the intentional use of language. In this new situation, speech itself speaks in the witty (*witzig*) modality of infinite parenthesis.

What is being said *parenthetically* must remain a mystery. The writer, Flaubert, can only recognize and acknowledge the power of this antecedent ground. He can speculate that it offers an abundance, an excess of possibilities (content), or, equally, that the parenthetical interior is an absolute lack of content, a pure form. The position itself, however, from which Flaubert grasps the distinction between form and content, has neither form nor content: it is the position of pure vertigo—not a hesitation between two samples of content or two formal options, but hesitation, *la syncope* as such, without form and without content.

Flaubert must also assume that the speech uttered in the condition of ironic self-oblivion is itself affected by the mystery of the productive transcendental subject. Flaubert understands that he cannot account for the source that enables him to produce the aesthetic object, the book; he knows that he is unable to specify whether he has, in fact, produced an object, for such a claim can be made only from the position of the transcendental subject. This position, however, is permanently antecedent to the finite subject whenever this subject speaks. The third position is more primordial than the relation between subject and object, for the subject becomes a subject, and the object becomes an object, only in the presence—or within the horizon—of this position. The anterior position, the transcendental repetition, is thus, precisely as anterior, indifferent to intentional production, for only in its horizontal perspective can intentionality appear for the first time. Precisely because his utterances now proceed from the enigmatic enclosure of parentheses, Flaubert cannot be sure what he is thus saying, nor can he specify what it is that he has thus produced. Uttered in the constitutive presence of the transcendental sanction, the work is a "book about nothing."[34]

One could say that the transcendental ground of unity makes the literary condition a laughable condition, since the writer is helpless to identify the original higher position that enables him to be a writer. Put differently, access to the parentheses can be gained only in a momentary fashion, in the spasm of serious/jocose laughter that shows, in a fleeting moment, the transcendental vista. The present analysis has come full circle and returned to the classroom in which Charles was humiliated by his fellow pupils. We can now interpret this laughter in the transcendental context as defined by Immanuel Kant. In Paragraph 54 of *Critique of Judgment,* Kant describes the content of laughter in the following words: *"Laughter is an affection arising from the sudden transformation of a strained expectation into nothing. This transformation, which is certainly not enjoyable to the understanding, yet indirectly gives it very active enjoyment for a moment."* (Kant's italics).[35] The momentary experience of the transcendental subject "is certainly not enjoyable to the understanding": the entry into parentheses, cliché, and *Witz* occasions loss of consciousness. But laughter also "indirectly gives [the understanding] very active enjoyment for a moment." Like bricolage, the pleasure and the pain of transcendental experience dissolve the subject. It is the threat of this experience that prompted the violent rejection and the trial of Flaubert's *dissolute* novel. *Madame Bovary* is an exotic fruit of transcendental hovering, a dissolved product "of a strained expectation suddenly transformed into nothing."

---

34. Victor Brombert ("Flaubert and the Status of the Subject," in *Flaubert and Postmodernism,* ed. Schor and Majewski, 100–15) says that Flaubert, faced, like every writer, with "the specter of eternal redundance" of his creative endeavors, still believes that there exists a viable subject matter, a "something-to-be-written," something that "can be communicated—though perhaps only in an enigmatic, or as Flaubert puts it, 'incomprehensible' manner. This indeed, for Flaubert, is the paradox of the subject: 'I have a need to say incomprehensible things' " (111).

35. Immanuel Kant, *Critique of Judgment,* trans. J. H. Bernard (New York, 1951), 177.

IV
Genre as Example in *Ulysses*

Did that first division, portending a second division, afflict him?

—*Ulysses*

In a well-known scene from the "Ithaca" episode in *Ulysses,* Leopold Bloom enters his house and carefully surveys the "frontroom."[1] As it glides over the interior of the room, Bloom's gaze lingers on the mantelpiece:

> What homothetic objects, other than the candlestick, stood on the mantelpiece?
>   A timepiece of striated Connemara marble, stopped at the hour of 4.46 a.m. on the 21 March 1896, matrimonial gift of Matthew Dillon: a dwarf tree of glacial arborescence under a transparent bellshade, matrimonial gift of Luke and Caroline Doyle: an embalmed owl, matrimonial gift of Alderman John Hooper.
>   What interchanges of looks took place between these three objects and Bloom?
>   In the mirror of the giltbordered pierglass the undecorated back of the dwarf tree regarded the upright back of the embalmed owl. Before the mirror the matrimonial gift of Alderman John Hooper with a clear melancholy wise bright motionless compassionate gaze regarded Bloom while Bloom with obscure tranquil profound motionless compassionated gaze regarded the matrimonial gift of Luke and Caroline Doyle. (*U,* 17.707)

1. James Joyce, *Ulysses* (New York, 1961).

Perhaps the most conspicuous aspect of this description is that it is powerfully affected by the agency of the mirror. As in fairytales, both the objects observed and the observer seem to have fallen under the spell of the looking glass, or to use a "modern" phrase, they have fallen under the spell of the mirror's alterity. For, clearly, the visually simple scene on the mantelpiece suddenly becomes complicated by the mirror's powers. The "interchanges of looks" take place both outside and inside the mirror. "Before the mirror," gazes roam aimlessly, humans lose their subjectivity, and objects acquire human properties: "The matrimonial gift of Alderman John Hooper with a clear melancholy wise bright motionless compassionate gaze regarded Bloom while Bloom with obscure tranquil profound motionless compassionated gaze regarded the matrimonial gift of Luke and Caroline Doyle." Within the mirror, "the undecorated back of the dwarf tree regarded the upright back of the embalmed owl."

But the two economies themselves are produced by and abide in a third space, the mirror itself, in whose catalytic presence alone the two conventional spaces, the inside and the outside, can be created and recognized. This dimension, which, plausibly, is the same agency that endows mirrors with magical powers in fairy tales, represents a synthesis of the purely physical and the purely imaginary spaces. It is perhaps this agency that gives, in the scene above, the impression of a presence that brings this scene into view and organizes it. This point of view, "looking" in all directions, cannot be reduced to the usual perception involved in ocular vision, for it exists both inside and outside the mirror, emerging from the mirror and returning to it. It switches liberally from three-dimensional space to planar reflection on the mirror's surface and freely combines these two in the supradimensional vehicle of reflection. This point of view brings forth *that which can be seen*, a possibility of vision infinitely identical with the visible itself. Because of this infinite identity, however, the synthesis that creates the arena of visibility at the same time remains excluded from it.

Still, although the magic of the mirror cannot be captured by mirrors, it is indissociable from the work of specular optics. This intriguing interdependence becomes the subject of the next passage, which describes the reflection of Leopold Bloom's personal library: "What final visual impression was communicated to him by the mirror? The optical reflection of several inverted volumes improperly arranged and not in the order of their common letters with scintillating titles on the two bookshelves opposite" (*U*, 17.708). Bloom's books occupy the same multiple spaces that claimed the objects on the mantelpiece. Thus, they stand "before" the mirror; they are lined up "within" the mirror; and they contemplate, like the "dwarf tree" and the "embalmed owl," their own reflection in the mirror. Moreover, the distortions in the books' ordering indicate that the books are claimed by the mysterious "point of view" concealed in the infinite space of the mirror. By examining the disorder among Bloom's books, we may probe with more precision the secret of mirror reflection.

The mirror affects the representation of the books in several ways. First, the volumes appear "inverted." Here, other types of inversion, not related to simple homothetic reflection, may also be intended: the books may have been inverted spatially (upside down, backside out), based on the size of the volumes (small books mixed with large ones), or they may have been inverted from the alphabetical order of title or author, or date or place of publication, or from Bloom's private classification by subject.

In addition to their inversion, the volumes appear "improperly arranged." Closely related to this distortion is a third mechanism. In an obscure verdict, the books stand "not in the order of their common letters." Both expressions carry a disconcerting ambiguity. First, the "community of letters" may refer to an ordering in groups of titles beginning with a specific letter—*A*, *B*, or *Z*—while these groups themselves may be placed on the shelves in random order. The phrase may also refer to alphabetical ordering, from *A* to *Z*.

The phrase "common letters" appears disconcerting, not only because of this ambiguity, but also because "order" and "community" imply opposed methods of arrangement, the ordinal and the cardinal series. If the books were originally intended to stand "in the order of their common letters," then their arrangement had obeyed both the ordinal and the cardinal regimens: the *set* of books was arranged in alphabetical *order*. At a certain point in the past, Bloom's books formed a sequence *and* a set—they entertained ordinal *and* cardinal relations simultaneously. In the infinity of the original order, the common denominator, a letter, assembled a *set* and, at the same time, "properly arranged" a *series*.

Taken together, the three distortions in the books' arrangement are, precisely as "improper" arrangement and as "inversion," the visible indicators of this original order. However, recovering this order with the help of these indicators is by no means easy, for the books may have departed either from a systematic ordering (one used in libraries) or from some empirical (and perhaps random) placement on the shelves. At any rate, it is evident that the original series—the unity of the empirical and the ideal orders in relation to which the distortions are perceived as distortions—is missing, although the books' "improper arrangement" echoes (precisely by its "impropriety") this unity's unrelenting summons. In the magical space of the mirror, the empirical and the systematic orders are one.

This property of optical reflection has been analyzed by Immanuel Kant in his treatise *Of the First Foundation of the Difference of Regions in Space* (*Von dem ersten Grunde des Unterschiedes der Gegenden im Raume*). Kant considers space and time as a priori particulars, that is, as things found in experience yet *not* perceived by the senses. To prove the existence of a priori particulars, Kant introduces the example of hand gloves. While symmetrical when placed against each other, the right and the left hand gloves are not superimposable (that is, although the left glove *symmetrically* matches the right hand, one cannot *put* the left glove on the right hand). This deceitful symmetry of what Kant calls an "incongruent counterpart" [*incongruentes Gegenstück*] proves the existence of absolute space as an a priori particular.

As Jean-François Lyotard shows in *Duchamp's TRANS/formers*, Kant is pursuing the philosophical implications of this analysis when he surmises that the incongruence of counterparts can be eliminated by inserting the mirror into their deceitful symmetry.[2] It is "enough to apply a mirror along the vertical axis of th[e] body in order to make the half presented to the mirror produce, in the form of its reflected image, an appendage that is fully congruent (superimposable) on the other half. If the specular image of the right hand is a left hand, the image of this image is a right hand" (52). However, Lyotard observes that *by themselves* mirrors neither introduce nor eliminate incongruence; rather, incongruence can be controlled by inserting an even or an odd number of mirror reflections: a reflected image "will be incongruent or congruent with the model according to whether it comes in an even or odd rank, respectively, in the series" (52). This approach differs radically from that of Claude Lévi-Strauss's structuralist method, which sets two mirrors "obliquely" against each other to reduce "the number of mirror images" and make structuralist analysis

---

2. Jean-François Lyotard, *Duchamp's TRANS/formers*, trans. Ian McLeod (Venice, Calif., 1990), hereinafter cited parenthetically by page number in the text.

manageable.³ Set facing each other, says Lévi-Strauss, two mirrors deemphasize the power of empirical representation and allow deduction (specular images) to play a more significant role in cognition. Lyotard's analysis of Kant's thought, on the other hand, allows for disorienting machinations of the "specular machine." This machine is "identifying when it is itself doubled (raised to an even power), but dissimilating when it functions alone or when assembled with itself in uneven quantities. You will observe that the first-named function, which we will call assimilating or specular, puts three objects in play: the object presented to the first mirror, its image in the latter, and the image of this image in the second mirror; for the dissimilating function to be exercised, on the contrary, the first two are sufficient: it is this latter function that Duchamp calls *mirrorish*" (53). Applied to Joyce's objects on the mantelpiece, this analysis would suggest that the perplexing "inversions" and "improper arrangements" arise from the *mirrorish* function: a mirror reflects not an object (not even another mirror) but the magical, dissimulating power of mirrors, reflexivity as such. It is *mirrorishness* that gives mirrors in fairy tales the power to reveal the future and to know who is the most beautiful woman in the world.

Hence, when with Leopold Bloom the reader tries to "catalogue these books," he should understand Joyce's catalog as an instance of Duchamp's discovery:

Thom's Dublin Post Office Directory, 1886.
Denis Florence M'Carthy's *Poetical Works* (copper beechleaf bookmark at p. 5).
Shakespeare's *Works* (dark crimson morocco, goldtooled).
The Useful Ready Reckoner (brown cloth).
The Secret History of the Court of Charles II (red cloth, tooled binding).
The Child's Guide (blue cloth).
When We Were Boys by William O'Brien M.P. (green cloth, slightly faded, envelope bookmark at p. 217).
Thoughts from Spinoza (maroon leather).
The Story of the Heavens by Sir Robert Ball (blue cloth).
Ellis's *Three Trips to Madagascar* (brown cloth, title obliterated).
The Stark-Munro Letters by A. Conan Doyle, property of the City of Dublin Public Library, 106 Capel Street, lent 21 May (Whitsun Eve) 1904, due 4 June 1904, 13 days overdue (black cloth binding, bearing white letternumber ticket).

3. Claude Lévi-Strauss, *Structural Anthropology*, trans. Claire Jacobson and Brooke Grundfest Schoepf (New York, 1967), 214–15.

Voyages in China by 'Viator' (recovered with brown paper, red ink title).
Philosophy of the Talmud (sewn pamphlet).
Lockhart's *Life of Napoleon* (cover wanting, marginal annotations, minimising victories, aggrandising defeats of the protagonist).
Soll und Haben by Gustav Freytag (black boards, Gothic characters, cigarette coupon bookmark at p. 24).
Hozier's *History of the Russo-Turkish War* (brown cloth, 2 volumes, with gummed label, Garrison Library, Governor's Parade, Gibraltar, on verso of cover).
Laurence Bloomfield in Ireland by William Allingham (second edition, green cloth, gilt trefoil design, previous owner's name on recto of flyleaf erased).
A Handbook of Astronomy (cover, brown leather, detached, 5 plates, antique letterpress long primer, author's footnotes nonpareil, marginal clues brevier, captions small pica).
The Hidden Life of Christ (black boards).
In the Track of the Sun (yellow cloth, titlepage missing, recurrent title intestation).
Physical Strength and How to Obtain It by Eugene Sandow (red cloth).
Short but yet Plain Elements of Geometry written in French by F. Ignat. Pardies rendered into Englifh by John Harris D. D. London, printed for R. Knaplock at the Bifhop's Head MDCCXI, with dedicatory epiftle to his worthy friend Charles Cox, efquire, Member of Parliament for the burgh of Southwark and having ink calligraphed statement on the flyleaf certifying that the book was the property of Michael Gallagher, dated this 10th day of May 1822 and requefting the perfon who should find it, if the book should be loft or go aftray, to reftore it to Michael Gallagher, carpenter, Dufery Gate, Ennifcorthy, county Wicklow, the finest place in the world. (*U,* 17.708–709)

It would seem that the catalog was meant to impose, by an arbitrary decree, an extrinsic order on the unruly "community of letters." The list has, then, either described Bloom's books ad hoc, to give an immediate idea of the library's content, or else it has, as a "catalog" in the strict sense of the word, prescribed the order in which the books should be arranged (or in which they had been arranged earlier). However, if the list merely describes the books as they stand on the shelves, then it cannot, strictly speaking, be a catalog. But examined as a catalog in the sense of a prescriptive list, the list shows no signs of ordering either: the *mirrorish* catalog prescribes a system, but the system in question cannot be found.

Placed in the space between reality and ideality, the transcendental catalog challenges the reader's patience by forcing him to read a descriptive prescription. In its penumbral semantics, the catalog implies order yet furnishes no evidence of having ordered the listed items. It coincides with any empirical placement of the books, and any empirical arrangement immediately answers to a "catalogical" formula. The identity of the empirical and the systematic, of randomness and order, suggests a peculiar logic: for Joyce, logic is nothing more than mere contiguity of objects, a *cata*-logic. In this strange "structure" of local meanings, the catalog *coincides with* sheer metonymic placement, and each random cast of the dice *exemplifies* the system. Joyce shows us his fiction, as Frank Kermode puts it, "fitting where it touches."[4]

But the question still remains: Where, or what, does Joyce's fiction touch that it is so felicitously "fitting"? *Mirrorishness* gives Joyce's catalog extraordinary powers of ordering that exceed the systems of semiotic and library *reference*. Bloom's books do not appear as an object in the field of representation defined by two mirrors; rather, in their incongruence they instantiate space considered a priori, *space in general*. Joyce shows what pure, Kantian space would look like if it were not smothered by empirical objects; the story told by the mirror is not mimetic representation but *transcendental presencing*. A synthesis of "the order of the common letters," the catalog presents space as an a priori particular in which random assemblage and ideal order, the scene presented and the instrument of presentation, attain identity—here the real is the rational, the mundane is the aesthetic.

Traditional critical analyses of *Ulysses* are systematically frustrated by the *akinetic* posture of the catalog, by what Hugh Kenner calls Joyce's "inventory."[5] Such criticism is quick to overlook this posture, preferring to analyze the novel in terms of narrative motion, one oriented teleologically or kinetically. The preference for the narrative option confirms the abiding influence on literary hermeneutics of Hegel's dynamic theory of truth developing across history. The Hegelian model can be traced to Aristotle's *entelechy*, a notion intended to explain an entity's development, to explain—to use a famil-

---

4. Frank Kermode, *The Sense of an Ending: Studies in the Theory of Fiction* (New York, 1967), 113.

5. Hugh Kenner, *The Stoic Comedians: Flaubert, Joyce, and Beckett* (Boston, 1963), 30–66.

iar image—how the seed becomes the tree.⁶ However, the entelechic model is so committed to the *result* of the historical process that it neglects the *process* itself. Because the explanatory framework is controlled by the *telos*, the intermediate stages will not be analyzed for their own sake: teleology finds the individual historical moment as such quite useless. In terms of the present analysis, a teleological reading will most likely skip the stationary catalog of Bloom's books and, instead, address a dynamic aspect of *Ulysses*.

Criticism of *Ulysses*, to the extent that it embraces the Hegelian concept of truth, is bound to perpetuate the teleological bias and subordinate the historical detail, the example, to the teleological framework. By limiting itself to temporal perspective, criticism of *Ulysses* misses an opportunity to analyze the novel and the example in the double perspective: as a detail separate from history and as a meaningful, systematic component of the larger process. This is a distortion to which Joyce's novel, a quasi-Hegelian "phenomenology" of the spirit, is eminently vulnerable.

In a certain sense, the teleological bias represents only a special case of a general perplexity that haunts the literary criticism of *Ulysses*. Under the influence of romantic aesthetics, modern literary criticism assumes that Joyce's novel is sustained by the model of organic unity; but this criticism has consistently struggled, and failed, to give an example of the novel's unity thus *organ*ized. The following discussion will attempt to explain precisely this impossibility of illustrating with examples the encompassing organic structure of Joyce's novel and, at the same time, to revive the romantic premise of novelistic unity. I will argue that for Joyce exemplarity is the locus of presentation of the unity of absolute time and space (the cardinal and ordinal series) in which history as such comes into existence for the first time.

Expressed in terms of Lyotard's analysis presented above, the critical debate over *Ulysses* follows the split between Hegel's specular and Duchamp's *mirrorish* conceptions of reflection: "The nature of the final product of the series of mirrors depends on a decision about the number, odd or even, of the mirrors. Such is the "solution" that the

---

6. "Entelechy: [fr. Gk. *entelecheia*] 1: the realization of form-giving cause as contrasted with potential existence."
"Teleology: [fr. Gk *tele-, telos* end—more at WHEEL] 2: the fact or character attributed to nature or natural processes of being directed toward an end or shaped by a purpose."

Socrates of Plato, and later Hegel, proposes for the *dissoi logoi* of the Sophists: the double discourses keep us in a state of incongruence, so we must, says the philosopher, find thirds for them in order to arrive at the unity of contrary theses" (*Duchamp's TRANS/formers*, 54). The *mirrorish* function of exemplarity can be developed in the context of the romantic theory of the novel, a theory preoccupied with the adequate presentation of the subject to itself. The following argument will develop the conception of *Ulysses* as a romantic novel in two steps. First, it will make a case for Joyce's exemplarity as a romantic arabesque. Second, it will seek to demonstrate *Ulysses'* affinity with the romantic theory of the novel on the basis of this arabesque nature. As an arabesque, *Ulysses* frustrates the reading experience with its unanalyzable structure because the complexity of this structure exceeds the model of organic unity described by the mechanism of the hermeneutic circle. In the arabesque the reader of *Ulysses* is confronted with a textual unity whose organizing principle remains hidden. Overwhelmed with a plethora of examples, the reader is unable to assemble these examples into a meaningful pattern. At the same time, however, the work does not slip into complete chaos. The arabesque structure of *Ulysses* presents the reader's mind with exemplarity as such, that is, with the general presence of an example in the text, but this comprehensive example is not separate from that which it exemplifies. In its incongruence, Joyce's exemplarity exemplifies, not a positive content, but itself: it is an example of exemplarity.

It is this unresolved, *mirrorish* circularity of presentation that renders the Joycean example compatible with the circular formula for the romantic novel offered by Friedrich Schlegel. The romantic novel is designed to bring the subject as such to presence in the form of presentation proper to itself. Like the forms of the romantic genre discussed in the other chapters, the genre of exemplarity in *Ulysses* represents a privileged place of disclosure of the self in its character as self. This presentation is infinite because, rather than presenting objective content, the example is only the minimal structure of the example's self-presentation. The only content presented is the self of the example. In keeping with Schlegel's reflective formula about the self-presentation of the self, Joyce's example is an example of exemplarity.

However, like Flaubert's bricolage in *Madame Bovary*, Joyce's example in *Ulysses* does not reach the complete presentation of the self intended by the romantic theory. The example only exemplifies the infinite circularity of the romantic presentation of the subject, without accomplishing the presence as such. Finally, at the conclusion of this analysis, I will argue that it is this incomplete reflective nature of exemplarity that makes it the universal reading technique of *Ulysses*. Instead of presenting the reader with conceptually transparent reading content, the presence of the example exposes the reader's mind to *the example of presence* in this infinite circularity. Rather than apprehending objective content, the reader of *Ulysses* is swept away by the non-objective encounter with *space and time in general*. History finds its universal ground and essence in this absolute generality.

In order to develop Joyce's conception of exemplarity it is first necessary to separate *Ulysses* from the teleological frames of interpretation because these frames reduce examples to the status of passive tokens of the historical process. With this goal in mind it may be appropriate to consider Joseph Frank's influential thesis about the nontemporal—*spatial*—option in modern literature.[7] The spatial option brings the hope of neutralizing the teleological interests that drive large-scale narrative structures (epic, history) and of restoring the example to its rightful place in the teleological enterprise. In our concrete analysis, the spatial option promises to render Joyce's hermetic catalog legible.

Frank locates the origin of the spatial option in literature in Gotthold Ephraim Lessing's *Laocoön*. Lessing freed the work of art from classical aesthetic rigors, reinterpreting aesthetic form in a framework of space and time, a framework that Immanuel Kant later developed into the model of the basic (empty) forms of perception. Frank's spatial reading relies on the technique of "reflexive reference" (14), which apprehends the work "spatially, in a moment of time, rather than as a sequence" (9). Frank illustrates the technique with the country fair scene (*comices agricoles*) in Flaubert's *Madame Bovary*. The "reflexive reference" is made among three levels: "the jostling mob" on the street level, "the speechmaking officials" on the platform, and the "amorous conversation" between Emma and Rodolphe in the city hall (14). The three plot segments occur simultaneously, and the reader is asked to adjust reading to this demand for simultaneity.

Frank argues that Joyce borrowed Flaubert's technique, composing *Ulysses* "of a vast number of references and cross references that relate to each other independently of the time sequence of the narrative" (16). At the point when the references must be connected together, however, Frank's proposal runs into problems that arise

---

7. Joseph Frank, *The Widening Gyre: Crisis and Mastery in Modern Literature* (New Brunswick, 1963), hereinafter cited parenthetically by page number in the text.

whenever "spatialized forms" are imposed on temporal constructs. Frank writes: "[Joyce's] references must be connected by the reader and viewed as a whole before the book fits together into any meaningful pattern" (16). A few paragraphs later, Frank adds: "Joyce desired in this way to build up in the reader's mind a sense of Dublin as a totality.... The reader is intended to acquire this sense as he progresses through the novel.... It might almost be said that Joyce literally wanted the reader to become a Dubliner" (18–19).

The two passages describe the two moments of the hermeneutic circle: the parts can be known only by their individual placement in the whole, while the whole can be apprehended only through a survey of individual parts. In real time, the reader begins by inductively assimilating the details of the work in the hope of accomplishing reading synthesis by deductively fitting the details into the whole. However, in a theoretical description of the hermeneutic circle, the two operations occur simultaneously. In other words, induction and deduction condition one another: parts are parts only in relation to their whole, and the whole is a whole only as an interrelation of parts. Read in terms of this theoretical account, Frank's synthesis yields the following circular formula: "One can *become* a real Dubliner by reading *Ulysses* only if one *is* a real Dubliner before reading it."[8]

Frank's reliance on a combination of inductive and deductive reading procedures in his description of the act of reading *Ulysses* reveals the lesson of Joyce's novel to be quite complex: the novel enacts the unity of the a posteriori order of induction and the a priori order of deduction. Strictly speaking, the problem is one of accomplishing the unity of induction and deduction, of stating at which point the leap

---

8. *Ulysses* criticism has, of course, applied induction and deduction in a variety of ways. The narrative-oriented studies of *Ulysses* seek to enter the hermeneutic circle at an appropriate thematic, dynamic, or stylistic moment, and to describe the novel in a developmental scheme—not only when the process is described as a stylistic journey, as in Karen Lawrence's *The Odyssey of Style in "Ulysses"* (Princeton, 1981), but also when it is taken, as in Hugh Kenner's *Ulysses* (Baltimore, 1987), for degenerative regression, or, as in Michael Groden's *"Ulysses" in Progress* (Princeton, 1977), for a stylistic progression and development. On the other hand, static readings of *Ulysses* relate the novel's textual units to literary or mythological prototypes. Robert Martin Adams' *Surface and Symbol: The Consistency of James Joyce's "Ulysses"* (New York, 1962) presents *Ulysses* as a layered text, a gesture also found in S. L. Goldberg's *The Classical Temper: A Study of James Joyce's "Ulysses"* (London, 1961), which places *Ulysses* parallel to Homer's *Odyssey*. In this category also belong comparative studies: William T. Noon's *Joyce and Aquinas* (New Haven, 1957), Bjørn J. Tysdahl's *Joyce and Ibsen: A*

from an accumulation of details to the encompassing whole becomes possible. Seen in this perspective, the solution offered by Frank addresses, not this theoretical point, but rather, only its practical consequence: Frank seeks to determine what historical individual is capable of fitting the details of *Ulysses* into a meaningful whole.

Only in this sense is his answer pertinent to the theoretical question asked above. Frank writes: "For this is what Joyce demands: that the reader have at hand the same instinctive knowledge of Dublin life ... that the Dubliner possesses as a birthright" (19). The notion of "instinctive knowledge," which suggests that the perfect reader of *Ulysses* is familiar with the novel because he knows Dublin, immediately brings up a second aspect essential to Frank's thesis: reading *Ulysses*, we merely *recognize* Dublin, for *memory is the condition of reading*. Frank defines the dependence of reading on memory in his famous dictum: "This, it should be realized, is the equivalent of saying that Joyce cannot be read—he can only be reread" (19). Since the citizen already knows the total context of Dublin's *hic et nunc*, his hermeneutic labors consist not in filling in the blanks but in *re-*filling them.

As we have seen, Frank bases this power of memory on the notion of "birthright," which "gives the native a knowledge of Dublin's past and present as a whole; and it is only such knowledge that would enable the reader ... to place all the references in their proper context" (19). First, it must be remarked that the "birthright" does not represent a synthesis of the hermeneutic operation but merely specifies an empirical candidate who has already accomplished such synthesis. Second, it can be seen that the mechanism of "birthright" bases the

---

Study in Literary Influence (New York, 1968), and Richard K. Cross's *Flaubert and Joyce: The Rite of Fiction* (Princeton, 1971). Here, too, belong the schemas of Gorman, Gilbert, and Linati, the explicit parallels to Shakespeare, Swift, Vico, Sterne, Blake, etc., and to mythical, medical, occult, and local Irish materials. Finally, one should not overlook Peter Bürger's impressive treatment of the synthesis of induction and deduction (*Theory of the Avant-Garde,* trans. Michael Shaw [Minneapolis, 1984]). Bürger is concerned with the hermeneutic status of a formalist work of art if it is assumed that the formalist work of art cannot be referred to a unifying whole. Bürger sees the possibility of unifying the meaning of a formalist work in a hermeneutic synthesis of both procedures, in what he calls "a critical hermeneutics," which "will replace the theorem of the necessary agreement of parts and whole by investigating the contradiction between the various layers and only then infer the meaning of the whole" (82). Bürger's "critical hermeneutics" closely resembles Frank's "reflexive reference."

ability to read *Ulysses* on the privilege of intimate familiarity with one's place of birth, the privilege of autochthony. These two moments define the direction of the present response to Frank's analysis. First, by giving a historically concrete instance of someone equipped to read *Ulysses*, Frank's proposal raises the question whether it is possible to define the conditions of such reading without relying on an empirical candidate capable of executing this task. Second, as a formula that excludes non-Dubliners from *Ulysses'* reading community, Frank's "birthright" offers a challenge to define the hermeneutic synthesis in the original sense; only such primordial synthesis can make Joyce's novel accessible to *all readers*. *Ulysses* is not "for Dubliners only."

Frank's model of *Ulysses* as a spatialized totality offers several extremely valuable insights. Besides opening up a richer perceptual scope for *Ulysses* in the spatial dimension, Frank can pose the question of the nature of reading more rigorously than the novel's teleological readings have posed it: his analysis has shown that understanding (reading) *Ulysses* requires the synthesis of induction and deduction and that the synthesis is based on recollection. Moreover, Frank has most fruitfully shown that only an attempt to "spatialize" (*cf.* 15) literary form can bring to light the properly hermeneutic problematics of the act of understanding a literary text, can, in other words, show that the proper domain of the synthesis, in the hermeneutic circle, of induction and deduction is the synthesis of *time and space*.

At the same time, however, the complexity of Frank's model highlights the difficulties provoked by spatial apprehension of narrative form. If anything, it has shown the need to accomplish the unity of induction and deduction independently of empirical correlates of such synthesis. In this sense, Frank's call to unify induction and deduction restates, in the context of literary analysis, an important philosophical problem. Presenting this problem, even in a synopsis, is indispensable for establishing our thesis that, as the phenomenology of human experience, *Ulysses* is universally accessible in the synthesis of time and space accomplished in exemplarity.

The problem of the relations between the deductive and inductive orders has an established tradition of inquiry. The problem was paradigmatically formulated, we have seen, by Lessing's study, in the *Laocoön*, of the temporal and spatial limitations of specific art forms. It was further transformed by Kant's notion of time and space as pure forms of perception and, after Kant, by the historical interests of nineteenth-century thought; finally, the problem received an original treatment in Nietzsche.

The problem can be formulated in the following manner. The tradition has been exploring history as the unity of two moments—the unity of the spatial moment of sameness and repetition with the temporal moment of novelty and teleology. The conflict between repetition and teleology creates the following dilemma. Repetition guarantees comprehension by placing discrete events in a schema of similarity. The need for repetition, however, contravenes the teleological postulate. Joyce captures the conflict between repetition and teleology, comprehensibility and purposiveness, in Mr. Deasy's famous formula. Mr. Deasy believes in the purposeful march of human history: " 'All history moves towards one great goal, the manifestation of God.' " The postulates of teleology, however, are at odds with those of historical understanding, for progress implies novelty, and novelty, in its turn, challenges and upsets the self-identity and self-understanding of each historical moment. Mr. Deasy completes his thought: " 'The ways of the Creator are not our ways' " (*U*, 2.34).

Stated simply, this is the antinomy of sameness and difference. At stake in resolving this antinomy is the very possibility of history—the possibility of the *progression* of history and the possibility of recognizing history as the *same* in all the transformations that it undergoes in time. This conflict became an urgent problem for Friedrich Schlegel, in his study of the ancient and the modern civilizations, as the antinomy of the organic, closed culture of classical antiquity and the dynamic, progressive culture of modern Europe. Schlegel, we may recall, sought the ground of the unity of both epochs in the transcendental sphere, as the condition of possibility for the historical occurrence of and interrelation between both cultural modalities, and he discovered this ground in the speculative synthesis of "transcendental poetry." We can also recognize the pressure of this conflict on Nietzsche, who placed the antinomy of being and becoming under enormous strain in his conception of "the eternal return of the same."

Despite different interests, Frank's circular thesis about the "Dubliner" belongs in this general area of inquiry. Frank recognizes the need for synthesis; however, while acknowledging this need, he elects to side with deduction, with history's sameness. Rather than seeking the universal formula for reading *Ulysses* in the original synthesis of induction and deduction, Frank seeks refuge in the restrictive formula of the "birthright," which leaves some readers simply ill-equipped to read Joyce's novel. Leaving aside the question of a progression from Frank to Nietzsche to Joyce, we may propose that *Ulysses* occupies an important place in the debate concerning the synthesis of the hermeneutic circle. The critically recognized importance of *Ulysses* can be enhanced by examining it as a model of universal reading, as a synthesis of induction and deduction performed on the hermeneutic circle. Defining the nature of this synthesis will unlock the secret of *Ulysses'* hermeneutics.

In order to investigate the nature of this unity it is first necessary to examine the difference between Frank's and Joyce's syntheses. Frank asks about the comparative suitability of induction and deduction for the act of reading in order to determine which one plays a more important role and then to choose the more suitable method. In a sense, Frank does not accomplish the synthesis—he cuts through it. He resolves the tension between induction and deduction that vibrates in the circular formula "One must possess the birthright in order to acquire the birthright" by an arbitrary incision into what threatens to become, not a *circulus hermeneuticus*, but a *circulus vitiosus*. Instead of seeking synthesis, Frank points to a Dubliner, a *world-historical example* of such synthesis.

Joyce's synthesis of induction and deduction has a different structure. Joyce examines, not the usefulness of deduction or of induction for the empirical act of reading, but the relation between the two insofar as they belong to each other in some implied form of encompassing unity. He is interested, not so much in determining why some people can read *Ulysses* and others cannot, but primarily in determining how those who can read it accomplish the synthesis in the first place. Joyce is interested in the conditions of possibility for reading *Ulysses*, in the transcendental relation (or, as Hegel says, speculative mediation) between induction and deduction in their relation to each other.[9] This unity defines the possibility of reading in general, independent of the concrete reading matter and of the concrete historical reader.

The Joycean unity requires its proper scene. While the hermeneutic circle defines the mechanism in which induction and deduction engage specific reading matter, the circle itself is powerless to effect,

9. Joyce wrestles with the problem of a priori and applied systems, whose history extends, as Peter Szondi writes, from Friedrich Schlegel's poetics of genres, through Hegel ("In Hegel, induction and deduction are mediated by each other"), to Walter Benjamin (*The Origin of German Tragic Drama*) and Georg Lukács (*The Theory of the Novel*) (Peter Szondi, "Friedrich Schlegel's Theory of Poetical Genres: A Reconstruction of Posthumous Fragments," in *TU*, 81–82).

hermeneutically, the unity of induction and deduction that constitutes it. This unity, inaccessible to the circle, is accomplished in another sphere. When Stephen sentimentalizes the firmament, Bloom rejoins "that it was not a heaventree, not a heavengrot, not a heavenbeast, not a heavenman. That it was a Utopia, there being no known method from the known to the unknown: an infinity, renderable equally finite by the suppositious probable apposition of one or more bodies equally of the same and of different magnitudes" (*U*, 17.701). The other sphere of knowledge, here called "Utopia," exceeds the efficacy of the hermeneutic circle. For the circle merely provides the frame in which induction and deduction can operate, while the transcendental sphere first produces the operations of induction and deduction—it produces them a priori. This is to say that only in "Utopia" can we know that the building blocks of the hermeneutic circle—parts and wholes—are parts and wholes in the first place, and that a circle is, indeed, a circle. But this "Utopian" realm of knowledge, the realm of the "known method," itself remains, in principle, inaccessible to hermeneutic circularity. If hermeneutics enacts the movement from the known to the unknown, the "utopian," *transcendental* realm offers the knowledge, the "known method," which makes the hermeneutic transition possible. The model has two levels of knowledge: the lower level of the hermeneutic movement from "the known to the unknown," and the higher, transcendental level of the "method" that renders this movement meaningful.

It is this difference that sets Joyce apart from Frank. Admittedly, this is a narrow difference, for it refers to the unity of induction and deduction as it appears in reading practice and to the same unity in the transcendental sense, as the condition of possibility of reading that necessarily precedes this practice. Although quite technical, the difference can be demonstrated in textual analysis with sufficient clarity and pertinence, and in most cases, it is required as a necessary complement to otherwise inadequate hermeneutic explanations of *Ulysses'* textual strategies. In what follows I attempt to examine the models of reading proposed both in *Ulysses* and in critical studies of the novel, in order to show how these models of reading appear in Frank's hermeneutic, and in Joyce's transcendental, versions, and in order to determine the nature of the transcendental unity developed by Joyce. The analyses that follow are intended to clarify the transcendental dimension as the proper content and function of Joyce's conception of exemplarity.

While Joyce recognizes the role of hermeneutic circularity in the act of reading, he does not fail to stress its limitations:

Did Stephen participate in his [Bloom's] dejection?
He affirmed his significance as a conscious rational animal proceeding syllogistically *from the known to the unknown* and a conscious rational reagent between a micro- and a macrocosm ineluctably constructed upon the incertitude of the void.
Was this affirmation apprehended by Bloom?
Not verbally. Substantially.
What comforted his misapprehension?
That as a competent keyless citizen he had proceeded energetically *from the unknown to the known* through the incertitude of the void. (*U*, 17.697; italics mine)

It would appear that Stephen and Bloom represent two possibilities equally permissible in the hermeneutic circle. Stephen follows the orthodox formula; he proceeds from the known to the unknown. Bloom, in his turn, shows an alternative possibility: it equally makes sense that the seeker, the "competent keyless citizen," should begin in ignorance, that he should initially reside in the unknown, and that it is *the known* that is sought. But we may assume that Joyce is criticizing hermeneutics: Stephen and Bloom, taken together, parody the hermeneutic method, demonstrating that it is impossible, from within the hermeneutic model, to determine the direction of the hermeneutic movement; hermeneutics is powerless to decide which of its two possible avenues is truly, properly *hermeneutic*. The passage shows that it is impossible to determine which direction makes more sense: one equally moves from the knowledge of what is known to the knowledge of what is unknown, or from the ignorance of the unknown to its cognition. The hermeneutic model reaches its impasse because the known and the unknown constitute, with equal relevance, the points of departure *and* of destination in any heuristic procedure.

In other words, on the sole basis of hermeneutic procedure it is impossible to determine whether what one already knows is indeed what one knows or what one seeks to know. At the same time, however, with the act of broaching this possibility, with becoming aware of the hermeneutic deadlock, the subject is freed from the hermeneutic impasse. This supreme, Socratic ignorance ("I know that I do not know") is possible only in the transcendental sphere, the sphere of infinite, preconceptual knowledge. Translated to the present context, this conclusion implies that, *taken together*, Bloom and Stephen, as they demonstrate the equivalence of induction and deduction, a movement of both vectors towards each other, place hermeneutic inquiry in the parameters of transcendental knowledge. What is known in this higher knowledge ("the known method") is not specific or empirically concrete, for this knowledge is an infinite, nonconceptual meaningfulness in general. Itself without direction, it gives direction; disoriented, it orients everything else.

Quite understandably, this preliminary critique, by Joyce, of inductive and deductive procedures may leave the reader of *Ulysses* stranded in the transcendental "Utopia" of the text and ready to panic. Let us examine other versions of this disorientation. As Fritz Senn proposes, *Ulysses* opens up a virtual Pandora's box of directions. Drawing parallels between Homer's *Odyssey* and Joyce's *Ulysses*, Senn observes that Homer's epic executes "many turns." The first verse of the *Odyssey* uses "two forms of 'much/many': *poly-* and *polla*, and lines 3 and 4, with *pollon* and another *polla*, emphasize even further that multiplicity that characterizes the *Odyssey*." Odysseus himself becomes the object of this plurality. He is called, in the first line, *polytropos* ("much turned," "of many turns"). The word describes Odysseus as "a man much traveled, 'much wandering,' " but as the language evolved, the word acquired positive meaning: "a man capable of turning many ways, a versatile character." It acquired a pejorative meaning: "shifty," "wily," "fickle," "changeable"; and a neutral one as well: "various" and "manifold."[10]

For Senn, the etymological versatility of "turning" produces the turn of the turn around its axis to create a sense of a oneness of turn, a uni-verse, out of the polytropic potential of the turns.[11] But one must proceed with caution. Rather than resolving hermeneutic circularity in an object, rather than assigning a concrete, empirical equivalent to this unity (the universe), one may proceed transcendentally and disclose a pure turning, turning as turning's proper meaning. Wherever the word *polytropos* turns, it finds more of itself, every meaning turning toward the word, where the act of turning away from one meaning reveals, in another "meaning," the *meaning of turning* as a revelation of infinite diversity. The reader, placed in the turn of the turn, experiences directions as pure turns. (The infinite dimension of the turn invites extension to Frank's "rereading": rereading does not

10. Fritz Senn, *Joyce's Dislocutions: Essays on Reading as Translation,* ed. John Paul Riquelme (Baltimore, 1984), 128–29.
11. Ibid., 130.

merely retrieve a former content—it infinitely discovers the meaning of reading by reading itself.) The transcendental moment precipitates geographical disorientation, showing that *Ulysses* makes infinite the simple manoeuver of "turning."

The reader of *Ulysses* might hope to find relief from the cornucopia of directions in the enthymemic model of reading.[12] Like Frank's model of rereading, enthymeme treats reading as reconstruction.[13] An enthymeme withholds certain parts of the argument in order to intensify listener-participation. As a gigantic enthymeme, *Ulysses* is understood to induce reader participation by withholding crucial elements of the exposition; it leads the listener out of the unknown (or the false) to the known (or the true). This model understands the novel as a truncated syllogism of a forensic proof: "The audience constructs the proofs by which it is persuaded."[14] The infinity of the transcendental moment changes enthymemic reading from extrapolative reconstruction to an interdependence between inference and the original totality. The available fragment does not imply a totality to which it belongs; it only indicates totality as that concept in whose terms the fragment will be comprehended as a fragment in the first place.

In its reliance on extrapolation, enthymeme resembles the concept of the transit of Venus, a topic very likely to appear in Sir Robert Ball's volume *The Story of the Heavens*, which features in Leopold Bloom's library. As Barbara DiBernard points out, the transit of Venus relies on parallax: a contrast of two places distant in space will offer the system of triangulation. As Joyce himself puts it, in parallax the "infinity" of the universe is "renderable equally finite by the suppositious probable apposition of one or more bodies equally of the same and of different magnitudes" (*U*, 17.701). The operation extends the promise of establishing the basic unit of measure for Joyce's novel. As DiBernard argues, with this one distance secured through parallactic measurement, "all others can be computed in relation to it," and the scale of the so-

---

12. Phillip Tompkins, "James Joyce and the Enthymeme: The Seventh Episode in *Ulysses*," *James Joyce Quarterly*, V (1968), 199–205.

13. Joseph Frank writes: "All the factual background summarized for the reader in an ordinary novel must here be reconstructed from fragments, sometimes hundreds of pages apart, scattered through the book" (*The Widening Gyre*, 18). Kenner adds: "The arranging presence . . . enjoys a seemingly total recall for exact forms of words used hundreds of pages earlier, a recall which implies not an operation of memory but access such as ours to a printed book, in which pages can be turned to and fro" (*Ulysses*, 65).

14. Tompkins, "James Joyce and the Enthymeme," 201.

lar system can be known. The reader of *Ulysses* would apply parallactic displacement to measure *Ulysses'* tropological system.¹⁵

In the transcendental dispensation, however, parallactic displacement determines the relation of two measures *to each other*. Any two measures offer a sense of proportion, of "finitude," but this proportion makes sense only for this internal relation, while the measure of measure itself cannot be thus inferred. In *Ulysses*, measure plays with measure. The novel provides the space for this play; it founds the possibility of measure, but as such constitutive locus, as the transcendental realm, it itself remains incommensurable.

The technique of extrapolative measure also underlies the model of reading *Ulysses* as catechetical recitation. Like enthymeme, catechism bases reading on recollection. As Hélène Cixous writes, "the *echo* marked in cat*ech*ism" repeats to the subject the fundamentally impenetrable mysteries of the Revelation. In Cixous' own analysis the simple sense of recollection immediately assumes transcendental character. The catechetical "echo" denotes a content so deeply embedded in the subject that it can be retrieved only in a mechanical interrogation that bypasses normal cognitive channels. The tedious repetition of the catechetical routine renders the subject oblivious to language, predisposing the subject to experience the *ineffability* of absolute truth: the infinite repetition of the echo hypnotizes the subject with "unending symmetries" that erase language and open the subject up to infinity.¹⁶ What is thus retrieved is not empirical content that can be memorized and repeated, but the subject itself as *the pure capacity of the subject to memorize itself as this ungraspable "echo" of the ineffable divine truth*.

"Perfection" offers yet another extrapolative measure for *Ulysses*. In this model, the knowledge of the world's perfection is inferred from its imperfections. Still, how can one first know that the world is, indeed, imperfect? How can one deduce perfection from imperfection,

---

15. Barbara DiBernard, "Parallax as Parallel, Paradigm, and Paradox in *Ulysses*," *ÉIRE*, X (1975), 70–71. DiBernard offers her candidate for the transit of Venus in the universe of *Ulysses:* "The transit of Venus observed in *Ulysses* is that of Molly Bloom and May Dedalus ... Stephen's problems stem to a great extent from his guilt over his mother, and Bloom sees all women in terms of Molly. Because both Stephen's and Bloom's behavior patterns are largely a result of their attitudes toward these women, *Ulysses* is thus given scope" (72).

16. Hélène Cixous, "The R(use) of Writing," in *Post-Structuralist Joyce: Essays from the French*, ed. Derek Attridge and Daniel Ferrer (New York, 1984), 27.

the ideal from the actual? The irreducible distance is usually bridged in the "gnomon," a word that Joyce used for the world's imperfections,[17] on the logic that, as Cixous writes, the gnomon is "the part of a parallelogram left when another parallelogram . . . has been taken from it, the spike . . . of a sundial."[18] Etymologically a synecdoche, gnomic wisdom is a form of accommodation, of philanthropic, "philosophical" resignation:

> He believed then that human life was infinitely perfectible, eliminating these conditions?
>   There remained the generic conditions imposed by natural, as distinct from human law, as integral parts of the human whole: the necessity of destruction to procure alimentary sustenance: the painful character of the ultimate functions of separate existence, the agonies of birth and death: the monotonous menstruation of simian and (particularly) human females extending from the age of puberty to the menopause: inevitable accidents at sea, in mines and factories: certain very painful maladies and their resultant surgical operations, innate lunacy and congenital criminality, decimating epidemics: catastrophic cataclysms which make terror the basis of human mentality: seismic upheavals the epicentres of which are located in densely populated regions: the fact of vital growth, through convulsions of metamorphosis from infancy through maturity to decay. (*U*, 17.697)

Gnomic wisdom is poised between resigned acceptance and idealistic rebellion. This is Leibniz's logic of the "best of possible worlds," the philosophical gnomic wisdom par excellence; it confers on what is contingent and finite the dignity of the necessary and the normative. That which *is* becomes the standard for that which *ought to be:* imperceptibly, the ideal capitulates to the actual.

The margin separating gnomic wisdom from transcendental knowledge is very narrow. Gnomically speaking, humanity hesitates between the actual and the ideal, between accepting its fate and rebelling against it, a dissonance of tone that can be sensed in the passage above. This duality is a result of the lack of sobriety and precision. As a result of this false tone, gnomic wisdom fails to recognize in its discourse the simultaneous presence of the prescriptive and the descriptive visions of *la condition humaine;* deaf to the false tone in its

---

17. Fritz Senn, " 'All the errears and erroriboose': Joyce's Misconducting Universe," in *International Perspectives on James Joyce*, ed. Gottlieb Gaiser (Troy, N.Y., 1986), 164.

18. Cixous, "The R(use) of Writing," in *Post-Structuralist Joyce*, ed. Attridge and Ferrer, 27.

own message, gnomic wisdom is convinced that philanthropic reaction is the noblest response.

This is to say that gnomic wisdom fails to analyze the relation between perfection and imperfection and that it merely contaminates its acceptance of the world as it is with the noble impulse to improve it. Although the gnomic dispensation understands the world, it does so in the manner of the naïve mind, only in its worldliness, as unmediated presence and field of activity. In this understanding, every element is unproblematically assimilated in a total (but unexamined) sense of the world, on the assumption that everything in this world is naturally comprehensible. The gnomic frame of mind uncritically extrapolates the *pars* of the sundial, the gnomon, onto a larger totality, without thinking through, criticizing, the consequences of the hermeneutic difference between parts and whole. In the language of classical philosophy, gnomic wisdom is a failure to be bewildered, to experience Aristotle's *thaumadzein*. In the language of modern philosophy, it is a failure to note the ontico-ontological difference, the difference between Being and beings.

Considered transcendentally, the relation of imperfection to perfection is not intended to determine a measure that would provide the basis for practical initiatives to improve the human lot. Rather, imperfection is the initial precondition under which all efforts to improve the world can begin to make sense. Gnomically speaking, philanthropy persists, although the death of all mankind is inevitable. But speaking transcendentally, it is this inevitability that renders all philanthropic concerns *meaningful* in the first place. As imperfect, the world is perfectible. Considering that neither dispensation can change anything in the sublunar world, the difference may seem pedantic. But it is worth insisting on: the transcendental sense takes priority in this futile enterprise, as it renders the gnomic discourse about "the best of possible worlds" meaningful in the first place.

Before addressing the transcendental sense of Joyce's exemplarity, we must first discuss one more strategy frequently given prominence in *Ulysses* criticism. The hermeneutic relation between parts and whole presupposes a minimum degree of similarity—Cixous' "echo"—between the members of the pair, to allow for extrapolation. In some fundamental way, extrapolation and reading are structured on this "echo." The cliché captures the very essence of reading as echo, as rereading, in that it embodies a circularity so rigorous that it resists hermeneutic interpretation. Considered as a reading strategy appropriate for *Ulysses*, the cliché comes far closer than do the empirical models of reading *Ulysses* to the structural rigor and economy of operation that characterize Joyce's exemplarity.

The mechanism of the cliché is such that the original instance cannot appear otherwise than as repeated. The cliché is language used in complete adequacy with the original communicative context to such an extent that the original context of the phrase asserts itself as forcefully as does its conceptual meaning. However, precisely because of this accompanying ballast of usage, a simple reading of the cliché becomes problematic: cliché's original context swallows up its encoded meaning. As a result, the order of priority between context and meaning becomes obscured. The cliché comes to the reader, even to the first reader, as worn out, no longer and not yet an origin.

The essentially incomplete nature of the cliché strands the reader in the infinite gap between the cliché and its original milieu. The access to the originating situation is possible only in the repetition of the cliché, but each time it is repeated, the cliché's *clichéd* aspect asserts itself with equal insistence. The cliché can now express only its organic relation to the original context; it can, that is, express neither the pure conceptual meaning that it carries as a phrase nor the pure context in which it originated, but only the fact of the relation, of the bonding, between concept and context. The cliché belongs to its origin so fundamentally that it cannot demonstrate this relation; it is a language that gets in its own way. Originless and original at the same time, the cliché traps the reader in the vicious circle of hermeneutics.

This trap proves even more challenging for the writer. Can the subsequent use of the cliché be distinguished from its original occurrence? How can Joyce re-mark the boundary of the cliché? How can he use language frozen in the infinite loop of its occurrence? How can Joyce *quote* it? As Robert Janusko shows, "Oxen of the Sun" exploits the logic of allusion to the utmost, making it impossible for the reader either to arrive at a supposedly "Joycean" surface or to savor the original sources in their purity.[19] The restorative nature of Joyce's language redefines the structure of literary allusion (from Latin *alludere*, "to play with") from the orthodox sense of a stable, identifiable echo to a cacophony of contextual clues: speaking with the voices of the assorted sources, *Joyce's voice fails to remark its specificity*. This absence of the properly "Joycean" signature plays the allusions in

---

19. Robert Janusko, *The Sources and Structures of James Joyce's "Oxen"* (Ann Arbor, 1983).

Ulysses off against one another in a ludicrous (*ludere*) display of allusions. In the textual spectacle, Joyce's words "sound" familiar, but the first verbal instance that founds this familiarity is missing, supplanted by the always second word. In Joyce's textual performance, the "rehearsal" of clichés beckons, infinitely, to an origin unable to be born and unable to die, to a perpetually interred origin, to the "hearse."[20]

As infinite, this sense of cliché, quotation, and allusion gives prominence, not to the content of the device, but to the infinite moment responsible for the content's function. Joyce's language operates within cliché's monadically enclosed circuit of recurrence. In regurgitating language Joyce presents the mechanism of the cliché as essential to language operation. In order to be a phenomenology of the human spirit, *Ulysses* must possess a residue recognizable for any reader: in the loop of the cliché, every instance of language appears as the echo of a language once used properly and familiar to everyone. Just as Bloom's library is "inverted" and "improperly arranged" in relation to an absent but pertinent organizing system, so *Ulysses* stands opposed to the totality of language, re-presenting it as its miniature sample. The terms sustain extrapolative homology in virtue of the "echo," and to that extent Frank's analysis is confirmed—"one cannot read *Ulysses*, one can only reread it"—however, in a Joycean twist, the "echo" is infinite—it invites familiarity but withholds recognition. Transcendental rereading is nonconceptual.

As an encyclopedia of clichés, *Ulysses encircles* the reader: language in its totality must be a cliché in order to stabilize meaning and in order to be each time *re*-cognized, in the "echo," as such a totalizing system. *Ulysses* exposes the hermeneutic circle as the cliché par excellence of the human sciences, and it can do so by reaching, in the transcendental critique of cliché, behind the sense of science developed in the nineteenth century. *Ulysses* beckons to the philosophical sense of "science" in Kant, Fichte, Schelling, and Hegel as the transcendental system of knowledge, a sense lost in the days when the empiricist, objective, positivist laws of the physical world dominate intellectual inquiry.

The previous analysis has attempted to show that transcendental vertigo significantly alters the objectifying, empirical thrusts of the different reading strategies found in, or proposed for, *Ulysses*. Objective,

---

20. "Rehearse: [ME *rehersen*, fr. MF *rehercier*, lit. to harrow again, fr. *re* + *hercier* to harrow, fr. *herce* harrow—more at HEARSE]" (*Webster's New Collegiate Dictionary*).

empirical measurements rest on transcendental infinity, which itself, however, remains immeasurable. We can now return to the central problem of the unity, in the hermeneutic circle, of induction and deduction, with the goal of establishing this original unity of time and space as the domain of Joyce's transcendental exemplarity. The unity of induction and deduction is, as we have said, the question of the unity of the hermeneutic circle itself. Nowhere is the inexorable power and the absolute claim of transcendental analysis more apparent than in relation to this question. The question addresses the very possibility of knowing that the circle is *a circle.*

We have seen that the hermeneutic circle merely organizes the interaction of induction and deduction but that it itself is powerless to constitute these operations in their essence or to bring about their synthesis. This constitutive privilege is reserved for the transcendental realm. Just as induction and deduction stand in relation to each other and disclose each other in their essence in this "mediation," so also the hermeneutic circle itself requires its counterpart in order to come into its own. However, the hermeneutic circle lacks the means of positing its own completing *gestalt.* The question arises, therefore, What figure can enter into transcendental transaction with the circle so that the circle can be known to be a circle? This is the transcendental task par excellence, intimated by Bloom's utopian "known method": the circle is a circle *only with a square.*

As Helen Georgi argues, the riddles presented in *Ulysses* systematically indicate that the novel as a whole is a puzzle.[21] Assuming that the central puzzle of *Ulysses* is the puzzle of "squaring the circle," the inquiry carries considerable promise: the operation—ridiculous, futile—can square *Ulysses,* can square, that is, naïve (inductive) reading with competent (deductive) rereading. It can combine the inductive process of discovery with the deductive routine of recollection; it can reconcile teleology with repetition—it can give the hermeneutic circle its true unity.

In order to see how the operation works in a concrete passage, we can analyze a sentence from "Aeolus" (following Murray McArthur).[22] The passage, which enacts Mr. Deasy's antinomy of repetition and

21. Helen Georgi, "Covert Riddles in *Ulysses:* Squaring the Circle," *Journal of Modern Literature,* XIII (1986), 329–39.

22. Murray McArthur, *Stolen Writings: Blake's "Milton," Joyce's "Ulysses," and the Nature of Influence* (Ann Arbor, 1988), hereinafter cited parenthetically by page number in the text.

teleology, carries important implications. First, it shows that the unity of induction and deduction in the hermeneutic circle is the work of transcendental vertigo. In addition, the complexity of the passage helps differentiate the conceptions of circularity in Frank, Nietzsche, and Joyce. And, finally, the passage helps formulate the fundamental questions that transcendental vertigo inevitably provokes:

GENTLEMEN OF THE PRESS

> Grassbooted draymen rolled barrels dullthudding out of Prince's stores and bumped them up on the brewery float. On the brewery float bumped dullthudding barrels rolled by grossbooted draymen out of Prince's stores. (*U*, 7.116)

The two sentences deploy the same meaning: both are derived from one semantic core. This is the deductive structure of sameness built on the analogical construction of history. When Stephen says, in the conversation with Mr. Deasy, "History is a nightmare from which I am trying to awake" (*U*, 2.34), he is referring to the prison of repetition based on this structure. But a teleological reading can also claim this fragment for its purposes, revealing a temporal, inductive aspect of the cluster. Teleology can argue that the second sentence, while recognizably derived from the first, induces a sense of "development," that it "advances the plot" with the play of stylistic modulations, and that it seems somehow "better" because it is closer to the (novel's) end.

The cluster's adaptability to both the repetitive and teleological readings has several implications. For one, it may be indicating that teleological explanation represents for Joyce a "nightmare" as, if not more, harmful than the nightmare of history's vicious cycles. The teleological vision of history targets humanity's natural need for purpose, and the sentences are carefully crafted to exploit this need. They are skillfully constructed to elicit an inquiry into the "purposes" of history and, simultaneously, to divert the reader from a transcendental inquiry into history's original ground. To awaken from the "nightmare," one must ignore the decoy question, "Where is history *going?*" and pursue the real—as Nietzsche calls it, *genealogical*—issue: "Where does history *come from?*"

In order to prepare an answer—and this is the second lesson of the passage—we must concentrate on the interaction of repetition and teleology staged in the cluster. Let us look at the passage once again. We have, in the inductive dispensation, a return of the circle ("on the brewery float. On the brewery float") and, in a deductive schema, a restatement of the first sentence by the second. The passage enacts a tension of the two orders. In an uncanny repetition, in an intratextual *echo*, the second sentence invokes the first sentence. Just as, in the quoted passage, two sentences move parallel to one another with a slight displacement, so *Ulysses* moves parallel to some previously uttered sequence, restating the "original" story in a slightly displaced, "reversed" order. Just as Leopold Bloom's library stands "inverted" and "improperly arranged" in relation to an absent but insistent order, *Ulysses* stands "inverted" in relation to an ordering principle that rules over it *in absentia*. The intimations of this absent order that exceeds repetition and teleology enable the subject to "awake" from the repetitive and teleological nightmares. Only a squared unity of the ordinal and the cardinal orders, only the synthesis of the catalog can reveal history's true origin. As transcendental, this synthesis is of little use to the historicism of Frank, and it concerns even less the "untimely" (*unzeitgemäß*) Nietzsche. For Joyce, history's origin will emerge as a result of the unity between space and time, between deduction and induction. I will hope to show that Joyce's transcendental exemplarity is the locus and figure of this unity, a generative nexus capable of squaring the antinomy of sameness and teleology that haunts history as its "nightmare."

In our search for a figure of this squaring, it may be helpful to retrace some of the steps in Murray McArthur's attempt, in *Stolen Writings*, to unify the metonymic and the metaphoric dimensions in *Ulysses* (104–107). McArthur's study is especially pertinent here because it seeks to establish the unity in question in an analysis of one of Joyce's puzzles and, for this reason, implicitly addresses the problem of the quadrature of the circle.

McArthur concentrates, in his discussion of the "Aeolus" episode, on the episode's symmetrical middle—in the thirty-second section of the sixty-three total sections (107). In a previous section (marked "? ? ?"), Lenehan poses his riddle: "Silence! What opera resembles a railway line?" (*U*, 7.132). In the thirty-second section he answers it: "*The Rose of Castille.* See the wheeze? Rows of cast steel. Gee!" (*U*, 7.134). The complex pun contains a metaphor and a metonymy. It is a metaphor "signifying a flower from Spain" (a woman), and it is a metonymy signifying "fixed-bed systems of transportation" (*Stolen Writings*, 107). In view of this duality, McArthur raises the crucial question: "Given this conjunction of contiguity and similarity, one has to ask if either quality has priority" (112). Is *The Rose of Castille* "a metaphoric metonymy or metonymic metaphor?" (112).

At the center of the "Aeolus" episode, the reader finds a textual moment, Lenehan's puzzle, which allows for two figural interpretations. The puzzle is both a metaphor and a metonymy, and it is tempting to decide that the phrase is a matter of only one of these rhetorical figures. This is the path of empirical solutions, which are mainly concerned with determining the relevance of these figures of speech for organizing reading matter. But it is also possible to pursue the question of priority between metaphor and metonymy in transcendental rhetoric. The transcendental nature of the question asserts itself in the following form: How are metaphor and metonymy related *to each other*? This rhetoric inquires about the reciprocal relation of the two figures, not only with the goal of determining which of them is first or more important, but primarily with the goal of describing the form of mediation that allows them to form Lenehan's complex pun. The problem is similar to the dilemma of Kant's "incongruent objects," the pair of gloves, as well as to the one we have encountered in the case of the hermeneutic circle. While the circle moves from the known to the unknown, the site on which—or the form in which—the "known" can meet the "unknown" can be "known" in the "higher," transcendental realm.

Keeping the goals of transcendental rhetoric in mind, we can now proceed to examine the consequences of adopting specific solutions to the relation between metonymy and metaphor in *Ulysses* with respect to the synthesis of the act of reading. The synthesis of metaphor and metonymy, because it entails the harmony of space and time, and of deductive and inductive orders, because, in other words, it establishes the continuum of space and time, is a synthesis of history. In this sense, history has figural structure, and for this reason each specific resolution of the unity of metonomy and metaphor, their "squaring," will constitute a concrete conception of history. Let us sketch out three solutions: the synthetic, the complementary, and the exemplary relations between sameness and teleology, deduction and induction.

For Richard Ellmann, McArthur argues, the figures clash in a triadic economy: *Ulysses*, the novel-epic, brings the reader to the other shore, ending "the nightmare of history" of the epic itself (*Stolen Writings*, 145). In this historical *epoché*, spatial and temporal dimensions, metaphor and metonymy, come together in a third moment, elevated (*aufgehoben*) to an extra-historical realm in the eschatology of the other world. However, the triad that elevates history above itself is unable, as McArthur correctly argues, to "subsume [the novel's] structural difficulties" (145), unable, that is, to unify "the necessity and positive energy of sameness and the accidental and negative force of difference" (145).

In McArthur's model of complementarity, Lenehan's pun is a dynamic process in which both figures of speech participate equally (141). The point between metonymy and metaphor designates the moment of transition of opposites into their counterparts, the chiasmus of Bloom's wit: "The complex rose of Castille/rows of cast steel is a case of figural parallax. Seen from one perspective, the phrase designates a parallelism of properties; from the other perspective, it signifies a parallelism of location. Both perspectives are necessary for the rhetorical parallax to work ... The parallel figures of metaphor and metonymy ... actually exist in ... equal balance, sharing their qualities in the rhetorical vibrations of wit" (113). Taken together, metaphor and metonymy balance, "like the tuning fork," the temporal and the spatial, the ordinal and the cardinal orders: contiguity and similarity form a vibrant simultaneity of *Ulysses*' "rhetorical infrastructure" (113).

In the present proposal the relationship between metonymy and metaphor is resolved in the exemplary relation understood as the transcendental comportment of the two figures to each other. Before clarifying this solution, we must first describe McArthur's proposal in greater detail. McArthur's parallactic relation unites metaphor and metonymy in complementarity to yield harmony and vibration (*Stimmung*). McArthur finds this model organizing the "Sirens" episode, where metaphor and metonymy produce the sound (sirens' song) that achieves a perfect balance between the temporal and the spatial, between the ordinal and the cardinal arrangements. In McArthur's terms, "Aeolus" and "Sirens" enact in the realm of the audible what "Cyclops" achieves in the realm of the visible. Just as the monocular vision of the Citizen is absorbed within "Cyclops"'s binocular narrative planes, the spheres of contiguity and similarity in "Aeolus" are fused into the time-space continuum of vibrant omnipresence.

In general terms, the solution offered by McArthur tends to describe the relation between the two figures in substantive, concrete terms as productive relations that assume a perceptible form existing empirically in time and space. Here lies the central difference between complementarity and exemplarity. The figure of exemplarity appears, not in the empirical sphere, but in Kant's "absolute space." It only denotes the minimal relation between metaphor and metonymy (the right glove and the left glove) insofar as they can be related to each other in actual space. This relation cannot be positively described except by saying that together the two figures constitute a whole that does not produce anything extrinsic to this relation. The relation is infinite. In their mutual, exemplary comportment, metaphor and metonymy create a lack by taking away and then supplement that lack by giving back. Both are constituted not by movement but by *removal*, not by sample but by *ex*-ample.

Still, exemplarity faces critical interrogation from other quarters. The transcendental sense of exemplarity has been established with an eye to proposing a universal formula for reading *Ulysses*. In that case, however, how can reading, which engages an object, be based on examples, which, enclosed in infinite interiority, remain intransitive? And if reading is, as Frank has shown, based on memory, what does exemplary retrieval, as empty and infinite, bring to mind? What happens by way of example?

To see how exemplarity furnishes a universal model for reading *Ulysses*, we shall begin with a short sketch of Joyce's critique of the traditionally conceived example. Examples serve as units of comprehension supervised by *teleo*logic. Ordinal logic singles out examples from the mass of meaningless, nonexemplary, insub*ordinate* episodes. Examples illustrate a thesis about history only because they have been stripped of their individuality and pressed into the service of history to be the *phonemes* of history's discourse. Individual episodes can attain this status—they can appear in the Book of History, only if they fit into the teleological agenda, only, that is, if they *exemplify* a preconceived grand design. All other episodes end up (as in Hegel) on the trash heap of history.

Up to a point, the Joycean example cooperates with this process of historical selection and with this conception of exemplarity fashioned to satisfy particular ideological interests. A segment is "taken out," isolated from the organic continuum of the process. But it is precisely the momentarily extrinsic placement of example in relation to history that gives Joyce the opportunity of unexpected redefinition. As it stands out, the new example leaves nothing behind, no nonexemplary detritus. A linguistic analogy may help here. Joyce extends the phonemic function of the exemplary episode to those historical moments that have been judged useless for teleological thesis. By replacing phonology, the study of sounds as productive of meaning, with phonetics, the study of sounds without regard for meaning, Joyce abolishes meaning based on difference and introduces general meaning—meaningfulness in general. In Joyce's phonetics of history, every historical moment resonates with a measure of significance. Joyce's *cata*logic makes *every* moment exemplary.

Clearly, then, the new example is not produced by a process of selection. Its new significance has little to do with the "epiphanies" of Joyce's early aesthetics, with the moments of a heightened perception that makes every detail exquisite. The aesthetically pleasing examples presented in *Ulysses*, unlike the moments of epiphany in *Stephen Hero* and *A Portrait*, no longer glorify the detail in a poetics of luminous shining forth. In *Ulysses* the examples, in defiance of entelechic regime, become so exemplary, so singular, as to obtain, like the books in Bloom's library, *exemp*tion from the overall historical matrix they were supposed to represent. Like Bloom's books, Joyce's examples cannot be *ordered around*. Their splendor (if, indeed, it is splendor) cannot be understood with reference to any recognizable matrix—something easily done in the case of epiphanies, where the unique moment stands out by way of contrast with the gray monotony of the world. The exemplary moment stands out intransitively.

But what happens in the space of the example? We have seen that the space of Bloom's library was affected by the mysterious power of the mirror, which accounted for a series of systematic distortions and intriguing absences. The books listed in the catalog implied, in their distorted arrangements, a certain ordering principle that itself remained undemonstrable. Joyce's example defines this "echoing" relation: the individual moment enjoys a relation to the original order, yet it is impossible positively to determine the nature of this relation.

The catalog, we may recall, presented the books in an apparently chaotic arrangement in such a way as to postulate that the original order was immediately realized in this arrangement, although the reader lacked the means to identify it. This immediate indwelling of the original order in the aggregate of Bloom's books helps define the nature of the relation between example and totality intended by Joyce. The extrapolation, or the infinite recognition, between the example and the totality of history makes it impossible to separate the historical moment from this moment's encompassing totality, for in the example, the detail and the totality, the origin and the echo, are unified immediately.

Exemplary repetition offers exemption from the vicious repetition of the cycles of history. How does this repetition differ from the wisdom of Mr. Deasy, from Frank's proposal, from "the eternal return of the same," or from the truism that "history repeats itself"? This question brings us back to Mr. Deasy's antinomy. Historical understanding, we have seen, is at odds with itself. To claim intelligibility, it relies on repetition; to claim teleological progression, it invokes variation in excess of repetition. The Joycean example is constituted by this duplicity and can, indeed, be very easily drawn into its debilitating play: it can either represent history, acting as a lowly servant (to the neglect of its own individuality), or else it can stand emancipated from the totality of relations called history, "signifying nothing."

However, as it hovers at the center of this conflict, the Joycean example manages to avoid both extremes—complete submission to history's meanings and complete separation from historical relevance. Etymology confirms this ambivalence (Latin *exemere* to "take out"): the example is excluded from history's analogical rigors but still manages to remain historically pertinent. The ambivalence allows it to occupy a dynamic—we might say *impertinent*—position in relation to the antinomy of history. This ambivalence frees the category of "meaning" from iteration and fills the discrete moment with a meaning alien to history's teleological interests; it exempts meaning from the logic of sameness and gives the lie to history's shrill warning that the only alternative to "law and order" is unbridled chaos. The vibrant duplicity defines the first outlines of the example as the universal model of reading. The example can exempt the historical moment from repetition and teleology, and it can found Stephen's "awakening," because it is informed by the simultaneity of order and chaos. It hails from a prehistorical logic, from *cata*logic.

What is the nature of this logic? Joyce's conception of exemplarity is a modernist version of the romantic arabesque. In proposing his arabesque, Joyce is attracted neither by the whole (history) from which the segment is taken, nor by the content of the item (example) thus taken out, but exclusively by the operation of taking out, of "exampling." This is the difference between an empirical and a transcendental example. Neither outside nor inside history, the example *impertinently* dwells on the threshold of conceptual understanding.

In its familiar sense, the example possesses meaning because it is placed in the totality of history. Here, however, the example, "taken out" of its context, loses this comforting reference and, in the moment of this separation, its meaning is, for a split-second, taken out, exampled, meaning-less. But the phrase "meaning-less" invites caution. It does not designate the simple negative, "the lack of meaning"; rather, it indicates exemplary meaning as "something-less-than-meaning." The example says, infinitely, transcendentally: "I know that I do not know." This emptiness has important consequences. As it exits from history, the example does not leave history's fraudulent meaning behind, nor does it save in its interior some authentic truth from history's prevarications. Exemplary meaning has humble aspirations: it appears *in, and as, the moment of exit* from the historical matrix. Conceptually empty, the example *means* only because it has survived—except that in exemplary logic survival entails, not a fortunate escape, not a sparing from danger, but a *living-on* (or *-over* [*sur-vivre*]) history's external/internal threshold.

It is this peripheral quality that colors Joyce's exemplarity with a tone of negativity. And while this negativity is, in principle, impossible to conceptualize, it nevertheless operates in a systematic manner. "Example" shares its privative logic with the etymologically related "redemption"; together with "salvation" and "exception," the words form a cluster that creates a disconcerting give and take based on infinite interiority, which is also infinite externality. The usage of "to save" suggests various forms of the exclusionary gesture. One can "save money"; "save oneself the trouble"; one "saves the leftovers"; or, in the same logic, "two passengers were saved" (the others were lost). The logic of exclusion works most explicitly in the prepositional form: "All perished save two." The point is this: in every act of saving, somebody or something is *lost*. Only because "exception is taken" can one proceed to save everybody, but then somebody will always be left out, for in offering salvation we act under the incision of *sauf*, which always leaves behind a leftover: someone (something) who could not be saved but, also, precisely that in virtue of which we *could* bring someone (else) to safety.

"Redemption," in its turn, concretizes the externality of example as a taking back (*re* + *emere*).[23] A quick glance at etymology suggests the following scheme. While we are now buying (taking) something back, we do not know how we had originally become owners, nor can

---

23. "Redeem: [ME *redemen*, modif. of MF *redimer*, fr. L *redimere*, fr. *re-*, *red-* re- + *emere* to take, buy; akin to Lith *imti* to take] 1 a: to buy back: REPURCHASE b: to get or win back" (*Webster's New Collegiate Dictionary*).

we recall how we managed to lose what had been originally ours; we have no memory or record of the acquisition or loss. While "redemption" carries within its *re-* an echo of the originary event (*der Sprung*), it leaves the memory of the initial transaction veiled in darkness. Redemption reinstitutes the initial order, but only as a re-taking: the first *taking*, the *Urnehmung* (and *Wahrnehmung* means "taking for true"), or simply the *Nehmung*, remains in obscurity; one can neither re-take (redeem) it nor simply take (deem) it, for it is "deemability" itself.[24]

The privative logic of the cluster is captured by Michel Serres: "*Example* is a word whose prefix says 'difference' and whose root says 'buying' and 'selling.' As if it were a way of getting out of exchange, something taken away, something removed from the purchase."[25] The privative moment indicates exemplarity's preconceptual origin: something is always lost as a condition of saving; one meaning always disappears for another meaning to come to light. It would be futile to insist that something stable always abides, always *remains* after the operation of saving. "Remaining" (related to "mansion") itself brings the remainder to presence only in the repetitive modality of *re-*. To ensure that the house stands firm, the foundation must first be dislodged. Stability is first established by originary, transcendental upheaval.

We can now return to the difference between Joyce's conception of exemplarity and McArthur's conception of complementarity. The example differs from complementarity in virtue of its constitutive emptiness: it makes room for metaphor and metonymy; it constitutes their separate functions and organizes their proper interaction. While the example is their original unity, it itself does not constitute another figure in the rhetorical repertoire; it remains as their relation, itself empty, a relation in general. Joyce's example is aligned, not with Hegelian dialectic, not with figures (like *Aufhebung*), but with Kantian philosophy, with minimal relations, "conditions of possibility." Hence the exemplary unity, or synthesis, of the two figures does not constitute a third moment, a composite figure that unites them, but is a process of doubling, of a *mirrorish*, dissimulating give and take, of ex-ampling.

24. Nietzsche speaks of this original barter for which no currency, no *valuation*, has yet been created, in Book II, Sections 8–11, of *The Genealogy of Morals*.
25. Michel Serres, *The Parasite*, trans. Lawrence R. Schehr (Baltimore, 1982), 29.

This empty figure has extremely important consequences for the model of reading *Ulysses*, for the notion of history that it entails, and for the relation with totality that it entertains. In the first place, exemplarity underlies Joyce's conception of history. History, we have seen, is a figural construct, since metonymy and metaphor are rhetorical equivalents of time and space, repetition and teleology, deduction and induction. What, then, is history if, as the unity of time and space, it is constituted in the empty figure of exemplarity? How can the fullness and unity of history be found in the infinite emptiness of the example?

Transcendental exemplarity, as the minimal relation between metaphor and metonymy, probes the origin of history; indeed, it founds history because it pertains to the question of *the origin of the relation of priority as such*, for in exemplarity metaphor and metonymy infinitely determine each other, without either of them emerging as a dominant figure. Rather than describing history's diverse empirical shapes, exemplarity interrogates the ground of history as the unity of time and space. It describes that which makes history *history*. It is, therefore, of immense importance to recognize the infinite nature of the exemplary relation between metaphor and metonymy. As a transcendental relation, exemplarity creates history as an enclosed exchange without externality, as an infinite relation that contains its external moment, its other world, or teleological fulfillment, already, and always in advance, in itself. As a pure relation of the two figures, exemplarity comes both before and after history, as the excessive identity of history *as* history.

A similarly infinite relation holds for Joycean redemption. Redemption, rather than restoring reality to pristine condition, designates the restorative power of redemption as the pure movement of repetition itself. Joyce foregrounds this repetition in the archaic forms of "agenbite of inwit" for "remorse," and "Agenbuyer" for "Redeemer." The formation dwells, not on the concrete sense of restoration to perfection, and not on the repetition of the same activity ad infinitum, but on the infinite relation between the pristine reality and the imperfect one, on the redemptive relation between fall and paradise. For origin to *be* a first, the *second* moment is structurally indispensable. Return makes origin—origin constitutes return; metonymy calls for metaphor—metaphor summons metonymy. Exemplarity stands at the center of these transactions as the pure "taking" and "giving," as the originless relation between origin and return, between metaphor and metonymy.

It is important to stress here that the exemplary model differs from the allegorical explanation of history developed by the biblical scholarship of the Church Fathers. This sense of figurality has structured Western thinking since its inception in the figural relation between the Old and the New Testaments. As Erich Auerbach shows in his essay "Figura," the patristic tradition derived the meaning of historical events from a *comparison* of two events in biblical history. The earlier event was seen as the prefiguration of the later event, as this event's "type," while the second event fulfilled the first one. Moreover, the second historical event itself merely prefigured the ultimate, eschatological meaning of these historical events (the model of elevation we have encountered in Ellmann).[26]

While related to the allegorical scheme, exemplary figurality differs from it in one significant respect. In the biblical model, one event is fulfilled in another event, and this fulfillment itself finds its completion in the eschatological moment, which transcends history. The first event exists in history only insofar as it prefigures the second event, only insofar as its lowly meaning is subordinated to the more excellent meaning of the second event. We can recognize in this subordination the manipulation of examples by teleological interests. In contrast, the exemplary relation between two events does not subordinate the detail to the later event or to a transcendent interpretive scheme. The example exists both transitively, for history, and infinitely, for itself: it belongs to history and transcends it. The example is both more and less than history; it is history's original ground. While in the patristic tradition the letter of the Old Testament prefigures the spirit of the New Testament, in the exemplary relation the two dispensations stand in a relation of mutual origination; they stand under the law of the exemplary give and take of origin. Origin (the old) and its derivative moment (the new) come into existence only in, and as, the example, the mutual give and take of Jew and Gentile: "Jewgreek is greekjew" (*U*, 15.504).

In its emptiness, Joyce's exemplarity is the supreme figure of salvation and redemption within history. In accordance with the logic of these operations indicated by their etymology (*sauf, reemere*), the figurative meaning of history is not eschatological, as history's end, but sublunar, as history's folding in upon itself in the mutual, infinite

---

26. Erich Auerbach, *Scenes from the Drama of European Literature* (Minneapolis, 1984), 11–76, 53, 58.

comportment of two historical events. Joyce founds history as a universal event, or as the event of universality, accessible to all human beings, in the past, in the present, and in the future. In contrast to the teleological model of history, in which the meaning of history is postponed until Doomsday, the meaning of history for Joyce occurs at every moment as the exemplary synthesis of the temporal and spatial coordinates, a synthesis that posits the world-hood of the world in its historicity and by which history can become the history *of* the world.

As a figure that founds history, Joyce's figure of the absent origin, the example, resembles Hölderlin's figure of the lack of destiny, *dysmoron* ("without destiny").[27] Hölderlin reasoned that, to the extent that the essence of modernity is founded on its difference from antiquity, modernity is condemned to repeat Greece in order to imitate it or even surpass it. However, dissatisfied with the classicist understanding of this repetition of antiquity, Hölderlin conceived an alternative model. He assumed that what remained to be repeated, or imitated, in Greece was not the great achievement of Greece but that which Greece failed to achieve, that which had never taken place there.

Because Greece was distinguished by its destiny as a philosophical, artistic, and political people, and because it possessed a strong sense of identity as a complete cultural organism, Hölderlin concluded that modernity will properly imitate Greece only if it repeats that which did not happen there in these respects. Consequently, the modern, Hesperian world is exiled, without art, without gods, without identity, and without destiny. This desolate condition is, for Hölderlin, the supreme form of modern repetition, the only one that can bring us close to the gods.

Joyce's exemplary ground of history invites parallels with Hölderlin's notion of *dysmoron*. Because Hölderlin saw the meaning of history in the relation of modernity to antiquity, and because he saw in Greece a lack constitutive of modernity, he concluded that modernity must *repeat what was absent in Greece* and that this repetition will assume the form of a perpetually increasing differentiation and distancing. Hölderlin's figure of history never achieves a concrete form because it enacts the infinitely increasing differentiation; it remains without synthesis.[28] Joyce, for his part, saw the possibility of estab-

---

27. A most illuminating discussion of Hölderlin's concept of *das Schicksallose* (without destiny), which occurs in his *Notes to Antigone*, can be found in Philippe Lacoue-Labarthe's essay "Hölderlin and the Greeks," in *TM*, 246.

28. See Lacoue-Labarthe, "The Caesura of the Speculative," in *TM*, 231.

lishing a historical relation between Jews and Gentiles as an infinite relation of universality founded on the lack of origin, on the absence of *arché*. The universal relation, the relation that ignores the empirical accidents of time and place, can be established only in the synthesis of time and place, in the exemplary interiority *that absolutely pre exists* time and place—universality as origin-less, *an-archic*. In this exemplary synthesis of time and space, the particulars of time and place do not come into play *yet*. Joyce's example reveals the meaning of history, not in the simple, exemplary meaning of a chosen event, in teleological prefiguration, but in archaeological restoration of universality understood as the erasure of origin, an erasure that, like Hölderlin's synthesis without term, lacks a positive *gestalt*. The motif of "the Wandering Jew" is an exemplary actualization of this erased content, of universality in a concrete figure, the ever-shifting, formless, uprooted occurring of history itself.[29]

The infinite, exemplary formation "jewgreek is greekjew" accomplishes the erasure in two ways. First, the formation enacts the circular movement of reference and identity without origin and without term: "What, reduced to their simplest reciprocal form, were Bloom's thoughts about Stephen's thoughts about Bloom and Bloom's thoughts about Stephen's thoughts about Bloom's thoughts about Stephen? He thought that he thought that he was a jew whereas he knew that he knew that he was not" (*U*, 15.682). Second, the formation "jewgreek is greekjew" obliterates origin in the infinite, irreversible exit of Stephen and Bloom from the house of bondage, Bloom going first, and Stephen second, the firstness of the first and the secondness of the second both appearing as the function of this originless "order of precedence," of "the order of their common letters." This exemplary relation of Jew and Gentile makes salvation conceivable:

> In what order of precedence, with what attendant ceremony was the exodus from the house of bondage to the wilderness of inhabitation effected?
> Lighted Candle in Stick borne by
> BLOOM
> Diaconal Hat on Ashplant borne by

---

29. Joyce describes this wandering in the following way: "Would the departed never nowhere nohow reappear? Ever he would wander, selfcompelled, to the extreme limit of his cometary orbit, beyond the fixed stars and variable suns and telescopic planets, astronomical waifs and strays, to the extreme boundary of space, passing from land to land, among peoples, amid events. Somewhere imperceptibly he would hear and somehow reluctantly, suncompelled, obey the summons of recall" (*U*, 17.727–28).

STEPHEN
With what intonation *secreto* of what commemorative psalm?
The 113th, *modus peregrinus: In exitu Israël de Egypto: domus Jacob de populo barbaro.*

(*U*, 17.697–98)

The passage places the candlestick, the symbol of the Jewish Temple, in the exemplary relation with the "ashplant," the symbol of the new dispensation. Both Testaments "exit" history into the "wilderness of inhabitation"; they experience redemption in the empty semantics of exemplary "taking." Exemplarity "takes," nullifies, the historical origin and the cultural specificities of ethnic and religious groups. The exemplary formation "jewgreek is greekjew" removes specific origin while giving universal community in return. The exemplary exit, the disappearance (the "taking") from "secular" history (*in exitu*) is compensated by the "gift" of "sacred" history, of the transcendental ground of history, of history in its totality, in this concrete moment of exemplary *exodus*. Exemplary meaning appears in the moment of exit.[30] The chiasmus "jewgreek is greekjew" shows the cosmopolitan condition, the *absence of origin*, to be the minimal condition of universality.

This is to say that the exemplary formation "jewgreek greekjew" presents the condition of universal reading (of reading *Ulysses*) as the cosmopolitan condition. As a formula for universal reading, the example possesses such an expansive mandate by virtue of its tenuous relation to analogical meaning. The example is opposed to the etymological series prefixed by *para-*: paragon, paradigm, parallel. These terms, particularly the term "paradigm," imply an exclusionary moment: para-

---

30. Here we may return to the assertion made earlier that Joyce's novel is "the quasi-Hegelian phenomenology of the spirit." We have seen what interpretive problems arise in connection with the teleological models of *Ulysses* based on Hegel's dynamic conception of totality as the product of the historical process. The additional meaning of the relation between Joyce and Hegel, and the power of the exemplary solution to Joycean hermeneutics, can be brought out with Jacques Derrida's thesis that Joyce is "the most Hegelian of modern novelists" ("Violence and Metaphysics: An Essay on the Thought of Emmanuel Levinas," in *Writing and Difference*, trans. Alan Bass [Chicago, 1978], 153). Derrida explains Joyce's Hegelian affinity in the following manner. The origin of, but also the crisis in, philosophy lies in philosophy's encounter with alterity. The two responses to alterity, the Hellenic and the Hebraic, define the two essential attitudes available to thought. From the two mutually dependent and mutually constitutive accounts of the Other there arises the fundamental undecidability:

digms denote in linguistics the verbal units existing *in potentia*, eligible to enter the syntagmatic chain but, for some reason (for some logic, *logos*), not selected for this particular utterance. In his idiosyncratic analysis of the relations *in absentia* and *in praesentia* during his walk on the Strand ("Proteus"), Stephen contemplates the possibility of preventing this exclusion, of uniting the paradigm with the syntagm in *kata-logos*. Following Stephen's terminology, the language of *Ulysses* can be defined as universality in concrete form, as the synthesis of similarity (spatial placement [*nebeneinander*]) and contiguity (temporal sequence [*nacheinander*]), a synthesis of deduction and induction.

The formation "jewgreek greekjew" overcomes Frank's restrictive formula of a "Dubliner." It overcomes, in other words, the exclusionary logic of language operation by which every syntagmatic chain utilizes only one item from the linguistic paradigm (a Dubliner) while excluding others. Joyce's example grants the items excluded from the syntagmatic chain (Muscovites, Parisians, Londoners) entrance into *Ulysses'* Dublin. The example unifies syntagm and paradigm, metonymy and metaphor, induction and deduction; it transcendentally squares the hermeneutic circle. But here an important distinction must be made. Joyce does not understand universality as the ability to identify the contextual allusions, the merely empirical skill available to Frank's Dubliner or to the erudite reader. The synthesis accomplished in the pages of *Ulysses*, because it is "grounded" in the absence of origin, reveals the universal condition of reading to be independent

---

> Are we Greeks? Are we Jews? But who, we? Are we (not a chronological, but a pre-logical question) *first* Jews or *first* Greeks? And does the strange dialogue between the Jew and the Greek, peace itself, have the form of the absolute, speculative logic of Hegel, the living logic which *reconciles* formal tautology and empirical heterology? Or, on the contrary, does this peace have the form of infinite separation and of the unthinkable, unsayable transcendence of the other? To what horizon of peace does the language which asks this question belong? From whence does it draw the energy of its question? Can it account for the historical *coupling* of Judaism and Hellenism? And what is the legitimacy, what is the meaning of the *copula* in this proposition from perhaps the most Hegelian of modern novelists: "Jewgreek is greekjew. Extremes meet"? (153)

The hesitation of this alternative energizes the circular, inconclusive synthesis of reflexivity, in the mutual gaze of Jew and Gentile: "He thought that he thought that he was a jew whereas he knew that he knew that he knew that he was not" (*U*, 15.682). Derrida adds: "We live in the difference between the Jew and the Greek, which is perhaps the unity of what is called history" (153).

of the specific historical circumstances—or the privilege—of erudition, education, or autochthony.

We have seen that the unity of syntagm and paradigm, of metonymy and metaphor, discloses the ground of history. It follows that exemplary reading embraces the whole of history: the totality of history, conceived spatially, like the Bayeux tapestry, can be grasped only by somebody who has seen *all of it*. However, properly speaking, remembering the totality of history *as* totality implies a position external, both antecedent and final, to the historical process as a whole. Reaching the ground of history is possible only in this external placement; this external placement, however, renders universal reading indifferent to specific historical content—rereading the empirical details of history becomes impossible in principle. Although Frank's model can explain the transitive reading of *Ulysses* as a rereading of particular historical content, it is powerless to describe reading not determined by a specific object, reading as total recollection.

The excessive power to remember everything in general but nothing in particular is disconcerting: it recovers, remembers, in each event, the completeness of history in which this event has now found its place and which has made it historical. This dimension of completeness hidden in every historical event is the condition of possibility for this event's historical character. As such a condition, it cannot be specified by any criterion relevant in the study of history; no mnemonic device can retrieve it from the reader's memory. Rather than retrieving history, this original memory first posits history as a meaningful concept.

The power to remember that dimension of the empirical event that constitutes this event in its historicity is the transcendental power of hypermnesia.[31] Hypermnesia remembers, in each historical event, the unity of space and time without which this event could not have occurred. Hypermnesia remains indifferent to the empirical content of the event, for it first remembers the ground of history, history's condition of possibility. The example's hypermnetic powers enable the reader to hyper-read the syntagmatic chain, to retrieve (*reread*) the substitutions from the inexhaustible paradigm. Because *exemplary*

---

31. "Can one pardon this hypermnesia which *a priori* indebts you, and in advance inscribes you in the book you are reading?" Jacques Derrida, "Two Words for Joyce," in *Post-Structuralist Joyce*, ed. Attridge and Ferrer, 147.

hyper-reading unifies syntagm and paradigm, it is equipped to remember more than is empirically given; it can penetrate history beyond the teleological horizon. It first re-members the ground of history, *historicity as such*—the pure "night" and the pure "mare"; only when it is subjected to a *telos* does history become a repetitive system, the "nightmare."

However, while among the many reading strategies discussed for *Ulysses* exemplarity alone can unite induction and deduction, it can do so only with the essential ambivalence implied in its etymology. Although it establishes proportions between the detail and the historical corpus and, in this relation, seems to assure extrapolation, it remains intransitive, both more and less than this whole. In the asymmetrical relation, in the squared hermeneutic circle, the example easily embraces history's teleological syntax, while its penumbral semantics resists assimilation into history's interior. The asymmetry provokes a radical incalculability. Although individual segments invite extrapolation, extension proves impossible in view of the example's infinite relation to the whole. Instead of bringing us to a familiar place, Ulyssean aesthetics keeps us infinitely returning. The exemplary surplus prevents the closing of the hermeneutic circle *just yet.*

Joyce offers the example as a part of the whole, but the whole collapses whenever the example is "taken." The reader experiences this collapse as the Kantian sublime; he experiences in the example the idea of totality that, properly speaking, is inaccessible to sensory experience. This sublime experience presents *exemplary meaninglessness*, a discontinuity between the isolated detail and the echo of the detail's framing totality. Sampled, the example's contextualizing totality, the whole, is momentarily lost. Only this transcendental loss, however, makes empirical reconstitution possible.[32] Just as the bricolage of *Madame Bovary* attracts the mind with an idea of order but withholds the specific shape of that order, so *Ulysses*, structured on exemplarity,

---

32. Joyce's pursuit, through the arabesque, of the romantic notion of the whole (*die Ganze*), resembles another such effort close in time to historical romanticism. As Maurice Blanchot indicates ("Literature and the Right to Death," in *G*, 21–62), for the Marquis de Sade the momentary loss of totality constitutes the revolutionary gesture par excellence. De Sade investigates the negative as the power of language: language speaks from the totality of relations but, insofar as it speaks from the totality, it annihilates the concrete existent each time it is uttered (see also 41–43). The essence of literature is established, for de Sade and for Joyce, on this need for absolute negation.

implies a universe but denies its clear triangulation. As romantic arabesques, both works expose the mind to transcendental vertigo.[33]

The preceding analyses have identified the potential objects of the example's arabesque reference. We have established that exemplarity describes the conditions for a universal reading of *Ulysses*. We have also seen that the universal character of exemplarity is indispensable, not only for an understanding of history, but above all for history's constitution. Finally, we have established that exemplarity (re-)deems both the reader and history.

We have been able to venture these hypothetical identifications because exemplarity is a structure of referral that, "grotesquely," implies a framing totality. But the essentially ambiguous nature of the example must be accounted for in the most rigorous fashion. On the one hand, as an example of itself, Joyce's exemplarity is a reflexive structure; it is transcendental in strict fidelity to the romantic theory of the novel: in the momentary breakdown of hermeneutic unity, *Ulysses* presences itself, it is an example of itself. Within the romantic formula for the subject's self-presentation, the example aspires to complete generative circularity and self-presence. It is not concerned with determining the meaning of its grounding totality; rather, as an arabesque, it represents the minimal condition of knowledge, for it suspends the mind's hermeneutic operation. *Ulysses*, considered as a systematic network of relations, as a text, is a gigantic *example* of itself. Exemplifying itself, it both suggests and denies an external form of its identity—the formula of universal reading, the constitution of history, and redemption. The arabesque reflexivity of Joyce's exemplarity fails to say not only what order Joyce's catalogue imposes on Bloom's books but also *what objects* are cataloged in this catalog.

On the other hand, Joyce's example also exhibits certain essential limitations in its character as a reflexive structure of self-presentation, for precisely as an arabesque, the example manages to retain the mo-

---

33. To gain a more immediate sense of the exemplary experience, we may return to Goethe's notion of arabesque. Goethe incorporated the experience of the arabesques he had seen during his Italian journey into *Wilhelm Meister's Apprenticeship* (ed. and trans. Eric A. Blackall in cooperation with Victor Lange [New York, 1983], Book 8, Chap. 5), as the "Hall of the Past" (which is also the Hall of the Present and of the Future). The novel's narrator comments: "If we could only describe how admirably everything was arranged, how everything appeared as it should, by combination or contrast, uniformity or variety of color, and thereby produced a perfect as well as clear effect—if we could do that, we would be transporting the reader to a place he would never wish to leave" (332).

ment of external reference to an absent grounding totality. In other words, although the emptiness of the example necessarily transcends any objective figures and inclines towards self-presentation, its arabesque nature preserves the echo of a hypothetical whole and of a potential object thus presented. In sum, in *Ulysses* Joyce explores exemplarity as the last possibility, the most minimal one, of bringing the conceptual and the sensible (to use Kant's terms) into proximity and harmony. Joyce uses exemplarity as a schema for "saving the phenomena" in a systematic structure of description and accounting; as such a "saving" structure, his exemplarity sides with the phenomena and not with the system. However, the example is still a specific option, an elected solution; in *Finnegans Wake* this optionality is nullified in a complete dissolution of example in itself.

Ulysses' arabesque self-presentation becomes visible in the exemplary, intransitive reading. The simultaneous actualization of syntagm and paradigm, the squaring of induction and deduction (which is, in hypermnesia, the operative structure of exemplarity), incapacitates language practice with a Ulyssean *dyslexia.* "Metempsychosis" implies the analogical structure of history—the subject exists in different individuals in recognizable historical cycles. In the exemplary alternative, Molly's "met him pike hoses" injects the surplus of memory into history's analogical grid (*U,* 4.64). In Cixous' words, "The reiteration of the signifier ["metempsychosis"—"met him pike hoses"] . . . comes out of the play that makes the text the producer of its own reflection . . . making it impossible to set up a subject and intentionality, in that it is so difficult to extricate language as such from what language says to itself across the words of the subject."[34]

Leopold and Molly Bloom respond to the dyslexia induced by exemplary reading in different ways. Leopold seeks to bring the infinite mystery of reading to a condition of transparency. First, as he restores the books in his library to their "original" order, he muses on "the necessity of order, a place for everything and everything in its place: the deficient appreciation of literature possessed by females: the incongruity of an apple incuneated in a tumbler and of an umbrella inclined in a closestool: the insecurity of hiding any secret document behind, beneath or between the pages of a book" (*U,* 17.709). Second, Bloom devotes "an entire year to the study of the religious problem and the

---

34. Cixous, "The R(use) of Writing," in *Post-Structuralist Joyce,* ed. Attridge and Ferrer, 27.

summer months of 1882 to square the circle and win that million. Pomegranate! From the sublime to the ridiculous is but a step" (*U*, 15.514–15). "From the sublime to the ridiculous is but a step": the sublimity of the example renders all efforts to read it ridiculous.

Molly, on the other hand, respectfully enters exemplarity's intransitive mechanism. In the passage quoted below, Molly can read the example only in dyslexia, and dyslexia, *a fortiori*, prevents a transitive reading, leaving the example's content out of grasp. Exemplarity frustrates interpretive desire, making it impossible to distinguish the example from what it exemplifies.[35] Above all, Molly is attuned to the exemplary give and take; she knows that the hypermnetic surplus of

---

35. This impossibility is a function of Joyce's understanding of linguistic ideality as *oblique* as opposed to Husserl's *clarity*. At stake here, according to Jacques Derrida (*Edmund Husserl's "Origin of Geometry": An Introduction*, trans. John P. Leavey, Jr. [Lincoln, 1989]), are two ways of understanding the transcendental foundation of comprehensibility. The first option entails the reduction of the "manifold of experience" to a formula untainted by experience (Husserl): "to reduce or impoverish empirical language methodically to the point where its univocal and translatable elements are actually transparent" (103). The second option entails the expansion of the opacity of experience to make it coincide with the very vital chaos of sense-perception (Joyce):

> to repeat and take responsibility for all equivocation itself, utilizing a language that could equalize the greatest possible synchrony with the greatest potential for buried, accumulated, and interwoven intentions within each linguistic atom, each vocable, each word, each simple proposition, in all worldly cultures and their most ingenious forms (mythology, religion, sciences, arts, literature, politics, philosophy, and so forth). And, like Joyce, this endeavor would try to make the structural unity of all empirical culture appear in the generalized equivocation of a writing that, no longer translating one language into another on the basis of their common cores of sense, circulates throughout all languages at once, accumulates their energies, actualizes their most secret consonances, discloses their furthermost common horizons, cultivates their associative syntheses instead of avoiding them, and rediscovers the poetic value of passivity. In short, rather than put it out of play with quotation marks, rather than "reduce" it, this writing resolutely settles itself *within* the *labyrinthian* field of culture "bound" by its own equivocations, in order to travel through and explore the vastest possible historical distance that is now at all possible. (102)

This excellent description refers primarily to *Finnegans Wake*, whose circularity repeats the original instance with its context without loss of totality. But the exemplary relation to totality that operates in *Ulysses* can also be detected in *Finnegans Wake*. In *Ulysses*, Joyce stresses the example's power to save and redeem: exemplarity functions as the condition of possibility for language. *Finnegans Wake*, on the other hand, emphasizes exemplarity's other side, that which is impossible for language to articulate but

the novel offers redemption only because it simultaneously holds something back.³⁶ Stopping short of the pure presentation of *Finnegans Wake*, *Ulysses* disrupts the syntagmatic chain with exemplary intrusions of items buried in the absolute past of the universal paradigm:

> With what success had he attempted direct instruction?
> She followed not all, a part of the whole, gave attention with interest, comprehended with surprise, with care repeated, with greater difficulty remembered, forgot with ease, with misgiving reremembered, repeated with error.
> What system had proved more effective?
> Indirect suggestion implicating self-interest.
> Example?
> She disliked umbrella with rain, he liked woman with umbrella, she disliked new hat with rain, he liked woman with new hat, he bought new hat with rain, she carried umbrella with new hat. (*U*, 17.687)

As an arabesque, *Ulysses* exemplifies its grounding totality. This exemplification, however, is hermeneutically inaccessible. Although (or, perhaps, *because*) Joyce's novel offers *only* examples, the reader will find it impossible to ex-emplify (*ex-emere*, take out) the novel's operative mechanism; and while only exemplary reading of *Ulysses* can redeem us (*re-emere*, take back), it will also prevent us from ever grasping our good fortune in reflection.

---

which founds articulation. In its eternal wakefulness, in its insomnia, *Finnegans Wake* presents the totality of relations, salvation as such, beyond the arabesque, the grotesque, the nightmare, and the awakening. Julia Kristeva (*Powers of Horror: An Essay on Abjection*, trans. Leon S. Roudiez [New York, 1982]) traces the continuity between *Ulysses* and *Finnegans Wake* in terms of the different approaches to the "abject." For Joyce "it is verbal communication, it is the Word that discloses the abject. But at the same time, the Word alone purifies the abject, and that is what Joyce seems to say when he gives back to the masterly rhetoric that his *Work in progress* constitutes full powers against abjection. A single catharsis: the rhetoric of the pure signifier, of music in letters—*Finnegans Wake*" (23).

36. Kristeva (*Powers of Horror*) explains Joyce's subterranean exemplarity as a function of the feminine *abject* by focusing on Molly's monologue: "The writer approaches the hysterical body so that it might speak, so that he might speak, using it as springboard, of what eludes speech and turns out to be the hand to hand struggle of one woman with another, her [Molly's] mother of course, the absolute because primeval seat of the impossible—of the excluded, the outside-of-meaning, the abject Atopia" (22).

V

The Genre of the Neuter in *The Trial*

> What exceeds the system is the impossibility of its failure, and likewise the impossibility of its success. Ultimately nothing can be said of it, and there is a way of keeping still (the lacunary silence of writing), that halts the system, leaving it idle, delivered to the seriousness of irony.
>
> —Maurice Blanchot

At the end of *The Trial* we witness the scene of K.'s execution.[1] K. is momentarily distracted from his plight by a human figure in the distance, probably a woman, who seems to be intrigued by the mysterious spectacle. Last desperate and dark thoughts race through K.'s mind as he attempts to comprehend his fate: "But the hands of one of the partners were already at K.'s throat, while the other thrust the knife into his heart and turned it there twice. With failing eyes K. could still see the two of them, cheek leaning against cheek, immediately before his face, watching the final act. 'Like a dog!' he said: it was as if he meant the shame of it to outlive him" (*T*, 172). The simple simile at the end of Kafka's novel, "like a dog" [*wie ein Hund*] implies, as do all similes, a common frame of reference in which everybody knows how a dog is treated. Still, this reference to universal or communal experience contradicts the theory of metaphor under which Kafka chose to labor. The specific nature of Kafka's theory of metaphor and the un-

---

1. Franz Kafka, *The Trial*, in *The Penguin Complete Novels of Franz Kafka*, trans. Willa and Edwin Muir (New York, 1983). The parallel references in German can be found in Franz Kafka, *Der Prozess*, ed. H. F. Brookes and C. E. Gawne-Cain (London, 1969).

usual sense of the common ground that this theory invokes are defined by the following dilemma: What does a comparison of the type "like a dog" actually say in a language that, as in Kafka's case, is not based on the logic of similarity? Or, more generally, What is the *use* of using a comparison in a system that does not recognize comparative operations?

In any theory of metaphor it is of paramount importance to determine the ground that gives this theory the capacity to generate figurative language. Whatever specific solution a given theory might adopt, it always recognizes the fundamental division into the literal and the figurative dimensions as central to the metaphorical mechanism. Kafka's simile "like a dog," for instance, sets out to describe the humiliating death of K. in terms of insensitive and cruel treatment of dogs. The reader can see what manner of death K.'s lot was because he understands the ground of this simile, the wretched manner of death that is the lot of some dogs. The metaphorical mechanism works under several conditions. It presupposes two entities (a human person, a dog) that in their separate individualities possess a pool of attributes and properties. Moreover, the possibility of comparing the manner of death of a person to the manner of death of a dog rests on the assumption that a person can be put in the place usually reserved for a dog (and *vice versa*). In this substitution, the literal (the human) acquires the properties of the figurative (the animal).

At the heart of the exchange of places and properties lies a metaphysical conception of language. The metaphysical character of this conception is displayed by two moments: first, the premise that the identity of a given item is defined by a set of distinctive properties (the *essence*); and, second, the assumption that language possesses a literal and a figurative level, a circumstance that allows one thing (human) to be understood in terms of (to be transferred to) another (animal). The present analysis will explore the following possibility: while in its verbal form, "like a dog," Kafka's simile conforms to the figurative language made possible by the metaphysical model, it describes a relation between "human" and "animal" in a nonfigurative and nonmetaphysical manner. If this assertion is true, it would imply that Kafka's language violates the two assumptions that underlie the metaphysical understanding of language: the principle of stable properties, which allows for similarity, and the principle of substitution, which permits comparative operations. Rather than comparing K.'s wretched death to the insignificant death of a dog, the simile "like a dog" describes the network of language as a series of similes capped by a final term, "dog," standing for *insignificance as such*. This insignificance, this "shame," the absence of metaphysically defined properties, terminates everything by infinitely "outliving" it.

If Kafka's metaphor violates the first assumption—the principle of stable properties—then the "dog" is not a dog. In that case, what is it? On the face of it, the negation leads to a dead end—the absence of the dog. But it may be that this absence of the dog is still the result of the metaphysical conspiracy; if the properties of an entity are negated, then this entity simply ceases to exist. To escape metaphysics, negation itself must be placed outside of the metaphysical logic. The possibility of such placement emerges in Maurice Blanchot's discussion of literary language. In literature a cat *can* metamorphose into a dog:

> Everyday language calls a cat a cat, as if the living cat and its name were identical. . . . Even if the word excludes the existence of what it designates, it still refers to it through the thing's nonexistence. . . . To name the cat is, if you like, to make it into a non-cat, a cat that has ceased to exist . . . but this does not mean one is making it into a dog, or even a non-dog. That is the primary difference between common language and literary language. The first accepts that . . . the word restores to the cat all the certainty it had on the level of existence. . . . But literary language is made of uneasiness. . . . Its only interest in a thing is in the meaning of the thing, its absence, and it would like to attain this absence absolutely . . . to grasp in its entirety the infinite movement of comprehension. What is more, it observes that the word cat is not only the nonexistence of the cat, but a nonexistence made *word*, that is, a completely determined and objective reality. . . . Thus is born the image that does not directly designate the thing, but rather, what the thing is not; it speaks of a dog instead of a cat. (*G*, 44–45)

Blanchot describes a certain moment in the metaphysical theory of language that escapes this theory even as it submits to its operation. Every name differs from the thing it names: when I say "cat," the real cat is absent from language. The name makes the thing present through its negation, its absence. Hence the possibility of non-metaphysical language is already contained in the metaphysical mechanism of language. Negation attends upon all naming and constitutes the meaning of the thing *in language.*

Indeed, for Blanchot negation can become the sole "content" of language, as the absence that makes all naming possible. In this model, language, instead of finding a name for another name ("dog" for "man"), seeks to attain the thing as it negatively exists in language, to attain the dog as a word, so that the dog is "like a dog." It can be seen how the alternative understanding of the negation that operates in language can also destabilize the second assumption of the metaphysical theory of language. Instead of stable properties and identities, language uses the negation of properties as the condition of presentation of a thing in language. Even the literal presence of a dog in language presupposes a negation of this dog's properties. In some fundamental way, the literal level of traditional rhetoric itself can first emerge only in this process of negation, the non-metaphysical negation brings the dog to language, for by being negated the real dog becomes language, it becomes the word "dog." The simile "like a dog" is Kafka's metaphor for the real world's coming to language in negation.

It follows that Kafka's rhetoric is driven, not by the optional transposition of the literal ground into figurative forms, for such a simple operation would presuppose stable properties; rather, the simile "like a dog" expresses the initial movement in which an object comes to presence in language by being negated as a thing, by being made absent. Kafka's metaphors do not follow the movement of representation in which the literal and the figurative meanings operate on already constituted sets of properties; rather, they follow the infinite movement in which the properties of objects are stripped away for presentation in language.

The following analysis will seek to trace the genealogy of Kafka's nonmetaphysical metaphorics to the romantic theory of the novel. This genealogy is composed of several distinctive stages. Kafka frees his language from metaphysical parameters by eroding the logic of properties and by arresting the movement of substitution. First, in place of the properties operative in language, Kafka introduces the absence of properties in general—the logic of the neuter. It must be stressed, however, that the neuter underwriting Kafka's language is not a middle value lodged between two opposite terms. In the genre of the neuter, an item refers to itself, as this item's movement towards its identity in language. Hence Kafka's nonmetaphysical language is not distinguished by a mere absence of properties but by the *becoming proper* of properties, the item's arrival into its own identity not defined by extrinsic properties but by the item's "essence."

This movement towards one's proper identity, however, exceeds the boundaries of metaphysically understood representation. As the presence of self-sameness, Kafka's language achieves presentation, it effectuates the presence of the proper in its proper form as its shame, its inessence. It is here that the nonmetaphysical interests of Kafka's literary enterprise can be articulated with the strategic interests of the romantic theory of the novel. Kafka's presentation of the self as such—discussed here in the framework of Maurice Blanchot's *récit*—coincides with the romantic postulate to achieve the presentation of the subject in the form adequate to this subject. Insofar as it rigorously achieves the presentation of the subject in the reflective movement that generates itself as its proper content, Kafka's nonmetaphysical language of the *récit* faithfully conforms to romanticism's original project.

Besides realizing the romantic theory of the novel, the *récit* also brings out the extreme possibility of such realization. As it effectuates the presence of the subject to itself, the *récit* also demonstrates in a concrete fashion the intractable surplus necessarily implied by such presentation. What emerges in the movement of the proper towards itself is the excessive presentation that romanticism encountered in the theory of the fragment. The identity of the self with the idea of this self, rather than producing a transparent overlapping, yields a moment of identity that cannot be absorbed in the speculative formulas of identity of the type $A = A$. As it realizes its dream of self-sameness in the *récit*, romanticism arrives at the extreme possibility contained in the question of the subject; conceived as identity, and accomplished strictly according to this requirement, the self-sameness of the subject exceeds the theory that helped produce it. The initial formulation, the romantic principle of identity stating that "every theory of the novel must itself be a novel," yields, now, the situation of romantic equivocity in which the self-identical subject *lies outside its theory* as its exergue. Let us now retrace the steps of this genealogy in greater detail.

The nonmetaphysical possibility opened up by Kafka in the metaphysical mechanism of language has provoked many critical commentaries. However, while criticism's range of response has been defined by the horizon of this essential option between metaphysical and nonmetaphysical senses of language, criticism has all too frequently stopped short of broaching the nonmetaphysical possibility. Instead, the discussion of Kafka's metaphorics has opted to present the exhaustion of the metaphysical potential of language as an extreme, border case of the metaphysical mechanism.

The theories of Kafka's metaphorics based on the orthodox metaphysical premises assume that the metaphorical dimension of language depends on a solid ground of literality that can never be absorbed in the figurative escapade. The assumption of a solid premetaphoric foundation guides authors like Walter Sokel and Günther Anders, who seek the stable metaphorical level of language in language itself. Anders, for instance, maintains that Kafka, unlike Nietzsche or Wagner, does not create a private mythology: "He does not invent images, but uses those which already exist, taking their visual content, their 'real' meaning and scrutinizing it under a microscope." Conceding that "even the smallest and apparently abstract parts of everyday speech consist of metaphors," Anders envisions Kafka's style as a revival of "some forgotten visual or literal significance in a word or phrase."[2] Sokel emphasizes the archaeological thrust of this approach in his thesis that Kafka reenacts metaphors buried in language, "not only in the German language in which he wrote but also in the universal symbolism of prerational thought."[3]

An opposite thrust guides those accounts of Kafka's metaphor that present the dissolution of the metaphysical model of language as an erosion of metaphysics. Beda Allemann, for example, argues that Kafka's language does not rely on a solid ground for figurative transposition but that, instead, this ground is produced by the figural application of language: paradoxically, rather than enabling metaphor, the literal level issues from the metaphorical transfer.[4] Allemann illustrates this notion of Kafkan metaphor with the parable "Prometheus":

> There are four legends concerning Prometheus:
> According to the first he was clamped to a rock in the Caucasus for betraying the secrets of the gods to men, and the gods sent eagles to feed on his liver, which was perpetually renewed.
> According to the second Prometheus, goaded by the pain of the tearing beaks, pressed himself deeper and deeper into the rock until he became one with it.
> According to the third his treachery was forgotten in the course of

---

2. Günther Anders, *Franz Kafka*, trans. A. Steer and A. K. Thorlby (New York, 1960), 45, 44. Anders offers a classical formulation of this view: "In the absence of that community of belief which gives birth to and sustains symbols, all that Kafka has to work with is the common possession of language; for even he, the outsider, has this at his disposal still, in all its range and depth" (43).

3. Walter H. Sokel, *Franz Kafka* (New York, 1966), 45.

4. Beda Allemann, "Metaphor and Anti-Metaphor," in *Interpretation: The Poetry of Meaning*, ed. Stanley Romaine Hopper and David L. Miller (New York, 1967), 103–23, hereinafter cited parenthetically by page number in the text.

thousands of years, forgotten by the gods, the eagles, forgotten by himself.
According to the fourth everyone grew weary of the meaningless affair. The gods grew weary, the eagles grew weary, the wound closed wearily.
There remained the inexplicable mass of rock. The legend tried to explain the inexplicable. As it came out of a substratum of truth it had in turn to end in the inexplicable.[5]

The four-stage attrition of the myth, an attrition leading to the "inexplicable mass of rock" in which Prometheus himself disappears, defines the impoverishment of the traditional treatment of the simile. Poetry has eroded metaphor and has attained what Allemann calls the "absolute metaphor," a transfer of meaning apparently without any figurality (115).

While the two accounts of Kafka's tropology proceed from opposite assumptions, they reach the same conclusion, insofar as they both remain within the metaphysical horizon. In these accounts language is built on a firm ground of meaning. In the first account, the original ground precedes language and founds its operation, while in the second it denotes a metaphysically "inexplicable" entity that, nevertheless, becomes absorbed by the metaphysical mechanism that produced it. Language already presupposes in its structure a solidity that only later allows for expressive molding, or else the solid "inexplicable mass of rock" denotes the terminus, the result, of a process in which language has exhausted all possibilities of transfer and is no longer sensitive to similes. Both approaches view the erosion as a valuable aesthetic innovation, as a terminal moment of metaphorical language that marks "the crisis of the modern world." The metaphysical horizon itself, however, remains intact.

Kafka's simile *"like a dog"* covers the distance of this development but is irreducible to its possibilities. In order to mark off this difference it is first necessary to make more explicit the intimate connection between the figural use of language and language's metaphysical structure. The parallels between the nonmetaphysical implications of Kafkan metaphor and the exhaustion of metaphysical possibilities in philosophy can be brought out with the help of Allemann's model of modern metaphor as reference to an inexplicable meaning. As Allemann shows, these parallels are genealogical in nature (105). Allemann locates the origin of the conception of language pushed to the edge of metaphysics—neither literal nor figural—in Nietzsche's

---

5. Franz Kafka, "Prometheus," trans. Willa and Edwin Muir, in *The Complete Stories*, ed. Nahum R. Glatzer (New York, 1976), 432.

famous critique of classical tropology in "On Truth and Lying in an Extra-Moral Sense."[6] In the essay Nietzsche argues that figurative language stands only at a third remove from the original metaphorical transaction, after the transposition of sensory data into an image and then of the image into language. Nietzsche suggests that in this economy the literal level is derived from the metaphorical level. He speaks of *pia fraus*, the higher truth of poetic deception, to indicate that the truth of language rests on the figurative, rather than on the literal, dimension.

But Nietzsche's account of the origin of language, as it merely reverses the order of priority between the literal and the figurative levels, loses sight of yet another possibility of arranging the relation between literal and figurative aspects of language. As Allemann notes, a Kafkan parable is a text without any local metaphors. While a vague "aura" of metaphor hovers over the text, the reader is unable to identify any verbal content as the literal ground that would be suitable for originating the process of metaphorical interpretation. In Allemann's exegesis, Kafka's "inexplicable mass of rock" not only does not rely on a transposed meaning, but it also destabilizes the very nature of metaphor as a bridge, or transfer. First, Allemann says, the "absolute metaphor" is a contradiction because metaphors assert relative comparisons. And second, since, as Allemann writes, "metaphors are based upon relations the reader has to know beforehand, either through his own experience or through the literary conventions familiar to him ... [a] text like Kafka's prose parables ... which has torn down the bridges of metaphor, necessarily becomes a metaphor whose only frame of reference is itself" (114). The rock of the mountains will resist any *tertium comparationis*, for the inexplicable cannot be compared to anything, not even to itself (*cf.* 113).

The eroding movement of the parable about Prometheus characterizes Kafka's antimetaphorical style in general. By avoiding local metaphors, Kafka creates, according to Allemann, texts that "become a kind of metaphor themselves; this new metaphor, however, is without a definite level of meaning outside of it, a level on which its 'real,' nonfigurative, *eigentliche* meaning may be found" (113–14). The Kafkan text eliminates all metaphor; it becomes an unanalyzable construct no longer relatable to the duality of figural and literal levels. Impertinent to the rhetorical opposition, the new metaphor hovers

---

6. Sander L. Gilman, Carole Blair, and David J. Parent, eds. and trans., *Friedrich Nietzsche on Rhetoric and Language* (New York, 1989), 246–57.

infinitely over the dialectic of literal and rhetorical expression as the parable of this dialectic. Clasped by the parabolic arch, the text is both the literal ground of the parable and its transposed referent.[7]

The transformation of the metaphorical operation, from an operation on the solid ground of literality to the production of an all-encompassing figure of this ground, duplicates on the level of metaphorics the transformations that have taken place in the strictly philosophical sphere of metaphysics. In Plato the meaning of sensible reality was grounded in the ideal realm; in Nietzsche the relation was inverted, and the ideal meaning was grounded in the sensible. As it ends the metaphysical possibilities of thought, Nietzsche's "inverted Platonism" announces the need for thinking a different relation between the "visible" and the "invisible." Kafka's metaphor solicits interpretations that would more or less adequately reflect this new economy. Rhetorical tropes, which are based on a metaphysical *Entscheidung* (decision), operate in Kafka without (outside) this metaphysical frame; they hover between the figurative and the literal terminus of the simile in an endless suspension of the metaphysical poles of language without ever accomplishing the meta-phor. The metaphysical *Ent-scheidung* (de-cision) provokes the infinite transfer; it urges the reader both continuously to "go over" and constantly to "give it up": *gehe hinüber* and *gibs auf*.[8]

The parabolic relation between the literal and the figurative dimensions has serious implications for the metaphysical model of language. Having annulled all mediating similarity, the new economy makes metaphorical speech impossible in principle. However, if the stable ground of properties and the principle of their substitution are no longer in place, what is the meaning of the simile *"like a dog"*? If speech now parabolically hovers over the literal and the figurative di-

---

7. Criticism has reflected this shift in the conception of Kafka's metaphor—from the metaphysical schematization (into the literal and the transposed meaning) to the suspension of metaphor and of its metaphysical foundation—in a variety of ways. Allemann replaces the dialectic of literal and figurative meanings with their *"Antithetik"* as more appropriate for Kafka's discourse (Beda Allemann, "Kafka: Von den Gleichnissen," *Zeitschrift für deutsche Philologie*, LXXXIII, Special Issue 3 [1964], 102). Kafka's parables are not parables, writes Allemann, in the sense that the phrase determines the essence of a parable as *not being* one (*cf.* 99). Marthe Robert writes that Kafka "incessantly incarnates all the possible lies in order to reveal, on the black bottom of appearances, the negative truth" (*Kafka* [Paris, 1960], 80–81), hereinafter cited parenthetically by page number in the text. For Walter Benjamin, Kafka's parables, ruled by "diathesis," "are *more* than parables" (Walter Benjamin, "Some Reflections on Kafka," in *Illuminations*, 144).

8. "Go Over!" appears in Kafka's "On Parables," in *Parables and Paradoxes* (Bilingual ed.; New York, 1961), 11. "Give It Up!" in *CS*, 456.

mensions but is not identified with either of them, what is speech? What is that hovering itself?

To answer this question it is necessary to recognize that the hovering of Kafka's self-sufficient parable has emerged as a direct consequence of the erasure of the logic of properties. The nonmetaphysical implications of the erasure are forcefully presented by Charles Bernheimer in his analysis of Kafka's parable "On Parables" ("Von den Gleichnissen").[9] Speaking of parables in terms of parables abolishes the metaphysical difference that organizes tropology, for as Bernheimer notes, "the goal of the *Gleichnis* is to promote *gleich-werden,* the dissolution of conscious difference into the self-expression of words" (49). Bernheimer presents the loss of articulation in the figure of the "metatextuality" of Kafka's self-referential parable. The "assimilation" of parable by parabolic economy brings about the merger of both levels. Since the parable's meaning cannot be distinguished from the process of its narration, the metaphysical difference is abolished, and the parable begins to speak without relying on the metaphysical distinctions that underlie language. As the aestheticization of logical relations in language, Kafka's parables, says Bernheimer, "parabolize" their relation to the parabolic operation; hence, if there are any metaphors in Kafka's language, they were not selected in a conscious process of comparing properties but occurred impersonally and involuntarily in the aleatory process of blind betting (49).

Like Bernheimer, Allemann interprets the loss of linguistic properties in Kafka in terms of aestheticization of logic. In the absence of qualities and properties that make metaphorical attribution possible, the aesthetic *translatio,* writes Allemann, occurs simply between words, under the sheer pressure of their physical proximity: "Two words stand in a relationship to each other; they exert a mutual influence, and this kind of *translatio* and correlation opens up a dimension in which an understanding of this verbal structure becomes possible" (120). The movement of figurality based on similar properties becomes a tentative transfer, what Nietzsche calls a "stammering translation" [*andeutende Übertragung*] (*Nietzsche on Rhetoric,* 252). Instead of a movement *of* interpretation that chooses among objectively preexistent options, Nietzsche posits a movement *to* interpretation that enacts and contains interpretation exclusively as this movement.

9. Charles Bernheimer, *Flaubert and Kafka: Studies in Psychopoetic Structure* (New Haven, 1982), 45–55, hereinafter cited parenthetically by page number in the text. This study is particularly important as an expansion of Allemann's thesis about Kafkan antimetaphor because it refines Allemann's analysis of Nietzsche's essay.

At this point it appears that Kafka's hovering metaphor has ceased to perform a strictly tropological function and has, instead, assumed a postmetaphysical and posthermeneutic role. Lacking the literal level on which a figurative meaning could be erected, the reader no longer encounters a preexistent and constituted entity called "text" whose meaning would be available for interpretation, but an entity whose very nature as a text needs to be interpreted in order to become a text. In other words, the reader must perform an act of interpretation to decide, simultaneously and reciprocally, first, that Kafka's text is a metaphor and, second, that Kafka's intended metaphor is a text. The metaphorical operation, irreducible to local intratextual moments, embraces the text as a whole in its nature as a text. This metaphor interprets that which lies in front of the reader as a text; it metaphorizes the literal level (reading matter) as the only transposed content of its operation, and it comes into its own, it "itself becomes a metaphor," in the figure of text.

Reading, in other words, constructs textuality as the locus in which interpretation will begin to make sense. Kafka completes Nietzsche's thought and shifts it from the fringes of metaphysics into the extrametaphysical ("extra-moral" or "non-moral"—*aussermoralisch*) arena: the textuality generated in the self-reference of metaphor is no longer a solid entity subjected to metaphorical transfer but the very essence of metaphor in a situation where metaphor has ceased to function metaphysically. What is produced in the metaphorical relation once the metaphysical dispensation has been rendered ineffective is not the tropological transfer from one meaning to another but textuality, or text, as the fabric (texture) in which (a) meaning will be placed.

This structure radically changes the relations between the two levels that the metaphysical theory of metaphor schematizes into the literal and figurative dimensions. The structure also affects the metaphysical schematization in philosophy between the sensual and the ideal realms. In its choice of the category of "text," the Western philosophical and literary tradition intended to denote a container of possible interpretations in accordance with the metaphysical model. The new text, however, no longer opens itself up to literal and figural interpretations but only solicits the question of its identity. For Kafka and Nietzsche the term *text* denotes the reflective act in which meaning is generated as the infinite identification of something as text. The nonmetaphysical category of "textuality" is a circular and reciprocal structure in which metaphor interprets something as a text and in which text—the woven texture—is a metaphor for this process of interpretation (or else the interpretation of this process of metaphorization).[10]

Having collapsed metaphor and the metaphysical scheme that underwrites it, Kafka's texts can no longer be subsumed in the hermeneutic model of understanding. For example, the nonmetaphysical character of Kafka's language makes it impossible to develop the unity of *The Trial* in the process of hermeneutic synthesis of parts and whole. By giving the parable "Before the Law" the ambiguous status of both an autonomous piece and a part of *The Trial*, Kafka proposes the notion of the whole as a field of interaction of two components that interchangeably encompass each other. As mutual containers, the novel and the parable eliminate any clear sense of externality that would encompass them both; rather, they "contain" the outside exclusively in their relation to each other as the potential of one element to be enclosed by the other.[11]

The immeasurable, infinite totality implied in this model prevents simple empirical judgments concerning the status of *The Trial* as an unfinished work. The infinite relation of containment enacted between the parable and the novel posits the completion, the idea of totality for this particular work, not as an external measure, but as the infinite internal determination of Kafka's novel *as a novel*, solely in relation to the parable. In the infinite relation, *The Trial* is an intrinsi-

10. Shimon Sandbank, in his article "Action as Self-Mirror: On Kafka's Plots" (*Modern Fiction Studies*, XVII [1971], 21–29), suggests that Kafka's tautological expressions and situations have none of a traditional tautology's "normal logical inevitability." Because Kafka's stories, like mathematical strings in Gödel's theorem, mirror themselves parabolically, Kafka's statements are both tautological and informative, both true and false (*cf.* 25–26). Allemann ("Metaphor and Anti-Metaphor," in *Interpretation*, ed. Hopper and Miller, 111) observes that Kafka uses similes only immediately to acknowledge them in phrases like "but this is only an image"; his "as if" performs a similar, metalinguistic, function.

11. The question is, Does *The Trial* provide the hermeneutic home for the parable, or does the parable represent the novel? According to Henry Sussman (*Franz Kafka: Geometrician of Metaphor* [Madison, Wisc., 1979], 20, hereinafter cited parenthetically by page number in the text), "Freedom has not been wrested from the context of the novel. The parable's a priori freedom has instead submitted the novel to a retrospective ordering; and, in the process, has determined a place for the parable. The framework has crystallized only too late around the hole in the parable—a space it can then only leave empty." Rainer Nägele ("Kafka and the Interpretive Desire," in *CCP*, 24–25) examines the parable's contextuality in the framework of its metonymic determination, concluding that fragment and whole are bound to each other only tentatively.

cally unfinished work (the order of chapters is not definitive, and several chapters still remained to be written)[12] so that one can construe a finite conception of its meaning (in the concrete arrangement of chapters by Max Brod).

Neither can the new economy be reduced to the purely formal models of unity offered by functional or geometrically regular patterns. For instance, the physical proximity of rooms to the "main" room does not entail any functional plan, architectural or otherwise. The room adjacent to the main room (*das Nebenzimmer*) in *The Trial*'s opening scene, solely by virtue of its proximity to something else, implies an infinity—not only an endless series of other rooms, but the possibility of otherness visible in the hole (*die Lücke, die Tür*) through which the room's finitude escapes into some vast expanse (*T,* 9). Similarity and contiguity fail to support the organic and the formal conceptions of the meaningful whole.

Finally, the nonmetaphysical character of Kafka's metaphorics is responsible for Kafka's unusual relation to literary tradition.[13] Literary tradition is a form of language to the extent that it presupposes similarity among successive authors who create and perpetuate it. As we have seen, Kafkan metaphor systematically puts its literal ground into question and is unable to recover the literal meaning that precedes it. With the removal of similarity, Kafka can neither follow a predecessor nor bring forth a successor; he can neither inaugurate nor belong to a literary tradition identifiable in positive stylistic terms of trends, movements, and schools.[14] Kafkan metaphor makes it impossible to

---

12. The editorial history of Kafka's *Nachlass*, particularly of *The Trial*, is indeed educational. The ordering of the novel's chapters has been revolutionized, after Brod's first attempt, by Herman Uyttersprot's provocative article "*The Trial*: Its Structure" (*Franz Kafka Today*, ed. Angel Flores and Homer Swander [Madison, Wisc., 1958], 127–44). The ramifications of this proposal have been discussed by Dieter P. Lotze in "One Commentator's Despair: Notes on the Structure of Kafka's *The Trial*," *Journal of Modern Literature*, VI (1977), 389–97.

13. Alan Udoff's question about what constitutes a complete text, a question he raises in his analyses of "The Problem of Our Laws" ("Before the Question of the Laws: Kafkan Reflections," in *CCP*, 178–213), has posed perhaps the most serious challenge to date to Max Brod's role in the process of editing Kafka's works. The essay subjects contextuality to a close scrutiny from the point of view of Kafka's relation to canonical works, a question asked in light of the parable's own imagery of the Law. Udoff persuasively argues that the attitude of supplication adopted by "the Man from the Country" expresses Kafka's position in relation to the "door" to literary tradition.

14. The acknowledged "greats" in Kafka's private reading: Kierkegaard (briefly), Goethe, Kleist, Flaubert, Dostoevsky. Robert Martin Adams (*Strains of Discourse: Studies in Literary Openness* [Ithaca, 1958], 168) draws an analogy between Kafka and Swift

determine tradition as a linguistic construct, to determine it in language, and to determine it *for literature*. In this sense, Kafka is inimitable; his work bears no relation to external, "similar," instances of writing, and neither is self-identity, resemblance with itself, this work's constitutive relation.[15]

To develop this assertion concerning Kafka's relation to tradition it may be helpful to summarize Jorge Luis Borges' analysis of Kafkan tradition in his short meditation "Kafka and His Precursors."[16] Borges claims that he "could recognize [Kafka's] voice, or his practices, in texts from diverse literatures and periods" (L, 199). For Borges the chronologically anterior texts resembling Kafka's style enter Kafkan

---

in their use of animals to achieve the effect of defamiliarization, reflecting a generally accepted view that Kafka works from within eighteenth-century rationalism (cf. Theodor Adorno ["Notes on Kafka," in *Prisms*, trans. Samuel and Shierry Weber (London, 1967), 268] on the eighteenth-century sources of the genre of parable). Alberto Spaini ("The Trial," in *The Kafka Problem*, ed. Angel Flores [New York, 1946], 143–44) finds it hard to identify a literary niche for Kafka in the contemporary German tradition, suggesting Max Brod's *Tycho Brahe*, Meyrink's *Green Face*, and Martin Buber's Jewish mysticism. Robert (*Kafka*, 85) argues that Kafka has a preference for minor genres, only indirectly linked with artistic expression, subverting the power of the logic of similarity in the process of tradition-formation and canonical fossilization. Finally, any study of Kafka's stylistic singularity should take into account Roland Barthes' analysis of the "death of the author" in terms of the erosion of stylistic registers—ideological, authorial, social wisdom, etc. ("The Death of the Author," in *Image-Music-Text*, 142).

15. This is the primary sense of Robert's formula: "Virtuose de l'imitation, Kafka est à la fois inimitable et 'inclassable', si fort qu'on soit tenté de l'imiter et de lui chercher dans l'histoire littéraire une place qui lui convienne vraiment" [Virtuoso of imitation, Kafka is at the same time inimitable and "unclassifiable," so strong that one would be tempted to imitate him and to find for him in literary history a truly fitting place] (*Kafka*, 85; translation mine). Considered in relation to tradition, Kafka resembles the dog from his story "Investigations of a Dog" (cf. 78). The dog, as Robert notes, ponders the world in a solitude elected freely, for his choice of solitude lies in the very nature of dogs: "Le Chien ne peut pas rompre avec l'espéce canine, il est solitaire, mais à la manière des chiens, son choix de la solitude est encore une manière d'être chien" [the Dog cannot break with the canine species; it is solitary, but in the manner typical for dogs, its choice of solitude is one more way of being a dog] (135; translation mine).

16. Jorge Luis Borges, "Kafka and His Precursors," in *L*, 199–201. Borges' list of Kafka-like authors includes: Zeno of Elea, Han Yu, "a prose writer of the ninth century" (L, 199), two parables by Kierkegaard, Robert Browning's poem "Fears and Scruples," a story by Léon Bloy, and a story by Lord Dunsany. It should be added that in the Borgesian theory of Kafkan tradition the similarity of style obtains between an individual writer and Kafka, but it does not necessarily obtain among the writers themselves: "If I am not mistaken, the heterogeneous pieces I have enumerated resemble Kafka; if I am not mistaken, not all of them resemble each other" (L, 201).

tradition because Kafka retroactively brings out in these works those features that without Kafka's centering impact would have remained imperceptible: "If Kafka had never written a line, we would not perceive this quality [of Kafka's echo]" (*L*, 201). Kafka retroactively constitutes the history of these texts. As Borges concludes, "Every writer *creates* his own precursors. His work modifies our conception of the past, as it will modify the future" (*L*, 201).

Conspicuously lacking in Borges' short treatise on Kafka and in his famous theory of literary and historical hermeneutics presented in "Pierre Menard, Author of the *Quixote*," is the attempt to specify what it is about this particular author (Kafka, Cervantes) that permits the conceptualization of the hermeneutics of rereading as such? (While Borges does explain the special status of Cervantes in literary history, his commentary is intended to establish his transcendental *similarity*; in the case of Kafka, however, we are after transcendental *difference*.) In the present case, why is the "precursor principle" most transparently present in Kafka, rather than in, say, Robert Musil, Marcel Proust, or Gertrude Stein? In other words, what makes Kafka paradigmatic in the formulation of literary-historical networks of precursorial affinities?

Borges' original insight can be further elaborated in the context of Kafka's unique conception of metaphor as no longer based on similarity and metaphysics. This erasure of similarity is well explained by Allemann's reading of Kafka's parable "Prometheus." In closing in upon itself, the rock on which Prometheus has suffered swallows the victim, the wound, *and the subsequent readings of the myth's significance*; it erodes the series of hermeneutic attempts that Kafka deploys (everything grows "weary"). Beyond signifying a punctual moment in literary history (as Borges has it), beyond representing an individual interpretive consciousness that determines a tradition of one's precursors, Kafka—Allemann's reading would seem to imply—disappears into the very sequence that he has brought to life. The paradigmatic author has become yet another moment in the life of a transpersonal, anonymous sequence.

The uniquely Kafkan potential (or danger) of this process consists in the disappearance of the paradigm—which confers order on historical flux—into the very order that it has effectively brought forth. Kafka develops the contours of this structure of disappearance in a story entitled "The Cares of a Family Man" (*CS*, 427–29). "At first glance it [the creature Odradek] looks like a flat star-shaped spool for thread," but "it is not only a spool, for a small wooden crossbar sticks out of the middle of the star" (*CS*, 428). The father of the story's "family" is concerned that the peripheral existence of Odradek does not conform to the cycle of generational succession. The father worries that Odradek simply will not die:

> I ask myself, to no purpose, what is likely to happen to him? Can he possibly die? Anything that dies has had some kind of aim in life, some kind of activity, which has worn out; but that does not apply to Odradek. Am I to suppose, then, that he will always be rolling down the stairs, with ends of thread trailing after him, right before the feet of my children, and my children's children? He does no harm to anyone that one can see; but the idea that he is likely to survive me I find almost painful. (CS, 429)

The creature "Odradek" specifies the manner of a given author's presence in tradition as that of "survival": a Kafkan "survival" (the "outliving" from *The Trial*'s final scene) determines an author's distinctive marks to be in excess of this author's empirical and literary biography. "Odradek" defines the mode in which the paradigmatic author, having retrospectively constituted his precursors, enters this group as one of its members—becoming, in effect, *one of his own precursors*. The anticipation of an author *by this very author* points to a meltdown of the conception of literary tradition centered around the paradigmatic author; the relationship between Kafka as the originator of his tradition and Kafka as a member of the tradition thus originated is simultaneously that of self-origination and self-effacement.[17]

17. As Rüdiger Bubner has argued ("Über einige Bedingungen gegenwärtigen Ästhetik," *Neue Hefte für Philosophie*, V [1975]), canons—the backbone of tradition—have so far been constructed primarily along two avenues (40–41; 62). A representative work is selected as an *organon* from among the existing works (*e.g.*, Goethe), in "a hypostatizing canonization of the 'classic' work"; secondly, and more basically, each "classic" work is selected for its conformity with the truth-concept (fragments translated by Jürgen Naeher in his article "Philosophical Concepts in Literary Criticism," in *Literary Criticism and Philosophy: Yearbook of Comparative Literature*, ed. Joseph Strelka, X [University Park, Pa., 1983], 104–105). The former method invites vicious circularity (a historical work defines a paradigm for all historical works), while the latter subjects the literary canon to an extrinsic criterion borrowed from philosophy. In exposing circularity and methodological externality in canon-formation, and in thus highlighting an absolute gap between the canon and the empirical series, Bubner shows that tradition cannot be based on truth or *organon*. This impossibility of framing continuity in syllogistical modes suggests, not only that the continuity of tradition is expressed metaphorically, but that it is *a metaphorical expression*, *a simile*. Because the cohesion of tradition rests on figural, unmotivated constructs, the truth of every canon originates in tropology—every new work "belongs" to tradition only and necessarily in a manner of speaking.

What distinguishes the efficacy of "Odradek" from that of Borgesian retroactive hermeneutics and from Borges' solution in Menardian hermeneutics is that "Odradek," in his (its?) capacity to "outlive" the author, denotes not only Kafka's individual properties of style (which are used to identify Kafka *as Kafka*), and not only those features of Kafka that help identify *his precursors*, but, most centrally, a pool of impersonal features (although derived from the historical writer called Kafka) useless for any positive identification whatsoever. This pool, which Stanley Corngold calls "the surplus-subject," regulates the relation between Kafka and his precursors without being itself assimilated to either pole of this transaction.[18]

It is conceivable that precisely this moment of the loss of distinctive properties, of "impersonality," motivates Borges in his choice of Kafka for delineating the theory of literary precursors. Borges can erect the fable about Kafka and his literary precursors only on Kafka's figure of "outliving": tradition is sustained only from within the life-giving domain of survival secured by "Odradek." Borges may be saying that Kafka can be properly honored only by a writer who has understood the Kafkan mode of precursorship and that only those possessing this understanding (Borges, for example) can legitimately (*i.e.*, impersonally) continue Kafka's literary enterprise. This is not merely to reiterate Kafka's "originality" but to emphasize that, while a Kafkan tradition is a self-regulating mechanism, it at the same time has not been set in motion by similarity. It has no identifiable originating rationale—it simply does not exist.

As he speaks the language of "allusive transference" and "stammering translation," the language in which properties are no longer proper nor properly his, Kafka does not *use* language but brings language to explicit articulation. Instead of saying something in conformity with the metaphysical structure of language, Kafka says the saying itself. The former kind of speech may be called transitive: it presupposes the possibility of drawing comparisons, of establishing analogies, and of precise denotation of objects and conditions. Here speech accomplishes itself outside of itself. The latter type of speech, on the other hand, is intransitive: it "asserts" the relation of speech to speech. Intransitive speech does not assert relations among objects based on similarity but, as Marthe Robert writes, "alludes" to the nature of speech *as speech*

---

18. Stanley Corngold, *The Fate of the Self*, 165.

(*Kafka*, 110–36). Robert claims that, whenever he speaks, Kafka "alludes," not to a solid literal ground, but to the nature of language itself as "a manner of speaking" [*façon de parler*] (132). In allusion Kafka uses language, not to effect reference or communication, but to bring pure speech to itself. He alludes to language as repetition of the totality of language.[19]

In Robert's analysis, Kafka recites linguistic icons, the set phrases of language, its habits of thought (good and bad), prejudice as well as folk wisdom. However, while Kafka may, like Nietzsche, see language as an impenetrable network of expressions linked by the mirror of now forgotten similarity, and while, in the manner described by Allemann, Sokel, and Anders, he may be deriving a ground of meaningfulness from the semantic core of language, he is also attacking—as Robert argues—language's function of naming. But rather than restoring language to innocence by shearing off the crust of clichés, Kafka changes the denomination of things by baptising them with forgotten names (*à l'aide de noms anciens, de nomes désaffectés, usés* [135–36]). Kafka's speech alludes to the forgotten truth of the totality of language, whether the purity of the individual's speech (Robert) or the story-teller's community, lost after the myth of the individual became dominant (Benjamin).[20]

The simile "like a dog" enacts such a change of denomination; it denotes a search for the forgotten name. It is impossible to escape the tautological overtones of this project. Because speech is used here to remark its nature as speech, this identity has to be somehow presented in a medium that would, in some hypothetical, allusive sense, be different from the object thus presented. Kafka's allusive language labors under this inner contradiction. In the manner of intransitive speech, it seeks to express only the speech of speech, but this immediate relation can at any time degenerate into referential language and be expressed as objective content.

19. Roland Barthes ("Kafka's Answer," in *Critical Essays*, trans. Richard Howard [Evanston, 1972], 136) offers the following formula for Robert's understanding of Kafkan allusion: "K feels he has been arrested, and everything happens *as if* K were really arrested (*The Trial*)". Robert writes that Kafka uses the hypothetical in order to test words, without drawing any positive results from such a procedure, even in the form of disillusionment or of a critique of language. The test has a hypothetical relation to reality (*cf. Kafka*, 124). Alwin L. Baum speaks, in this context, of Kafka's "interminable *vielleicht* [perhaps]," which weakens his judgment and statement ("Parable as Paradox in Kafka's *Erzählungen*," *MLN*, XCI [1976], 1330).

20. Walter Benjamin, "The Story-Teller," in *Illuminations*, 83–109.

The paradigmatic simile *"like a dog"* suffers the fate of precisely this ambiguity, for it can be interpreted within both the transitive and intransitive models of speech. In the first model, one can seek help in the externality guaranteed by the metaphysical structure of language. One could, for instance, attempt to save the dog from the jeers of the anonymous group by separating the word from other speaking subjects and by restricting it to private use by a sensitive individual. In this solution, however, the removal of the word to a private language separated from common usage also prevents the speaker from using similes ("like"), for our ability to make comparisons is based on a universally shared world of identifications and substitutions.

An intransitive reading of Kafka's simile is possible in what Robert has called Kafka's *"récit allusif du Chien"* (135). For Robert this non-metaphysical language can dissociate the meaning of the word "dog" from the nearly universal, collectively imposed pejorative sense by using the phrase, not in its intended pejorative meaning, but in a "manner of speaking." In this "allusive" use Kafka allows the phrase "like a dog" to speak, not from an individual subject, who could manipulate the simile for positive or negative meanings, but from the totality of language, which has no intentions. The opposition in Kafka's solution, then, is not one between private (positive) and collective (pejorative) but between transitive and intransitive use of similes.

Articulated by language itself, the Kafkan simile operates very much like the parable of Prometheus in Robert's enlightening exegesis: it proceeds out of habit and in the name of a forgotten link that integrates the logic of similarities and endows the simile with sense. The forgotten name can be brought to consciousness only through a baptism, a secondary ceremony of naming where the first name is already only a substitute for an irretrievable "original" term (*cf.* 135). The object brought forth by the language of allusion is not an entity identifiable in the objective network of similarities but the unity of language that is anterior, or posterior, to the logic of similes. Kafka's language still inhabits the speech of the group, but its allusive bridge transfers it beyond conceptual meanings into a sphere that lacks the ordering hierarchies required to sustain and exploit rhetorical and metaphysical distinctions.

In allusion, the logic of the general and the particular, the tension between the individual and the community, and, finally, the metaphysical distinction within language between the literal and the figurative levels are accommodated by a source that is equipped with both the plural and the singular dimension but that is reducible to neither—the genre of *Hundschaft*. Kafka's genre of "doghood" stands in the same relation to traditional classifications of genre in which Kafka's eroded metaphor stands to traditional rhetoric. In the commonly accepted terminology, genre is regarded as a general category that subsumes items of the same kind. The relation is well captured in Goethe's canonical description: "There is a great difference, whether the poet seeks the particular for the general or sees the general in the particular. From the first procedure arises allegory, where the particular serves only as an example of the general; the second procedure, however, is really the nature of poetry: it expresses something particular, without thinking of the general or pointing to it."[21] "Seeking the particular for the general" designates an allegorical operation (the general contains the particular), while "seeing the general in the particular" designates the economy of the symbol (the particular functions "without thinking of the general or pointing to it").[22] In both cases, the relation is, properly speaking, a relation of *representation*.

Kafka's genre of *Hundschaft* suspends this distinction. *Hundschaft* circumscribes the space in which generality, community, and metaphor cannot deploy the logic of relations, referrals, subsumptions, and, most importantly, representation. "Doghood" implies unlimited extension of relations, a general reference to totality that exceeds the logic of properties and is, for this reason, the death of similarity. In Goethe's terms, Kafka's genre is symbolic rather than allegorical. But there is a difference between Goethe's and Kafka's symbol. Although in Goethe the particular functions "without thinking of the general or pointing to it," the definition implicitly asserts the original relation and unity of the two; the initial unity of the particular and the general must first be sundered and the separation must be maintained for the

21. Johann Wolfgang von Goethe, "Maxims and Reflections," trans. René Wellek, in *A History of Modern Criticism* (6 vols.; New Haven, 1955), I, 211.

22. Coleridge's terms *symbol* and *allegory*, although they reverse Goethe's terminology, recognize the same basis for this distinction. In addition, one should remark, if only parenthetically, the indebtedness of Goethe's language to Kant's terminology of analytical and synthetic judgments. Kant writes: "In all judgments in which the relation of a subject to the predicate is thought . . . this relation is possible in two different ways. Either the predicate B belongs to the subject A, as something which is (covertly) contained in this concept A; or B lies outside the concept A, although it does indeed stand in connection with it. In the one case I entitle the judgment analytic, in the other synthetic" (*Critique of Pure Reason*, B10). The similarity between Goethe and Kant lies in the use of the metaphor of "containing" to denote representation.

symbol to work. In Kafka, however, the separation is not needed, because the particular has never entertained any relation to the general.

Kafka's model of representation does not stand in relation to Goethe's theory of symbol and allegory as a third option; it is, rather, a third moment within the traditional economy, a moment that constitutes this economy but is irreducible to it. As critical literature has frequently observed, Kafka suspends the symbolic and the allegorical relations of representation in the simultaneous presence of two ambiguous denotations. One should note, for example, the ambiguity in the verb *deuten* ("to point to something" and "to interpret") and the ambiguity of *der Prozess*, "trial" and "process." Theodore Ziolkowski analyzes in this context the double meaning of *Schuld*, either "guilt" or "fault."[23] Sussman observes the play on *tauschen/täuschen* (to exchange/to deceive—*Geometrician of Metaphor*, 100) and the double sounding of *graben* (to bury), which allows for the difference between "grave" and "to engrave" (152).

Kafka injects ambiguity into the paired terms to make one term infringe on the other's semantic prerogative, resembling it and standing different. Thus, one interprets the meaning of the word *deuten* as "to point out," and each trial (*Prozess*) is a (due) process (of law). It is not clear whether the meaning thus arrived at can be determined outside of the pair, for the words point at each other, yet they also differ, and this is why the pointing out must take place, and so on. In a similar way, K. arrives at the quarry—where he is to be executed—by chance or by design, that is, by both. He arrives as the sum of these two semantic options, but the sum of the two meanings itself is devoid of meaning: "In complete harmony all three [K. and his two guards] now made their way across a bridge in the moonlight ... [In the quarry] they came to a standstill, whether because this place had been their goal from the very beginning or because they were too exhausted to go farther" (*T*, 170–71). In the pairings, the interpretations are brought forth in relation to each term, for the meaning of interpretation can be either a "pointing out" or an "explanation," and the decision can be made solely within the semantic field permitted and generated by these terms. The structure that generates the meanings of meaning is infinite, for the interpreting subject has come to understand that the meaning of one word emerges in the light of the second term. Both

---

23. Theodore Ziolkowski, *Dimensions of the Modern Novel: German Texts and European Contexts* (Princeton, 1969), 50.

terms achieve the "complete harmony" of reference to each other, their meaning generated in the infinite circularity of semantic reciprocity. As such an enclosed circuit, the paired terms become Kafkan allegories/symbols of (their mutually determined) meaning, dwelling in an originary extratropological meaninglessness.

Kafka's representation is defined by the ambiguity of this infinitely circular mechanism. The suspension in *Hundschaft* of (Goethe's) symbolic and allegorical moments discloses a possibility of representation that does not depend on the relation of a general term to a specific moment. The original event, the presentation, occurs in the infinite allegorical reciprocity of "re-" and "-presentation." Re-presentation makes the totality present as a repeated event, in the ambiguity of the pristine and the belated.

In order to see what exactly happens to representation in Kafka's genre of *Hundschaft* it may be helpful to explore the term "allegory" as defined, not by Goethe, but by etymology. "Allegory" denotes a reference to another meaning.[24] This reference, however, must be rigorously distinguished from the reference of word to thing or concept that characterizes denotation. Denotative reference always points to something specific, and when the reference fails, it has a positive term for this failure (error). Allegorical reference, on the other hand, defines the pure mechanism of meaning as referral, the pure difference between saying and meaning. In language, *cat* is not a cat: for a thing to enter language the thing itself must be made absent. Allegory is the name of this constitutive absence. As such an indication of otherness, allegory is related to the *ainigma* and the riddle. Most importantly, allegory indicates an *other* meaning; it indicates a meaning that always accompanies explicit linguistic articulation but exceeds it and remains concealed from it. In this sense, allegory defines the mechanism of irony.[25]

A few examples may, perhaps, shed more light on this ironic sense of allegory. In a characteristic episode in *Madame Bovary*, Emma, intending to break off her renewed affair with Léon, writes him a letter declaring that she is unable to keep the appointment in the Cathedral the next morning. With the letter already sealed, she realizes that she

24. "Allegory: [ME *allegorie*, fr. L *allegoria*, fr. Gk *allegoria*, fr. *allegorein* to speak figuratively, fr. *allos* other + *-agorein* to speak publicly, fr. *agora* assembly—more at ELSE, GREGARIOUS]" (*Webster's New Collegiate Dictionary*).
25. See Angus Fletcher, *Allegory: The Theory of a Symbolic Mode* (Ithaca, 1964), 2.

does not know Léon's address and decides to deliver the letter in person. Her meeting with Léon is impossible, and this impossibility must be affirmed in a meeting. In the Rouen Cathedral, Emma will comment on her words sealed in the envelope. The content of the letter, the writing, is both indispensable and superfluous; the letter must be delivered, for it contains the central message—yet it is also redundant, since Emma can *tell* Léon *what the letter says.* If she did this (and she does not), it would be unclear whether she would be telling Léon about her decision (direct speech), or retelling the message already written in the letter (reported speech). The letter is infinitely other, its speech neither direct nor indirect, but neutral.

In *The Trial*, K. expects to meet a colleague visiting from Italy and show him the sights of the city, but K.'s inadequate knowledge of Italian leads to a misunderstanding. Instead of the Italian friend, K. meets the Priest. In the ensuing conversation the Priest tells K. the parable "Before the Law" as if it applied to K. When K. asks for an explication of the parable, the Priest explains that the parable is only a preamble to the law. Overwhelmed by the conditional clauses and preliminary definitions, K. vanishes in the abyss of infinite exegesis.

As Georg Lukács argues, Søren Kierkegaard sought to encompass his turbulent relationship with Regine Olsen in the *gesture.* The purpose of the Kierkegaardian gesture—the arbitrary and inexplicable rejection of Regine—is "to make unambiguous the inexplicable," to preserve the usefulness of the finite language of symbolic human acts for the rigor of ideal meanings. The gesture unites the fragility of finite life with immutable form, in whose "rigid permanence" alone every evanescent moment becomes true reality.[26] When Kierkegaard constructs his life on the gesture, he presupposes the system that articulates this gesture. Still, after the gesture, he continues to seek ways to solidify and correct it, as if the gesture controlled the system and not the other way around. He rejects Regine, yet he continues to write explanatory notes in order to determine, to clarify, and to confirm the intended, proper meaning of this rejection.

Elias Canetti associates Kafka's cancellation of the engagement to Felice Bauer with the intensive work on *The Trial* that soon followed, the novel's trial standing for the family judgment on Kafka's worth-

---

26. Georg Lukács, "The Foundering of Form Against Life: Søren Kierkegaard and Regine Olsen," in *Soul and Form*, trans. Anna Bostock (Cambridge, Mass., 1974), 28, *cf.* 29, hereinafter cited parenthetically by page number in the text.

lessness.[27] Kafka himself had special sympathy for writers who freely broke off their engagements because of some connection with their writing careers.[28]

In all these encounters, fragile appointments and abortive reunions take place in the lateral presence of a textual piece—letters, the book, and the Law. The paths of the characters diverge, derailed by the persistent elusiveness of the texts that accompany the meetings, the written word preceding (Flaubert), accompanying (Kierkegaard), and succeeding (Kafka) the event itself. In Flaubert, the letter remains virginal, its reading an impossible task: " 'Read this,' she [Emma] said, holding out a sheet of paper—'No, don't!'—and she snatched her hand back again." In her letter Emma delivers that which can be neither communicated orally nor sent *as* a letter: pure writing, not yet and no longer legible. Kierkegaard and Regine interpret their letters without opening them, interpret them *one way or another*, and send them back with the undecipherable message of the conjectural interpretation. In *The Trial* Kafka fully exposes the parable "Before the Law" to a comprehensive reading that can no longer be interpreted. The parable, when fully interpreted, translates K. to pure textual reality—before/behind the door of the Law, K. disappears.

27. Elias Canetti, *Der andere Prozess: Kafkas Briefe an Felice* (Munich, 1969). (English: *Kafka's Other Trial: The Letters to Felice*, trans. Christopher Middleton [New York, 1982]).

28. Erwin R. Steinberg ("Kafka's 'Before the Law'—A Reflection of Fear of Marriage; and Corroborating Language Patterns in the Diaries," *Journal of Modern Literature*, XIII [1986], 129–48) draws attention to Kafka's familiarity with the case of Franz Grillparzer's broken engagement to Katherine Fröhlich. Canetti (*Kafka's Other Trial*, 6, 39) makes a passing reference to Grillparzer and to Kafka's sympathy for Dostoevsky, Kleist, and Flaubert, of whom only Dostoevsky married, and of whom Kleist alone, according to Kafka, did the only right thing by committing suicide. In his biography of Kafka, Peter Mailloux briefly mentions as "indeed striking" the parallels between Kafka's engagement to Felice Bauer and Kierkegaard's to Regine Olsen, both affairs lasting five years before being brought to a sudden and final end (*A Hesitation Before Birth: The Life of Franz Kafka* [Newark, 1989], 417, and 600, n. 66). Jean Wahl's "Kierkegaard and Kafka" (*The Kafka Problem*, ed. Flores, 269–70) briefly analyzes the two writers' engagements in the context of philosophical affinites and the role of their fathers. John Kelly, in "*The Trial* and the Theology of Crisis," (*The Kafka Problem*, ed. Flores, 151–71) pursues the relation between Kafka and Kierkegaard in a discussion of *The Trial* that uses Karl Barth's notion of theological "crisis." Maurice Blanchot ("Kafka and the Work's Demand," in *The Space of Literature*, trans. Ann Smock [Lincoln, Nebr., 1982], 61) distinguishes between Kierkegaard's rejection of Regine, conceived as a shift from the aesthetic to the ethical, and Kafka's rejection of Felice, conceived on the analogy with Abraham's sacrifice of Isaac.

In all cases, writing's "ambiguous" efficacy is both impenetrable and absorptive. Emma's correction of her mistake is futile, and so are Kierkegaard's letters to Regine, Kafka's explanations to Felice, and the Priest's exegesis of the Law to K. The characters of these textual dramas remain blind to the writing they seek to interpret. They mistake writing for an object of investigation, while the writing is that which brings them together. They have unwittingly become parables themselves, *sind Gleichnisse geworden*;[29] they belong to the unrepresentable genre of *Hundschaft* without a possibility of appeal, beyond interpretation, beyond comparison.[30]

The reading—the interpretation—of meaning is confronted in Kafka with the allegorical, other meaning. Kafkan hermeneutics invokes the totality of meaning but withholds the concrete meaning. It asserts the Law but prevents the application of the Law in concrete instances. Each specific law exists in the allegorical relation to its *allos*, its other; hence, it is the Law of each law that it should point to the other Law as this law's own meaning.

The Law is unified but inaccessible; conversely, the Law forfeits its unity when it becomes ostensible in a law. K. is very surprised, in Chapter 8, when the Commercial Traveler reveals to him that Advocate Huld also has "an ordinary practice": "This alliance between business and equity seemed to him uncommonly touching" [*ungemein beruhigend*—uncommonly reassuring] (*T*, 131). Advocate Huld expresses a similar split in the Law: he portrays himself as the dutiful student of "every precept of duty, piety, and tradition" [*Anstand, Pflicht und Gerichtsgebrauch*] (*T*, 146).

---

29. Kafka, *Parables and Paradoxes*, 10–11.
30. Charles Bernheimer ("On Death and Dying: Kafka's Allegory of Reading," in *CCP*, 87–96) examines the Kafkan paradox that the erosion of similarity (death) might itself be the last opportunity (or the temptation) for the writer to find some founding or productive meaning. On the one hand, Kafka is driven by the Kierkegaardian gesture, by the eros of writing: "[Kafka's desire for wholeness, for *Vollkommenheit*] is the desire for death to be clearly definable as the absence of life and for writing to be free to elaborate its fictional inventions on the basis of their analogy to life's limited organic form and constricted temporal extension" (92). On the other hand (and this is the Kafkan "gesture"—*allegory*), in Kafka's fiction "the protagonist wishes to tell a story of mastery, as if from the point of view of his death, of his reflection in the heavenly plane.... He wants to reach the imaginative space of his own death and thereby to achieve the authority to narrate his life, but he is repulsed by the, to him, unimaginable activity of his own death impulse" (94).

The Law, which governs all existents and all exegesis, is internally unified, and its unity is, properly speaking, pretextual; that is, it exists before the commentary, and even before the scripture itself, for the scripture merely records the Law. Udoff refers to this quality of the Law as "unalterability" (*Unveränderlichkeit*), "the radical exclusion of any constitutive or interpretive alterity" (*CCP,* 203). The unchangeable Law requires that explanation (exegesis) demonstrate the Law's inner stability, but it also prevents exegesis and exegetes as its legitimate representatives. Sussman makes a similar argument: "The law has space only for its readings, not for its readers or most devoted servants. The end of this allegory of successive readers is that the interpreters are all expendable, although interpretation is the nature of the law" (*Geometrician of Metaphor,* 104).

The allegorical condition of interpretation clarifies both the inner complexity of the Law and Kafka's technical choices in presenting this complexity. The Priest in the cathedral scene (Chapter 9) seeks to obey both demands, the unpresentability of the Law and the presentability of its specific provisions, by telling the parable—one of the introductory commentaries to the code.[31] Intended to furnish a *preparatory explanation,* the commentary alters the story's argument from without. Still, the deception of the Man from the Country must be explained *in subsequent exegesis,* even though the parable was originally intended to forestall textual deception. The preliminary commentary and the subsequent exegetical debate alter the text in its textuality; they announce it in advance and remark its passing away. They merely serve as premature or belated indices of the unalterable Law that controls alterability.

The new situation of the reader is presented in Leni's reported speech to Advocate Huld about the behavior of Block as he awaits an audience with the officers of the Court:

"What has he been doing all day?" went on the Advocate. "I locked him into the maid's room," said Leni, "to keep him from disturbing me at my work, that's where he usually stays, anyhow. And I could peep at

---

31. The significance of this parable for any study of Kafka is indicated in the following four exemplary treatments: Ingeborg Henel's "Die Türhüterlegende und ihre Bedeutung für Kafkas *Prozess*" (*Deutsche Vierteljahrsschrift,* XXXVII [1963], 50–70); Rainer Nägele's "Kafka and the Interpretive Desire" (*CCP,* 16–29); Alan Udoff's "Before the Question of the Laws: Kafkan Reflections" (*CCP,* 178–213); and Jacques Derrida's "Devant la Loi" (*CCP,* 128–49).

him now and then through the ventilator to see what he was doing. He was kneeling all the time on the bed, reading the book you lent him, which was spread out on the window-sill. That made a good impression on me, since the window looks out on an air-shaft and doesn't give much light. So the way Block stuck to his reading showed me how faithfully he does what he is told." (*T*, 147)

An allegorical reading of this scene makes reading depend on a perpetually revised and perpetually receding anterior decision. As long as it lets the reader (Leni) observe Block without his knowledge that he is perceived as a reader, the allegory serves extrinsic, exegetical ends; that is, it hegemonically (as the etymology of *exegesis* indicates)[32] leads the reader out of darkness to interpret Block's activity *as* reading. *We* can, critically, see Block reading only when *he* cannot see to read. Someone can read only because someone else cannot; something can be read as text only because something else cannot be read.

The exegetical reading of this scene of reading "leads the reader out into clarity"; it serves to "throw light" on the scene, so that it will become visible. In this visibility, the activity of Block can appear only as reading. By extension, we (and Leni) can read only that which we construe to be a patient attempt at reading, and those behind *Leni*'s (and our) back must construe her reading as an allegory of reading. However, observed (read) without exegetical guidance, Block, submerged in exegesis and suppliance, leads himself in and out of the reading of reading. Indifferent (blind) to the truth that allegory is indispensable for reading to take place, he inhabits allegorical otherness itself, for he is reading and/or praying. True to his allegorical nature, Block becomes a suppliant dog before the Law.[33]

The exegetical battle between the Priest and the Man from the Country in the cathedral's dim interior shows, in a parallel fashion, the need for an external observer to throw light, to determine the two opponents' activity *as* interpretation and as exegesis. In this configuration, the Text of the Law Itself is the ever-receding other. Only systematic disappearance makes possible the determination of a reading as reading; only the absence, the lack (*die Lücke*) allows the reader to

---

32. "Exegesis: [NL, fr. Gk *exegesis* fr. *exegeisthai* to explain, interpret, fr. *ex* + *hegeisthai* to lead—more at SEEK]" (*Webster's New Collegiate Dictionary*).

33. The "dog-role" structures the scene in Chapter 8, when Block is finally granted audience with Advocate Huld. In the course of the session, "The client ceased to be a client and became the Advocate's dog" (*T*, 147).

understand the dialogue between the Priest and K. as interpretation. Language itself can come to language only in this allegorical withdrawal of language's essence.

The Trial allegorically refers to something that is both inadequate and excessive in relation to the reading matter. Kafka writes his novel as a belated occurrence, as a trace of an earlier event. The obscure event is neither an object nor a spatio-temporal occurrence, but the totality of speech. Because it occurs simultaneously with, or in, every instance of speech, this event cannot be narrated in direct or indirect speech. The original event is neutral.

In one of the episodes in the court's attics, K. undergoes an attack of suffocation. He is led away by two court functionaries, the group composing a trio: "At last he noticed that they were talking to him, but he could not make out what they were saying, he heard nothing but the din that filled the whole place, through which a shrill unchanging note like that of a siren seemed to ring" (*T,* 60). In the realistic context of the scene there emerges a moment of allegorical referral to some other meaning—an otherness beyond determinate interpretations in the manner of parable, symbol, or implication. The scene is permeated with a "ringing" voice to suggest a significance other than the realistic description, but specific reference is denied. What survives in the reference is only the imperative that meaning is a function of a general reference to otherness.

As it refers to the original event, Kafka's "reported speech" is neither direct nor indirect but is used "in a manner of speaking." What speaks *in* (locative) "a manner of speaking" is not only referential content of communication but the speech of speech. This interference of the subject of speech with language's referential register exposes realistic material to systematic distortions. It foils anticipation of events, disfigures the time-space continuum, and upsets synchronic coordination. Advocate Huld talks with Block: " 'You've come at the wrong time.' 'Wasn't I called for?' said Block, more to himself than to the Advocate. . . . 'You were called for,' said the Advocate, 'and yet you've come at the wrong time [*Du wurdest gerufen . . . trotzdem kommst du ungelegen*].' After a pause he added: 'You always come at the wrong time' " (*T,* 144).

In the presence of the invisible anteriority it is impossible to determine "speech acts" and syntactic categories with any precision. During his first interrogation, K. talks with the Examining Magistrate:

" 'Well then,' said the Examining Magistrate... 'you are a house-painter?' 'No,' said K., 'I'm the junior manager of a large Bank'... 'This question of yours, Herr Examining Magistrate, about my being a house-painter—or rather, not a question, you simply made a statement [*Ihre Frage ... vielmehr, Sie haben gar nicht gefragt, sondern es mir auf den Kopf zugesagt*]—is typical of the whole character of this trial that is being foisted on me' " (*T,* 36–37). The confusion as to the type of speech act, as to its *genre,* makes it impossible to determine precisely what kind of a trial is "foisted" on K., and in the name of what law it is thus "foisted." In its reference to the constitutive other, language seems to imply an object (the defendant), an objective condition (guilt), a purposeful activity (the trial), in a coherent system of identifiable categories (Greek *kategorein,* to accuse), yet the other of language is the possibility by which language possesses any meaning, and as such a constitutive ground it distorts the referential aspect it seeks to evoke. Embroiled in a trial (*Prozess*), K. is swept away by the process of language coming to presence.

As intransitive speech, Kafka's language is engaged in the continuous process of its resurgence. We have said that Kafka's intransitive language risks expressing its comportment to the constitutive otherness as the content of transitive speech, of objective reference. Kafka's images of the Law operate under the weight of this infinite duplicity. For example, the Law can *admit itself* (to be a law) only through a door that belongs exclusively to it. When ushering K. into the interrogation room, the woman tells K.: "I must shut this door after you, nobody else must come in" (*T,* 34–35). The door is the genre of specificity—individual, but not objectively known as determined individually. The door (and the law) is intended specifically for K., but it becomes specific only after K. passes through it. In other words, K. can have no prior objective knowledge of the door as intended for him; he can only pass through the door that becomes specifically his only in the moment of this passing. The door does not preexist the subject as an objective category, iterable in legal codes (clause, loophole) or in spatial reference (door), but is an opening that only becomes one upon entry. As the door to the *Rumpelkammer,* the entrance into genre becomes an entrance only when it is opened (*T,* 67). In a concrete sense, the door is its own opening. The self-admitting nature of genre is evident in the studio of the painter Titorelli. Although located "in a suburb which was almost at the diametrically opposite [*vollständig entge-*

gengesetzt] end of the town from where the Court held its meetings" (*T*, 108), it is equipped with a *second* door leading directly to the Court's quarters. In the universal opening onto everything, the allegorical third opens (onto) itself.

In the novel's opening passage Kafka establishes the plot in relation to an absent order; from this moment on, the story occurs in the shadow of this formative order. This order is constantly present in the realistic content as an anterior determination that cannot be represented but without which the events described in the novel could not take place. Since the event is the original event of the totality of speech, Kafka's prose repeats the occurrence of speech as "a manner of speaking."

The repetition in question indicates Kafka's understanding of representation when representation no longer follows the mechanism of subsumption, conceptualization, and repetition based on the metaphysical foundation of similarity. The original event comes to presence as repetition; its original presence is presented as re-presencing. Repetition is the mode of the text's self-presencing, the momentary presencing of textuality in the indeterminate economy of the prefix *re-* that conceals, in *re-petition*, the original event, the defendant's (the speaker's) *-petition*. The petition can come to presence only as premature and belated; its original presence in the present can be indicated only in the infinity of the prefix *re-*. The *-petition* defines the only content of *The Trial* as the infinite *Prozess* of the presencing of what is present.

"The man did not submit to this scrutiny for very long, but turned to the door and opened it slightly so as to report to someone who was evidently standing just behind it [*der offenbar knapp hinter der Tür stand*]." The tentative presence of someone behind the door anticipates the parable "Before the Law"—it opens up onto Kafka's allegorical anterior reality. But the status of this reality is, at best, suppositional and speculative. " 'He says Anna is to bring him his breakfast.' A short guffaw from the next room came in answer [*Ein kleines Gelächter in Nebenzimmer folgte*]; one could not tell from the sound whether it was produced by several individuals or merely by one [*es war nach dem Klang nicht sicher, ob nicht mehrere Personen daran beteiligt waren*]." The source, if one assumes it to be real, is inarticulate (laughter), and it resists a determination of number (How many persons laughed?). Moreover, it carries pure repetition; it contains no new information: "Although the strange man could not have learned anything from it that he did not know already, he now said to K., as if passing on a statement: 'It can't be done.' " Kafka's reported speech is reported in a fundamental sense of the term: the totality of language cannot be determined as original or as reported; hence, it can now be, reportedly, in a third, allegorical sense, neither direct nor indirect but *only* reported.

The scene is controlled by such fundamental distortions in other aspects as well. For example, K., "put out and hungry . . . rang the bell. At once there was a knock at the door." The ring of the bell coincides with the knock on the door; it *causes* the knock, almost bringing about the arrest itself. The same mechanism controls the exchange that soon follows between K. and the warders, Willem and Franz: " 'I'd better get Frau Grubach—' said K., as if wrenching himself away from the two men (though they were standing at quite a distance from him [*die aber weit von ihm entfernt standen*]) and making as if to go out. 'No,' said the man at the window, flinging the book down on the table and getting up. 'You can't go out, you are arrested' " (*T,* 10). Although standing apart, K. seeks *to distance himself from this distance.* Moreover, K. is arrested in a perpetual moment: he is arrested *before* the morning has dawned, after he has woken up, immediately after he has rung the bell, and at the moment when he has made the first movement beyond the invisible boundaries of his confinement. Finally, he is arrested *when* he tries to step outside or *because* he has tried to do so. The immediacy of the response (*sofort*) eliminates the time lapse between cause and effect, between sequence and con-sequence; it preempts all possibility of action and reaction, of impulse and interpretation, all possibility of hermeneutics.

Presented in reported speech, K.'s arrest resists all interpretation. And this not only because K. is innocent and the arrest appears to be unjustified, a terrible mistake of objective knowledge, but because the speech of the third cannot be interpreted. When speaking of someone's guilt, we rely on a logically simple predicate of attribution. Innocence, on the other hand, lacks attributes; it is a natural condition belonging to the prelapsarian world of undifferentiated existence. Innocence not only does not require positive determination; it cannot supply one, for, like *cat* in language, it is an infinite concept: it *cannot* be positively predicated. Innocence exists, then, solely in relation to guilt, in the sense that it is accessible to language, it is *sayable,* only as the opposite of guilt, as *in*-nocence. But if no predicate is available for innocence, how can guilt itself, the opposite of innocence, be attributed, except as a *determination,* a curtailment, a delimiting of the infinity of innocence? Language is locked into the calculus of determinations, unable to indicate innocence or guilt independently of each other. Language, as metaphysical, imposes the supreme metaphysical distinction: it can speak only about the guilty and the innocent. What agency attributes—speaks—pure, infinite innocence? Would it come in direct speech, indirect speech? The voice that would defend the innocent—the third voice—must speak in the neuter. The original event that befalls K. is the uninterpretable event of the innocent—that is, undemonstrable, unprovable—totality of language. K. has no alibi.

Perhaps the most revealing aspect of the original event of language emerges in K.'s attempt to interpret his arrest as "a rude joke" [*ein großer Spaß*] prepared by his colleagues from the bank (*T,* 11). Kafka's recourse to the "act of speech" called "joke" to attempt an interpretation of the totality of language must be placed in the ambiguity of Kafka's destruction of the metaphysical structure of language and in the context of his allegorical understanding of language. In his conversation with the Inspector, K. defines the limits and the conditions of a joke: " 'I won't say that I regard the whole thing as a joke, for the preparations that have been made seem too elaborate for that. The whole staff of the boarding-house would have to be involved, as well as all you people, and that would be past a joke. So I don't say that it's a joke' " [*das ginge über die Grenzen eines Spaßes. Ich will also nicht sagen, daß es ein Spaß ist*] (*T,* 16). In order to place his arrest in a meaningful frame, K. resorts to both a hermeneutic and an allegorical notion of totality. Defined hermeneutically, within the metaphysical boundaries of language, a joke can be a joke only if the joke's participants constitute a small congregation. If the whole staff at the bank, the whole world, the whole human community were to conspire to make up a joking situation, then it would be impossible to tell a joke, impossible, that is, to *tell* it *from* a nonjoke.

In the latter case, when the boundaries are erased, language begins to operate nonmetaphysically. In other words, seen from the point of view of the possibility of telling a joke, language presupposes a group of persons, a contingent extrinsic to the context in which the joke can be told. The joke, then, is not constituted, as in empirical models of linguistic communication (Jakobson's addressor, addressee, message, code), by the teller and the audience, but, as in transcendental philosophy (Kant's conditions of possibility) by those who, in their radical externality, remain fundamentally indifferent to joking: either those who can never become privy to a joke or, which amounts to the same thing, those who have heard all the jokes ever uttered.[34]

As he speculates about the conditions of possibility for his arrest, K. inadvertently formulates the ironic condition of possibility for language in general. K.'s hypothesis about the conditions of the joke implies the same external, allegorical "someone" who (that?) is implied in *The Trial*'s initial hypothesis, "Someone must have been telling lies about Joseph K." In both passages, the extrinsic position—while it remains extrinsic to the joke and to truth—is nevertheless essential for jokes and the truth to be told. The extrinsic audience, the "someone," is essentially indifferent to the seriousness and the jocosity that it makes possible, indifferent to the truth and the slander that it originates. This excessive reserve of language cannot be expressed in the joke; it cannot appear in language except, as in *The Trial*, in the transgression, the allegorical transfer beyond the conditions of speech: "and that would be past a joke" [*das ginge über die Grenzen eines Spaßes*].

Finite language can perform its transitive function of communication only because there is an audience that it fails to reach, only because there is an infinite and incomprehensible meaning that it cannot express. In this sense, the *allos*, the constitutive externality of language, cannot be determined in a concept. It may equally denote a joke (*Spaß*) or a lie (*Lüge*). K.'s hypothesis presupposes a third community, anterior to the occurrence of the joke and of truth, a surplus community that, left outside of the boundaries of communication, makes all communication and miscommunication, all truth and lie, possible.

The anterior third, that which cannot be spoken, is overshadowed in everyday language by the referential aspect. Speech, diverted from the other, becomes preoccupied with objective relations, oblivious to its source that speaks before it, that speaks, as Blanchot says, in the

---

34. For Nägele ("Kafka and the Interpretive Desire") Kafka's episodes describe struggles "between two figures, but the duality is possible only in relation to a third agency, before which it takes place, by which it is shaped.... Kafka's triadic constellation has the structure that Freud discovered in the joke; and many of his stories, particularly 'Before the Law,' with its pointed surprise at the end, indeed can have the effect of the joke" (*CCP*, 25).

neuter.³⁵ It is this neutral community (and its voice) that is Kafka's sole preoccupation in his literary project and that gives the distinctive profile to his narratives. Kafka's narratives tell the story of the origin of language; they narrate the relation of transitive language to language's allegorical origin.

In order to see how Kafka understands the surplus external to language it may be helpful to examine the dynamics of Kafka's narrative voice as analyzed by Blanchot. In his description of Kafka's narrative impersonality, Blanchot argues that writing becomes possible for Kafka only in the condition of an inability to write. If Kafka writes, "I cannot write," he is lying, for he has just written. Experience can be expressed only when it no longer belongs exclusively to the experiencing subject, only when the personal world recognizes the external constraint. The incapable *I* expresses itself only in the shift to *him*, in this disappearance, in the power of this lack.³⁶ In the process of this shift (which must be distinguished from the metaphorical shift in rhetoric), there emerges the infinite moment that hovers between the grammatical *I* and *him*. Blanchot calls this third term the *neuter*. Blanchot writes, in the essay "The Narrative Voice (the 'He,' the Neutral)," that the shift from *I* to *him* "designates 'its' [the neuter's] place as both the place from which it will always be missing and that will thus remain empty, but also as a surplus of place, a place that is always too many places: hypertopia" (*IC*, 379–87, 462). The shift stretches the speaking position, not between a determinate origin (*I*) and a determinate destination (*he*), but in "the alteration occasioned by another kind of speech or by the other as speech (as writing)" (*IC*, 384). The "excess" is extrinsic to speech—it goes past the boundaries of the joke (of language).

It is here that the significance of the narrative voice for Kafka's allegorical narratives comes to light. Blanchot writes: "The narrative 'he' [or 'it,' *il*] . . . marks the intrusion of the other—understood as neutral—in its irreducible strangeness and in its wily perversity" (*IC*, 385).

---

35. Blanchot formulates the notion of the neuter in his meditation "René Char et la pensée du neutre," *L'Arc*, XXII (1963), 9–14. I am using here the translation as found in *IC*, 298–306. The specifically Blanchotian notion of neutrality, or impersonality, in its differences from dialectical models of writerly communication, is discussed by Paul de Man ("Impersonality in the Criticism of Maurice Blanchot," in *Blindness and Insight*, 60–78).

36. Maurice Blanchot, *The Sirens' Song*, ed. Gabriel Josipovici, trans. Sacha Rabinovitch (Bloomington, 1982), 38.

The shift from *I* to *him* marks the "intrusion" of the other by remarking the repetition that lies at the basis of language. The "I" can express itself only by becoming "Him," by re-counting, in self-oblivion, the other that underlies the production of this re-counting. In "narrative space," writes Blanchot, "something happens" to the "bearers of speech . . . that they can only recapture by relinquishing their power to say 'I.' And what happens has always already happened: they can only indirectly account for it as a sort of self-forgetting, the forgetting that introduces them into the present without memory that is the present of narrating speech" (*IC*, 384–85).

The narrative voice makes the intrusion of the other possible by suspending the attributive function of speech. The voice "would establish the center of gravity of speech *elsewhere* [*ailleurs*], there where speaking would neither affirm being nor need negation in order to suspend the work of being that is ordinarily accomplished in every form of expression" (*IC*, 387 italics mine). The passage locates the negation of the "dog" outside of the language of metaphysics. We may recall that Kafkan metaphors, because they eliminate similarity, radically change representation to the extent that representation involves subsumption and generalization. Rather than referring to objective content, Kafka's nonmetaphysical language of the genre of *Hundschaft* presents the speech of (the other of) speech.

The radical change of the meaning and mechanism of representation carries important consequences: "In this respect, the narrative voice is the most critical voice that, unheard, might give to be heard" [La voix narrative est, sous ce rapport, la plus critique qui puisse, inentendue, donner à entendre] (*IC*, 387).[37] Kafka's "recounting," his narrative voice, and his rhetoric, to the extent that they do not enter into the metaphysical play of similarities, disrupt "most critically," as Blanchot would say, the continuity of logical subsumptions and destabilize the conceptual basis of human intellection. The quality of the Kafkan tale as the perpetual self-reassertion of the forgotten bears out the suspended, *neutral* relation of presentation; it bears out the essence of language as an allegorical evocation of absolute indeterminacy in the midst of finite content: "Negation cannot be created out of anything but the reality of what it is negating; language derives its value and its pride from the fact that it is the achievement of this

---

37. The French is quoted from "La voix narrative (le 'il,' le 'neutre')," in *De Kafka à Kafka* (Paris, 1985), 184.

negation; but in the beginning, what was lost? The torment of language is what it lacks because of the necessity that it be the lack of precisely this. It cannot even name it" ("Literature and the Right to Death," in *G*, 45–46). In his destruction of metaphor, Kafka seeks to uncover precisely this constitutive lack. As a figure of transcendental repetition, Kafkan metaphor momentarily re-presents the irretrievable origin.

The Trial's opening clause *allegorizes* language, in the sense that it places language in relation to an anterior constitutive totality of meaning that remains unrepresentable. The in-forming totality for a brief moment suspends conceptual reference; only in the lacuna of this suspension, however, does objective reference become possible. In this direct comportment to its allegorical origin, Kafka's language enacts the pure repetition of the absence that speaks in language *qua* language.

Kafka's notion of language as a purely repetitive relation to origin, as repetition without conceptual content, can be presented in the context of Banchot's theory of narratives. According to Blanchot, language always occurs in the presence of a constitutive externality. In his essay "Wittgenstein's Problem," Blanchot, making a reference to Flaubert, describes the externality invoked by language in the following way:

> The problem defined by Flaubert is the question of the *Other* of speech. Now, ever since Mallarmé, we have sensed that the other of a language is always posed by this language itself as that by way of which it looks for a way out, an exit to disappear into or an Outside in which to be reflected. Which means not only that the Other is already *part* of this language, but that as soon as this language turns around to respond to its Other, it turns toward another language; a language that, as we ought not ignore [*sic*], is other, and also has its Other. At this point we come very close to Wittgenstein's problem, as corrected by Bertrand Russell: every language has a structure about which one can say nothing *in* this language, but there must be another language that treats the structure of the first and possesses a new structure about which we cannot say anything, except in a third language—and so forth. (*IC*, 337)

Speech always occurs in the presence of the other, but this otherness cannot be securely stabilized. On the one hand, speech, precisely as expressed, conceals that which must thus always remain unexpressed. The other is "unexpressed because covered over by expression" (*IC*,

390). At the same time, the other of speech now dwells in advance of language, as something always implied by expression and lying ahead of it as its unattainable goal.

Speech is therefore always haunted by the other, preceded and followed by it. The other is a lack: language becomes language only by suppressing the unsaid. But the other is also excess; speech now also pursues the other that always outpaces it. Language, lodged between the other it has suppressed and the other it cannot attain, carries the other as already sunk into oblivion. It repeats the other as already forgotten, unable to re-call that which as language it repeats. Blanchot calls the most direct, and most exclusive, relation of speech to this external source "literature": "A work says what it says by silencing something. . . . Literature moreover says this by silencing itself. There is in literature an emptiness of literature that constitutes it" ("Wooden Bridge [Repetition, The neutral]," *IC*, 390).

The incessant comportment of language towards its other, always calling for a supplementation of the lack that itself has provoked the initial covering over, follows the logic of the constitutive lack as elaborated by the romantic notion of origin. We may recall that in its study of antiquity romanticism detected an original division; the always-lost unity of ancient Greece calls for a supplementary completion. What makes this mechanism of supplementation specifically romantic is the infinite nature of the completion in question. The romantic completion is not a pragmatic or effective filling in of vacant space, after which the unity is restored and becomes functional again; rather, it is infinite because it cannot even become a movement of completion without the lacuna as the anterior condition of this movement. The negativity of the lacuna constitutes the possibility of the positive gesture of completion. Romantic completion becomes possible because it corresponds to the original absence, to the absence of origin: it repeats the absent moment of incompletion in its effort to close it off and fill it in. As original, the incompletion persists as the "for the sake of which" of completion, not as a positive or objective lack or hole, but only as the submerged, absent "object" of the efforts at effecting completion.

Hence the Blanchotian work of literature is, literally, the work of infinite completion in the mode of repetition. The repetition of the work (of completion) is inescapable, for the work is not an object (a book) but the occurrence of origin in the act of completing the absent origin. The romantic work only repeats the operation of language: "The necessity of repeating can in no way be eluded since it is not superadded to the work nor imposed solely by the habits of social communication" (*IC*, 390). Among the different types of repetition actualized in literary history (episodic repetition in the epic, literary criticism), Blanchot singles out the type of repetition that only responds to the initial doubling, the doubling that originally constitutes the minimal relation of language *qua* language to what Blanchot calls its "enigmatic" source. The enigma, the romantic absent origin that constitutes language, is the neuter. The affinity of Blanchot's concept of the neuter with the romantic notion of transcendental poetry emerges in the following definition of the neuter in Blanchot's essay on René Char: "For what belongs to the neuter is not a third gender opposed to the other two and constituting for reason a determined class of existents or beings.... It refuses to belong to the category of subject as much as it does to that of object. And this does not simply mean that it is still undetermined and as though hesitating between the two, but rather that the neuter supposes another relation depending neither on objective conditions nor on subjective dispositions" (*IC*, 299). The neuter, as neither a subjective nor an objective category, operates in the transcendental fashion: neither real nor ideal, it is the constant occurring of itself in terms of itself. Kafka's transcendental, nonmetaphysical language repeats the neuter in the duality of otherness, as the suppressed point of its origin and as the postulated object of its comportment.

As a relation to the neuter, Kafka's language narrates only the original event of its own occurring; it is a *récit* (tale). As indicated in the introduction, Blanchot develops the notion of the *récit* in the essay "The Song of the Sirens" (*G*, 105–13). The essay divides the *Odyssey* into two distinct sections, separated by the episode of Odysseus' encounter with the sirens. Odysseus' journey until this encounter proceeds as infinite striving, as the "tale" (*récit*), while after the encounter the narrative turns into the "novel" (*roman*). According to this distinction, the "tale" infinitely pursues its goal of becoming a tale. The "novel," on the other hand, forgets the infinite goal of its journey, dispersing itself into objective, determinate themes. Blanchot's distinction between the *récit* and the "novel" describes, arguably, the transition from what is known in the history of narrative literature as the poetics of "romanticism" to the poetics of "realism," a qualitative loss, according to Blanchot, in which the *récit*, "an ode," has "turned into an episode" (*G*, 107).

In a development perhaps central to his thought on narratives, Blanchot understands the *récit* as the privileged locus of disclosure of the neuter, of the other "as such." This unique power of the *récit* to bring language "face to face" with the "enigma" of its origin lies in the necessary relation of *récit* to repetition, to re-citation ("The Wooden Bridge"). The repetition of citation in the re-citation of *ré-cit*, the infinite proximity of both terms, describes the original immediacy with which the constitutive lacuna of the other envelops language, the infinitely recurring relation of language to its transcendentally absent source. Without citation, there could be no re-citation; yet citation, the originary event, can only come to presence in the infinity of the prefix, in and as re-citation. Without the other, there could be no speech, yet the other appears only as absence, now and forever inaccessible because already covered by speech and always in advance of it. The word *récit* comports itself rigorously towards the lacuna of the neuter, allowing the neuter to precede it and to come after. The *récit* cites the original event as already a re-citation—in it the neuter infinitely re-occurs in and as language.

What is re-cited in *récit* is the nonconceptual nature of Kafka's narrative voice. Blanchot writes that the words of the neuter "are not concepts in the sense of either Aristotelian or Hegelian logic, nor are they ideas in the Platonic sense or, to be precise, in any sense at all" (*IC*, 299). The *récit* instantiates the other of speech *both as insufficient and excessive in relation to* conceptual otherness understood as mere negativity. The repetition that characterizes Blanchot's *récit* defines the specific manner in which Kafka's language is independent from metaphysical schematization. Conception, the attributive aspect of language, is determined by what remains, allegorically, unconceptualizable: conception is made possible by what Emmanuel Levinas calls de-ception, a momentary shutdown of the conceptual field.[38] De-ception, or de-con-ceptualization, denotes the infinite content, the indeterminate surplus that cannot be encompassed by conceptual subsumption, that cannot be exhausted by (Goethe's) symbolic or allegorical *representation*. De-conception is the pure otherness that secures the work of concepts: de-conception founds concepts and the familiar solidity of the attributive aspect of language. The familiar conceptuality of language presupposes the *critical*, momentary excess

38. Emmanuel Levinas (*Collected Philosophical Papers*, trans. Alphonso Lingis [Boston, 1987]) develops the term as an index of alterity with reference to the ego: "The conception according to which the data of our senses are put together in the ego ends, before the other, with the de-ception, the dispossession which characterizes all our attempts to encompass this real" (59).

or lack, what Jacques Derrida has called in his essay on Blanchot's *récits* the "blink of the eye": "the eyelid closes, but barely, an instant among instants, and what it closes is verily the eye, the view, the light of day. But without such respite, nothing would come to light."[39]

Because language is understood as language only in its concurrent reflection in another language, in whose terms alone it can first emerge as language, the story, the *récit*, of language cannot be told *sensu stricto*; it can only be re-told, re-cited as this simultaneous, infinite relation. *The Trial* is a story of this *Prozess*, of the infinite relation of language to what has already happened. It repeats the original event by making it come to presence in the infinitely supplementary relation of re-citation (re-presentation). Insofar as it repeats the original event, the event of its origination in the other language always simultaneous with it, *The Trial* is not a belletristic tale about fictive events told for the sake of representing these events but *an example of romantic literature* that tells the story of telling, a re-citation of citation. Deliberately distinguished from a realistic *Roman*, which narrates events, Kafka's romantic *récit* repeats, tells the story of, the event that constitutes language. As a recitation of the citation, Kafka's *récit* is the unpresentable speech in "a manner of speaking."

Considered in the context of the romantic theory of the novel, the theme of repetition reaches in the *récit* perhaps its highest point of saturation. As the proper place and mechanism of the presentation of the subject to itself, the romantic theory of the novel sought to effect the transcendental condition of the subject's infinite self-grasping and self-production. In this endeavor, the romantic theory of the novel aspired to nothing less, and nothing more, than making the subject of speech itself present in what speaks. The project has considerable potential for tautology: what speaks is the subject of speech itself.

We have seen the tautological and repetitive dimensions of this operation in Flaubert and Joyce. There, repetition is elaborated as a procedure that might still be applied to objects and that might still be construed as a stylistic strategy of satire. The total and pervasive nature of Flaubert's and Joyce's repetition alerts the reader to the source of language but stops short of bringing this source itself to presence. In the modernist poetics of Flaubert and Joyce, *Madame Bovary* and *Ulysses* place the subject of speech at the threshold of absolute presentation, indicated negatively in the poetics of the romantic arabesque.

---

39. Derrida, "The Law of Genre," 212.

Kafka and Melville, on the other hand, realize the project of the romantic novel by making the subject of speech present as such. In Melville, we have seen, the subject coincides with the figure of what is considered to be the human subject. But the coincidence of the reflexivity that characterizes the romantic theory of the novel with the structure of human subjectivity is accidental. The subject's self-presentation in Melville is realized as the self's becoming a self, where the self is less the structure of human subjectivity than that of the self's grasping itself as such. This state of being the "object" of one's own grasping corresponds to Friedrich Schlegel's formula that "every theory of the novel must itself be a novel": that which does the grasping exists only because it grasps itself in this very activity of grasping. The Melvillean presentation is the infinite arrival of the Same into its own so that it can become its self and exhaust its being in this internal, enclosed relation of self-sameness.

The reflexive formula of the romantic novel approaches its limits in the repetition of Kafkan *récit*. Here, there is no danger of confusing the generativity of romantic reflection (and the presence of the subject it effects) with any structures known in the empirical world. As it repeats the suppressed enigma of language, the *récit* immediately cites that which exceeds it. The subject, here, belongs immediately in the very locus of its occurrence: the subject of repetition occurs in repetition as such. This occurrence, or this presence, cannot be confused with an extrinsic form or object, not even with the figure of the "subject," for it is the subject *of repetition* that is being repeated. As it dwells buried in re-citation, the subject of repetition as such comes to presence in its immediacy. Beyond the relevance to the real and the ideal, this repetition enacts the transcendental presence of the subject of repetition in the form appropriate to itself. What is revealed as this subject is not an objective figure but the very condition of objective meanings, the principle of iterability that guarantees the recognizability of objects as self-identical. The subject of repetition itself, however, is not self-identical, for, as the subject *of* repetition, it is the ground of repetition and of identity.

Interpreted in strict conformity with Schlegel's formula, the identity of what is being repeated with what does the repeating institutes the subject of repetition as completely dissolved. This subject is nothing subjective, for it is both more and less than itself, the excess of the work of the subject, the exergue. No history can occur in this self-sameness; the subject reaches itself as a being-subject and disappears in the surplus of its self-sameness. The surplus renders the subject *untimely* for history: too original and too late, and too identical to be *made by* it. No longer generative of history and no longer history's subject, repetition stands outside history, unable to return and recur within it. It is the happening-outside-of-history, the unhistorical happening—*befalling*—of self to itself, the distinctly postmodern legacy of the romantic project to construct modernity and, through this construction, to escape repetition.

BIBLIOGRAPHY

Adams, Robert Martin. *Strains of Discourse: Studies in Literary Openness.* Ithaca, 1958.
——. *Surface and Symbol: The Consistency of James Joyce's "Ulysses."* New York, 1962.
Adorno, Theodor W. *Prisms.* Translated by Samuel and Shierry Weber. London, 1967.
Allemann, Beda. *Ironie und Dichtung: F. Schlegel, Novalis, Solger, Kierkegaard, Nietzsche, Thomas Mann, Musil.* Pfullingen, 1956.
——. "Kafka: Von den Gleichnissen." *Zeitschrift für deutsche Philologie,* LXXXIII, Special Issue 3 (1964), 97–106.
Anders, Günther. *Franz Kafka.* Translated by A. Steer and A. K. Thorlby. New York, 1960.
Attridge, Derek, and Daniel Ferrer, eds. *Post-Structuralist Joyce: Essays from the French.* New York, 1984.
Auerbach, Erich. *Scenes from the Drama of European Literature.* Minneapolis, 1984.
Bahti, Timothy. "Fate in the Past: Peter Szondi's Reading of German Romantic Genre Theory." *Boundary 2,* XI (1983), 111–25.
Bakhtin, Mikhail. *Dialogic Imagination: Four Essays.* Edited by Michael Holquist. Translated by Caryl Emerson and Michael Holquist. Austin, 1981.
——. *Problems of Dostevsky's Poetics.* Translated by Caryl Emerson. Minneapolis, 1984.
Barthes, Roland. *Critical Essays.* Translated by Richard Howard. Evanston, 1972.
——. *Image-Music-Text.* Translated by Stephen Heath. Glasgow, 1977.
——. *S/Z.* Translated by Richard Miller. New York, 1974.

Baudelaire, Charles. "*Madame Bovary*, by Gustave Flaubert." *L'Artiste*, October 18, 1857.
Baum, Alvin L. "Parable as Paradox in Kafka's *Erzählungen*." *MLN*, XCI (1976), 1327–47.
Beaujour, Michel. "*Genus Universum*." *Glyph*, VII (1980), 15–31.
Behler, Ernst. "Friedrich Schlegel und Hegel." *Hegel-Studien*, I (1963), 203–50.
Benjamin, Walter. *Gesammelte Schriften*. Edited by Rolf Tiedemann and Hermann Schweppenhäuser. 7 vols. Frankfurt am Main, 1972.
———. *Illuminations: Essays and Reflections*. Edited by Hannah Arendt. Translated by Harry Zohn. New York, 1969.
———. *The Origin of German Tragic Drama*. Translated by John Osborne. London, 1985.
Bernheimer, Charles. *Flaubert and Kafka: Studies in Psychopoetic Structure*. New Haven, 1982.
Bernstein, J. M. *The Philosophy of the Novel: Lukács, Marxism, and the Dialectics of Form*. Minneapolis, 1984.
Berthoff, Warner. *The Example of Melville*. Princeton, 1962.
Blanchot, Maurice. *De Kafka à Kafka*. Paris, 1985.
———. "*The Gaze of Orpheus*" *and Other Literary Essays*. Translated by Lydia Davis. Barrytown, N.Y., 1981.
———. *The Infinite Conversation*. Translated by Susan Hanson. Minneapolis, 1993.
———. "René Char et la pensée du neutre." *L' Arc*, XXII (1963), 9–14.
———. *The Sirens' Song*. Edited by Gabriel Josipovici. Translated by Sacha Rabinovitch. Bloomington, 1982.
———. *The Space of Literature*. Translated by Ann Smock. Lincoln, Nebr. 1982.
Bloom, Harold, ed. *Franz Kafka: Modern Critical Views*. New York, 1986.
———. *Modern Critical Interpretations: Gustave Flaubert's "Madame Bovary."* New York, 1988.
Borges, Jorge Luis. *Labyrinths*. Edited by Donald A. Yates and James E. Irby. New York, 1964.
Brodhead, Richard H. *Hawthorne, Melville, and the Novel*. Chicago, 1973.
Bubner, Rüdiger. "Über einige Bedingungen gegenwärtigen Ästhetik." *Neue Hefte für Philosophie*, V (1975), 38–73.
Bürger, Peter. *Theory of the Avant-Garde*. Translated by Michael Shaw. Minneapolis, 1984.
Canavaggio, Jean. "Cervantes en primera persona." *Journal of Hispanic Philology*, II (1977), 35–44.
Canetti, Elias. *Der andere Prozess: Kafkas Briefe an Felice*. Munich, 1969.
———. *Kafka's Other Trial: The Letters to Felice*. Translated by Christopher Middleton. New York, 1982.

Cascardi, Anthony J. "The Logic of Moods: An Essay on Emerson and Rousseau." *Studies in Romanticism*, XXIV (1985), 223–37.
——. "Totality and the Novel." *New Literary History*, XXIII (1992), 607–27.
Castro, Américo. *Hacia Cervantes*. Madrid, 1957.
Cervantes Saavedra, Miguel de. *Don Quixote*. Translated by Anna Ludwika Czerny and Zygmunt Czerny. II of 2 vols. Warsaw, 1986.
——. *Don Quixote*. Edited by Joseph R. Jones and K. Douglas. The Ormsby Translation, revised. New York, 1981.
——. *Don Quixote*. Translated by John Ozell. New York, 1967.
——. *Don Quixote de la Mancha*. Translated by Tobias George Smollett. London, 1986.
——. *El ingenioso hidalgo Don Quijote de la Mancha*. Edited by Joaquín Casalduero. Madrid, 1984.
——. *The Ingenious Gentleman: Don Quixote de la Mancha*. Translated by Samuel Putnam. II of 2 vols. New York, 1949.
Corngold, Stanley. *The Fate of the Self: German Writers and French Theory*. New York, 1986.
Cross, Richard K. *Flaubert and Joyce: The Rite of Fiction*. Princeton, 1971.
Culler, Jonathan. *Flaubert: The Uses of Uncertainty*. Rev. ed. Ithaca, 1985.
de Man, Paul. *Blindness and Insight: Essays in the Rhetoric of Contemporary Criticism*. 2nd ed., rev. Minneapolis, 1986.
——. "Hölderlin and the Romantic Tradition." In *Romanticism and Contemporary Criticism*, edited by E. S. Burt, Kevin Newmark, and Andrzej Warminski. Baltimore, 1993.
——. *The Rhetoric of Romanticism*. New York, 1984.
Derrida, Jacques. *Edmund Husserl's "Origin of Geometry": An Introduction*. Translated by John P. Leavey, Jr. Lincoln, 1989.
——. "The Law of Genre." *Glyph*, VII (1980), 202–32.
——. *Margins of Philosophy*. Translated by Alan Bass. Chicago, 1982.
——. "The Politics of Friendship." *Journal of Philosophy, Law and Society*, LXXXV (November, 1988), 632–44.
——. *Writing and Difference*. Translated by Alan Bass. Chicago, 1978.
DiBernard, Barbara. "Parallax as Parallel, Paradigm, and Paradox in *Ulysses*." *Éire*, X, (1975), 69–84.
Dryden, Edgar A. *The Form of American Romance*. Baltimore, 1988.
——. *Melville's Thematics of Form: The Great Art of Telling the Truth*. Baltimore, 1968.
Efron, Arthur. *Don Quixote and the Dulcineated World*. Austin, 1971.
Eichner, Hans. *Friedrich Schlegel*. New York, 1970.
——. "The Supposed Influence of Schiller's *Über naive und sentimentalische Dichtung* on F. Schlegel's *Über das Studium der griechischen Poesie*." *Germanic Review*, XXX (1955), 260–64.

———, ed. *"Romantic" and Its Cognates: The European History of a Word.* Toronto, 1972.
Flaubert, Gustave. *Correspondence.* Edited by Louis Conard. Vol. VII of 9 vols. Paris, 1926–33.
———. *Madame Bovary.* Norton Critical Edition. Edited, with a substantially new translation, by Paul de Man. New York, 1965.
———. *Madame Bovary.* Edited by Victor Brombert. Paris, 1986.
Fletcher, Angus. *Allegory: The Theory of a Symbolic Mode.* Ithaca, 1964.
Flores, Angel, ed. *The Kafka Problem.* New York, 1946.
Flores, Angel, and Homer Swander, eds. *Franz Kafka Today.* Madison, Wisc., 1958.
Flores, R. M. "The Role of Cide Hamete in *Don Quixote.*" *Bulletin of Hispanic Studies,* LIX (1982), 3–14.
Foucault, Michel. *Language, Counter-Memory, Practice: Selected Essays and Interviews.* Edited by Donald F. Bouchard. Translated by Donald F. Bouchard and Sherry Simon. Ithaca, 1977.
———. "Le langage à l'infini." *Tel Quel,* XV (1963), 44–53.
———. *The Order of Things.* New York, 1973.
Frank, Joseph. *The Widening Gyre: Crisis and Mastery in Modern Literature.* New Brunswick, 1963.
Frank, Manfred. "The Infinite Text." *Glyph,* VII (1980), 70–101.
———. *Was ist Neostrukturalismus?* Frankfurt am Main, 1984.
———. *What Is Neostructuralism?* Translated by Sabine Wilke and Richard Gray. Minneapolis, 1989.
Gaiser, Gottlieb, ed. *International Perspectives on James Joyce.* Troy, N.Y., 1986.
Garber, Frederick, ed. *Romantic Irony.* Budapest, 1988.
Gasché, Rodolphe. "Foreword: Ideality in Fragmentation." In *Friedrich Schlegel's "Philosophical Fragments."* Translated by Peter Firchow. Minneapolis, 1991.
———. "The Sober Absolute: On Benjamin and the Early Romantics." *Studies in Romanticism,* XXXI (1992), 433–53.
———. *The Tain of the Mirror: Derrida and the Philosophy of Reflection.* Cambridge, Mass. 1986.
Genette, Gérard. *Figures of Literary Discourse.* Translated by Alan Sheridan. New York, 1982.
———. "Genres, 'Types,' Modes." *Poétique,* VIII (1977), 389–421.
Georgi, Helen. "Covert Riddles in *Ulysses:* Squaring the Circle." *Journal of Modern Literature,* XIII (1986), 329–39.
Gilbert, Stuart. *James Joyce's "Ulysses."* New York, 1955.
Gilman, Sander L., Carole Blair, and David J. Parent, eds. and trans. *Friedrich Nietzsche on Rhetoric and Language.* New York, 1989.
Giovannini, G. "Melville's *Pierre* and Dante's *Inferno.*" *PMLA,* LXIV (March, 1949), 70–78.

Girard, René. *Deceit, Desire, and the Novel.* Translated by Yvonne Freccero. Baltimore, 1985.
Goethe, Johann Wolfgang von. *Maximen und Reflexionen.* Edited by Max Hecker. Weimar, 1907.
———. *Wilhelm Meister's Apprenticeship.* Edited and translated by Eric A. Blackall in cooperation with Victor Lange. New York, 1983.
Goldberg, S. L. *The Classical Temper: A Study of James Joyce's "Ulysses."* London, 1961.
Gollin, Rita. "*Pierre*'s Metamorphosis of Dante's *Inferno.*" *American Literature,* XXXIX (1968), 542–45.
Green, Otis H. "El *ingenioso* hidalgo." *Hispanic Review,* XXV (1957), 175–93.
Groden, Michael. *"Ulysses" in Progress.* Princeton, 1977.
Haig, Stirling. *Flaubert and the Gift of Speech: Dialogue and Discourse in Four Modern Novels.* New York, 1986.
Harari, Josué V., ed. *Textual Strategies: Perspectives in Post-Structuralist Criticism.* Ithaca, 1979.
Hart, Clive, and David Hyman, eds. *James Joyce's "Ulysses": Critical Essays.* Berkeley, 1974.
Heidegger, Martin. *Basic Writings.* Edited by David Farrell Krell. New York, 1977.
———. *On the Way to Language.* Translated by Peter D. Hertz. San Francisco, 1971.
Henel, Ingeborg. "Die Türhüterlegende und ihre Bedeutung für Kafkas *Prozess.*" *Deutsche Vierteljahrsschrift,* XXXVII (1963), 50–70.
Henrich, Dieter. "Fichte's Original Insight." *Contemporary German Philosophy.* I. Translated by David R. Lachterman. University Park, Pa., 1982.
Higgins, Brian, and Hershel Parker, eds. *Critical Essays on Herman Melville's "Pierre; or, The Ambiguities."* Boston, 1983.
Holder, Alan. "Style and Tone in Melville's *Pierre.*" *Emerson Society Quarterly,* LX (1970), 76–86.
Hopper, Stanley Romaine, and David L. Miller, eds. *Interpretation: The Poetry of Meaning.* New York, 1967.
Jameson, Fredric. *The Political Unconscious.* Ithaca, 1981.
Janusko, Robert. *The Sources and Structures of James Joyce's "Oxen."* Ann Arbor, 1983.
Joyce, James. *Ulysses.* New York, 1961.
Kafka, Franz. *The Complete Stories.* Edited by Nahum R. Glatzer. New York, 1976.
———. *Der Prozess.* Edited by H. F. Brookes and C. E. Gawne-Cain. London, 1969.
———. *Parables and Paradoxes.* Bilingual ed. New York, 1961.
———. *The Trial.* In *The Penguin Complete Novels of Franz Kafka.* Translated by Willa and Edwin Muir. New York, 1983.

Kant, Immanuel. *Anthropology from a Pragmatic Point of View.* Translated by Victor Lyle Dowdell. Revised and edited by Hans H. Rudnick. Carbondale, 1978.

———. *Critique of Judgment.* Translated by J. H. Bernard. New York, 1951.

———. *Critique of Pure Reason.* Translated by Norman Kemp Smith. New York, 1965.

Kenner, Hugh. *The Stoic Comedians: Flaubert, Joyce, and Beckett.* Boston, 1963.

———. *Ulysses.* Baltimore, 1987.

Kermode, Frank. *The Sense of an Ending: Studies in the Theory of Fiction.* New York, 1967.

Kierkegaard, Søren. *The Concept of Irony: With Constant Reference to Socrates.* Translated by Lee M. Capel. Bloomington, 1965.

Knox, Norman. *The Word "Irony" and Its Context, 1500–1755.* Durham, 1961.

Kristeva, Julia. *Powers of Horror: An Essay on Abjection.* Translated by Leon S. Roudiez. New York, 1982.

LaCapra, Dominick. *Madame Bovary on Trial.* Ithaca, 1982.

Lachterman, David R. "*Die Ewige Wiederkehr des Griechen:* Nietzsche and the Homeric Question." Manuscript of a lecture delivered at the comparative literature department of SUNY-Buffalo, February, 1991.

Lacoue-Labarthe, Philippe. "Poetry as Experience." *SubStance,* LX (1989), 22–29.

———. *The Subject of Philosophy.* Edited by Thomas Trezise. Minneapolis, 1993.

———. *Typography: Mimesis, Philosophy, Politics.* Edited by Christopher Fynsk. Cambridge, Mass., 1989.

Lacoue-Labarthe, Philippe, and Jean-Luc Nancy. *The Literary Absolute: The Theory of Literature in German Romanticism.* Translated by Philip Barnard and Cheryl Lester. Albany, 1988.

Lawrence, Karen. *The Odyssey of Style in "Ulysses."* Princeton, 1981.

Lee, A. Robert, ed. *Herman Melville: Reassessments.* New York, 1984.

Levinas, Emmanuel. *Collected Philosophical Papers.* Translated by Alphonso Lingis. Boston, 1987.

Lévi-Strauss, Claude. *Structural Anthropology.* Translated by Claire Jacobson and Brooke Grundfest Schoepf. New York, 1967.

Lotze, Dieter P. "One Commentator's Despair: Notes on the Structure of Kafka's *The Trial.*" *Journal of Modern Literature,* VI (1977), 389–97.

Lovejoy, Arthur O. *Essays in the History of Ideas.* New York, 1955.

Lukács, Georg. *Die Seele und die Formen: Essays.* Berlin, 1971.

———. *Soul and Form.* Translated by Anna Bostock. Cambridge, Mass., 1974.

———. *The Theory of the Novel.* Translated by Anna Bostock. Cambridge, Mass., 1987.

Lyotard, Jean-François. *Duchamp's TRANS/formers*. Translated by Ian McLeod. Venice, Calif., 1990.

———. *The Postmodern Condition: A Report on Knowledge*. Translated by Geoff Bennington and Brian Massumi. Minneapolis, 1984.

McArthur, Murray. *Stolen Writings: Blake's "Milton," Joyce's "Ulysses," and the Nature of Influence*. Ann Arbor, 1988.

McKeon, Michael. *The Origins of the English Novel, 1600–1740*. Baltimore, 1987.

Mailloux, Peter. *A Hesitation Before Birth: The Life of Franz Kafka*. Newark, 1989.

Melville, Herman. *Pierre; or, The Ambiguities*. Edited by Harrison Hayford, Hershel Parker, and G. Thomas Tanselle. Evanston, 1971.

Milder, Robert. "Melville's 'Intentions' in *Pierre*." *Studies in the Novel*, VI (1974), 186–99.

Morrissey, Robert. "Breaking In (Flaubert in Parentheses)." *SubStance*, LVI (1988), 49–62.

Nancy, Jean-Luc. "*Menstruum universale* (Literary Dissolution)." *SubStance*, XXI (1978), 21–35.

Nelson, Lowry, Jr., ed. *Cervantes: A Collection of Critical Essays*. Englewood Cliffs, N.J., 1969.

Newmark, Kevin. "*L'absolu littéraire:* Friedrich Schlegel and the Myth of Irony." *MLN*, CVII (1992), 905–930.

Niess, Robert. "On Listening to Homais." *French Review*, LI (1977), 22–28.

Noon, William T. *Joyce and Aquinas*. New Haven, 1957.

Parker, Hershel. "Why *Pierre* Went Wrong." *Studies in the Novel*, VIII (1976), 7–23.

Pascal, Blaise. *Works of Pascal*. Translated by O. W. Wight. N.p., 1866.

Polheim, Karl. "Spätzeiten als Frühzeiten." *Wirkendes Wort*, XI (1961), 74–82.

Prendergast, Christopher. "Flaubert: Quotation, Stupidity and the Cretan Liar Paradox." *French Studies*, XXXV (1981), 261–77.

———. *The Order of Mimesis: Balzac, Stendhal, Nerval, Flaubert*. New York, 1986.

Rivers, Elias L. "Cervantes' Art of the Prologue." In *Estudios literarios de hispanistas norteamericanos dedicados a Helmut Hatzfeld con motivo de su 80 aniversario*, edited by J. M. Solà-Solé, A. Crisafulli, and B. Damiani. Barcelona, 1974.

Robert, Marthe. *Kafka*. Paris, 1960.

Rosenberry, Edward H. *Melville and the Comic Spirit*. Cambridge, Mass. 1955.

Rousset, Jean. *Forme et signification: Essais sur les structures littéraires de Corneille à Claudel*. Paris, 1962.

Sallis, John C. "Art within the Limits of Finitude." *International Philosophical Quarterly*, VII (1967), 285–97.

Sandbank, Shimon. "Action as Self-Mirror: On Kafka's Plots." *Modern Fiction Studies*, XVII (1971), 21–29.

Schlegel, Friedrich. *Friedrich Schlegel, 1794–1802: Seine prosaischen Jugendschriften.* Vol. I of 2 vols. Edited by J. Minor. Vienna, 1882.

———. *Friedrich Schlegel: "Dialogue on Poetry" and Literary Aphorisms.* Translated by Ernst Behler and Roman Struc. University Park, Pa., 1968.

———. *Friedrich Schlegel: Schriften zur Literatur.* Edited by Wolfdietrich Rasch. Munich, 1970.

———. *Friedrich Schlegel's "Lucinde" and the Fragments.* Translated by Peter Firchow. Minneapolis, 1971.

———. *Charakteristiken und Kritiken I, 1796–1801.* Edited by Hans Eichner. Munich, 1967. Vol. II of *Kritische Friedrich-Schlegel-Ausgabe*, edited by Ernst Behler. 21 vols.

———. *Literary Notebooks, 1797–1801.* Edited by Hans Eichner. Toronto, 1957.

Schor, Naomi, and Henry F. Majewski, eds. *Flaubert and Postmodernism.* Lincoln, Nebr. 1984.

Sedgwick, William Ellery. *Herman Melville: The Tragedy of Mind.* New York, 1962.

Senn, Fritz. *Joyce's Dislocutions: Essays on Reading as Translation.* Edited by John Paul Riquelme. Baltimore, 1984.

Serres, Michel. *The Parasite.* Translated by Lawrence R. Schehr. Baltimore, 1982.

Shepherd, Gerard W. "Pierre's Psyche and Melville's Art." *Emerson Society Quarterly*, XXX (1984), 83–98.

Sokel, Walter H. *Franz Kafka.* New York, 1966.

Sollers, Philippe. *Writing and the Experience of Limits.* Edited by David Hayman. Translated by Philip Barnard and David Hayman. New York, 1983.

Spitzer, Leo. "Linguistic Perspectivism in the *Don Quixote*." In *Cervantes: Modern Critical Views*, edited by Harold Bloom. New York, 1987.

———. "On the Significance of *Don Quixote*." In *Cervantes: A Collection of Critical Essays*, edited by Lowry Nelson, Jr. Englewood Cliffs, N.J., 1969.

Steinberg, Erwin R. "Kafka's 'Before the Law'—A Reflection of Fear of Marriage; and Corroborating Language Patterns in the Diaries." *Journal of Modern Literature*, XIII (1986), 129–48.

Stern, Milton R. *The Fine Hammered Steel of Herman Melville.* Urbana, 1957.

Strelka, Joseph, ed. *Literary Criticism and Philosophy: Yearbook of Comparative Literature*, X. University Park, Pa., 1983.

Sussman, Henry. *Franz Kafka: Geometrician of Metaphor.* Madison, Wisc., 1979.

Szondi, Peter. *"On Textual Understanding" and Other Essays.* Translated by Harvey Mendelsohn. Minneapolis, 1986.

Tanner, Tony. *Adultery in the Novel: Contract and Transgression.* Baltimore, 1979.

Todorov, Tzvetan. *Genres in Discourse.* Translated by Catherine Porter. New York, 1990.

———. "La réflexion sur la littérature dans la France contemporaine." *Poétique,* XXXVIII (1979), 131–48.

Tompkins, Phillip. "James Joyce and the Enthymeme: The Seventh Episode in *Ulysses.*" *James Joyce Quarterly,* V (1968), 199–205.

Tysdahl, Bjørn J. *Joyce and Ibsen: A Study in Literary Influence.* New York, 1968.

Udoff, Alan, ed. *Kafka and the Contemporary Critical Performance: Centenary Readings.* Bloomington, 1987.

Warminski, Andrzej. "Dreadful Reading: Blanchot on Hegel." *Yale French Studies,* LXIX (1985), 267–75.

Watt, Ian. *The Rise of the Novel.* Berkeley, 1957.

Weber, Samuel. "Criticism Underway: Walter Benjamin's *Romantic Concept of Criticism.*" In *Romantic Revolutions: Criticism and Theory,* edited by Kenneth R. Johnston, et al. Bloomington, 1990.

———. "It." *Glyph,* IV (1978), 1–31.

Weiger, John G. "*Don Quixote:* The Comedy in Spite of Itself." *Bulletin of Hispanic Studies,* LX (1983), 283–92.

———. "The Prologuist: The Extratextual Authorial Voice in *Don Quixote.*" *Bulletin of Hispanic Studies,* LXV (1988), 129–39.

Wellek, René. *A History of Modern Criticism.* Vol. I of 6 vols. New Haven, 1955.

Wheeler, Kathleen, ed. *German Aesthetic and Literary Criticism: The Romantic Ironists and Goethe.* New York, 1984.

Willis, Raymond S., Jr. *The Phantom Chapters of the "Quijote."* New York, 1953.

Willson, A. Leslie, ed. *German Romantic Criticism.* New York, 1982.

Wright, Nathalia. "*Pierre:* Herman Melville's *Inferno.*" *American Literature,* XXXII (1960), 167–81.

Ziolkowski, Theodore. *Dimensions of the Modern Novel: German Texts and European Contexts.* Princeton, 1969.

INDEX

Absolute: literary, 21–22, 24, 29; poetic, 25–26, 29, 54, 60, 61; romantic, 28; sober, 33; reflection in Benjamin, 27; saying in Manfred Frank, 50–51
Adorno, Theodor, 260n
Allegory: in Paul de Man, 51n; in *Moby-Dick*, 99, 101; in *Pierre*, 138; in Flaubert, 178–80; in biblical hermeneutics, 237; as otherness, 269; in Kafka, 273, 274, 278, 280, 281, 282, 286
Allemann, Beda, 253; and absolute metaphor, 255, 256n, 259n, 262
Apostrophe, 82n; and parabasis, 84–85, 98, 107
Apperception: empirical, 4; pure, 4, 22, 24; as condition of possibility of the subject, 4
Arabesque, 18, 56, 57; in Goethe, 160, 244n; in Flaubert, 169, 287; in *Ulysses*, 172, 210, 233, 244, 245, 246n, 247, 287
Aristotle: and entelechy, 208; *thaumadzein* in, 223
Auerbach, Erich, 237
Austin, John Langshaw, 174, 196n

Bakhtin, Mikhail: and Greek antiquity, 9n; and hybrid genre, 36; and novelistic discourse, 190–91

Barthes, Roland: and death of the author, 54, 260n; on Kafka, 265n; and lisible and scriptible literature, 72
Baudelaire, Charles, 174
Bauer, Felice, 270–71, 271n
Benjamin, Walter, 3, 32; and medium of reflection (*Reflexionsmedium*), 24, 26, 28, 61; poetic absolute in, 25–26; and absolute reflection, 27; on Kafka's dialectic, 256n; the storyteller in, 265; "The Concept of Art Criticism in German Romanticism," 26, 102n; and the translator's task (*die Aufgabe des Übersetzers*), 88–89
Bernheimer, Charles, 257, 272n
Bild: in Kant, 5; *Bildung* (in Schiller), 125
Blanchot, Maurice: and writing, 73n; and literature, 188–89; on de Sade and Joyce, 243n; and absence (of the Book), 35, 41–44, 53; and *récit*, 46, 285–86; and *roman*, 46–47, 285; on Flaubert, 194, 198, 199; and negation in language, 250; and the neuter, 281n; and language and the other, 283–85; repetition in, 284; "The Athenaeum," 34; "The Song of the Sirens," 46; *The Madness of the Day*, 49; "The Narrative Voice," 281; "Wittgenstein's Problem," 283; "Wooden Bridge," 284

Borges, Jorge Luis: on Cervantes, 59–60, 105–107; and Kafka, 261–70
Brentano, Clemens, 17
Bricolage, 56, 157, 162, 166–67, 189, 243; infinity of, in Flaubert, 168–69, 171, 177, 184; and hermeneutics, 159, 177; and phenomenology, 182–84
Brod, Max, 260, 260n
Bubner, Rüdiger, 263n
Bürger, Peter, 212n
Burton, Robert: *The Anatomy of Melancholy*, 100–101

Canetti, Elias, 270–71
Cardinal order, 204, 228, 230
Cascardi, Anthony, 2, 3, 119n
Celan, Paul, 181n
Cervantes, Miguel de Saavedra: and *ingeniosidad*, 70, 71; and "First Prologue" to *Don Quixote*, 70–76; anti-prologue in, 71; and transcendental prologue, 73, 74; irony in, 75; romantic irony in, 76; and antiphrasis, 75, 76, 84; and periphrasis, 82; and intention and instinct, 75, 76, 80; and conscious and unconscious, 79, 108; speculative (proximate) involution in, 76, 78, 79, 80, 84, 85, 88, 89, 102, 161; and mimesis and originality, 77–78; and transcendental mimesis, 78, 90, 92, 104, 108; and quotation and originality, 79–80; translation in, 86, 88–89, 99; and translation from Arabic, 86n; as transcendental (romantic) poet, 18, 83, 134; and neo-Aristotelian aesthetics, 90; *le mot juste* in, 90; interpretation in, 86–88; origin in, 55–56, 88, 97–98, 103–104; and originality, 76–78, 79–80; *es opinión* cluster in, 93–95, 94n, 102; margin in, 96–98, 107; laughter in, 96–98; genre in, 103; and the romantic theory of the novel, 109–12
Char, René, 281n, 285
Chiasmus: in Melville, 124, 138–40; in Joyce, 230, 240

Church Fathers, 237
Cixous, Hélène, 221, 222, 223, 245
Cliché: in Flaubert, 178–80, 184, 190; in Joyce, 223–24
Coleridge, Samuel Taylor: and "The Ancient Mariner," 106; symbol and allegory in, 267n
Comices agricoles, 195, 196, 211
Corngold, Stanley, 119n; and "the surplus-subject" in Kafka, 264
Cretan liar paradox, 169, 198
Culler, Jonathan, 163

Dante: as romantic author, 18, 55, 134; and *Commedia* and *Inferno*, 134–39, 138n; and *oeconomia divina*, 136; and Paolo and Francesca, 134, 134n
De Man, Paul, 10n, 51n, 281n
De Montaigne, Michel, 82n
Derrida, Jacques: on Blanchot's *récit*, 48–50, 287; on apostrophe, 82n; on tropology, 146n; on Joyce, 240n; on hypermnesia, 242–43, 246, 246n; mentioned, 196n
De Sade, Marquis, 243n
Diderot, Denis, 18
Donato, Eugenio, 100, 171n
Dostoevsky, Fyodor: poetics of, 9n; and Kafka, 260n; and marriage, 271n
Duchamp, Marcel: mirrorish in, 206, 209–10, 235; "Nude Descending a Staircase," 183; *TRANS/formers*, 205

Eichner, Hans, 7, 160
Ellmann, Richard, 229, 237
Emerson, Ralph Waldo, 119n
Epic, 6, 13, 33, 36, 38, 229; Homeric, 14, 61, 63, 64; as subjective or objective genre, 15; and the novel, 16; *Odyssey*, 39, 46–47, 285; repetition in, 285
Eschatology, 229, 237

Fichte, Johann Gottlieb: positing (*setzen*) of subject in, 22–23, 33; and Ur-Form of reflection, 26–27; and self-determination of reflection (*Selbstbestimmung*), 27;

and self-delimitation (*Selbstbeschränkung*), 27n; and reciprocal determination (*Wechselbestimmung*), 31; and the self-manifesting subject, 42; mentioned, 3, 21

Flaubert, Gustave: *Madame Bovary*, 56–57, 210, 269–70; and neuter in *Madame Bovary*, 270; *la syncope* in, 56, 161, 178, 180, 185, 200; *bêtise* in, 170; irony in, 167, 188, 191; and classical rhetoric, 172; philosophy of language in, 172; parentheses in, 184–87, 186n; jokes and puns in, 196, 196n; and form and content, 186, 189, 194–95, 198, 199; and realism, 187; and romantic aesthetics, 188; quotation in, 185n, 191n; repetition in, 79; *le mot juste* in, 197; *Bouvard and Pécuchet*, 100; *Dictionary of Received Ideas*, 189–90; and Kafka, 260n; and marriage, 271n; transcendental resemblance in, 177; transcendental speech in, 196; transcendental subject in, 200–201; transcendental repetition in, 190, 198

Foucault, Michel, 47n, 92n

Frank, Joseph: and spatialized literature, 211–14; reflexive reference in, 211; and re-reading in Joyce, 213, 227, 231, 233, 242

Frank, Manfred, 12n, 47n; and absolute saying, 50; and textuality, 50–51

Freud, Sigmund, 196n

Gasché, Rodolphe, 26, 28, 29, 32, 35

Gautier, Théophile: and *bovarysme*, 174

Genette, Gérard: and genre theory, 48–49; on bricolage, 158; mentioned, 168, 170, 198

Genre: dissolution of, in romanticism, 41, 49; and *Mischgedicht*, 41; transcendental theory of, 32, 36, 36n, 38, 44; taxonomic theory of, 48–49; in Melville, 131

Girard, René: mimetic desire in, 9n, 134, 174; romantic *mensonge* in, 134–35; and novelistic and romantic writers, 135; and *Launcelot*, 134

Gödel's theorem, 259n

Goethe, Johann Wolfgang von: and Friedrich Schlegel, 18n; arabesque in, 160; and *Dichtarten*, 36n, 48; and *Dichtweisen*, 48; and canon formation, 263n; and symbol and allegory, 267–68, 269, 286; *Wilhelm Meister's Apprenticeship*, 42, 244n; mentioned, 18

Grillparzer, Franz, 271n

Grotesque, 160, 169, 246n

Hegel, Georg Wilhelm Friedrich: speculative mediation in, 216; and absolute knowledge, 21; Spirit in, 21; on abstract totality, 29, 61; and criticism of romanticism, 29–31; sublation (*Aufhebung*) in, 31, 235; and speculative dissolution, 31, 32; the Concept (*der Begriff*) in, 32, 45–46, 61, 110; end of history in, 62; unhappy consciousness in, 133; and phenomenology in Joyce, 209, 240n; historical truth in, 208–209; *The Philosophy of Fine Art*, 30; *Phenomenology of Spirit*, 73n; mentioned, 3, 21, 225, 231

Heidegger, Martin: language in, 45; and *Ereignis*, 45–46, 65; and ontico-ontological difference, 223; and ontology, 119; and anxiety, 119; and existential analysis, 119; "The Origin of the Work of Art," 130n

Herder, Johann Gottfried: philosophy of history in, 6, 8, 15n

Hölderlin: and poetry of poetry (speech of speech, hyperbolic poetics), 3, 10n, 15, 37, 44, 51n, 54, 62, 65; and aorgics, 41, 53; as translator of *Oedipus Rex* and *Antigone*, 112–13; Hesperian in, 113, 238; experience in, 181n; *dysmoron* in, 238

Homer, 39

Hopkins, Gerard Manley, 51

Husserl, Edmund, 246

Intuition: sensory, 3, 5, 23, 24–25; intellectual (conceptual), 19, 24–25, 25n, 29; as *anschauen* or *Anschauung*, 5, 19, 23

Jakobson, Roman, 279
Joyce, James: *Ulysses*, 57–58, 172; *Ulysses* as phenomenology of experience, 209, 225; exemplarity in, 57, 172, 209, 231–35; exemplarity and history in, 233–34, 236, 242; memory and reading in, 213; history in, 227; philanthropy in, 222–23; allusion in, 224; transcendental rhetoric in, 229–31; enthymeme in, 220–21; parallax in, 221; catalog in, 207–208; catechism in, 221; perfection in, 221; gnomic wisdom in, 222–23; metempsychosis in, 245; epiphany in, 232; redemption in, 234–35, 236, 247; salvation in, 234; exception in, 234; repetition in, 79, 172; universality in, 239–40; and the Wandering Jew, 239; and de Sade, 243*n*; "Ithaca," 202; "Oxen of the Sun," 224; "Aeolus," 226, 228, 230; "Sirens," 230; "Cyclops," 230; "Proteus," 241; *Stephen Hero*, 232; *A Portrait of the Artist as a Young Man*, 57, 232; *Finnegans Wake*, 57, 245, 246*n*, 247; mentioned, 47
—hermeneutics (induction and deduction) in, 212, 212*n*, 215, 229, 245; transcendental hermeneutics in, 217; hermeneutic circle in, 212*n*, 218; squaring of hermeneutic circle in, 226, 229, 243; *Stimmung* in, 230

Kafka, Franz: *The Trial*, 59; theory of metaphor in, 248–49, 252–55; metaphysics in, 254–59; and parables, 253–57; language and metaphysics in, 249; text and interpretation in, 257–59, 272, 273; text in, 277; and literary tradition, 260–64; and survival ("outliving"), 263–64; impersonality in, 264; genre in, 267, 276–77, 282; irony in, 269; and Felice Bauer, 270–71, 271*n*; and Kierkegaard, 272*n*; and the neuter, 59, 251, 275, 279; and repetition, 77; joke in, 279–80; transcendental language in, 285; "Prometheus," 253–55, 262; "On Parables," 257; "Before the Law," 259, 277; "The Cares of a Family Man," 262–64; and Odradek character, 262–64

Kant, Immanuel: and origin, 82; and sensory intuition, 119*n*; and unity of cognition, 158; pure reason in, 3; system of, 3–4; subject in, 3; aftermath of, 3, 17, 91; reflective judgment in, 5; transcendental imagination in, 5; free play of imagination in, 5, 20; and historical aesthetics, 6, 13; philosophy of history in, 6, 8, 15*n*; asymptotic dialectic in, 6, 10; and the sublime, 57, 243; judgment of taste in, 81; and *sensus communis*, 81; and conditions of possibility, 4, 5, 83, 235, 280; and congruent counterparts, 205, 229; and a priori particulars, 205; space and time in, 5, 19, 205, 214; absolute space in, 205, 230; intussusception in, 35; and Goethe, 267*n*; *Critique of Judgment*, 5, 81, 201; *Anthropology from a Pragmatic Point of View*, 68*n*; *Of the First Foundation of the Difference of Regions in Space*, 205; mentioned, 225

Kierkegaard, Søren: and Socratic irony, 36–37; and Kafka, 260*n*; and Regine Olsen, 270–71, 271*n*, 272

Kleist, Heinrich von: and Kafka, 260*n*; and marriage, 271*n*

Kristeva, Julia, 246*n*, 247*n*

LaCapra, Dominick, 175
Lacoue-Labarthe, Philippe, 30–31
Leibniz, Wilhelm: empirical apperception in, 4; and the best of possible worlds, 222, 223
Lessing, Gotthold Ephraim: *Laocoön*, 211, 214
Levinas, Emmanuel, 286
Lévi-Strauss, Claude, 205–206
Lovejoy, Arthur O., 18
Lukács, Georg: and *The Theory of the Novel*, 2, 9*n*; and the gesture, 270
Lyotard, Jean-François, 57, 205
Lyric, 6, 8, 13, 14–15, 36, 62; and Sappho, 62, 63, 64; and Hölderlin, 62, 63

McArthur, Murray, 228–31
Marin, Luis, 76
Melville, Herman: *Pierre*, 58–59; mood in, 58, 122, 132, 161; and hermeneutics, 142, 147, 148–49; tautology in, 58, 121; romantic tautology in, 150–52; metaphor in, 116, 131; Nature and Culture in, 118, 122, 132, 140, 149; irony and subject in, 120–21, 134–39, 140–42; and omniscient narrator, 120n, 154n; metaphysics and language in, 144–48; and postmodern literature, 155; portraiture in, 128–30; and Enceladus, 124–26, 131, 132n, 139, 155–56; face in, 126, 128–30; transcendental mimesis (similarity) in, 123, 126–28, 131; self in, 132–34; text in, 123, 140–42; and menippea, 155; suicide in, 141n; *Moby-Dick*, 99, 100–101
Meno's paradox, 147
Metaphor: in Joyce, 228–31; in Kafka, 248–49, 252–55
Metonymy, 228–31
Mimesis: and *phusis* and *tekhne*, 11, 54, 122; and diegesis, 38
Modernity: in Friedrich Schlegel, 8, 10; in Melville, 125; and the romantic novel, 288–89
Musil, Robert, 262

Nancy, Jean-Luc, 31
Nägele, Rainer, 259n, 280n
New Testament, 237, 240
Nietzsche, Friedrich: and Dionysian element, 12; "Homer and Classical Philology" and the Homeric question, 39; and eternal return of the same, 54, 63, 215, 233; death of God in, 54; lack of history in, 62; genealogy in, 227; as untimely (*unzeitgemäß*), 228; "On Truth and Lying in an Extra-Moral Sense," 255–56, 258; stammering translation, 257; *Genealogy of Morals*, 235n; *pia fraus* in, 255; interpretation in, 257–59; and Kafka, 253, 265; and Plato, 256

Novalis, 16n, 20, 43n, 44, 51n; *menstruum universale* in, 31, 35, 46; mentioned, 17
Novel, 1, 2, 17; as *der Roman*, 2, 17, 83, 109, 171, 200, 287

Old Testament, 237, 240
Olsen, Regine: and Kierkegaard, 270–71, 271n, 272
Ordinal order, 204, 228
Other, 44, 46, 55, 111–12, 136, 194, 196, 198, 199, 240n, 269, 275; as *allos*, 280; in Blanchot, 283–85

Paradigm, 164, 241–42, 245, 247
Pascal, Blaise, 70, 123
Picasso, Pablo: "Girl Before a Mirror," 183
Plato: and romanticism, 64–65; and Nietzsche, 256
Poe, Edgar Allan, 106
Postmodernity: and Friedrich Schlegel, 9, 54–55; and romantic theory of the novel, 289; and romantic dissolution, 60–61; in Melville, 125, 126, 149, 154
Presentation, 6, 17, 20, 55, 60, 104; or presence, 99–102; in Melville, 116, 120, 129–30, 133, 148; in Flaubert, 191; in Joyce, 208, 247; in Kafka, 251, 269
Proust, Marcel, 47, 262

Rabelais, François: and *Gargantua and Pantagruel*, 99, 100
Récit: and genre theory, 48–50; and romantic theory of the novel, 252, 285; and the other, 285–86, 287
Repetition, 54, 215, 277, 284; subject of, 288
Representation, 127, 129, 140, 206, 251, 267, 268, 269, 277, 286
Richter, Jean Paul: circular wit in, 150–52; mentioned, 17, 18, 58
Rimbaud, Arthur: "Bateau ivre," 106
Robert, Marthe, 256n, 261n, 265n; on allusion in Kafka, 264–67
Romanticism: Golden Age in, 7, 13, 63, 65; completion (and incompletion) in, 10, 64, 284; irony in, 12; criticism in, 12, 12n, 102n; and translation, 106; and Nietzsche and the Orient, 12;

and Hölderlin and the Orient, 113; reflection in, 17, 27n, 83, 91, 107; potentiation in, 18–19; theory in, 2, 19, 20, 21, 23–24, 54; fragment in, 20, 35, 252; dissolution in, 21, 24, 27, 30–31, 32, 41, 60, 64, 65, 102n, 288; and classicist aesthetics, 25–26; and *Sturm und Drang*, 26; Idea of Art in, 26, 102n, 107; profanation in, 29, 32, 41, 54, 65; Hegel's criticism of, 29–31; *Witz* in, 31, 197, 200; and prose, 32–33; literature in, 33–34, 42; equivocity in, 34, 35, 42, 62; exergue in, 36, 44, 60, 61, 65, 252, 288; and Socrates, 36; and the Book, 40, 40n, 42, 52–54; and the Book in Cervantes, 101, 105–106; and the Book in Melville, 148–50, 152–54; and manifesto and the French Revolution, 42; and language, 44–46; unworking (*désouvrement*) in, 53, 62, 65; and the lyric, 63; and history, 64–65; organicism, 53, 209; and formal and hermeneutic unity of the work, 41; and symbolism, 105

—transcendental poetry (*poiesis*, hyperbolic poetics, poetry of poetry), 14, 18, 43–44, 49–50, 54, 83, 110, 285; in Melville, 131; in Flaubert, 169, 191; in Joyce, 215; in Kafka, 275, 282

—identity in, 31–32; in *Don Quixote*, 91, 101; in Kafka's language, 252

Romanticization, 83; of the classical epic, 16–17, 62; of dialectic, 110–12

Rousseau, Jean-Jacques: *Confessions*, 18n; original contract in, 81, 82, 83

Russell, Bertrand, 169–70, 198

Sallis, John, 182–83
Sand, George, 192
Sappho, 63–64
Schelling, Friedrich Wilhelm Joseph von, 3, 21, 225
Schiller, Friedrich: and dialectic, 9, 9n, 10; and Schlegel, 9–10; "Über naive und sentimentalische Dichtung," 7, 9, 10, 122; *Aesthetic Education of Man*, 125

Schlegel, Friedrich: and the real and ideal in Flaubert, 199; and classical studies, 6; and Schiller, 9–10; and Nietzsche, 39; and Socratic irony, 37–38, 62; on Homeric epos, 39; and postmodernity, 9, 54–55; permanent parabasis in, 51n, 84, 88, 98, 107; and permanent parabasis and apostrophe, 84–85, 107; and the poetic ideal, 91, 91n; and genre theory, 19, 109–12; and *Lucinde* and Hegel, 30–31; "Über das Studium der griechischen Poesie," 7, 9, 10, 13; "The Letter on the Novel," 18, 83n; "On Incomprehensibility," 27n, 34n, 140n

—instinct and intention in, 38–39, 54, 62, 110–11; in Flaubert, 199

Searle, John, 174, 196n
Serres, Michel, 235
Shakespeare: as romantic author, 18, 55, 134; *Hamlet*, 134–39, 138n
Smollett, Tobias George: as translator of *Don Quixote*, 88
Socrates: and romantic genre, 36–39; and ironic knowledge, 76, 218; and Kierkegaard, 36–37; and *ekon* and *akon*, 70, 75; and *daimon*, 36, 70; in Cervantes, 76
Solger, Karl, 17
Sollers, Philippe: "The Novel and the Experience of Limits," 47; and romantic genre, 48
Sophocles, 112
Speculative absolute, 42
Speculative idealism, 21, 28, 65
Speculative metaphysics, 109
Spitzer, Leo, 100n, 101n
Stein, Gertrude, 262
Stendhal, 51n
Sterne, Laurence: *Tristram Shandy*, 99, 100; mentioned, 17, 18
Supplementarity, 11, 284
Surrealism, 193
Sussman, Henry, 259n, 268, 273
Swift, Jonathan, 84, 260n
Syntagm, 164, 241–42, 245, 247
Szondi, Peter, 14n, 109, 216n

Teleology, 209, 215, 227, 231, 237
Tieck, Ludwig: as translator of *Don Quixote*, 88; mentioned, 17, 51
Todorov, Tzvetan, 48
Tragedy (or tragic), 6, 8, 13, 62

Udoff, Alan, 260*n*, 273
Uncanny (*unheimlich*): in Flaubert, 171–73, 177, 189, 200

Vico, Giambattista, 6, 39
Voltaire, 84

Wagner, Richard: and romantic textuality, 253; mentioned, 51
Walton, Izaak: *The Compleat Angler*, 100
Warminski, Andrzej, 73*n*
Watt, Ian, 2
Weiger, John, 86, 93–98
Winckelmann, Johann Joachim, 11